**WITHDRAWN
UTSA Libraries**

European Employment Models in Flux

Also by Jill Rubery

WOMEN'S EMPLOYMENT IN EUROPE: Trends and Prospects
(*with M. Smith and C. Fagan*)
MANAGING EMPLOYMENT CHANGE: The New Realities of Work
(*with H. Beynon, D. Grimshaw and K. Ward*)
THE ORGANIZATION OF EMPLOYMENT: An International Perspective
(*with D. Grimshaw*)
SYSTEMS OF PRODUCTION: Markets, Organizations and Performance
(*co-editor with B. Burchell, S. Deakin and J. Michie*)
FRAGMENTING WORK: Blurring Organisational Boundaries and Disordering
Hierarchies (*with M. Marchington, D. Grimshaw and H. Willmott*)

Also by Gerhard Bosch

LOW-WAGE WORK IN GERMANY (*co-editor with C. Weinkopf*)
Arbeiten für wenig Geld: Niedriglohnbeschäftigung in Deutschland
(*co-editor with C. Weinkopf*)
WORKING IN THE SERVICE SECTOR: A Tale from Different Worlds
(*co-editor with S. Lehndorff*)
BUILDING CHAOS: An International Comparison of Deregulation in the
Construction Industry (*co-editor with P. Philips*)
WORKING TIME PREFERENCES IN SIXTEEN EUROPEAN COUNTRIES
(*with H. Bielenski and A. Wagne*r)

Also by Steffen Lehndorff

*Das Politische in der Arbeitspolitik: Ansatzpunkte für eine nachhaltige Arbeits- und
Arbeitszeitgestaltung (editor)*
Weniger ist mehr: Arbeitszeitverkürzung als Gesellschaftspolitik
FLEXIBLE WORKING IN FOOD RETAILING: A Comparison between France,
Germany, the United Kingdom and Japan (*co-editor with C. Baret,
S. Lehndorff and L. Sparks*)

European Employment Models in Flux

A Comparison of Institutional Change in Nine European Countries

Edited by
Gerhard Bosch, Steffen Lehndorff and Jill Rubery

Selection and editorial content © Gerhard Bosch, Steffen Lehndorff and Jill Rubery 2009
Individual chapters © their authors 2009

All rights reserved. No reproduction, copy or transmission of this publication may be made without written permission.

No portion of this publication may be reproduced, copied or transmitted save with written permission or in accordance with the provisions of the Copyright, Designs and Patents Act 1988, or under the terms of any licence permitting limited copying issued by the Copyright Licensing Agency, Saffron House, 6-10 Kirby Street, London EC1N 8TS.

Any person who does any unauthorized act in relation to this publication may be liable to criminal prosecution and civil claims for damages.

The authors have asserted their rights to be identified as the authors of this work in accordance with the Copyright, Designs and Patents Act 1988.

First published 2009 by
PALGRAVE MACMILLAN

Palgrave Macmillan in the UK is an imprint of Macmillan Publishers Limited, registered in England, company number 785998, of Houndmills, Basingstoke, Hampshire RG21 6XS.

Palgrave Macmillan in the US is a division of St Martin's Press LLC, 175 Fifth Avenue, New York, NY 10010.

Palgrave Macmillan is the global academic imprint of the above companies and has companies and representatives throughout the world.

Palgrave® and Macmillan® are registered trademarks in the United States, the United Kingdom, Europe and other countries.

ISBN-13: 978-0-230-22355-4   hardback
ISBN-10: 0-230-22355-9   hardback

This book is printed on paper suitable for recycling and made from fully managed and sustained forest sources. Logging, pulping and manufacturing processes are expected to conform to the environmental regulations of the country of origin.

A catalogue record for this book is available from the British Library.

A catalog record for this book is available from the Library of Congress.

10 9 8 7 6 5 4 3 2 1
18 17 16 15 14 13 12 11 10 09

Printed and bound in Great Britain by
CPI Antony Rowe, Chippenham and Eastbourne

Contents

List of Figures	vii
List of Tables	viii
List of Contributors	ix
Acknowledgements	xiv

1. European Employment Models in Flux: Pressures for Change and Prospects for Survival and Revitalization — *Gerhard Bosch, Steffen Lehndorff and Jill Rubery* — 1

2. Revisiting the UK Model: From Basket Case to Success Story and Back Again? — *Jill Rubery, Damian Grimshaw, Rory Donnelly and Peter Urwin* — 57

3. The Swedish Model: Revival after the Turbulent 1990s? — *Dominique Anxo and Harald Niklasson* — 81

4. From the 'Sick Man' to the 'Overhauled Engine' of Europe? Upheaval in the German Model — *Steffen Lehndorff, Gerhard Bosch, Thomas Haipeter and Erich Latniak* — 105

5. Is Institutional Continuity Masking a Creeping Paradigm Shift in the Austrian Social Model? — *Christoph Hermann and Jörg Flecker* — 131

6. Crisis of the Post-Transition Hungarian Model — *László Neumann and András Tóth* — 155

7. Capitalizing on Variety: Risks and Opportunities in a New French Social Model — *Isabelle Berrebi-Hoffmann, Florence Jany-Catrice, Michel Lallement and Thierry Ribault* — 178

8. Continuity and Change in the Italian Model — *Annamaria Simonazzi, Paola Villa, Federico Lucidi and Paolo Naticchioni* — 201

9	From a State-Led Familistic to a Liberal, Partly De-familialized Capitalism: The Difficult Transition of the Greek Model *Maria Karamessini*	223
10	The Transformation of the Employment System in Spain: Towards a Mediterranean Neoliberalism? *Josep Banyuls, Fausto Miguélez, Albert Recio, Ernest Cano and Raúl Lorente*	247

Index   270

Figures

Figure 1.1	Pressures for change on EU national employment models	13
Figure 1.2	Composite indicator of production market regulations, 1998–2003, selected countries	33
Figure 1.3	Labour input into social services and female full-time equivalent employment rate	35
Figure 1.4	Gross public expenditure on social services as a percentage of GDP	36
Figure 4.1	Regulation of the segments of the German employment model in the 1980s	110
Figure 4.2	Changes in the German employment model by employment segments	116
Figure 6.1	Annual changes of basic economic indicators	159
Figure 7.1	Activity rate, employment rate, unemployment rate in France, 1975–2006 (%)	187
Figure 7.2	Relative unit labour costs in manufacturing, 1970–2005 (year 2000 = 100)	189

Tables

Table 1.1	The location of the 'DYNAMO countries' in existing typologies according to different studies	10
Table 1.2	Elements of the production, employment and welfare regimes studied	19
Table 1.3	Pen sketches of national employment models	21
Table 1.4	Female employment rates (as a percentage of population aged 15–64 and in full-time equivalents), 1995 and 2006	38
Table 2.1	Features of change in the UK model between the early 1990s and 2008	60
Table 2.2	Real expenditure on selected major areas of public spending, 1992/93 to 2006/07 (£ billions)	63
Table 2.3	Proportion of skilled employees among the non-managerial workforce in the workplace, by sector	72
Table 4.1	Quantitative shifts in employment between and within employment segments, 1985–2004	115
Table 6.1	Lisbon employment targets of Hungary (2004, 2006)	173
Table 7.1	Labour productivity, 1987–2005	188
Table 7.2	Annual variation in the French consumer price index, 1981–2005	190
Table 8.1	GDP, employment and unemployment in Italy, 1961–2006 (annual percentage change, unless otherwise stated)	205
Table 8.2	Structure and dynamics of manufacturing exports in Italy and in the world, 1996 and 2002	211
Table 8.3	Employment rates by sex and geographical area, 1977–2003 (percentage of population aged 15–64)	214
Table 9.1	Main economic indicators, Greece	236
Table 9.2	Labour market and social indicators, Greece	238
Table 10.1	Employment by economic activity (in percentages), Spain 1976–2006, EU-15 2006	249
Table 10.2	Temporary employment rate (percentage of wage earners with a fixed-term contract), Spain, 1987–2006	257

Contributors

Dominique Anxo is full Professor in economics at the Departments of Economics and Statistics, University of Växjö and Director of the Centre for Labour Market Policy Research (CAFO). His research interests fall broadly into the areas of labour economics, industrial relations, gender economics, time allocation and evaluation of employment and labour market policy.

Josep Banyuls is a Lecturer in Labour Economics and Employment Policy at Valencia University (Spain). Major areas of interest are in sector change and employment effects, and in international comparative studies on labour management and work organization. He has participated on projects funded by different institutions, including the European Commission and the Valencia Local Government.

Isabelle Berrebi-Hoffmann is a sociologist and a Researcher at the CNRS, in the Interdisciplinary Laboratory for Research in Socio-economics (Lise-CNRS), CNAM, Paris. She has led several research projects and publications on experts and elites in a knowledge economy, service multinational firms models of organizations and knowledge workers. She has taught at Wharton, University of Pennsylvania and HEC group, France.

Gerhard Bosch is an economist and sociologist, Professor at the University Duisburg-Essen and Director of the Institute Work and Qualification (IAQ). He has published widely in the areas of comparative employment systems, low wages, industrial relations and vocational education and training, Recent publications include Bosch, G. and Weinkopf, C. (eds), 2008, *Low-Wage Work in Germany*, New York: Russell Sage Foundation, and Bosch G. and Lehndorff S. (eds), 2005, *Working in the Service Sector: A Tale from Different Worlds*, London: Routledge.

Ernest Cano is an economist and a Lecturer in the Department of Applied Economics at Valencia University (Spain). Research activities cover labour flexibility, new forms of employment and job quality, labour market segmentation and employment policy. He has published several articles and coordinated research projects in Spain on the topic of precariousness in employment.

Rory Donnelly is a Postdoctoral Research Fellow at Manchester Business School. His research interests are in comparative employment systems, the employment relationship, changing career dynamics and the implications of a knowledge-driven economy.

Jörg Flecker is Scientific Director of Forschungs- und Beratungsstelle Arbeitswelt (Working Life Research Centre, FORBA) and External Professor (Universitätsdozent) at the University of Vienna. His main research areas are work organization, industrial relations, flexibility and internationalization. Recent publications include (as editor) *Changing Working Life and the Appeal of the Extreme Right* (published by Ashgate, Aldershot).

Damian Grimshaw is Professor of Employment Studies at Manchester Business School and Director of EWERC (European Work and Employment Research Centre). Recent publications include a policy report for the Equal Opportunities Commission, Undervaluing Women's Work and a co-authored book published by OUP, *Fragmenting Work*.

Thomas Haipeter is Senior Researcher at the Institute Work and Qualification/IAQ (Working Time and Work Organization Department) and Lecturer at the University of Duisburg-Essen. His main research areas are industrial sociology and industrial relations. Recent publications include *Arbeitgeberverbände in der Metall- und Elektroindustrie* (together with Gabi Schilling, published by VSA-Verlag Hamburg).

Christoph Hermann is Senior Researcher at the Working Life Research Centre (FORBA) in Vienna and a lecturer at the University of Vienna, specialized in comparative political economy with a focus on work and employment. Recent publications include *Brüche und Kontinuitäten im österreichischen Beschäftigungs- und Sozialsystem* (edited with Roland Atzmüller, Published by Sigma in Berlin).

Florence Jany-Catrice is Assistant Professor at the University Lille 1, researcher in the laboratory Clersé-CNRS and member of the Institut universitaire de France. Her research fields are oriented on service economies, international comparisons, and social indicators. She is the author or co-author of several books on these aspects, among which is *New Indicators of Well-Being and Development* (with J. Gadrey, published by Palgrave Macmillan in 2006).

Maria Karamessini is Associate Professor in Labour Economics and Economics of the Welfare State at Panteion University of Social and Political Sciences, Athens. Her publications and research interests cover labour market analysis and policy, gender and employment, youth transition from education to work, industrial restructuring, employment reorganization and industrial policy, social policy and social models.

Michel Lallement is Professor of Sociology at the CNAM, Paris. His research affiliation is with the Lise-CNRS. He has written numerous books and articles on work, employment, industrial relations and working-time policies, including *Temps, travail et modes de vie* (PUF, 2003) and *Le Travail. Une sociologie contemporaine* (Gallimard, 2007).

Erich Latniak is Senior Researcher at the Institute Work and Qualification/IAQ (Working Time and Work Organization Department), University of Duisburg-Essen. His main research areas are work organization and work design, human resource management and work and health aspects, especially in the IT industry.

Steffen Lehndorff is Director of the Working-Time and Work Organization Department at the Institute Work and Qualification/IAQ, University of Duisburg-Essen. Areas of interest include international comparative studies on employment and working-time structures, and working-time, work organization and industrial relations in services and manufacturing. He has published widely in these areas and has been co-ordinator of various EU projects (including the project on dynamics of national models on which this book draws).

Raúl Lorente is Lecturer in Sociology at Valencia University, Spain. He was previously lecturer at two Mexican universities (UAT and ITESM). His research focuses on the sociology of work and labour economics and on part-time work in Spain. He has published articles on these topics and a book *La precariedad laboral de trabajar a tiempo parcial* published by Plaza y Valdés editores.

Federico Lucidi is PhD student in economics at the University of Rome 'La Sapienza' and researcher at the Fondazione Giacomo Brodolini. His main research interests are in labour economics and labour market policies.

Fausto Miguélez is Director of the Centre d'Estudis Sociològics QUIT and University Professor at the Autonomous University of Barcelona. His main research areas, in which he has published extensively, are the social structure, industrial relations and the relationship between time, work and everyday life. He has been involved in a large number of comparative research projects for the last 20 years.

Harald Niklasson is full Professor (since 2005 emeritus) in economics at the Departments of Economics and Statistics, Växjö University, Sweden and active member of the Centre for Labour Market Policy Research (CAFO) founded by him in 1987. His research has included the development and application of methods for the economic evaluation of labour market policy means and programmes.

Paolo Naticchioni is a Postdoctoral Researcher at the University of Rome 'La Sapienza'. His research is in labour economics.

László Neumann is Sociologist, PhD, and Senior Research Fellow at the Institute for Social Policy and Labour and at the Institute for Political Science, Hungarian Academy of Sciences. Current research interest embraces several fields of labour market policy and industrial relations: decentralized collective bargaining, employment practices and labour relations at foreign-owned companies, and labour market impacts of Hungary's accession to the European Union.

Albert Recio is Professor at the Department of Applied Economics at the Autonomous University of Barcelona and a member of QUIT. His research interests fall broadly into the areas of labour economy, employment structure, union and social movements and labour policies. He has also published numerous articles and book chapters addressed to the labour economy issue.

Jill Rubery is Professor of Comparative Employment Systems at Manchester Business School and founder and Co-Director of EWERC (European Work and Employment Research Centre). She has published widely in the areas of comparative employment systems, gender equality and labour market segmentation. She is joint author of *The Organization of Employment: An International Perspective* (with Damian Grimshaw, published by Palgrave Macmillan). In 2006 she was elected a Fellow of the British Academy.

Thierry Ribault has a PhD in economics and is a Researcher at the CNRS, in the laboratory Clersé-University of Lille 1. He has published in the areas of labour segmentation and gender issues in the service economy in a comparative perspective, especially in relation to Japan. In 2008 he contributed to a book on care and domestic services in France.

Annamaria Simonazzi is Professor of Economics at the University of Rome 'La Sapienza'. She is Scientific Director of the Fondazione Giacomo Brodolini and co-editor of *Economia & Lavoro*.

András Tóth, PhD, is Research Director of the Centre of European Employment Studies at the Institute of Political Sciences. He has written extensively on issues related to industrial relations, labour law and sociology of work.

Peter Urwin is an Organizer for UNISON, the UK's largest public sector trade union. Between 2005 and 2007 he was a Research Associate at EWERC

(European Work and Employment Research Centre) at the University of Manchester.

Paola Villa is Professor of Labour Economics at the University of Trento (Italy) and an expert on gender studies and labour market in comparative perspectives.

Acknowledgements

This book is based on the results of a research project entitled 'Dynamics of National Models of Employment' (Dynamo) which was conducted over the period 2004–07. The project was set up to investigate the external and internal pressures for change on national employment models in Europe and to consider the implications for the future of national models of this process of change and restructuring. A particular question was whether we would find a tendency for EU member states to develop new specific solutions or a process of convergence towards a European Social or a European Market Model.

The project as a whole involved ten national teams and three interrelated themes and methodologies. This book reports on the first of these, namely the changes in national employment models that can be observed to have been taking place in nine European countries over recent decades. The implications of these developments are not only crucial for our understanding of processes of institutional change and the extent of convergence or divergence within the European community, but also because the survival and indeed revitalization of distinctive national employment models is crucial if Europe is to be able to generate decent work for its citizens. This first theme covered the whole field of production and welfare systems. More detailed work on changes in production systems was undertaken as a second stage through studies of sector-specific changes, taking the examples of IT-services, construction, elderly care, hotels and the motor industry. The third theme focused on change in welfare systems through a comparative analysis of the sources of support provided by the national models – from the state, the labour market and the family – to citizens at key life-course stages. The results of these production and welfare themes are to be published at a later stage.

The editors would like to express their thanks to all the 45 researchers who contributed to the success of the project, including the Irish team who unfortunately, due to illness, could not contribute to the present book. We have enjoyed the collective work process in the course of the project and the inspiring discussions at project meetings. We benefited from various thematic contributions of individual team members which gave us a chance for a better understanding of key issues underlying the present publication, such as the notion of a European social model, of EU economic policy issues and of immigration, or of regional developments in southern and in central and eastern Europe. We experienced a wonderfully supportive attitude of all co-authors in the production process of the present volume and we would like to thank each contributor for their efforts and patience.

We thank the EU Commission, Directorate General Research, for financial support and particularly Heiko Prange and Ronan O'Brien who supported our project and helped in many ways. We would like to make special mention of Gerry Rodgers, former Director of International Labour Institute (ILS), who gave us the opportunity to present earlier versions of some of the papers of this volume at the ILS conference on 'Decent Work, Social Policy and Development' from November 20–December 1, 2006 in Geneva and for Lydia Fraile, also from the ILS, whose astute questions and valuable suggestions contributed considerably to the European country studies. Many thanks also to Andy Wilson from Manchester, who provided translation services to his usual high level, and to Virginia Thorpe from Palgrave who, in managing the production of the book, proved to be extremely flexible, helpful and cooperative.

1
European Employment Models in Flux: Pressures for Change and Prospects for Survival and Revitalization

Gerhard Bosch, Steffen Lehndorff and Jill Rubery

Introduction

Institutions are the building blocks of social order; they shape, govern and legitimize behaviour. Not only do they embody social values but they also reflect historical compromises between social groups negotiated by key actors. It thus comes as no surprise to find major differences in the institutional arrangements of today's capitalist societies. These differences apply especially to employment institutions, which shape the exchange of human labour. Employment contracts are necessarily incomplete contracts, since the actual performance required and rewards offered are constantly subject to new decisions after the contract has been initiated. To put some limits on this uncertainty, institutions, both formal and informal, have been established to influence not only the contractual conditions but also the rights of employees or their representatives to engage in some shared determination of their working conditions and the organization of the work process. The employment relationship is also a pivotal institution in economic systems, with consequences as much for social and family organization as for the production system. It not only shapes the terms under which labour is supplied to and utilized within firms, but also underpins systems of social stratification and determines standards of living. Furthermore, as welfare states have developed and provided support for citizens not in employment, so the employment relationship has become integrated into welfare arrangements, with time spent in an employment relationship often the basis for accumulated entitlements to benefits. The employment relationship is also a key political relationship, both shaping and shaped by the power dynamics between capital and labour and the distribution of incomes within society.

It is the employment relationship embedded within this multiplicity of interlocking institutions that gives rise to what we call national employment models. These multiple interfaces and interactions between employment and other societal arrangements mean that national employment models are pivotal elements in the development and maintenance of distinctive varieties of capitalism (Hall and Soskice, 2001; Whitley, 1999) or what Maurice et al. describe as societal effects (Maurice et al., 1986; Maurice and Sorge, 2000). One of the main tenets of the societal effect school is that the interlocking nature of institutions both shapes and constrains processes of change within a societal system. This interlocking of institutional arrangements also creates the possibility of spillover effects from one sphere to another, potentially increasing the scope of change through ripple or domino effects. Thus, change to the nature of the internalized employment relationship has implications for the survival of the welfare system or the traditional family form. Likewise, pressures for change within the employment model may originate in different spheres: for example in changes in the production system from manufacturing to services, in changes in family and gender relations in line with changes in women's aspirations and labour market behaviour or in changes in the welfare state, including changes to the mode of financing or to the criteria of eligibility for benefits. It is these interconnections that place the employment relationship at the centre of processes of restructuring and change in national models.

There is a great diversity among European employment models. However, for outsiders – for example observers from the United States – it is often the commonalities that are more evident and that have given rise to the notion of the European social model. For much of the post-war period there has been a shared view in most of Europe that, within the constraints of capitalism, there is still scope for the development and maintenance of a public space and for the protection of rights for employees and citizens. It is these shared beliefs that are the basis for the European social models.[1] However, these beliefs are now under challenge from both within and outside the nation states. Pressure to change stems from increased globalization and financialization of markets, the development of new technologies, new forms of governance and the dominance of the service economy, all of which may erode the comparative advantages of distinctive national models that have their origin in outmoded or nationally-specific production models. These production challenges to established models coincide with more internal pressures to reform welfare and employment regimes in line with the long-term changes in demography and social attitudes, manifest in both an ageing society and the feminization of the economically active population. These pressures to change are being articulated not only at the national level by national actors but also through the various policies – both hard and soft – of the European Union (EU) and other supranational organizations such as the Organisation for Economic Co-operation and Development (OECD) or the World Trade Organization (WTO).

It is in this context that this book takes as its theme the challenges to the national employment models in Europe and the impact of responses to these challenges in maintaining, reshaping, revitalizing or indeed destabilizing national employment models. This theme takes on policy significance, as these responses will have implications for the continued survival of the core principles of public space and employee and citizen rights and protections that underpin the concept of the European social model or models. Authors from nine European countries analyse how actors in their respective countries have responded to the above-mentioned challenges and how the national employment models have changed over recent decades. Thus, the focus of this book is on change in employment models. There are good reasons to expect that the outcome of these changes will not be the same in all countries, since not only the starting points but also the capacity of actors to respond differ substantially. However, just stating that European employment models are nearly as diverse as 20 years ago is not in itself a satisfactory analytical result. Our interest is in considering whether these changes are likely to lead to improvement or deterioration in social cohesion and the quality of work. The reference point for understanding changes in social cohesion and quality of work is the concept of 'decent work' as set out by and promoted by the International Labour Organization (ILO).[2] We choose this reference standard over the currently fashionable flexicurity concept in European policy circles. While the flexicurity approach does overlap with our interests in the sense that the objective is to seek ways of adjusting to challenges while maintaining social protection and security, its concerns are nevertheless narrower than those addressed here and in practice it promotes flexibility over security. As Keune and Jepsen (2007) argue, the introduction of flexibility is considered justified provided there is some improvement in social protection for flexible workers, even if the overall outcome is reduced protection. Furthermore, we are also concerned with the impact of the quality of work on comparative advantage, a dimension that is missing from flexicurity where the focus is primarily on smooth and efficient reallocation of labour, not on pushing out the boundaries of the production function or establishing comparative advantage in the global economy (Rubery, 2008).

Obviously there is a danger in such a complex exercise that we will get lost in details. To understand the linkages between employment, production and welfare we draw on the various typologies developed in the broad literature on varieties of capitalism. Such 'typologizing is not an academic game but an essential first step in creating some order out of the chaos of international diversity and providing a framework within which meaningful comparisons can be made' (Fulcher, 2005, p. 178). Typologies are ultimately heuristic instruments and abstractions from national specificities. All the authors in this volume have used these typologies to bring order to the details of their empirical research.

Plan of the chapter

In what follows we first outline the variants of European social models, drawing upon the main typologies of national models in the literature covering production, employment and welfare systems. These typologies were not developed specifically for European economies but in practice are largely based on European reference models, whether as exemplars of coordinated market economies or social democratic welfare systems. Problems with typologies are identified, including their focus on only one element of the model – for example production or welfare – and their emphasis on supply-side characteristics to the neglect of other factors influencing employment performance. The typologies of employment models have increasingly been recognized as static and functionalist, offering little room for understanding tensions, conflicts and change. Recently, however, the literature on national models has been redirected and is now concentrated on challenges to employment models and the processes, forms and outcomes of change. We follow, therefore, this discussion of typologies with an analysis of both the types of pressures for change and the forms of change taking place within national models. Here we suggest that the recent focus on incremental change within national models is insufficient and that more attention needs to be paid to potential ruptures, linked to pressures both external and internal and emanating not only from the production and finance system but also from the social and welfare system. These challenges, we argue, tend to have different impacts according to variations in the architecture of the national models and according to differences in the constellation, roles and attitudes of actors. This highlights the importance of the exercise of political will and choice in the reshaping of national models. To explore these issues further we first provide pen sketches of the main trajectories of change in the nine country case studies (described in the country chapters) before outlining some examples of the importance of architecture, actors and political will in shaping the outcomes of processes of restructuring and change. In the conclusions we summarize our thoughts on how to analyse the dynamics of change in national models before turning to the need to develop a new agenda for institution building if European employment models – and the associated European social model providing both a public space and employee and citizen rights – are not only to survive the current phase of restructuring but also to be revitalized to meet the new challenges.

Typologies of European employment models

Over recent decades, the stream of literature that has contributed to the concept of what we call national employment models has evolved from a broad range of institutional starting points (cf. Coates, 2005 for a thoughtful and both historical and analytical account). Their basic and shared underlying question has been why different national trajectories of capitalist development continue to be reproduced over time. By and large there are two broad streams of research and discussion. The first stream focuses on national competitiveness and how this is embedded in country-specific institutions. The objective is to reach a better understanding of the factors explaining differences in the pace and structures of both economic and employment growth. Greatest attention has been given to the manufacturing sector and the major research topics addressed include capital structures, corporate governance, work organization, vocational training and industrial relations. The second research stream focuses on developing a better understanding of different welfare regimes, which are interpreted as comprising institutions such as the welfare state, the system of labour market protection and the family system. Variations in the service economy also falls within this area of study, since outsourcing of family work into paid services is one of the drivers of growth in service employment. While the issues covered by these two research approaches have only recently started to overlap to any significant degree, in part because of the increasing importance of the service economy where welfare and family systems are crucial to production models, one commonality in the two approaches has been the use of high-profile country examples as material for typologies. These ideal types are utilized to highlight contrasting basic trajectories among developed capitalist countries. Irrespective of the fact that the multitude of national models consists of empirical hybrids and must therefore not be confounded with these ideal types (Crouch, 2005), the value of the typologies is largely found in their use as an analytical tool through which to identify major institutional commonalties among groups of countries and their divergence from other groups.

The core hypothesis of the 'varieties of capitalism' approach (referred to in what follows as 'VoC') is that economic and productivity growth may be fostered to an equal degree by institutions which provide a large amount of elbow room for the influence of the 'free forces of the market' and by institutions which impose 'beneficial constraints' (Streeck, 1997) on the same market forces. The focus of the analysis is on companies and on the implications of the institutional settings in which they are operating for the patterns of growth and competitiveness among national economies. Drawing on various comparative studies of these areas (for example Hollingsworth and Boyer, 1997; Ebbinghaus, 1999; Whitley, 1999), Hall and Soskice (2001) distinguish two contrasting trajectories among developed capitalist countries, labelled as 'liberal' versus 'coordinated market economies' ('LME' and 'CME' respectively). Firms in liberal market economies coordinate their activities internally primarily by means of hierarchies and externally by means of markets. Markets and hierarchies also play a key role in coordinated economies. Here, however, firms in addition rely heavily on non-market relations and 'strategic interactions' for external coordination, which may be used to extend both the time span and the range of possible courses of action.

The most important difference between these two types lies in their respective 'comparative institutional advantage'. By way of example, in coordinated economies the protection of employees' voice is stronger and collective actors, such as employers' associations and trade unions, play significant roles in establishing cooperative relationships. Thus, institutions may offer greater opportunities for the formation of strategic alliances between actors and this may induce capital to be 'patient' in the short run for the sake of higher revenues in the long run (Hall and Soskice, 2001). At the core of this interaction are institutional complementarities, a mutual reinforcement of institutions governing the capital, labour and product markets. In contrast, liberal market economies rely on institutional complementarities of a different nature. Here, high economic and employment growth rates are more likely to be driven by high profit margins and to be based on fluid labour markets, compatible with firms following a more short-term and market orientation. These conditions are said to facilitate a more radical kind of innovation and a faster pace in the conquering of new fields of economic activity. One could debate whether the modernization of existing companies should be labelled as less 'radical' than innovation achieved via high turnover of companies. That said it is nevertheless the case that each of the two systems offers specific strengths (and weaknesses, for that matter) in terms of developing comparative advantage. The outcomes of these paths may vary, in both economic structure and specialization (Sorge, 1991) and in forms of social relations, resulting for example in differences in social inequality and risks. However, there is one commonality amidst these fundamental differences: the respective strengths of both models lie in institutional complementarities (or 'institutional ecologies' as Hall [2007, p. 80] has it) which give rise to 'comparative institutional advantages'. As Hall and Gingerich (2004, p. 29) summarize their consecutive data analyses based on various sets of indicators, 'when complementary institutions are present across spheres of the political economy, rates of economic growth are higher'. The nub of the argument, as phrased by Hancké et al. (2007, p. 7), is that, 'there is no "one best way", as in arguments for neoliberal convergence, but "two", on which middle-spectrum countries (with muddled institutional architectures) may "divergently converge"'.

Undoubtedly the VoC approach has been particularly fruitful in making both a strong point against 'one best way' thinking and in setting a research agenda on the development paths of national economies. One weakness of this stream of literature,[3] however, is that most of the key studies have been focused on manufacturing industry. This weakness was not of great significance as long as manufacturing could be considered the dominant benchmark for international competitiveness and the pacesetter for advancement in work organization, as it was in the 1970s and into the 1980s, and indeed as long as other key sectors of the economy, such as banking and insurance and the mainly publicly owned utilities, were organized in a similar fashion to manufacturing. In today's world of developed capitalisms this perspective is no longer adequate. The structure of labour demand has changed following large-scale job losses in manufacturing. Governance structures and work organization have also changed as a consequence of both the push to privatization in traditional sectors, such as public utilities and other publicly owned companies, and the emergence of new services and knowledge-intensive 'vanguard' industries such as information technology (IT), telecommunications and biotechnology. There have also been significant changes on the labour supply side, with an increase in women's employment, an ageing population and an expansion of entrants from higher education. For all these reasons a broader perspective has become necessary.

Part of that broader perspective is provided by the parallel development of typologies of varieties of welfare capitalism. Traditionally, it was aspects such as the protection against major social risks that were taken as the central issues for the analysis of welfare states. Esping-Andersen (1990), too, took this starting point when he developed his influential and widely debated typology of liberal, social-democratic and conservative (or continental) welfare regimes in EU countries. His typology is based primarily on two criteria: to what extent, and by what means, the welfare state contributes (a) to the 'decommodification' of labour, and (b) to reducing social and status inequality. Under these two criteria, the different types of welfare regime not only work on different principles, they also produce different outcomes. Compared to Nordic social democratic welfare regimes, conservative welfare regimes, as encountered in some continental European countries, provide fewer comprehensive and universal social rights in the way of benefit entitlements; indeed levels of benefits are linked to employment status. Nevertheless, they still provide higher levels of decommodification of labour compared to 'liberal welfare regimes'.[4] A similar hierarchy among welfare regimes applies in the level of protection provided against life-course risks and in the degree to which class and intergenerational inequalities are reduced (Esping-Andersen, 1990, p. 77). Between the social democratic and conservative welfare states, however, a further, and decisive, distinction has been identified: the extent to which welfare obligations are assigned to the household, rather than the state. In this perspective, most continental EU countries tend to provide strong incentives for married women to stay at home, focusing strong welfare guarantees on the male breadwinner (a regime branded as 'familialism' in the wording of Esping-Andersen, 1999, p. 45). In further debates much emphasis was laid on different gender contracts and child-care regimes (for example Germany versus France; Lewis, 1992; Anxo and Fagan, 2005) and on the particular characteristics of southern European countries. Here protection is afforded to the male sole breadwinner in full-time employment, in line with the conservative regime, but the family remains an important production unit and a key institution in the system of social protection. This role is reinforced by the importance of small firms with family workers, the low level of social protection beyond core workers and the marginal labour market status of many young and female workers (Ferrera, 1996; Karamessini, 2008).

Esping-Andersen (1999) highlighted how the characteristics of the welfare system, including the extent of 'de-familiarization' and the degree of income inequality, influenced patterns of service-employment growth. While this approach is crucial to the understanding of different service economies, it applies primarily to social services; that is, services that are outsourced from households as a consequence of rising participation rates among women. These include child or elderly care services that may be provided by either public or private providers, and some consumer services such as restaurants which in part substitute for domestic labour, as well as contributing to the leisure economy. Other service industries, in particular business services, grow for completely different reasons. The explanation of growth in these sectors, in turn, is located much more in the realm of the VoC approach, including different innovation systems and national specialization patterns in the European and global economy. Castells (1996) distinguished between countries that had adopted a service economy model (US, UK, Canada) that emphasizes capital management services over producer services, in contrast to the industrial production model (Germany, Japan) where producer services are more important than financial services. To better understand growth patterns in the service economy, Bosch and Wagner (2005) used Esping-Andersen's typology but enriched it with indicators from the production and service models. According to this hybrid typology the social democratic model combines high levels of social services (gender equity, modern welfare state) with high levels of producer services (specialization in high-value products accompanied by high shares in research and development [R&D] and investments in education and training) but relatively low levels of consumer services (to the extent that Baumol's [1967] argument holds that high wage costs will reduce demands for labour-intensive, low-productivity services). For the same reason, the continental model shows high levels of producer services but, because of the conservative welfare state, low levels of social services. The European liberal models have comparative advantages in financial services and have medium levels of social services. The southern European models have low levels of employment in social, producer and financial services but high levels in consumer services due to their specialization in tourism. In addition, the authors point to the problems of comparisons of employment structures between smaller and larger countries because the former may be able to specialize in only a few industries, an option which is not possible for larger countries. This applies especially to comparisons between the USA and European countries which are often the size of a US state.

Up until now the debates on VoC in manufacturing and in services, and on welfare regimes, have largely taken place on different, if neighbouring, playgrounds. However, these playgrounds are not separated from one another by strong fences. Major aspects of VoC typologies, such as employment protection and other elements of labour market regulation, are also crucial for welfare regime typologies; for example, employment protection and employment security policies influence the patterns and forms of welfare state support for the unemployed. Note, however, that in this stream of literature any linkage between institutions, such as the impacts of welfare states on industrial relations and training systems, is viewed through the lens of its importance for coordination among firms, identified as the core actors in any variety of capitalism. Consequently Hall (2007, p. 40), in commenting on variations across welfare states in his VoC analysis, expressed the view that 'social policy is a crucial adjunct to coordination'. This approach is undoubtedly legitimate within a research agenda focused on explaining firms' interests in the reproduction of institutions that depart from clear-cut 'free market' environments. However, other research questions require different appreciations of the interplay of institutions.

Thus, a more integrated approach to the analysis of national employment models, comprising production, employment and welfare regimes, could yield substantial benefits. Amable (2003) took up this challenge by developing a typology based on cluster analyses. To this end, he used numerous sets of indicators on the organization of product and labour markets, of financial systems, and of systems of education and social protection. He ended up with five types, namely 'market-based', 'Asian', 'Continental European', 'Social-democratic' and 'Mediterranean' models of capitalism.[5] In contrast to the typologies based on ideal-types, a cluster-based grouping is necessarily inclusive and, therefore, does not leave countries marooned between competing typologies. This could in principle resolve the problems of applying typologies to 'deviant countries', most strikingly France which 'finds itself in a typological purgatory, neither CME fish nor LME fowl' (Levy, 2006, p. 23), or Italy which is called a 'deviant' case within the VoC literature, characterized by 'a mix of logics, a high degree of institutional incoherence and an apparent absence of complementarities' (Molina and Rhodes, 2007, p. 223). However, in practice Amable's 'Continental European' cluster, although containing Germany as the standard reference case that combines a 'coordinated market economy' with a 'continental welfare regime', is otherwise composed of countries that are primarily notable for the heterogeneity of their characteristics and an absence of clearly identifiable common elements (Amable, 2003, p. 224).[6] The clearest and most homogenous clusters in Amable's analysis were in fact the 'market-based' economies, followed by the 'social-democratic' cluster. This suggests that, while some ideal-type models may be representative of a group and may even act as a model for imitators, others may in practice stand alone. While we would not necessarily agree with Amable that this lack of homogeneity among the continental cluster countries implies a lack of institutional coherence at the individual national model level, this outcome nevertheless underscores the need to go beyond existing typologies when analysing change in, or of, national employment models. The underlying concern of this book is how to understand basic trends of change within and across countries, rather than just 'categorizing' them.

Table 1.1 The location of the 'DYNAMO countries' in existing typologies according to different studies

Country	Esping-Andersen	Hall/Soskice	Coates	Amable
Sweden	Social-democratic	Coordinated	Negotiated	Social-democratic
UK	Liberal	Liberal	Market-led	Market-based
France		Mixed	State-led	Continental
Germany	Continental	Coordinated	Negotiated	Continental
Austria				Continental
Hungary		Emerging		
Spain		Mixed		Mediterranean
Italy	Continental (Southern)	Hall: Mixed Thelen: Coordinated		Mediterranean
Greece				Mediterranean

Source: Own compilation based on Esping-Andersen (1990 and 1999), Coates (2000), Hall and Soskice (2001) including Thelen (2001), Amable (2003) and Hancké et al. (2007)

Table 1.1 locates the national employment models studied in the present book within these various typologies of models and demonstrates that the nine cases cover the full range of varieties of (welfare) capitalism identified in the literature, thereby providing an appropriate sample for the exploration of the nature of change within categories of national models. Before moving on to this task, however, we need to take into account a number of factors that impact upon employment performance of models that are not normally included in the dominant literature on verities of capitalism.

Beyond typologies: Some missing factors shaping the performance of models

The analysis of change at an individual country level requires consideration of some dimensions and country characteristics additional to those used to construct typologies. These factors may be able to explain differences both in countries' capacities to adapt and change over time and in perceptions of models as failing or succeeding.

A first example of such variables is the macroeconomic management of the economy, including wage setting and monetary and fiscal policies. Just as innovative firms cannot succeed without a good marketing strategy or strong financial management, so national economies must also be well managed. Under Keynesian economic policy some institutions of macro-economic management (for example a coordinated pay policy) were regarded as integral to the employment models. With the change from Keynesian to a more liberal or monetarist approach, the notion of an employment model became firmly associated with supply-side characteristics. However, the high employment growth in the UK (and also in the USA) in the last decade, prior to the financial crisis in 2008, cannot really be explained without taking into account the UK's expansive fiscal policy; similarly the unfavourable employment situation in some countries of the Euro zone has to be viewed also in the context of the Maastricht criteria and the growth-constricting interest rate policy adopted first by the German Bundesbank and then by the European Central Bank. The housing boom served in some Euro zone countries, especially Spain, as a functional equivalent to an expansive macroeconomic policy by driving up internal demand. (cf. Banyuls et al., Chapter 10). However, certain approaches to macroeconomic policy may also be inherent to individual national models. Liberal economies such as the UK but also the US appear to have become dependent for continuing growth and employment on ever-increasing consumer credit, external debt and bank-financed property booms. Likewise centralized pay bargaining, which had traditionally operated as a cornerstone of the Swedish mode, had to be re-established from 1994 onwards in response to the crisis of the 1980s and the early 1990s. This crisis was in part attributable to a policy of allowing the financial discipline that had been built into the core of the original model and exercised through centralized wage policy to weaken (cf. Anxo and Niklasson, Chapter 3).

A second factor that may explain a divergence of country experience within typologies is that national employment models have their cycles. They represent historical compromises that are successful during a particular period but then have to be renewed. Very rarely are models changed as a part of a preventive strategy, in accordance with a master plan agreed by the actors involved; more commonly, the changes are enforced by crises. Crises in employment models usually last longer than cyclical economic crises because the restructuring process can be extremely conflict-ridden. In the course of institutional restructuring, however, new decisions are made with regard to distribution and participation. These decisions naturally produce winners and losers, which in turn may create obstacles to reform. Germany's employment model, at least before the 2008 crisis, was showing signs of recovery after a long crisis; the productive system, including the associated producer services, had already been successfully modernized, but the reform of the welfare state was still in process. Crises are often, quite wrongly, only interpreted negatively. They can also provide the impetus for revitalization through reform of a national employment model. As such, the classification of a national model as a success or as a failure may be highly context specific and dismissing a model as an example of a failed or outdated system may prove premature. This institutional rebuilding, which is part of the life cycle of models, draws upon existing and historical institutional resources, but also provides considerable scope for more specific and contingent political factors to influence and shape outcomes. In consequence we differentiate ourselves from the current widespread understanding of 'models' as *role* models. Among not only national but also European and wider international actors, there is increasing interest in the sharing of examples of both good and bad experiences across national boundaries. This interest reflects the ups and downs of 'models' in both the political and academic debates. However, as Fulcher (2005, p. 190) notes, 'model status can change rapidly as economic fortunes and international judgements shift'. He refers to the examples of Japan which 'went from model in the 1980s to basket-case in the 1990s', and to the USA that 'went from competitive failure in the 1980s to become the model of shareholder capitalism in the 1990s but now, post-Enron/Worldcom and hugely burdened with debt, is it still a model?'. More recent European examples of changing 'model status' which are addressed in the present volume include the UK, Sweden and Germany. Rubery et al. (cf. Chapter 2) put their analysis of the UK model under the headline 'From Basket Case to Success Story – and Back Again?', indicating the fluctuating fortunes of the UK model. Anxo and Niklasson (cf. Chapter 3) remind us that, according to the literature of the early 1990s, the Swedish model was doomed to demise, whereas for many observers today Sweden ranks among the best-performing EU member states, as far as the Lisbon targets are concerned. An equally striking example of the dramatic ups and downs experienced by national models is that of Germany (cf. Lehndorff et al., Chapter 4). Similarly, Eichengreen (2007, p. 414) summarizes his larger picture of European economic development, set against the United States, with the outlook that 'for anyone encountering forceful statements of American triumphalism and Eurosclerosis, history is a reminder that this too shall pass'.

A third factor that may lead to divergence in development is that, in a global economy with an increasingly complex division of labour, it may make sense to strengthen national particularities and not to follow a dominant model. As Hall and Soskice (2001, p. 60) note, 'because of comparative institutional advantage, nations often prosper, not by becoming more similar, but by building on their institutional differences'. As globalization proceeds, the development of comparative competitive advantages may well be a country's best chance of preventing the relocation of its productive activities. A major issue is whether new patterns of specialization will emerge that were not captured by previous categorizations of production or welfare models and which may lead to new sources of difference among countries. For example the UK, long seen as unable to move on to a high-road manufacturing path due to skill deficiencies, has increased its specialization in tradable as well as more domestically oriented services, a strategy that in the growth decade created sufficient jobs to more than compensate for the above-average loss of jobs in manufacturing. Thus, while the problem of the UK being stuck in a low-skill equilibrium (Finegold and Soskice, 1988; Rubery, 1994) continues in some respects,[7] this characteristic may no longer have the same significance as in the past. Another example of divergent specialization is provided by the southern European countries' specialization in tourism; opportunities for service sector development may be dependent upon a different set of contingent and institutional factors than applied to the development of comparative advantage in manufacturing.

A fourth factor influencing the capacity of countries to respond to change is size of country. Smaller countries in crisis tend to achieve a new consensus on a change of direction more quickly than larger ones, where the restructuring of the employment model tends to last longer (Auer, 2000). One reason may be that they find it easier to identify niches in the global market where they can exploit their comparative advantages. Another reason may be that it is easier with a smaller number of actors to build up the necessary trust for institutional change. These two reasons might explain why Austria developed its own mix of a liberal market economy and social democratic corporatism, thus avoiding the same increases in inequality as in Germany over recent years (cf. Hermann and Flecker, Chapter 5). This may be why the national models of small countries appear to recover more quickly from crises than those of large countries.

Challenges to national models: Pressures for change and forms of change

Pressures for change

Figure 1.1. provides an illustration of the most significant pressures for change in European employment models. Globalization is the general term commonly used to encapsulate external pressures for change. However, this term encompasses a range of external pressures associated with a variety of

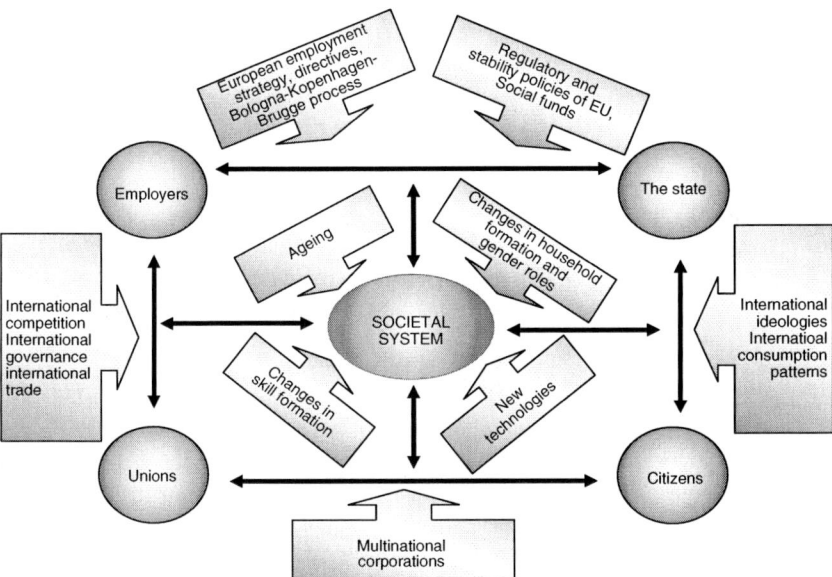

Figure 1.1 Pressures for change on EU national employment models
Source: Own representation after Rubery and Grimshaw (2003, p. 47)

institutional developments and new policy agendas as well as with changes in behaviour and attitudes. These various influences are depicted round the outer edge of the figure and include changes in international governance, including international agreements to open up markets (for example under the auspices of the WTO or as a result of EU directives on competition, including the freedom to provide services). Together they are calling into question traditional regulations and governance structures in national financial, product and of course labour markets. Public discourses are also being more strongly influenced by internationally dominant ideologies that call into question the compatibility of competitiveness with employment and social protection and promote the imperatives of change and modernization. The spread of international consumption patterns, through foreign travel, migration and the Internet, is speeding up pressures for change in national models of production and service delivery. Multinational companies also create pressure for change by importing forms of work organization developed abroad and by resisting national customs and practices.

National models also have to be responsive to general changes in new technologies – that is, to use Smith and Meiksins's (1995) distinction, there are some general universal changes, known as system effects, to which models have to respond. However, the mode of introduction of new technologies will be shaped by the second type of effects – societal-specific effects – as firms and indeed societies seek not just to absorb and implement the technologies but also to produce innovations to safeguard or build up comparative competitive advantage. Other internal challenges include the expansion of education systems, changes in household structures as a result of rising participation rates among women and the ageing of the population; all of these are not only changing the composition of labour supply but also creating new demands with which the welfare system will have to deal. Increased requirements for workers to be both more flexible and to raise their skill levels generate needs for new forms of support from the family, the state or employers to cope with longer and possibly more recurrent periods of education in a context of greater labour market uncertainty. Welfare systems not only have to adjust to extended life expectancy but also have to meet new demands for extended childcare services as fewer women are available to provide full-time care for their children.

Thus, the pressure for change is not only coming from deregulation of markets and globalization, as Streeck and Thelen (2005, p. 2) assume, but emanating simultaneously from within and from without. However, the dividing line cannot be precisely drawn. It is not only that public discourse has become more international or that international patterns of consumption and earnings may replace or be superimposed onto national patterns and expectations. It is also the case that the elites, whose fortunes until now were closely associated with the well-being of nation states, now have an increasing number of exit options (such as changing their place of residence or sending their children to private or foreign schools and universities), which may be weakening internal cohesion. In practice the decision-making bodies of international institutions such as the OECD, the WTO or the European Commission consist largely of national actors, and likewise many decisions at national level are influenced by international demands. Indeed one source of change in national models is that new configurations of actors may be emerging, reflecting the decline in influence of some actors but the rise of others, with new opportunities to influence models through action at international or national level (see for example Berrebi-Hoffmann et al., Chapter 7). National actors may seek, for example, to negotiate at international level arrangements that are binding on their country, thereby freeing themselves of the need to make compromises at national level. For example, the European Commission's decisions on the opening up of public utilities, which were ultimately taken by representatives of the national governments, would probably not have been passed by all national parliaments in their current form without the prior decisions at EU level. These differences may be the result of the greater attention paid to national rather than EU decision-making, the latter's processes remaining poorly understood by many national actors. Also, as Moravcsik (1994, p. 1) argues, the effect of the EU is to strengthen the power of the national executive 'permitting them to loosen domestic constraints imposed by legislatures, interest groups, and other societal actors'. National actors may also exaggerate the constraints imposed by globalization to justify policies for transforming national employment models (Weiss, 2003). Indeed, if one considers the range of reactions of nation states to the challenges of globalization, it is justifiable to retain a certain degree of scepticism towards those who argue that nation states are becoming increasingly powerless in the face of globalization. We would suggest that they still enjoy some degree of freedom to make choices and to take deliberate political action.

Forms of change: Some theoretical issues

Change turns out to be a challenge not just to the national models themselves but also to the theories on national models. It is only recently that change has become a prominent topic within the VoC stream of literature (Hancké et al., 2007). This move is an explicit reaction to one of the most pertinent critiques of the VoC approach. For Crouch and Farrell (2002) the approach brings with it a danger of 'institutional determinism', while Jackson and Deeg (2006, p. 37) note that 'the whole effort to describe and classify capitalism presumes institutional stability'. If we look at the history of existing national models, it is evident that this stability cannot be taken for granted. National models have developed out of conflicting interests and reflect a certain balance of power at crucial stages of development

(Hobsbawm, 1996; Thelen, 2003). Conflicts of interest and power relations are sources of both variation over time and variation across countries. As argued by Pontusson (2005, p. 165), 'conflicts of interest enable us to understand why institutional equilibria might come undone, and the power balance among political-economic actors provides the most obvious point of departure for an explanation of why institutions or policies change in a particular direction'. In Pontusson's view, 'the Hall-Soskice framework provides a solid foundation for exploring the institutional sources of comparative advantage, but leaves a great deal to be desired if we want to explain distributive labour-market outcomes or understand the politics of welfare-state restructuring in the current era. A more comprehensive and inclusive framework (which) might be built by treating efficiency/coordination and distribution/power as interrelated but separate, equally important analytical dimensions' (p. 165).

This perspective is difficult to incorporate within a VoC framework as a key VoC assumption is that leading actors in CMEs will keep seeking for ways to re-establish institutional complementarities wherever and whenever they are threatened. Of course under certain circumstances this may actually happen, as the chapter on Sweden (cf. Anxo and Niklasson, Chapter 3) in the present volume demonstrates. The chapter on Germany (cf. Lehndorff et al., Chapter 4) in contrast argues that the interest of major actors in the earlier institutional setting cannot be taken for granted. Shifting power relations that result from either new struggles between established actors or as a consequence of the emergence of new configurations of actors may produce cracks in the institutional architecture of the model. Diverging attitudes and strategies of actors vis-à-vis these institutions may result in a reshuffle of the interplay of institutions and actors in a given employment model. Changes in the overall economic, political or ideological environment provide opportunities to call into question historic compromises in which a national model has so far been rooted. As Crouch and Keune (2005) argue, deviant or dormant elements of a model may come into play and provide a resource to strengthen forces for change. For example, in the UK case the notion that the market does not need to be tempered by regulation and by redistributive social policy had been embedded in the values of the City of London over decades but only took hold as a dominant ideology and strategy under Thatcher.

Thus, the analytical challenge is to capture the interplay between changes in the economic, societal, political and ideological environment and foundations of national models on the one side, and the capacities of existing institutions to 'digest' these changes on the other. Changes in the foundations and environment may cause contradictions between elements of models (that is, between or within the production, welfare and employment regimes) and between attitudes of the public and the strategies of major actors vis-à-vis these institutions. These clashes may trigger institutional change, which in turn may lead to either the adaptation of institutions and actors to challenges or to new tensions and contradictions.

It is against this background that Streeck and Thelen (2005) have suggested a research agenda that turns attention onto how incremental change is taking place, leading either to 'reproduction by adaptation' or to 'gradual transformation'; that is, 'incremental change with transformative results'. To provide a more differentiated understanding, they distinguish five types of change. Of these arguably the most visible type of change is 'displacement', which is defined as a 'slowly rising salience of subordinate relative to dominant institutions'. A second type is called 'layering', which indicates an attachment of new elements to existing institutions, entailing a gradual change of their status and structure. Thirdly, 'drift' addresses a 'deliberate neglect of institutional maintenance in spite of external change resulting in slippage in institutional practice on the ground', whereas 'exhaustion' indicates a 'gradual breakdown' of institutions over time by way of 'depletion'. 'Conversion', finally, stands for a 'redeployment of old institutions to new purposes'.

As these authors take the 'broad process of liberalization' as the overarching context in which to identify 'the magnitude and significance of current changes', it follows that their reasoning is more about the *forms* and the *extent* of adaptation of these models to the universal mainstream than about the *content* and the actual *outcomes* of change. Incremental change is assumed to be primarily cumulative, towards liberalization. This approach tends not to focus on the room for manoeuvre for actors at critical junctures, for example the political choices that actors may or may not exercise to rebuild institutions in an environment where deregulation of product markets threatens the erosion of the social content of the employment models. Therefore it is not clear how the Streeck and Thelen approach can be applied in, for example, cases of revitalization of CME-type models through institutional reforms as we argue has occurred in Sweden (cf. Anxo and Niklasson, Chapter 3) and to some extent in Austria (cf. Hermann and Flecker, Chapter 5), or indeed with examples such as the UK case where there is evidence of a strengthening of the social dimension to LME-type models (cf. Rubery et al., Chapter 2).

Finally, the focus on incremental change draws attention away from possibilities of radical changes or ruptures with the existing employment model. In these pages accounts of fundamental ruptures in the development of national employment models are given for the cases of Spain (cf. Banyuls et al., Chapter 10) and Greece (cf. Karamessini, Chapter 9) after the periods of dictatorship, even if there remain important elements of continuity with the old models. Rupture is even more obvious for the case of Hungary (cf. Neumann and Tóth, Chapter 6). Similarly, the breakdown of the former socialist economy in East Germany exerted substantial pressure on the German model as a whole, which helped to push Germany away from its path-dependent development into the direction of the liberal employment models (cf. Lehndorff et al., Chapter 4). The cases of Hungary and East Germany also demonstrate how fragile institutions may be after a model change. This fragility reflects the fact that institutional complementarities have yet to develop and that so far no common or shared understanding has emerged among the main actors. This fragility might explain why Hungary is still in search of an employment model, oscillating between two options – the Rhenish and the Anglo-Saxon varieties of capitalism. Ruptures may also occur if a model is destabilized through the loss of an important pillar; an example here, which we turn to in more detail later, is the impact of changes to financial markets that are removing the 'patient capital' pillar on which the German model was built. Because of institutional complementarities, the consequences can be expected to be far reaching and indeed too much complementarity and interdependency of institutions may weaken or even endanger them. Deciding if a change is rupture or only a gradual adjustment may to a large extent depend upon an individual and subjective judgement, but we would contend that significant changes to a main pillar of a model has at least the potential to be considered a rupture if no countervailing measures are taken. The recent emphasis on gradual changes makes it difficult to understand the redirection of model changes that can be observed currently taking place in some countries, such as Germany. However, some countries had quite different employment models in the relatively recent past. The UK of the 1970s with its industry-wide bargaining and a strong nationalized sector was not the prototype of a liberal model. Rupture to this model may have been facilitated by the fact that, in the continuing conflictual UK industrial relations environment, the notion of social compromise had rather weak roots. The model was thus more vulnerable to short-term political cycles than for example the Swedish model.

A different recent approach to the change problematic is Hall's (2007, p. 41) suggestion to 'put the institutional changes occurring today into historical perspective': VoC should be 'best seen, not as a set of stable institutional models, but as a set of institutionally conditioned adjustment trajectories displaying continuous processes of adaptation'. The insights produced by this fruitful consideration, applied to critical periods of change in Sweden, Germany, France and the UK over the past 50 years, include the observation that similar developments, such as the 'liberalization' process, 'can have impacts that vary across institutional settings'. Therefore, 'despite important common trends, the political economies of Europe are not converging rapidly on a common liberal model' (Hall, 2007, p. 78). The open question here, in contrast to the position of Streeck and Thelen, is how to characterize those models which continue to diverge from the 'common liberal model'. By way of example, within his VoC perspective, Hall continues to characterize Germany as an exemplar of CME-type models, while acknowledging that over the past decade coordination among firms has been mixed and has involved increased dualization of the labour market. However, if the review of models had been conducted from the perspective of employment regimes, it would be questionable if it were still meaningful to characterize Germany as a CME.

Thus, while benefiting from the approaches to change discussed here, our interest is to go beyond them. The country studies in this book analyse the interplay between the main dimensions of the respective employment models; that is, the production, employment and welfare regimes on the one hand, and the handling of this interplay and the tensions involved by major actors on the other. The approach we are adopting can be called, for shorthand, 'architectures and actors'; thus we are concerned first with challenges to the architecture of models emanating from external or internal pressures and which may give rise to interactions between the main elements or pillars of national employment models – that is, the production, employment and welfare regimes (Table 1.2).[8] This perspective allows for the establishment of linkages between the two different and largely parallel streams of literature – that is, on the VoC and the 'worlds of welfare capitalism' – but also allows for differences in the specific architecture of models to result in divergent outcomes even within models that have previously been classified as sharing common elements and orientations. This wide approach is particularly important if the challenges to employment models are recognized to be emanating not only from changes in the world economy and in modes of economic and corporate governance but also from changes in demographics, in social arrangements and in individual aspirations and expectations.

The second focus is on actors. Much of the institutionalist literature is on the relationship between market and state. When it comes to understanding the dynamics of national employment models, however, it is necessary to bring the wider group of social, economic and political actors back in. This in turn entails aspects which may remain hidden if change is analysed from solely an institutionalist perspective. One aspect which has already been mentioned is the importance of changing power relations. Deviant or dormant models may come back into play once a turn of the tide in the economic or political environment fosters new political approaches and changes the constellation of

Table 1.2 Elements of the production, employment and welfare regimes studied

Production regime	Specialization patterns / value added base
	Ownership / governance
	Product market regulation
	Industrial organization / skill development / innovation
Employment regime	Labour market regulation / employment protection
	Education / training system
	Industrial relations system
	Unemployment insurance / labour market policy
Welfare regime	Welfare state / social protection
	Gender regime / role of family
	Social services

Source: Own compilation

significant actors. The emphasis on actors and conflicts of interest is also relevant for the social content or outcomes of a model. This reasoning leads us also to emphasize the importance of political choice. By way of example, there are important differences in the approaches of governments to the further development of the public infrastructure and to the macroeconomic management of the economy. Of course political choices are always constrained by the legacy of the traditional institutional context, the degree of consensus and trust and the economic situation within a country. An important part of the legacy is the type of state; that is, if it operates primarily on an arm's length or contractual basis or belongs to one of the types of promotional states that play a more direct role in coordinating and developing the economy (Whitley, 2007). But there are always turning points when pillars of the old models have to be changed to meet new external regulations or because they have lost legitimacy due to gradual erosion and/or because they are no longer in tune with the preferences of the population. This last factor highlights the importance of policy-making at the nation state level to meet citizens' needs and preferences. Even in a context of globalization and the influence of supranational bodies, most institutions of the welfare and employment model are still primarily determined by national legislation (Weiss, 2003). EU directives and employment strategy influence changes but within a wide frame which leaves open many possibilities for reactions by nation states. The hard laws on competition and the opening of product and labour markets leave much less leeway to social actors at the nation-state level. But to some extent, the implementation of this hard law can still be counterbalanced by nation states choosing to maintain or introduce regulations to guarantee social standards.

The focus on both architectures and actors is important for an assessment of the capacities of national models to change. Contradictions between major dimensions of employment models and the reopening of conflicts of interests may trigger institutional adaptations to changed environments, but adaptations in turn may also be the cause of new contradictions, tensions and conflicts (Wilkinson, 1983). While the focus of the institutionalist debates so far has been very much on institutional complementarities and their ability to foster both external comparative advantage and internal cohesion, we suggest that equal attention should be paid to the possibilities of the emergence of new incoherencies through the process of change in either competitive capacities or indeed in meeting internal needs and aspirations. The potential for institutional incompatibilities and comparative *dis*advantage thus requires equal attention.

Change in nine European employment models

Although the various European employment models we consider in this book are facing similar types of pressures, there are major variations both in the extent and force of the pressures and in the necessity for and extent and speed of response. The same pressures pose very different challenges for restructuring the national employment models.[9] Some countries have adopted a proactive policy – sometimes induced by a crisis in the national model[10] – and have already introduced modifications into their employment models in response to these pressures. Others have hardly begun the process of adjustment and, moreover, may be resistant to current orthodoxy on how to adjust since they fear major consequences for the employment model as a whole. However, there are also major variations within countries over time in the direction and pace of change, influenced by national political cycles and changes in the balance of power between actors. These variations are highlighted through pen sketches of the analysis of change presented in the nine country chapters of this book (see Table 1.3).

Table 1.3 Pen sketches of national employment models

	Type of model: VoC, variety of welfare state	Characterizing change	Continuing tensions/ unresolved issues
UK	LME Residual welfare state	Reinforcement of market model. Revitalization through new social pillars	Fragility of model based on financialization, housing and consumer credit. Segmentation of labour market continues even though improved public services/higher minimum social guarantees
Sweden	CME Social democratic	Revitalization through both re-establishment of model (macroeconomic controls, social contract) plus new pillars – such as innovation	Combining labour standards with product market deregulation but under threat from EU. High taxes still a political challenge
Germany	CME Conservative	Upheaval and fragmentation; neo-liberal reorientation of major actors in the wake of unification	Successful reform of production system but model challenged by rise of less regulated service sector, problems of unification, lack of universal labour standards and an outdated family/ welfare model
Austria	CME Conservative	Conversion – from demand-led to supply-led corporatism	Continuity of corporatism, with continuing regulation of labour standards associated with major changes in political context. Failure to modernize family and welfare policy

(Continued)

Table 1.3 (Continued)

	Type of model: VoC, variety of welfare state	Characterizing change	Continuing tensions/ unresolved issues
Hungary	Post-transition Legacy welfare state	In search of a model– oscillating between Anglo-Saxon/Rhenish model	Period of high FDI inflows has left country exposed to credit crisis; problem of reconciling demands for strong welfare state with poor value added base
France	CME/state-led Continental	Conversion – from state led to state enhancing	Privatization and decentralization of the state but the state has expanded role in providing minimum income guarantees and other forms of support for the unemployed, particularly the young
Italy	CME (north – under-developed in south) Familialist	Tensions between development and familialist model – shrinking core, enlarging periphery	Only 'limping reformism': problems of 'frozen specialization' in consumer goods vulnerable to delocalization; continuing problem of segmented/ incomplete welfare coverage Widening regional inequalities. Low tax base to support reform
Greece	State-led Familialist	Tensions between development and familialist model. From state-led to liberal, shrinking core and enlarging periphery	Liberal reforms not leading to new forms of comparative advantage. Limited welfare reform, in part because of low tax base
Spain	CME Familialist	From CME to liberal. Tensions between development and familialist model	Liberalization of model only resisted at national level by trade unions – limited influence at workplace. Some recent but limited changes to familialist welfare model. Reliance on housing market resulting in exposure to the credit crunch

Source: Own compilation
CME = coordinated market economy; FDI = foreign direct investment; LME = liberal market economy; VoC = variety of capitalism

Pen sketches of change in nine national employment models

The *UK* provides the European reference model for liberal market economies and for residual welfare states. However, a key observation made by Rubery et al. (cf. Chapter 2) is that the divergence between the UK and the US model, measured in social terms, is starker than in the early 1990s. Several of the social elements of the model have been strengthened, rather than weakened, and there is a higher commitment to public investment than in past decades. Particularly notable are the introduction of an effective minimum wage and the increase in public spending for health and other social purposes. This move, however, does not call into question the basic character of the UK as a 'liberal market economy'. First of all the economy has been one of the main promoters of the growth of deregulated financial services. Second, the expansion of public social expenditure implies a reinforcement of the liberal model as it is closely linked with a boost in outsourcing and tendering policies to expand the role of the private sector. The 'market state' is the concept in which both these aspects of this New Labour strategy of modernizing social services merge. Third, even the introduction of the minimum wage and the subsequent raising of its level can be explained in part by the reinforcement of means-tested benefits as the main anti-poverty policy, a hallmark of liberal welfare systems. Without an effective floor to the labour market, the adoption of in-work benefits could result in soaring public expenditures. The UK is a striking example of continuity *through* institutional change. As a consequence of structural changes resulting from a strengthening in the UK's position as a leader in globalization of services – both financial services and internationalized service production chains – the well-known problem of low skill equilibrium in manufacturing took on less policy significance than in the past. However, despite an increase in the share of new entrants with higher education, the UK model has still failed to improve the quality of employment for the mass of the working population. Inequality and segmentation are still inherent features of the labour market. The crisis of 2008 may temper the growth of inequality at the top end but its main impact is to reveal the fragility of the UK's prosperity, based as it has been on the growth of financialization, the speculative housing boom and high debts of consumers. The sustainability of the model is now very much in question.

Sweden, along with Germany, is often taken as the main reference country for 'coordinated market economies' and, further, as the most distinctive example of a social-democratic welfare state with comprehensive labour standards. After more than a decade of crisis, the Swedish model has emerged as another example of continuity through institutional change. Anxo and Niklasson (cf. Chapter 3) highlight the reforms of the collective bargaining and pension systems and point to the reorientation of active labour market policy as particularly salient aspects of this revitalization of the Swedish model – a revitalization aimed at providing long-term stabilization of the model. The breakdown of centralized bargaining from the early 1980s onwards not only threatened to reduce capacity for macroeconomic governance but also led to resistance from the public, concerned that the welfare state might be sacrificed on the altar of globalization. As a consequence, a new balance was sought between centralized and decentralized elements of collective bargaining in order to strengthen the capacity of the social partners to contribute to macroeconomic governance. A similar logic lay behind the pension reform, where the objective was to achieve a rebalancing of risks through a strengthening of the private elements in the system and an increase in the risks borne by employees so as to secure the long-term stabilization and survival of the still dominant public scheme.

International competitiveness in both manufacturing and in services has been reinforced by increasing investment in education and training as well as in research and development. The innovation system has been developed into a main pillar of the Swedish model and serves to ensure that high labour standards are still economically viable in a more competitive environment with open markets. The deregulation of product markets has not led to substantially increased income differentiation since wage-setting institutions appear to be functioning independently of product market regulation. Wages are effectively taken out of competition by high trade union density and high coverage of collective agreements. Sweden's employment rate in general, and the employment rate of women and of older workers in particular, are widely regarded as representing European best practice. The high taxes, combined with the broad tax base generated by the high employment rate, have made it possible not only to develop employment in social services but also to provide decent working conditions in these areas. Nevertheless, tensions over the high taxes and the unemployment rate, which is widely perceived as intolerable, have grown among the Swedish public over recent years.

Next to Sweden, *Germany* has been the second key exemplar of the 'coordinated market economy', but at the same time, in contrast to Sweden, a prominent example of a 'continental' or 'conservative' welfare state. The notions of change in, or of, the German model suggested by Lehndorff et al. (cf. Chapter 4) are not continuity but upheaval and fragmentation. This holds, according to their analysis, irrespective of the economic upswing before the financial crisis which turned Germany for a couple of years, as so many times in past decades, once again into the major economic engine within the EU. The manufacturing sector with its supporting institutions, such as the strong innovation and vocational training systems, has been and continues to be highly competitive. New forms of innovation-oriented cooperation between employers, unions and works councillors have been developed. However, the scope for 'coordination' – measured by the share of the whole economy affected – has been drastically reduced compared to the past. In the labour market it is the former dormant unregulated service model that has become equally important as the manufacturing segment which is no longer setting the pattern of labour standards for the whole economy. Alongside this dualism between the manufacturing and service production segments there is the strong geographical east-west divide which has proved to be far more resilient than expected after the catch-up process in the former East Germany came to a standstill some years ago. The German collective bargaining system also proved to be very vulnerable to external shocks stemming from German unification and the deregulation of product markets and has not been strong enough to avoid increasing wage inequality. Moreover, the continental welfare regime, which used to complement the production regime, nowadays channels women into precarious employment and no longer meets women's aspirations and preferences. The direction of future change is unclear since there is competition between not only two production models (manufacturing and services) but also between the old and the new emerging family models. Each of the model variants has powerful actors supporting them. The politics of reform seem often to be contradictory: on the one side there are efforts to promote further deregulation but on the other there is debate about introducing minimum wages and taking steps towards welfare state reforms to improve reconciliation of work and family life. Since such tensions probably cannot persist for very long, the German model is still at a turning point.

The diversity among CME countries appears even greater when we look at the *Austrian* case as presented by Hermann and Flecker (cf. Chapter 5) in this volume. In contrast to both Sweden and Germany, the traditional Austrian model was based on a combination of strong corporatism (the literally institutionalized 'social partnership') and a strong state that owned and governed key parts of the economy. The break from this sheltering is at the core of economic change over the past two decades. The highly protected economy has been transformed in a very short period into a flexible and competitive economy embedded into the upper segment of international chains of value added. The important aspect here is that corporatism has not only been preserved but has also contributed actively to this change. Demand-side corporatism, associated with neo-Keynesian policies, has been replaced by new forms of supply-side corporatism, supporting innovation and modernization. What is more, the state has been a key player in the process. It pushed the economy onto the new path and at the same time dismantled large parts of its own economic assets by waves of privatization, thus giving private capital a decisive boost. However, in contrast to Germany, nearly all employees are covered by collective agreements as membership of Chambers of Commerce remains mandatory for employers. In addition, the state has continued to promote collective bargaining by, for example, requiring the implementation of new employment regulations on flexible working to be based on collective agreements. The end result is that the social partners have been strong enough to agree on a comprehensive set of minimum wages without state intervention. As in Germany, the conservative welfare state has not been reformed, resulting in a similar negative impact on female employment and the development of social services. Overall much of the old institutional framework remains, although in part its content has changed. Austria seems to be an example of a 'conversion' from a protected towards an open market economy in which coordination is geared to support international competitiveness by preserving some social consensus. The political vulnerability of this top-down approach to the re-orientation of corporatism, however, has become obvious, once again, by the sweeping revival of right-wing populism in recent elections.

The four employment models sketched so far indicate that there is still a range of options under advanced capitalism to combine economic prosperity, social equity and welfare. For Neumann and Tóth (cf. Chapter 6) *Hungary* is a 'post-transitional' society still in search of a distinctive orientation for its economic and social model. The Hungarian employment model hovers between two conflicting sets of concepts: those associated with 'social Europe' and those associated with 'competitive Europe'. Over the past ten years the economy can be characterized as having been engaged in a race to 'catch up', with foreign direct investment (FDI), deregulation and privatization the main instruments deployed. After the deep post-transition crisis and the consequent dramatic employment losses, this policy resulted in a cycle of economic growth and employment recovery but accompanied by growing differentiation across the various strata of society. Some of the tensions arise out of the continuing strong expectations of welfare provision, stemming from the pre-transition era; yet for an applicant for Euro zone membership such expectations may be regarded as 'premature', relative to the state of Hungary's economic development. The absence of legacy institutions is inhibiting developments in other areas: political initiatives for social dialogue reflecting the EU policy have proved to be limited in impact owing to the weak development of capacities for self-regulation. However, given the toughening low-cost competition from neighbouring countries, the 'life cycle' of a low-road FDI-driven trajectory is coming to an end. This has become even more evident since the Hungarian chapter was completed because of the rapid withdrawal of FDI in the credit crunch leading to the need for Hungary to take on a major IMF loan. Skill-based and quality-oriented upgrading is needed but is hampered by the virtual dismantling of the vocational training system. The welfare system under the former socialist regimes promoted the employment of women and older workers. The problems of low employment for women and older workers arose after the political rupture caused by the process of restructuring and the associated extensive use of early retirement and by the weakness of labour demand ever since. These problems are not the same as the supply-side disincentives to participation found in the tax and welfare systems of Germany or Austria, but long paid leave periods do create problems for mothers reintegrating into work in Hungary.

France has always been placed in an ambiguous position within typologies of models: neither coordinated nor corporatist, but state-led, while its continental welfare state, in contrast to its German neighbour, has for decades fostered female labour market participation. As Berrebi-Hoffmann et al. (cf. Chapter 7) argue, the picture has changed substantially in many respects over the past 25 years. Private capital has gained a new and major role. The French model has moved from 'state-led' to 'state-enhanced' capitalism as an outcome of contradictory developments. Thus, huge waves of privatizations, the opening of the French capital market to foreign (in particular UK and US) investors and the priority given to supply-side oriented economic policies have been matched by an hitherto unprecedented expansion of public expenditure to support a general minimum income system and a wide range of active labour market programmes and subsidized jobs. Moreover, the state continues to make use of its regulatory power in the fields of industrial relations and minimum wages, thereby avoiding quite successfully the same breakdown in the regulated system of wage setting as found in Germany. The state has tried to delegate some of its power to social partners and, more recently, has also tried to foster corporatism, but with limited success as traditional elitist structures and fragmented industrial relations persist. One major change, however, is an increased decentralization of the state in France, through an increased role for regional government. It seems that many actors in the French elite would like to reduce the role of the state still further but at the same time are reluctant to give up state support for the big companies, the latter aspect being reinforced considerably by the financial crisis in 2008. In addition, owing to the weakness of the social partners, the state remains the principal actor able to forge social compromises and guarantee social peace in a tension-driven society, not least because the model is still unable to create sufficient employment for all social groups.

Interestingly, the fact that there used to be many more 'state-led' capitalisms in Europe than just the French has attracted limited attention among scholars dealing with the varieties of capitalism. In fact, if certainly for different reasons, the 'most' state-led capitalisms in Europe used to be (perhaps after Austria) southern European countries, analysed in the chapters on *Italy*, *Greece* and *Spain*. In these three countries the share of total value added produced by state-owned firms in the late 1980s exceeded even the French model (Karamessini, 2008). Moreover, these countries had, and continue to have, the strictest product market regulations (Amable, 2003). In stark contrast to France, however, the state was not geared to actually leading the economy but more to 'compensating' for failures elsewhere (Hancké et al., 2007, p. 26). Equally in contrast to the French case, a major common feature of these three countries is the persistence of the conservative 'familialistic' welfare state. In various other aspects, however, the diversity among the three countries is striking.

Italy has usually been presented in the literature as a key example of highly competitive 'industrial districts' in its northern part, and for a conservative 'family-based' welfare regime in the rest of the country. Simonazzi et al. (cf. Chapter 8) describe the Italian employment model of today as the intermediate product of a process of 'limping reformism'. While their assessment of the restructuring of the northern-based production system is rather optimistic, they underline a need to reshape the patterns of production and to upgrade skills to escape what some Italian economists call a problem of 'frozen specialization' in sectors now facing intensified international competition from China and elsewhere. They analyse the south of Italy as being locked into a low-efficiency and low-growth model. The persistent dualism of the Italian economy is accompanied by a dualism in the labour market which, after decades of substantial privatizations (leading to private monopolies rather than competition) and selective labour market reform measures, reflects the exacerbation of old segmentations and the creation of new ones. A shrinking core of well-protected workers are employed in what are referred to as the 'citadels of guarantees', namely the large manufacturing firms and the remaining public sector together with many of the large privatized utility companies. This core exists alongside a relatively unprotected but growing periphery. The large underground economy reduces the tax base and hampers the development of a more inclusive income support system or the provision of social services at the level that would be required to achieve a real break from the familialistic welfare regime. Instead, the familialist welfare system is maintained but reformed through, for example, the growth of informal workers employed by families to provide care for the elderly. Thus, rather than being a picture of stagnation, the Italian employment model is suffering from the effects of the limping reformism; that is, the combination of labour and product market deregulation, unbalanced and incoherent reforms and the unwillingness and incapability of major actors to tackle deeply rooted problems in Italian society and to counter vested interests.

Different to Italy, but similar to Spain, the employment model of *Greece* is a picture of dynamism following the break with the period of dictatorship. Departing from what Karamessini (cf. Chapter 9) calls a state-led familial capitalism, the Greek employment model has, since the early 1990s, been heading towards a form of liberal capitalism; in comparison, a process of gradual de-familialization of the welfare regime has begun only recently, encouraged by the European Employment Strategy and the availability of European social funds (ESF). Given the absence of strong traditions of class compromise, prospects for developing a coordinated market economy system are weak. What has evolved, in contrast, is an employment model that, although clearly in a state of transition, is not following a coherent reform path with a specified eventual goal. The industrialization model based on cheap labour has, as in Hungary, come to an end. Due in part to a comparatively low level of innovation, the Greek economy is losing ground in international competition. The outcome is increasing incoherence within the model; thus a drive towards privatization and deregulation has not provided for the development of comparative advantage vis-à-vis low-cost economies. Meanwhile, a dramatic mismatch has been allowed to develop between job expectations and the skill levels of large parts of the younger generation, arising from a major expansion of higher education and the availability in the labour market of low quality and often informal sector jobs. Consequently, many of these jobs are being taken up by the expanding immigrant population. Any more serious attempt to move away from a family-based welfare regime is being hampered by insufficient public social expenditures as the tax base is restricted by the large informal sector, a familiar story in other southern European countries and in Hungary.

The final chapter, by Banyuls et al. (cf. Chapter 10), draws a picture of continuous upheaval in the employment model of *Spain* since the end of the era of dictatorship. Against a background in which Spain is engaging in rapid economic catch-up, the Spanish model remains torn between 'short-term speculative capitalism' and continuing countervailing demands for employment and social protection. The predominant neoliberal approaches to labour market deregulation, social security reforms and public sector growth have been contested by trade unions and social movements. These have had some influence – albeit often temporary – on the general political agenda but hardly any impact at all at the workplace level. The result is a labour market that is highly segmented, with the highest levels of temporary employment in the whole EU. Although the family, despite changing family structures, continues to be regarded as the support mechanism of last resort, there has also recently been a stronger commitment to providing care for children and the elderly through a partial expansion of social services. Thus, although the Spanish model has experienced a period of rapid economic expansion, this boom has been based on partly fragile grounds, particularly a highly speculative housing boom. While internal consumption has been boosted and expansion has allowed for some public sector growth, the stability of the model is endangered by its limited basis for developing value added. The high rates of employment creation and economic growth have been achieved primarily by the expansion of low-quality services and construction. At the same time the Spanish economy has very low levels of R&D investment, a permanent external trade imbalance, and a low level of international competitiveness. Furthermore, the new prosperity is marred by poor labour conditions, limited development of social services and serious environmental problems.

Varieties of experience: A summary of the nine cases

The changes to individual national models, as described above, indicate the complexities of the processes taking place and the variety of actual outcomes. The contrasting cases of Sweden and the UK provide examples of revitalization of old models through the addition of new pillars (the revitalized innovation system and some decentralization of collective bargaining in Sweden and the strengthening of public expenditure and social guarantees in the UK). However, the extreme reliance on credit has meant that the revitalization of the economic part of the UK model has remained fragile. France and Austria are examples of conversion of the model from state-led to state-enhanced, even though there is a stark contrast between the complementary corporatist structures in Austria and the elitist structures in France. Hungary is still in search of a model. The most salient commonality among the three Mediterranean countries is found in the growing tensions between their economic and social development on the one side, and the maintenance of familialistic welfare regimes, supplemented by informal immigrant labour, on the other. With respect to other key features, their employment models continue to diverge. Germany may be regarded as the country experiencing the most distinct rupture to parts of its employment model, with competing and contradictory features under the surface of a coordinated market economy.

While the degree of change is high, it is often partial, incomplete and often moving in contradictory directions. The drivers for change are located in changes in the balances of power within the national model, through which the institutional structures may either be challenged directly or their use altered to reflect these new conditions. For each model there are different balances of power that are significant: for Germany it is perhaps the decline in the ability of the manufacturing sector to dominate that may be most salient, which is both a cause and a consequence of the declining power of trade unions relative to employers and the state; in France it is the changing role of the state vis-à-vis capital; for Austria the change is in the balance of power within continuing social partnership arrangements; and in Spain it is the continuing ineffectiveness of the trade unions at the level of the workplace that is most significant. While the prevalence of tensions between EU policies and national models is rather general, their impact is greater in some specific models; for example in Hungary the aspiration to join the Euro zone is creating barriers to developing a welfare and employment model that meets the aspirations of its citizens. Likewise the policy on free movement of labour pursued by the EU creates fewer tensions within national models which provide either full coverage of collective bargaining or statutory minimum wages – such as Sweden, Austria and the UK – than in countries like Germany where decreasing shares of the labour force are protected by statutory or contractual minimum standards.

While the dominant trend is towards a more liberal economic model, significant variations in the intensity of liberalism exist between the nine countries. National systems to protect labour standards – both legal and collective bargaining based – remain a continuing feature of the majority of the models. And, while access to social protection may have been tightened and linked more to employment-seeking behaviour and pension entitlements reduced, there is still a continuing commitment to state-based social protection in all of the nine examples explored here. There are even examples of positive developments to improve support in the labour market (the minimum wage in the UK) or to meet new welfare needs associated with change in gender and family relations (new care law in Spain, childcare as a new part of the welfare state in Greece, Italy and the UK, new approaches to paid parental leave in Germany). However, with the exception of the Swedish case, there is limited evidence within these selected countries of purposeful design or a clear view of how to revitalize the national/European employment model. Moreover, many of the stories of change are concerned with what can be regarded as negative changes; instead of new social compromises and the establishment of new social norms, the trend is more towards evasion of regulations and breaking with norms of fairness. For example, in Germany employers now seek to evade collective agreements and in Austria employers are switching from high to lower paying agreements. In both cases these opportunities were available in principle in past years but such action would previously have been regarded as underhand and against the norms of the national model. Another example of negative change concerns Italy and Greece where the dualism between the core and the periphery has effectively led to a shrinkage of the core, but with limited change in their relative privileges, alongside a growing periphery, often in informal employment. These changes exacerbate segmentation, particularly between younger and older generations, and fail to provide a core of middle-level quality jobs around which to build a strong but inclusive national employment and social model. There is thus possibly one common denominator in all the employment models considered here (except perhaps for the Swedish case) and that is the lack of clearly identifiable paths for their future development. We return to the issue of the future for these selected national employment models – and indeed for the whole of European member states – in the final section. First, however, we explore – again through selected examples – how these country cases can be analysed using the 'architectures and actors' framework we have proposed for understanding the dynamics of change in national models.

Coping with challenges: The importance of architectures and actors

Similar pressures pose very different challenges for restructuring national employment models as differences in the 'architecture of institutional arrangements' (Coates, 2000, p. 260) allow for divergent ways of coping with restructuring.[11] If key elements of employment models are changed or removed, it is their interactions with other elements of the model that will influence whether the result is a process of incremental change or a more fundamental rupture in the model. Moreover, the architecture of models is intertwined with political choice. This scope for choice may be crucial when it comes to decisions over reforms that could either revitalize or undermine the capacity of the model to generate decent work opportunities and provide social protection for citizens.

Both of these aspects can be demonstrated by examples of changes associated with the main external and internal challenges to employment models. We return here to the framework proposed earlier. First, we provide some examples of change induced through tensions between the different spheres of national models – across the production-employment and the employment-welfare nexus. We then turn to examples of the importance of actors and to new configurations of actors, before considering the scope for the exercise of political choice at the member state level, drawing on country-specific experiences.

Coping with challenges: The importance of model architectures

Challenges to national models across the production-employment nexus

One of the basic ways in which globalization and deregulation are challenging national models is through induced changes to ownership and governance structures, associated with the increasing importance of the stock market and the deregulation of product markets (Bosch et al., 2007). While control by stock markets has been a key feature of the UK economy for many decades, in France and Germany the rise in importance of the stock exchange is a much more recent feature. In both of these countries, this reshuffling in ownership structures has been promoted by both EU policies and by state action (privatization in France, changes in the corporate tax system in Germany) and in both cases it has been of strategic importance, albeit in different ways (see Chapters 4 and 7). In Germany these changes have called into question the supremacy of 'patient capital', which provided the capital ownership basis for investment and corporate strategies oriented to the long term. In France, where the internationalization of capital, reinforced by the waves of privatization over the past 20 years, is even greater, the main effect of this change is seen in the move from state-led to state-enhanced capitalism.

In many European countries the architecture of the models is such that labour standards have depended not only on employment regulations but also on structures and regulations of product markets. Deregulation of product markets has been a major preoccupation of the EU, particularly since the adoption of the aim in 1986 onwards of creating a single, competitive European market. It is this vision of the single European market that is not only opening up substantial parts of the public service or monopolies of publicly owned companies to private providers, but also allowing for more explicit regime competition among EU member states – through posted workers and the opening up of service markets and public procurement to other member states. These policies impact on national models in a number of ways. They open up competition to companies – particularly those from outside the member states – who have no commitment to sector level agreements and ways of managing employment. And by reducing the size of the public sector they also reduce the scope for unions to organize workers and negotiate collective agreements, since many governments are often more amenable to unions and collective bargaining than is the case with new private providers who may compete with the former state-owned companies by paying lower wages. Some European countries, especially the UK but also the Nordic countries, started the deregulation process in the 1980s before EU directives made it mandatory by privatizing public enterprises, abolishing entry barriers and other measures. Other countries, such as Germany, started to implement the directives primarily from 1995 onwards, whereas France and the southern European countries have continued to drag their feet (Conway and Nicoletti, 2006). An OECD indicator that summarizes the deregulation in energy, transport and communication demonstrates the low level of product market regulation in the Nordic countries, which is now hovering around that of the liberal economies (see Figure 1.2). The other three groups of countries – classified as continental, southern European and post-transition – can be seen in the figure to be moving more slowly and from a generally higher level of regulation towards the Nordic and liberal countries. The paradoxical observation, however, is that product market deregulation in the Nordic countries has so far not had a substantial influence on labour market regulations. Labour standards in these countries are based on statutory and collectively agreed regulations with extensive spheres of application and the same standards apply equally to state and private, domestic and foreign companies. Attempts by foreign service companies to undercut local pay rates have been successfully

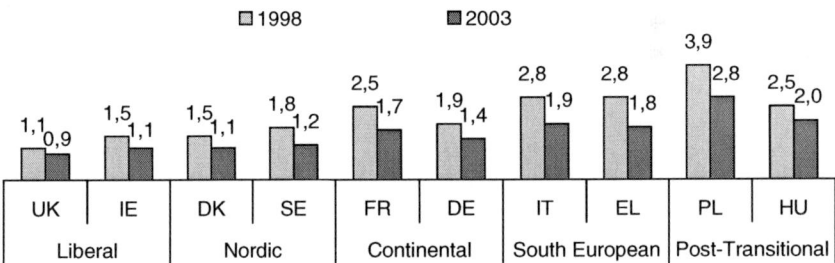

Figure 1.2 Composite indicator of production market regulations, 1998–2003, selected countries*
* This indicator is calculated as weighted average of a number of lower level indicators such as size and scope of public enterprises, barriers to entrepreneurship and barriers to trade and investment.
Source: Conway et al. (2005, p. 59)

contested by trade unions. As Anxo and Niklasson (cf. Chapter 3) argue, even the ruling of the European Court of Justice in the Laval case (EIRO, 2008), giving supremacy to free competition over labour standards, cannot harm – for the time being – the predominance of collective agreements in Sweden. This comprehensive and inclusive labour market regulation system, which is independent from the product market, is probably one of the reasons why deregulation of product markets has so far been widely accepted within the Nordic countries.

While generally binding collective agreements setting sector-level minimum wages have also served to maintain labour standards to a large extent in Austria and France, and to some extent also in Spain (European Commission, 2004, p. 33), in the UK, where there are no extension mechanisms, privatization of public utilities led to a deterioration in employment protection and conditions. The privatized companies were able in part to derecognize unions, particularly for managerial groups, and to outsource to non-organized firms, even if some still engaged in some collective bargaining at company level. Likewise in Germany the lack of generally binding pay conditions led in some industries, after the opening up of product markets, to an undercutting 'war' between those firms bound by collective agreements and those not so bound. In particular in labour-intensive industries or labour-intensive subsectors of industries (such as telecommunication call centres), competition based on wage costs triggered a wave of concession bargaining, resulting in a fragmentation of collective bargaining and a considerable increase in low-wage employment (Bosch and Kalina, 2008, p. 61).

The deregulation of product markets thus has the effect in some countries of removing key pillars of the model that have provided support for labour standards. Moreover, up till now these pillars of the employment systems have not been replaced by substitutes. Such substitutes could be provided either by generally extended collective agreements or through very high trade union density. The EU directives leave it to the member states to introduce, where necessary, new labour regulations to offset negative impacts on labour standards arising from the deregulation of product markets. So while national actors have choices, some actors may no longer see the need for national compromises and may regard the traditional employment system as a constraint on non path-dependent reforms. Thus, there are good reasons to argue that EU regulatory policies are endangering labour standards in some EU countries.

To summarize, the interdependence of product and labour market regimes used to be based, in some countries, on a balance between regulations in both areas. The more this balance is endangered from the production regime end, the more important becomes the employment regime as a counterbalance. If wages and employment security are less and less anchored in the production model, then they have to be secured through labour standards which take wages out of competition even in deregulated product markets. Since such standards are lacking at the EU level, these labour standards need to be developed by member states, based on national and sectoral frameworks that provide relatively comprehensive and inclusive coverage.

Challenges to national models across the welfare-employment nexus

Most of the literature on change in national models focuses on the challenges of globalization and deregulation to existing institutional arrangements. Equally important challenges are emanating from internal, societal changes, such as the ageing of society or the changes in gender roles. These challenges are to some extent linked as the birth rate has been falling in all societies, particularly those offering limited employment opportunities for women (Bettio and Villa, 1998; Esping-Andersen, 1999). National models will need to adjust to long-term social change if they are not to become increasingly out of step with the behaviour and aspirations of the population as a whole and women in particular. Such change includes higher female participation in education and employment and the changing preferences of men as well as women towards household and family formation. These developments pose challenges for national models across the whole production-employment-welfare nexus, although with different implications for different countries, dependent again upon the architecture of the model and the response by actors.

One challenge is how to develop the service economy; more services are needed in order to meet the problems of old age and to substitute for female labour in the home. Moreover, Figure 1.3 indicates that there is a relatively

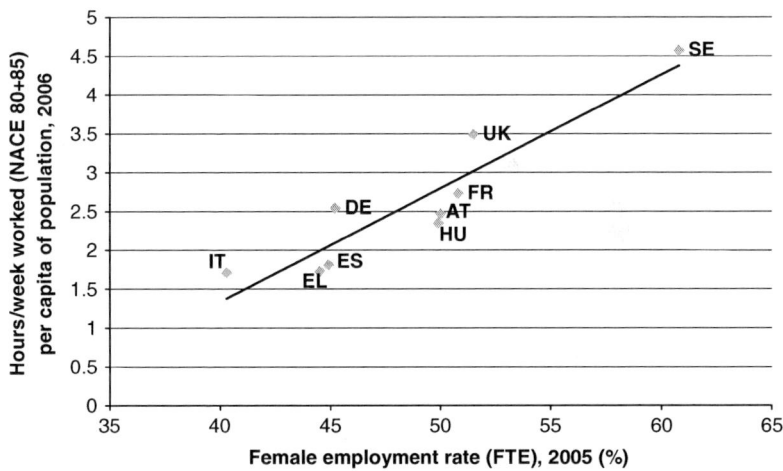

Figure 1.3 Labour input into social services* and female full-time equivalent employment rate**
* Total hours worked in education, health and other social services per capita of population, 2006
** 2005 (Correlation: 0,92*** significant at the 0,001 level)
Source: European Labour Force Survey, own calculation

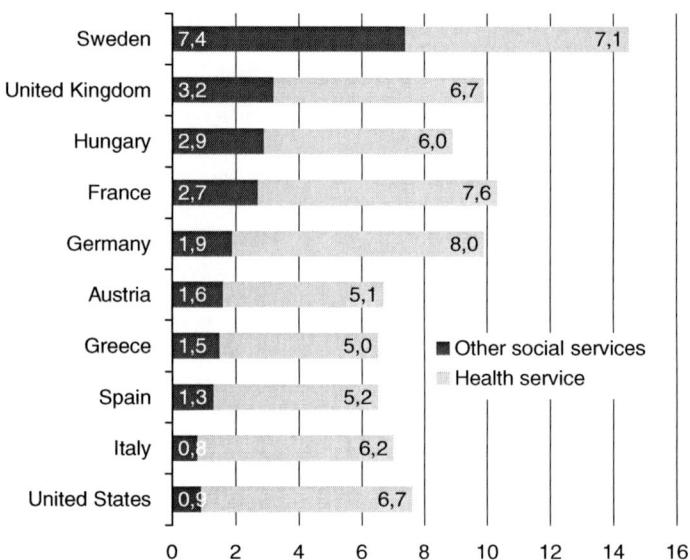

Figure 1.4 Gross public expenditure on social services as a percentage of GDP
Source: OECD (2007) 2003 data

strong correlation between female employment rates in full-time equivalents (FTE) and the share of employment in social services. These employment figures are reflected in variations among our nine country examples in public expenditure on social services, particularly on 'other social services' (that is, compared to health where expenditure shows less variation); shares of gross domestic product (GDP) spent on other services range from 0.8 per cent in Italy to 7.4 per cent in Sweden (Figure 1.4). Corresponding to the typologies of welfare systems, Sweden, as the flagship of the Nordic model, is at the top end,[12] and the southern countries at the bottom. The southern European countries in particular face a major fiscal challenge to develop public social services to both facilitate women's employment and increase employment opportunities in the services sector.

However, there is considerable diversity among the middle-ranked continental welfare regimes, with social expenditure in Austria and Germany close to the familialistic group of countries but much higher in France, thanks to the developed childcare system. Hungarian social services provision is similar, suggesting that in this post-transition economy social-democratic welfare state orientations coexist with an LME-type production regime. However, this disjuncture in orientations between the two systems is not necessarily in itself problematic; the UK as the LME flagship has, perhaps surprisingly, the second highest expenditure of the nine, but has a high per capita GDP to sustain it. It is more the mismatch between the welfare aspirations and a low value added production base that gives rise to the notion that Hungary has a 'premature' welfare state (cf. Neumann and Tóth, Chapter 6).

The UK case points to another issue, namely the terms under which people – mainly women – are employed to provide social services. There are a range of models through which welfare states can deliver care, but with major consequences not only for the quality of care but also for job quality and gender equality. The options being followed include improving the career track and prospects for care workers within the public sector (Sweden), switching to private sector providers (who pay much lower wages) while retaining public funding of the service (the UK), and providing cash payments that may fuel informal employment (Germany and Austria) except when tied into job creation programmes for the unemployed (France) (see Simonazzi, 2009). In the southern European countries the increasing gap in supply of service as women's availability for family care declines is met primarily through the employment by the family of female migrant workers to replace or supplement care provided by female family members. Thus, the policies adopted to respond to the declining availability of family-based care is having significant impacts on the evolution of employment and production models in Europe.

This brings us to a second challenge, namely to adjust national models to secure the increased integration of women without intensifying segmentation and undermining the capacity of the national models to maintain employment standards and social protection. The integration of women could, under one scenario, be associated with a general pulling down of labour standards through competition between new forms of employment outside of protective regulation. Alternatively, it could be associated with the development of more diversified but also more inclusive labour markets through the extension of protection to jobs and groups traditionally outside the core sectors.

As Table 1.4 demonstrates, there are highly divergent outcomes between the nine countries not only in achieved female employment rates but also in rates of growth over the ten-year period 1995–2005. Divergence between national models is even more apparent when comparisons are made between head count and full-time equivalent employment rates among women. Nevertheless, there is some evidence of recent convergence: the three southern countries have the highest growth rates from the lowest starting points. Moreover, Italy and Spain, two countries with historically very low rates of part-time working, have experienced above average rates of growth in part-time work, even if the part-time work share remains well below the EU average. This convergence in employment forms has been promoted by the EU in its belief that the diversification of employment forms can provide not only for employer flexibility but also meet work-life balance challenges and regularize informal work. However, the architectures of

Table 1.4 Female employment rates (as a percentage of population aged 15–64 and in full-time equivalents), 1995 and 2006

	1995	2005	Percentage increase in head-count employment rates 1995–2005	FTE 1995	FTE 2005	Percentage increase in FTE employment rates 1995–2005
Italy	35.4	45.3	*28.0*	33.8	40.3	*19.2*
Greece	38.1	46.1	*21.0*	36.9	44.5	*20.6*
Spain	31.7	51.2	*61.5*	28.9	44.9	*55.4*
Germany	55.1	59.6	*8.2*	46.1	45.2	*−2.0*
Hungary	45.2*	51.0	*12.8*	44.5*	49.9	*12.1*
Austria	59.0	62.0	*5.1*	53.4	50.0	*−6.4*
France	52.1	57.6	*10.6*	46.2	50.8	*10.0*
UK	61.7	65.9	*6.8*	47.0	51.5	*9.6*
Sweden	68.8	70.4	*2.3*	58.5	60.8	*3.9*
EU15	*49.7*	*57.4*	*15.5*	*42.3*	*47.4*	*12.1*
EU25	*51.1***	*56.3*		*n.a.*	*47.6*	

Source: European Commission (2007); own calculation
* 1996, ** 1997

national models differ in the significance attached to the full-time standard employment model. Resistance to regularizing and legitimizing part-time work has been stronger in societies – such as Italy and Greece – where social protection has been provided more by the protected standard employment relationship than by universal social benefits. Indeed in Greece there remains a preference for informal work over part-time work, despite financial incentives to employees to take up part-time working. Furthermore, in some national contexts, including for example France and Hungary where women's integration has been based on full-time, not part-time employment, the promotion of part-time work may be seen to marginalize rather than enhance women's employment position.

Germany and Austria also stand out for their declining employment rates for women, measured in full-time equivalent terms; here increased integration of women has been achieved through the promotion of low-paid part-time employment. Low wages are facilitated in Austria by wide differentials between collectively agreed sectoral minimum wages, while in Germany many of the mini-jobs are developing outside of collective agreements. Thus, in both cases the integration of women into the economy is part of the process of widening dispersion of labour standards, occurring in Austria within the framework of existing institutions but in Germany through a move from strong to weak coverage of collective regulation.

It is important to note that, while European law does provide for equality between part-time and full-time work within the same employing organization, there is no protection of employment standards across employers, thereby increasing the importance of the specific architecture of the national model in equality outcomes.[13] In Italy and Spain legislative reform promoted by the EU was aimed at increasing the integration of women into employment through regularizing informal work, but the outcome is a growth of non-standard employment forms offering much lower levels of social protection and the generation of new forms of segmentation, not only between women and men but also between younger and older labour market participants.

Much of the integration of women into the UK labour market in the 1980s and 1990s was also based on low-paid and unregulated part-time work, intensifying the characterization of the UK labour market as segmented and flexible. In the last decade, however, the national minimum wage has improved conditions, particularly for part-timers and those on maternity leave, and new rights to request flexible working within full-time jobs are enabling women to remain with the same employer after childbirth, thereby reducing the flow of women returnees into specific part-time jobs. These changes in employee rights in the UK again underline that it is not part-time work itself but how this employment form interacts with the architecture of the national model that matters. This is clearly demonstrated in Sweden where complementary institutions – in particular rights to reduced hours working – change the significance of part-time work for both labour market segmentation and for gender equality. In Sweden part-time work mainly takes the form of reduced hours working within standard full-time employment, with opportunities to return to full-time work once care responsibilities cease. In this context part-time work is a transition or temporary life cycle phenomenon, not associated with specific kinds of jobs, although the exercise of rights to vary hours has proved easier within the public sector.

A third challenge is how to develop tax and welfare policy in the light of changing gender roles and an ageing society. One issue of particular importance is pensions. Concerns over an ageing society in a context of macro-economic constraints is pushing countries to adopt later retirement based on longer employment. Younger people are often paying the penalty twice over in the form of lower entitlements to pensions and funding the retirement of existing pensioners and older workers whose rights have by and large been preserved. This policy also creates tensions with policies to encourage flexible working (as part-time work often leads to lower entitlements) and to provide women with better individual pension rights in light of changing family patterns. The architecture of the model again affects the options available; in Sweden the much closer matching between men's and women's employment histories and indeed incomes has allowed for a more consensus-driven approach to changing the pension system to retain solidarity between generations and the sexes. In contrast, in Italy pension reform has done nothing to deal with inadequate coverage and instead has largely increased differences by generation while maintaining inequalities in access according to labour market position, to the detriment of women. In the UK there have been efforts to improve the pension safety net, and more recognition of care work in access to the state pension, but the weakness of the LME model in providing old-age protection has been revealed by the collapse of company-based pension schemes. This is exposing middle and higher income workers for the first time to high levels of uncertainty over income in old age, tensions that could in the future promote a more radical rethink of the UK national model.

Role of actors in national model change

Conflicts of interest and actors' support of institutions

So far our focus has been mainly on how the challenges interact with the architecture of different national models. Implicit in the responses described to challenges has been the responses by actors and their choice of action within a set of alternatives, clearly still constrained by the architecture of the models. The scope for actors to play key roles in reshaping national models has been enhanced by the reduced pressures on some actors – particularly employers – to engage in compromises. This creates a particular threat to the coordinated economy model. As Hancké et al. (2007, p. 34) note 'the nature of the coordinated economy has become more contested and its reaffirmation and renegotiation less amenable to consensus-based solutions'. The consequence is that national employment models which diverge from 'liberal market economies' may need active support from major actors.

A key example of the importance of actors is found in the different attitudes of employers to the preservation of comprehensive coverage of collective agreements in Germany and Austria. The traditional German model was based on the notion that sector-level bargaining took wages out of competition and provided a basis for stable industrial relations, thereby providing comparative institutional advantage for small and large employers. The more recent German experience, however, tells a different story. Searching for opportunities to cut labour costs by avoiding the formerly 'beneficial constraints' of collective agreements has become an accepted part of behaviour for increasing parts of the business sector. This change in behaviour, motivated in part by the opportunity presented by declines in trade union power, is, implicitly or explicitly, challenging the compromise on industrial relations reached in the conflict-ridden early 1950s on which the West German model was established (Hall, 2007). As Thelen (2001, p. 74) points out, 'non-market coordination, far from being a self-sustaining feature of particular systems, in fact involves a political settlement and indeed one that has to be renegotiated periodically'. However, if trade unions are in decline, and there is no government action to fill the gap, fewer and fewer employers experience the need to negotiate, let alone *re*negotiate.[14] The result, as far as collective bargaining is concerned, is not only a coexistence of sheltered and unsheltered parts of the economy, but also a growing regime competition within individual industries.

Austria provides a contrasting example where the leading actors within the model appear to consider the stabilizing influence of existing institutions sufficiently valuable for them to continue to support the system of 'social partnership' and collective bargaining as one of its core institutions. The Austrian state has played an important part here too as new employment regulations were passed stipulating, for instance, that flexible work schedules must be based on collective agreements. This, in turn, gave rise to close to full coverage of collective agreements in the IT sector, where in most EU countries this kind of industrial relations is exceptional. Thus, in line with what the VoC approach suggests, there is evidence of what could be called a 'rub-off' effect from existing labour market institutions which cushions or curbs the destabilizing impacts of structural change in the production regime on those institutions underpinning the employment regime. Comparing the Austrian with the German case demonstrates, however, that the strength of this rub-off effect depends on the support from leading actors. If major actors draw back, thus leaving the employment model increasingly 'unsustained', the rub-off effect will eventually fade.

Sweden again provides an example where commitment from different sets of leading actors to the maintenance and revitalization of the model – particularly in the aftermath of the major crisis in the 1980s and early 1990s – facilitated the negotiation of reforms. The strongest example is in the reform of the pension system. This involved considerable changes to the benefits for citizens but was agreed to in the interests of maintaining a universal, decent pension system.

In contrast, although the industrial relations systems of the southern European countries have become less evidently adversarial of late, this reflects more the weakness of the trade unions than a move towards negotiated capitalism. In Greece, as Karamessini (2008) points out, most reforms are imposed after a trade union defeat and are thus far from negotiated. The position of trade unions in Spain is stronger and they have been engaged in new efforts to reform labour market institutions – particularly policies to promote the transformation of temporary into permanent employment – jointly with employers and the state. However, although Spanish trade unions have remained committed to engaging in national bargaining over social policy, at the same time they have been ready to challenge – though national strike action – some policies that take the reform movement to, in their view, unacceptable extremes. In both of these strategies they have had some success in shaping the path taken by the state. The trade unions at national level thus punch above their weight, as measured by active trade union membership, but their control over practices in the workplace has diminished as the sectors in which they had at least some presence at company level have declined, leaving employers by and large free to determine which aspects of collective agreements to implement.

These examples indicate that to the extent that the national models are the outcomes of historic compromises between conflicting interest groups, their long-term survival is under threat from the changes in both the composition and the power of different interest groups. These compositional effects include the changing balance between international and domestic capital and the changing labour force mix – from manufacturing to service employees and from manual to service and knowledge work. The outcome is in particular a reduction in the power of trade unions in most but not all national contexts. If the balance of power shifts, unilaterally imposed 'settlements' by the powerful actors, rather than compromises between conflicting interests, are likely to come to the forefront. This leads us to the third dimension of change in national models that we wish to stress, that of political will and action, particularly at the nation state level.

Political choice and the nation state

The national case studies provide a wealth of examples of situations in which there have been clear opportunities at national level to develop policies to revitalize national models or to change them in directions that were not simply following the liberalizing/deregulationist policy agenda.

It is also the case that in many instances the development of policies to revitalize or redirect models has not been easy and has required deliberate efforts to find new ways forward and agree new social compromises; this applies for example to the pension reform in Sweden as previously discussed, the wholesale reform of the vocational training system in Germany, or the negotiation of new social agreements in Spain on flexicurity policies (sometimes without the participation of employers). The mandate for change has in some cases come from a change of government; New Labour in the UK was elected on a commitment to introduce a national minimum wage and to address problems of child poverty through in-work tax credits and a more positive activation strategy – that is, to redress to some extent the excesses of the liberal model pursued since 1979. However, it was not until two years into office that it developed the political will to reject the funding straightjacket it had voluntarily accepted from the outgoing Conservative government and to adopt a policy to increase public expenditure to strengthen the health and education sectors.

The scope for political will and national choice to be exercised – even if in the case of responding to EU policy agendas – can also be found for example in the very French approach to introducing activation into its social policy. Here the focus is more on solidarity through minimum income guarantees and through public job subsidies to expand employment access to disadvantaged groups, rejecting the more punitive approaches to activation associated with a liberal model (cf. Berrebi-Hoffmann et al., Chapter 7).

Alongside these positive examples there are also many more negative cases of both partial or contradictory reforms and of policies and action likely to undermine the social objectives of the employment model. Political will can also obviously be exercised to dismantle cornerstones of national models. This was the case in Austria where the right wing government elected in 2000 first of all stopped effective negotiations under social partnership arrangements and then sold the remaining public sector interests in privatized enterprises. Likewise in Germany the reforms of the tax and unemployment insurance systems reversed the social orientation of the model architecture. In some cases the problem is not so much the state abandoning or weakening its commitments to an inclusive policy but the absence of such a policy in the first place, reflecting major variations in the extent to which states take active roles in shaping and directing economic development or in promoting inclusive systems (Whitley 2007). For example, in Italy the state has failed to extend welfare coverage and instead has continued to focus protection on a shrinking core of older and male workers in large organizations.

Another type of state failure is lack of political will. This can be observed in Greece where agreement cannot be reached on healthcare reforms and where blocking interests prevent the implementation of reforms. For example, working time laws have been passed allowing for flexible scheduling but have not been implemented as they require agreements with trade unions who are not minded to cooperate. Whether or not the specific policies would strengthen or weaken the social dimension in the longer term, there is a clear inability to act within this model, which increases uncertainty over its development path. It is also the case that some of the positive institution-building policies identified above have been constrained in either their design or implementation by external pressures or by the beliefs of key actors that models can only be revitalized within a broad neo-liberal framework. Thus, the child poverty and social infrastructure renewal programmes in the UK were implemented hand in hand with the development of the market state that may undermine the capacity of the reforms to deliver a more equal society.

Both the positive and the problematic examples presented here, as well as the impacts of the cross-cutting challenges from the production and welfare systems, as discussed in the first part of this section, lead us to one major conclusion. Actors at nation state level are faced with the need to promote institutional innovations which take into account the vulnerability of the existing models to both external and internal challenges.

Conclusions

The theme of this book is to understand the challenges to national employment models in Europe and the impact of the responses to these challenges in maintaining, reshaping, revitalizing or indeed undermining distinctive national employment models. This theme is of vital interest for the future development of Europe as the outcome will be critical for determining the survival of the core principles that, according to Wickham (2005), underpin European social models – namely, the notion of public space and the provision of rights and protections for employees and citizens. These social outcomes are also linked to whether there is a basis for Europe to maintain and develop comparative advantage in the world economy based upon production models supported by high-quality and high-performance employment systems. To a large extent the answers to these two related questions for future development remain open; the task in this book and in the project on which it draws was to develop further the theory and practice for analysing change in national models, particularly in a European context where the EU has a major influence on shaping action at national level. Nevertheless, our concern here is not simply with modifying and developing the theories of institutional change that have recently become somewhat of a preoccupation of institutional theorists (Campbell, 2004; Streeck and Thelen, 2005); our interest lies firmly in the political implications, defined in the wide political economy sense, of the changes we have observed and analysed. Thus, in these conclusions we first of all summarize the analytical and methodological contributions of the approach adopted here before returning to some thoughts on the future consequences of the changes we have observed and analysed.

Developing the analyses of change in national models

The nine country case studies in this volume provide analyses of changes that are taking place along different trajectories and within distinctive national employment models. Encompassed within the nine cases are examples from the whole range of national model categories as identified in the main typologies. Moreover, the collective experiences provide examples of exposure to very different types and intensities of internal and external challenges, related in part to the particular architecture of the national models.

The analytical and methodological contributions of the project in analysing change can be categorized as falling into four categories (Bosch et al., 2007). First, while taking the literature on typologies of national models as our starting point, we have argued that it is necessary to take into account factors other than supply-side institutional arrangements in explaining employment performance. It is in fact often the employment performance which underpins the changing evaluations of national models and the associated perceived need for model reform. Second, we have expanded on the range of challenges that are considered. Third, we have broken down the barriers between different typologies and focused on the interactions between changes in the production and welfare regimes in explaining changes in national employment models, paying particular attention to the specific architectures of models. Fourth, we have focused on the roles of actors and the associated scope for political will in the responses to challenges, albeit constrained by the environment in which political will or choice is exercised.

Expanding the factors accounting for employment performance

Debates on national models need to pay more attention to those factors that influence employment performance, other than the institutional arrangements normally emphasized in the literature on and policy analyses of national models. As we have argued, employment performance of national models cannot be understood without taking into account issues of macroeconomic management. Yet although the macroeconomic conditions are not necessarily linked directly to other aspects of the model, differences in macroeconomic arrangements and performance are often confused with the performance of institutional arrangements on the supply side. We have also called attention to potential differences in economic and employment performance according to the size of the countries, with small countries more able to find a niche in international markets or to organize political consensus for restructuring their national employment models. Further reasons for divergence relate to the fact that, in a global economy with an increasingly complex division of labour, the trend may not be towards convergence on a dominant model. Instead national particularities may actually strengthen or new specializations emerge, not captured by current typologies. Different specializations can be expected to follow different business cycles; for example the UK economy may be more strongly affected by the 2008 credit crunch, thereby changing the positive approval for the national model that built up from the late 1990s onwards. More generally, employment models may be considered to have their cycles. A model that has been successful in the past under specific conditions may need to be restructured if the internal and external environment is changing. This restructuring may, however, only come to fruition through a crisis that provokes a process of renewal and revitalization. History reminds us of the ups and down of models and of the dangers of strong and premature statements on the superiority of a specific model to create jobs.

Expanding the range of challenges

The need to conceptualize the process of change in national models as responses to pressures for change emanating from both external and internal challenges to national models provided a starting point for the development of this project. Our hypothesis was that contrary to much of the academic literature and policy debate, the pressures on national models should be seen as not simply the outcome of an inevitable process of globalization. Even within the globalization strand the challenges are not simply those of increasing international trade or the internationalization of production and finance; they also emanate from new institutional arrangements introduced by political processes, including new international trade agreements and the EU's implementation of competition law. More and more national regulations have been replaced by international regulations that tend to follow the liberal market model, certainly within the EU. These developments will have specific implications for different national models, requiring for example substantial changes in the various types of coordinated economies. But the primary focus on external challenges – wrapped up in the term globalization – not only provides a catch-all term that is often used to legitimize changes but also ignores the increasing internal challenges to national models. The main examples we have taken here are the challenges associated with changing gender roles and the ageing society. Responding to these challenges requires just as far-reaching and politically contested changes to important pillars of national employment models as responses to globalization. The ways new services are provided to meet the problem of old age and to substitute for female work at home is equally important for job creation, employment standards and social protection as regulations in the production sphere. The policies responding to these internal challenges could equally revitalize or destabilize or undermine the national model.

Towards more hybrid typologies and a greater focus on model architectures

The need to move towards more permeable or fluid boundaries within typologies is indicated by the fact that changes in models were found to be increasing diversity among particular groups of countries. Similarly we have identified a parallel need to develop more hybrid typologies, taking into account the characteristics in the different spheres, particularly between production systems on the one hand and welfare and family systems on the other. This need for a more integrated approach reflects the diversity of challenges to models, such that it is no longer possible – if it was ever the case – to focus on only one aspect of employment models. The existing country typologies each emphasize selected dimensions, which offer important explanations for national differences in employment in manufacturing (production typologies), in social services (welfare state typologies) and in the service sector as a whole (service typologies). All these typologies focus on particular elements of the employment models. In order to explore differences between countries in the dynamics of change in national models, future research requires progress in the development of more hybrid typologies incorporating all these various elements. The production, employment and welfare/family models are interlinked and challenges to the employment model may emanate from all directions; employment change may be induced outside of direct employment policies and has implications for welfare systems and production systems. However, it is also the case that performance may vary across elements of the model, such that a failure to resolve issues with respect to the welfare system may – as we have argued to be the case for Germany – lead to a momentum for change that could have negative implications for a successful production model. This suggests that attention needs to be paid to the specific architecture of the models, following Coates. The interactions between pressures for change and the reshaping of national models may depend on very specific elements – elements that are not shared across countries classified by typologies as being in the same category. Moreover, the interactions between the different spheres are likely to vary more than is allowed for in typologies that focus on one dimension primarily. Where there are high levels of mutual interactions between the spheres, pressures for change may be even more destabilizing than when the institutional arrangements are less closely interconnected.

The importance of actors and the exercise of political will

The fourth element that we have stressed is the role of actors and the scope for political will or choice in response to challenges. Since there are political choices the European social models might not so much be unsustainable as unsustained by certain configurations of actors at national and European level. Thus, our analysis supports Levy's (2006, p. 367 ff.) view that 'in the age of liberalization ... the state also rises'. This role for state actors has expanded to the EU level; the EU has taken over from the national states the power to regulate important segments of national employment models and has thereby become an important arena in which new constellations of national and supranational actors take decisions of vital importance for the future development of national employment models. Recent debates on change have tended to focus on incremental path-dependent changes, thereby highlighting the fact that institutions do not have to disappear in order for their function to change. However, this approach does not explain the choices that actors make over whether or not to revitalize the European social models or allow them to wither through neglect or destabilization. With the deregulation of product markets in many countries, important pillars of labour standards have been removed and choices have to be made as to whether to replace these pillars with new institutional arrangements. Likewise to adjust to the increasing participation of women and the ageing of society may require more than a process of incremental policy adjustment if the traditional model and its welfare and employment pillars are based on the presumption of stable male breadwinner households. Revitalization of social models requires in most cases the building up of new pillars, thereby changing the traditional institutional architecture. 'Institution building' has become a widely accepted concept for what needs to be done in those countries which joined the EU only recently. The core message of the analyses in the present book, however, is that even for the older members of the EU there is an urgent need to put institution building back on the agenda at both national and EU level. It is to the consequences of model change and the need for innovative institution building that we now turn.

Revitalizing national employment models in Europe: The need for multi-level institution building

The case for a programme of new and multi-tiered institution building to revitalize national employment models is based on the clear evidence that labour standards and social protection have positive progressive effects on the distribution of income and the quality of work. The relationship up for debate here holds not only for European models but also for the US; recent research has pointed to the importance of trade unions and social protection systems in developing higher-quality jobs and moderating income distribution in the US in the immediate post-war period and the impact of the erosion of these institutions in widening earnings equality from the 1980s onwards (Levy and Temin, 2007). Our argument is not only that of promoting fair distribution but also that social policy should be considered and developed as a productive factor (Hermans 2005), an approach highlighted in the initial development of the Lisbon strategy and in early stages of the European Employment Strategy. There is thus a need to design quality and productivity into jobs alongside measures to provide security and protection to individuals and households.

In the case of Sweden there is evidence of a capacity not only to maintain standards and protection but also to make innovative arrangements to shape the pattern of new service jobs, including promoting a new type of flexible standard employment relationship involving periods of socially protected part-time work or leaves from work. The survival of this model has up to now seemed assured, although new political developments may of course reopen these issues, leading to efforts to promote low-wage employment, as has already started to a limited degree with the change of government in Sweden. However, the other European countries covered in this project face much more serious problems in rebuilding institutional arrangements to develop inclusive labour markets that provide comprehensive employment and social protection. The challenge to labour standards arises out of the deregulation of product markets and, linked with the expansion of services, the growth of non-standard work forms outside the traditionally well-protected primary labour market segment. These developments fuel a competition between segments with high and with lower labour standards and social protection which may be deepened by outsourcing into less protected areas, or by the expansion of informal immigrant labour. Left to the market this insider-outsider competition is likely to undermine labour standards and increase social polarization. In some European countries this polarization within the formal labour market, or between formal and informal labour, may be replacing a previous system of segmentation between the employed and the inactive. If wages and employment security are less anchored in production markets then they have to be secured by comprehensive labour standards to take these factors out of competition, at least within the internal economy. In order to move towards a secure and inclusive service economy, there is a need not only for substantial reform of the welfare states to adjust to the changing gender roles, but also for policies to ensure the development of decent working conditions in the new service jobs. Arguments that globalization of markets and the increased potential for offshoring (even of service activities) preclude the development of new labour standards tend to exaggerate the sensitivity of offshoring decisions to Western wage levels; the gap in labour costs is simply too wide between developed and developing countries for Western countries to be able to reduce offshoring through competition on wage levels. Many jobs remain geographically tied and, while national models do have to be competitive in the world economy in their areas of specialization, the international fluidity of capital and labour is not such as to preclude the establishment of labour standards that are appropriate for the GDP and wealth of the society in which the jobs are located.

However, although in the nine country studies we can find some examples of positive renewal of institutions showing that there are political choices, on balance, with the exception of Sweden, there is little evidence of positive renewal of the whole institutional architecture of the models. Instead we find more a creeping deterioration and weakening of labour standards and protection without any clear positive embracing of an agenda of new institution building. Since institution building for the most part does not emerge as the outcome of a coherent plan and is politically highly contested, an argument could be made that the long-term outcome may be the development of a European-wide space based on a renewed set of employment and social protection standards. This could not be achieved in the short term as first there would need to be a process of transition during which the huge differences in wage levels across the EU, exacerbated by EU enlargement, are modified. The argument could be that, once the new member states are integrated and their development process kick-started, there may be new scope to rebuild labour standards and social protection. However, in another scenario, which is strongly supported by our country studies, the accumulation of gradual change could lead to ruptures within the European social models, constituting a type of change which cannot sufficiently be grasped by the different categories of incremental change developed by Streeck and Thelen (2005). The problem of finding a basis for renewal of national models appears to be being exacerbated by the reduced scope for action at the national level in two senses. First, national actors are more able to avoid the need to seek social compromise, in part because of changes in the balance of power between interest groups, with the weakening in particular of trade unions but also because of the involvement of the EU in national decision-making. The second factor is the direct constraints that the EU imposes on the scope for change in national models; these constraints are found primarily in the approach to macroeconomic policy and to competition policies that are enforced by hard law. In comparison, the hard law European employment rights agenda is both relatively minimal and weakly enforced (Wickham, 2005) while the soft law approach has up to now been more focused on promoting flexibility and activation than on the complementary security and job quality dimensions within the overall vision for the European social model.

Three problems emerge from this development of multi-level governance. First, if there is a reduced need for powerful actors to seek social compromises, then it is more likely that the reform process will be imposed on weaker groups, and the notion of public space and rights and protections for employees and citizens will not be preserved. Second, there is less likelihood that the reform process will emphasize the need for complementarities and coherence within the national model if there is undue pressure from external force for reform of one element of the model, without recognition of the whole set of challenges facing the national model. The EU has begun to address some of the interactions between policy areas, most notably in its concerns with flexibility and security, but these interactions still tend to be narrowly defined within the employment policy area and do not extend to the interactions between policy domains such as competition policy and employment policy. These changes in the balance of interests may also mean, as we have found in our studies, that there is a more widespread and universal response to the supranational agendas of globalization of financial markets, the international reorganization of value added chains, and competition policy. There are fewer examples where reform designed to provide either some counterweight in labour markets to deregulation in product markets or to develop more inclusive welfare systems to reflect changing family and employment patterns is given the same degree of emphasis or has brought about change on the pace or scale found in product and capital markets.

This point leads on to our third concern, namely the constraints on social innovation that multi-level governance arrangements may be inducing. The challenges to national models that we identified at the outset of the project clearly require the rebuilding of institutional arrangements to adjust to changing external and internal contexts and needs. However, the scale of innovation in institutional arrangements is constrained by the macroeconomic rules of the EU; the EU often points to innovative policies in some member states, such as the flexicurity systems in Denmark or Sweden, but the opportunity to emulate such models is constrained by the macroeconomic rules, such that the process of convergence across the EU is conceived as relating more to orientations of policies – towards activation, flexicurity and the like – but not towards a catch-up process through which welfare state systems converge not only on orientations but also on relative levels of benefits and degrees of coverage. The need for improved benefit coverage is being discussed within the flexicurity communication (CEC, 2007) but there is no discussion of how this squares with the macroeconomic constraints. The EU promotes the need to learn from best practice but pays little attention to the interactions between different institutional arrangements and the fact that policy performance in complex societies may depend more on these interactions than the simple trade-offs between the individual parameters normally used in economic theory. However, if models are to be revitalized and institution building put on the agenda, then much can undoubtedly be learnt by exploring examples of international best practice. This learning will only be effective if it is recognized that not only may individual policies need to be modified to fit different national contexts but also, where necessary, complementary and supporting institutional arrangements may need to be put in place.

Another deficiency in the EU approach is its focus on the employment-welfare nexus and neglect of the production-employment interactions. The importance of employment models for developing long-term comparative advantage in the knowledge economy is hardly articulated, except as an issue of individual skill development. The interactions between skills developed and innovation at the firm level does not form a central part of the EU's economic and employment policy agenda, where responsiveness to market signals coupled with good social policies for redeployment and retraining over the life cycle are deemed sufficient to promote Europe as a knowledge society.

In short the European market has been created mainly by negative integration policies. To sustain European social models and to avoid increasing divergence between European employment models, more emphasis on positive integration policies is needed by improving the capabilities of national actors to develop proactive policies and create new regulatory institutions at the European level (Hoskyns and Newman, 2000). This focus on the EU as a constraint on national actors does not and should not let national actors off the hook. There is still scope for national actors to take bold action to develop new and innovative institutional arrangements and indeed to promote these ideas at the European level. Indeed this scope could in principle be enhanced by the 2008 financial crisis to the extent that the abject failure of deregulation puts institution building back on the political agenda. However, it is also plausible that the impact of the associated state bailouts will be allowed to further squeeze out the social dimension of national models. Such an outcome is not inevitable and now, more than at any other recent time, is there a need for creative policy development and renewed political will.

Notes

1. We owe this notion to James Wickham whose work on the European social model (Wickham, 2005) has influenced our thinking on this topic.
2. Following the ILO definition, 'decent work' sums up the aspirations of people in their working lives. It involves opportunities for work that is productive and

delivers a fair income, security in the workplace and social protection for families, better prospects for personal development and social integration, freedom for people to express their concerns, organize and participate in the decisions that affect their lives, and equality of opportunity and treatment for all women and men. Decent work should be at the heart of global, national and local strategies for economic and social progress. It is central to efforts to reduce poverty and a means for achieving equitable, inclusive and sustainable development. The ILO promotes decent work through its work on employment, social protection, standards and fundamental principles and rights at work, and social dialogue.
3. Various aspects of the VoC approach have sparked controversial debates in recent years; cf. Hancké et al. (2007) for a critical account.
4. The fact that the UK is taken as a landmark here should not blind us to the differences between that country and the USA. By way of example, if the strong UK public sector, especially the National Health Service, is taken into account, the commonalities between the UK and other European welfare states are clearly visible, thus underpinning the notion of 'European social models' supported by the present authors (see Chapter 2 in this volume). In another publication, Rubery (2008) termed the UK employment model as 'liberal capitalism with a human face' to underline the differences from the US model.
5. When referring, in what follows, to Amable's typology we prefer to use the terms 'Nordic' and 'South European' purely for the sake of greater political and geographical precision, as justice should be done to Finland's Centre Party which can hardly be called Social-Democratic, and to Portugal which is located by the Atlantic Ocean rather than the Mediterranean.
6. This problematic has been taken on board by the VoC literature by creating a third type, namely 'mixed market economies/MME', which includes countries like Italy, Spain and France (Hall and Gingerich, 2004, p. 34). Quite obviously, however, this type is not much more than a residual category for the sake of statistical comparisons, quite similar to Amable's 'continental' cluster of countries. The respective economies are analysed as 'underperforming' (Hancké et al., 2007), thus making them interesting examples for the VoC case only insofar as they demonstrate how countries that lack strong institutional complementarities are drifting in the current environment. A similar concession to the lack of 'coverage' entailed by ideal-type-based typologies has recently been made by the establishment of a fourth type labelled as 'emerging market economies/EME', referring to the post-transition CEE economies. As Hancké et al. (2007, p. 4) acknowledge, the latter is 'less a separate "variety" of capitalism as such than a cluster of countries in transition with only partially formed institutional ecologies'.
7. It is also the case that the UK has significantly expanded its use of higher education as a means of building skills within its workforce. The outcome, however, may be to further reduce the status attached to non-higher education training and qualifications.
8. The term 'regimes' reflects the concept of 'institutions as social regimes' as elaborated by Streeck and Thelen (2005) as well as the move within the welfare state literature to a broader approach beyond just welfare *states* towards a wider set of institutions, including gender regimes or also education systems (Esping-Andersen, 1999; Kaufmann, 2003).
9. This observation may indeed apply to the financial crisis that has occurred since the chapters of this book were completed; at present the crisis is challenging all national models, with the intensity greatest in the UK and Spain (where

credit-based housing booms were very important) and Hungary (which has had to take out a major IMF loan due to withdrawal of FDI). However, the longer-term impacts are at present difficult to predict.
10. Examples of such crises inducing considerable change in the models include, as discussed earlier, the post-1990 Swedish model and the Dutch and Danish models in the early 1980s.
11. The concept of an 'architecture' of models does not suggest that national models have been designed or planned. This may be true in exceptional cases such as the Swedish 'Rehn-Meidner' model of the 1940s and 1950s, and maybe to some extent to the Austrian system of 'social partnership' after WW II. Rather the term architecture stands for the interdependence of its major elements which has evolved out of historic compromises and has provided for some stability for certain periods of time, without being necessarily coherent.
12. Sweden is an outlier even among Nordic countries but the ranking of these countries relative to other European nations remains unchallenged: public spending on 'other social services' as a percentage of GDP accounts for 6.3 per cent in Denmark, 4.9 per cent in Norway and 4.8 per cent in Iceland, while Finland with 3.7 per cent ranks way above the OECD average (OECD, 2007).
13. In the US, unlike in the EU, discrimination against part-timers in, for example, the provision of health benefits is allowed even within the same employer. This may explain the high rate of full-time work among mothers in the US, despite lack of childcare provision.
14. While Thelen (2001) is right to point to the importance of inter-employer conflicts of interest in destabilizing industrial relations in Germany, it is the story behind conflicts of interest among employers, namely the dramatic decline of trade union power in the post-reunification decade, that provides the clue for an understanding of the upheaval in the industrial relations system.

References

Amable, B. (2003), *The Diversity of Modern Capitalism*, Oxford/New York: OxfordUniversity Press.
Anxo, D. and Fagan, C. (2005), 'The Family, the State and Now the Market – the organisation of Employment and Working-time in Home Care Services for the Elderly', pp. 173–222 in G. Bosch and S. Lehndorff (eds), *Working in the Service Sector – A Tale from Different Worlds*, London/New York: Routledge.
Auer, P. (2000), *Employment Revival in Europe: Labour Market Success in Austria, Denmark, Ireland and the Netherlands*, ILO, Geneva.
Baumol, W. J. (1967), 'Macroeconomics of Unbalanced Growth: The Anatomy of Urban Crisis', *American Economic Review* 57: 416–26.
Bettio, F. and Villa, P. (1998), 'A Mediterranean Perspective on the Breakdown of the Relationship between Participation and Fertility', *Cambridge Journal of Economics* 22 (1998): 137–71.
Bosch, G. and Kalina, T. (2008), 'Low-wage Work in Germany: An Overview', pp. 19–112 in G. Bosch and C. Weinkopf (eds), *Low-wage Work in Germany*, New York: Russell Sage Foundation.
Bosch, G. and Wagner, A. (2005), 'Why Do Countries Have Such Different Service-sector Employment Rates?', pp. 74–102 in G. Bosch and S. Lehndorff (eds), *Working in the Service Sector – A Tale from Different Worlds*, London/New York: Routledge.

Bosch, G., Rubery, J. and Lehndorff, S. (2007), 'European Employment Models under Pressure to Change', *International Labour Review* 146 (2007): 253–77.

Campbell, J. (2004), *Institutional Change and Globalization*, Princeton, NJ: Princeton University Press.

Castells, M. (1996), *The Rise of the Network Society*, Oxford: Blackwell.

Coates, D. (2000), *Models of Capitalism: Growth and Stagnation in the Modern Era*, Cambridge: Polity Press.

Coates, D. (ed.) (2005), *Varieties of Capitalism, Varieties of Approaches*, Basingstoke: Palgrave Macmillan.

Commission of the European Communities (CEC) (2007), 'Towards Common Principles of Flexicurity: More and Better Jobs through Flexibility and Security –COM (2007), 359 final 27 June. http://ec.europa.eu/employment_social/employment_analysis/eie/com_2007_359_en.pdf.

Conway, P., Janod, V. and Nicoletti, G. (2005), 'Product Market Regulation in OECD Countries: 1998 to 2003', OECD Economics Department Working Papers No. 419, 1 April 2005, http://www.oecd.org/eco.

Conway, P. and Nicoletti, G. (2006), 'Product Market Regulation in the Non-manufacturing Sectors of OECD Countries: Measurement and Highlights', OECD Economics Department Working Papers No. 530, 7 December 2006, http://www.oecd.org/eco.

Crouch, C. (2005), Die Bedeutung von Governance für Vielfalt und Wandel im modernen Kapitalismus', pp. 101–26 in M. Miller (ed.), *Welten des Kapitalismus. Institutionelle Alternativen in der globalisierten Ökonomie*, Frankfurt/New York: Campus.

Crouch, C. and Farrell, H. (2002), 'Breaking the Path of Institutional Development? Alternatives to the New Determinism', MPIfG Discussion Paper 5/2002, Köln: Max-Planck-Institut für Gesellschaftsforschung.

Crouch, C. and Keune, M. (2005), 'Changing Dominant Practice: Making Use of Institutional Diversity in Hungary and the UK', pp. 83–102 in W. Streeck and K. Thelen (eds), *Beyond Continuity: Institutional Change in Advanced Political Economies*, Oxford: Oxford University Press.

Ebbinghaus, B. (1999), 'Does a European Social Model Exist and Can it Survive?', pp. 1–26 in G. Huemer, M. Mesch and F. Traxler (eds), *The Role of Employer Associations and Labour Unions in the EMU*, Aldershot: Ashgate.

Eichengreen, B. (2007), *The European Economy since 1945: Coordinated Capitalism and Beyond*, Princeton: Princeton University Press.

EIRO (2008), 'Unions Fear ECJ Ruling in Laval Case Could Lead to Social Dumping', European Industrial Relations Observatory, online: http:// www.eurofound.europa.eu/eiro/2008/01/articles/eu0801019i.htm.

Esping-Andersen, G. (1999), *Social Foundations of Post-Industrial Economies*, Oxford: Oxford University Press.

Esping-Andersen, G. (1990), *The Three Worlds of Welfare Capitalism*, Cambridge: Polity Press.

European Commission (2004), 'Industrial Relations in Europe', Luxembourg.

European Commission (2007), 'Employment in Europe 2006', Luxembourg.

Ferrera, M. (1996), 'The "Southern Model" of Welfare in Social Europe', *Journal of European Social Policy* 6 (1): 17–37.

Finegold, D. and Soskice, D. (1988), 'The Failure of Training in Britain: Analysis and Prescription', *Oxford Review of Economic Policy* Autumn 1988: 21–51.

Fulcher, J. (2005), 'Capitalisms', *Work, Employment and Society* 19 (1): 177–92.

Hall, P. A. (2007), 'The Evolution of Varieties of Capitalism in Europe' pp. 39–85 in B. Hancké, M. Rhodes and M. Thatcher (eds), *Beyond Varieties of Capitalism. Conflict, Contradiction and Complementarities in the European Economy*. Oxford/New York: Oxford University Press.
Hall, P. A. and Gingerich, D. W. (2004), 'Varieties of Capitalism and Institutional Complementarities in the Macroeconomy. An Empirical Analysis', MPIfG Discussion Paper 5/2004, Köln: Max-Planck-Institut für Gesellschaftsforschung.
Hall, P. A. and Soskice, D. (2001), 'An Introduction to Varieties of Capitalism', pp. 1–71 in P. A. Hall and D. Soskice (eds), *Varieties of Capitalism. The Institutional Foundations of Comparative Advantage*, New York: Oxford University Press.
Hancké, B., Rhodes, M. and Thatcher, M. (2007), 'Introduction: Beyond Varieties of Capitalism', pp. 3–38 in B. Hancké, M. Rhodes and M. Thatcher (eds), *Beyond Varieties of Capitalism. Conflict, Contradiction, and Complementarities in the European Economy*, Oxford/New York: Oxford University Press.
Hermans, S. (2005), 'The Social Agenda of the European Union and the Modernisation of the European Social Model', pp. 5–26 in *Towards a Modernisation of the European Social Model*, Collegium No.33, Winter 2005, College of Europe Bruges: www.coleurop.be.
Hobsbawm, E. (1996), *The Age of Extremes: The Short Twentieth Century, 1914–1991*, London: Abacus.
Hollingsworth, R. and Boyer, R. (eds) (1997), *Contemporary Capitalism: The Embeddedness of Institutions*, New York: Cambridge University Press.
Hoskyns, C. and Newman, M. (eds) (2000), *Democratising the European Union – Issues for the Twenty-first Century*, Manchester: Manchester University Press.
Jackson, G. and Deeg, R. (2006), 'How Many Varieties of Capitalism? Comparing the Comparative Institutional Analysis of Capitalist Diversity', MPIfG Discussion Paper 2/2006, Köln: Max-Planck-Institut für Gesellschaftsforschung.
Karamessini, M. (2008), 'Continuity and Change in the Southern European Social Model', *International Labour Review* 147 (1): 43–70.
Kaufmann, F-X. (2003), *Varianten des Wohlfahrtsstaats. Der deutsche Wohlfahrtsstaat im internationalen Vergleich*, Frankfurt am Main: Suhrkamp.
Keune, M. and Jepsen, M. (2007), 'Not Balanced and Hardly New: The European Commission's Quest for Flexicurity', pp. 189–211 in H. Jørgensen and P. K. Madsen (eds), *Flexicurity and Beyond*, Copenhagen: DJØF Publishing.
Levy, J. D. (2006), 'The State Also Rises: The Roots of Contemporary State Activism', pp. 1–28 in J. D. Levy (ed.), *The State after Statism. New State Activities in the Age of Liberalization*, Cambridge/London: Harvard University Press.
Levy, F. and Temin, P. (2007), 'Inequality and Institutions in 20th century America', NBER Working Paper 13106, National Bureau of Economic Research: http://www.nber.org/papers/w13106.
Lewis, J. (1992), 'Gender and the Development of Welfare Regimes', *Journal of European Social Policy* 2 (3): 159–73.
Maurice, M. and Sorge, A. (eds) (2000), *Embedding Organizations, Societal Analysis of Actors, Organizations and Socio-Economic Context*, Amsterdam: John Benjamin's Publishing Company.
Maurice, M., Sellier, F. and Silvestre, J-J. (1986), *The Social Foundations of Industrial Power. A Comparison of France and Germany*, Cambridge/Massachusetts: MIT Press.
Molina O. and Rhodes M. (2007), 'The Political Economy of Adjustment in Mixed Market Economies: A Study of Spain and Italy', pp. 223–52 in B. Hancké, M. Rhodes and M. Thatcher (eds), *Beyond Varieties of Capitalism*, Oxford: Oxford University Press.

Moravcsik, A. (1994), 'Why the European Community Strengthens the State: Domestic Politics and International Cooperation', Center for European Studies, Working Paper no. 52, Cambridge: Harvard University.

OECD (2007), 'The Social Expenditure Database: An Interpretive Guide', SOCX 1980–2003.

Pontusson, J. (2005), 'Varieties and Commonalities of Capitalism', pp. 163–88 in D. Coates (ed.), *Varieties of Capitalism, Varieties of Approaches*, Basingstoke: Palgrave Macmillan.

Rubery, J. (1994), 'The British Production Regime: A Societal-specific System?', *Economy and Society* 2 (23): 335–54.

Rubery, J. (2008), 'The UK as a Third Way: The US Model with a Human Face?', Industry Studies Conference, SSRN, online: http://ssrn.com/abstract=1134962.

Rubery, J. and Grimshaw, D. (2003), *The Organization of Employment*, Basingstoke: Palgrave Macmillan.

Simonazzi, A. (2009), 'Care Regimes and National Employment Models', *Cambridge Journal of Economics* (in press 10.1093/cje/ben043).

Smith, C. and Meiksins, P. (1995), 'System, Societal and Dominance Effects in Cross-national Organisational analysis', *Work, Employment and Society* 9 (2): 241–68.

Sorge, A. (1991), 'Strategic Fit and the Social Effect: Interpreting Cross-National Comparisons of Technology, Organization and Human Resources', *Organization Studies* 12 (1991): 161–90.

Streeck, W. (1997), 'Beneficial Constraints: On the Economic Limits of Rational Voluntarism', pp. 197–219 in R. Hollingsworth and R. Boyer (eds), *Contemporary Capitalism: The Embeddedness of Institutions*, New York: Cambridge University Press.

Streeck, W. and Thelen, K. (2005), 'Introduction: Institutional Change in Advanced Political Economies', pp. 1–39 in W. Streeck and K. Thelen (eds), *Beyond Continuity. Institutional Change in Advanced Political Economies*, Oxford: Oxford University Press.

Thelen, K. (2001), 'Varieties of Labor Politics in the Developed Democracies', pp. 71–103 in P. A. Hall and D. Soskice (eds), *Varieties of Capitalism. The Institutional Foundations of Comparative Advantage*, New York: Oxford University Press.

Thelen, K. (2003), 'How Institutions Evolve: Insights from Comparative Historical Analysis', pp. 208–40 in J. Mahoney and D. Reuschemeyer (eds), *Comparative Historical Analysis in the Social Sciences*, Cambridge: Cambridge University Press.

Weiss, L. (ed.) (2003), *States in the Global Economy: Bringing Domestic Institutions Back In*, Cambridge: Cambridge University Press.

Whitley, R. (1999), *Divergent Capitalisms: The Social Structuring and Change of Business Systems*, Oxford: Oxford University Press.

Whitley, R. (2007), *Business Systems and Organizational Capabilities*, Oxford: Oxford University Press.

Wickham, J. (2005), 'The End of the European Social Model – Before it Began?', Dynamo project thematic working paper, online: http://www.dynamoproject.eu/publications.php.

Wilkinson, F. (1983), 'Productive Systems', *Cambridge Journal of Economics* 7 (3/4): 413–29.

2
Revisiting the UK Model: From Basket Case to Success Story and Back Again?

Jill Rubery, Damian Grimshaw, Rory Donnelly and Peter Urwin

Introduction

When the UK took over the presidency of the European Union in July 2005, the then Prime Minister Tony Blair presented the UK model as a potential saviour for the European social model, a model for the rest of Europe to emulate. It had succeeded, it was claimed, not only in combining growth with high employment rates, facilitated by flexible labour and product markets, but also for using economic growth and modern approaches to public service and welfare reform to renew public services and to combat child poverty. Even at the time these claims were met with scepticism; for many the UK still represented the liberal or market version of capitalism which, if followed as the model for modernization, could not only sound the death knell for distinctively European varieties of capitalism (Wickham, 2005) but also promote a dangerously fragile form of expansion, based on extended consumer credit and a seemingly never-ending rise in house prices. From the perspective of autumn 2008, the grandiose claims by Blair to have developed a blueprint for Europe have been put in perspective by the financial meltdown and the state-led rescue plan for the jewel in the UK's crown, the City of London. This major collapse of the UK and world financial system is too new and its course as yet too unpredictable for this chapter to predict the characteristics of the next phase of model development in the UK. It is appropriate to note, however, that we are witnessing a clear demonstration of the cyclical volatility of the fortunes of national models (see Chapter 1 of this volume). The decade of New Labour could be argued to be the UK's glory years, with high employment combined with some renewal of its social model, even if the underlying weaknesses of the model could be clearly identified. The focus of this chapter is on understanding the factors behind the New Labour boom period and the extent to which its characteristics both reinforced and redefined the UK model as an example of neoliberal capitalism and a residual welfare state.

Typologies, change and the UK model

The literature on national socio-economic models provides a wide range of different typologies, dependent upon the research questions posed. Despite this variation there is a remarkable similarity in the positioning of the UK within the typologies. The common themes are the lack of institutions for economic coordination (Hall and Soskice, 2001), the dominance of financial constraints and shareholder power, and the correspondingly low power of labour, resulting in both flexible employment and weak employee voice (Pendleton and Gospel, 2005), the power of retailers over the manufacturing sector (Rubery, 1994), the low-skill base of UK production systems (Finegold and Soskice, 1988) and the provision of welfare as primarily a residual safety net (Esping-Anderson, 1990), despite high dependency on the state due to the weak and fragmented family system.

All of these features tend to put the UK into the US box of liberal market capitalism with only residual welfare protection. Such a classification can be regarded as an oversimplification of the history of the UK model. Its transformation into a neoliberal model is still relatively recent; up until the late 1970s it was known for a Keynesian consensus and a commitment to voluntary collective regulation and to a strong public sphere. The welfare system may have been Beveridge not Bismarckian – that is, based on targeted means-testing not insurance – but its social protection net has been extensive and long term, albeit ungenerous. Moreover, even if neoliberal ideology may always have been embedded in the values of the City of London (Crouch and Keune, 2005), the notion that the market did not need to be tempered by regulation and by redistributive social policy only took hold as a dominant ideology under Thatcher.

Nevertheless, by 1994 the neoliberal policy and the run down of the welfare system towards a residual model was well in train. An assessment of the characteristics of and prospects for the UK model by Rubery (1994, reprinted in Ackroyd and Fleetwood, 2000 and in Coates, 2003) considered it extremely unlikely that the UK would develop into a 'prosperous skill-based system' (Rubery, 1994, p. 347). This assessment reflected 15 years of continuous erosion of the welfare state and the public space that looked to be leading to long-term divergence between the UK and Europe. The interlocking institutional and social arrangements in the UK were generating a low-wage, low-skill economy that was reinforced by the short-termism of shareholder power and by the City's orientation towards international rather than British capital. British consumer manufacturing companies, under the control of dominant retailers, were unable to develop high value added strategies to compete under new international competition. Trade union power had been undermined not only by restrictive legislation but also by the rapid restructuring of production and ownership that came with de-industrialization and privatization and that deprived unions of their traditional strongholds. Plans to decentralize and fragment pay determination in the remaining public sector were expected to result in a further erosion of collective regulation. Work first policies were being combined with stricter and less generous benefit entitlements. No major renewal of the skill base appeared to be on the cards, either through education or training, and continuing lack of support for dual-earning families was trapping over-educated women in low-paid part-time jobs. The UK model appeared locked into a downward spiral.

However, the following decade or so did not live up to these predictions. Manufacturing industry did not recover but the period from the late 1990s until 2008 was characterized by a sustained high employment rate alongside low unemployment, a sustained expansion in young people attending higher education and by improvements in social safety nets, including a new and rising national minimum wage, higher benefits for the working poor and those with children, and higher minimum income guarantees for pensioners. The consequence has been significant reductions in poverty levels, particularly for pensioners and for children (Palmer et al., 2006). There have also been some responses to the needs of parents through new work-life balance initiatives. Moreover, far from moving further towards the US minimalist welfare system, the UK's commitment to both social safety nets and to social spending, particularly in health and education, has been reaffirmed. Thus, the assessment of this period cannot be entirely negative.

However, while the UK in its commitments to social provision moved more in line with the rest of the EU, in its economic revival it aligned itself even closer to the evolving US model. Both economies became exposed to the 2007/08 financial crisis due to their reliance on a large financial sector and high levels of both private indebtedness (especially in housing) and public indebtedness (large balance of payments imbalances) (Morgan Stanley, 2007). The UK also followed the US trend towards the development of a significant stratum of the super-rich. At the other end of the equality spectrum effective skill development opportunities are still not offered to those not entering higher education. Not only has little progress been made in training provision for this group, the UK also has a high share of school leavers who opt out of education, training and employment altogether. The question is thus whether this New Labour period marks another turning point, equivalent to the Thatcher turn, or should more appropriately be viewed as both moderating and intensifying an underlying neoliberal model.

Continuity and change in the UK model

In exploring issues of continuity and change we share the methodological approach outlined in Chapter 1. That is, we take change as necessarily path-dependent but that observation marks only the beginning of the analysis. We address factors that are normally considered within the debates on national models, such as welfare, industrial relations and regulatory and education systems. In addition, we examine factors that are often considered exogenous to national models but which impact on performance, including aspects of economic management. With respect to debates on the nature of change (see Chapter 1), we focus first on evidence for turning points – analogous to the Thatcher turn – while recognizing that even turning points may build upon existing, even if dormant or subordinate, values and norms within the society (Crouch and Keune, 2005). In some cases, changes in the model reflect changes in the significance attached to existing features, both as barriers to development and as facilitators or promoters of development. Most changes are incremental (Streeck and Thelen, 2005) but we distinguish between incremental change that reinforces the model's long-term features and that which modifies these characteristics. Particularly important here is cumulative incremental change that may lead to tipping points in the evolution of the model. Table 2.1 sets out the major changes we

Table 2.1 Features of change in the UK model between the early 1990s and 2008

Type of change	Situation in 2008	Situation in 1990s
Change in factors exogenous to model	Macroeconomic management – more stable and more expansionary from mid-1990s until 2008	More volatile
Turning points	Expansion in welfare state – particularly health and education infrastructure	Very limited expenditure on infrastructure and future commitment to welfare state uncertain
	Commitment to reduce child poverty	No commitment to reduction in poverty
	Involvement of private sector in public services delivery firmly established as key principle	
Continuity		
i) Reinforcement of features of model	Reinforced dominance of finance and of UK-led international retailing supply chains	City of London one of main strengths of model; retail sector dominant over British manufacturing
	Reinforcement of product market deregulation and intensification of globalization/ FDI flows in services	At forefront of product market deregulation and globalization but less FDI in services
	Expansion of personal credit and reinforcement of importance of housing assets	Personal credit already high by international standards; housing yet to recover from crash in 1989
	Increased means testing of benefits	Low flat rate benefits supplemented by means-tested benefits

(*Continued*)

Table 2.1 (Continued)

Type of change	Situation in 2008	Situation in 1990s
	Continued increase in inequality at top end	Rapid increase in inequality in 1980s and 1990s
ii) Change in significance of features	Ability of labour market to absorb increasing number of graduates – due to weak requirements to match jobs to qualifications	Fewer graduates – issue of absorption less important
	Comparative advantage increased by dominance of English language in services	Less trade in services/ less use of internet – so language less of a natural advantage
Incremental change		
i) Modification of features of model	Some evidence of stronger links between shareholders and management	More fluid capital markets
	Minimum floor of employment rights to compensate for decline in voluntary regulation	Opposition to EU social chapter, minimum rights and national minimum wage
	Return to more national collective bargaining in public sector	Decentralization of wage bargaining in public sector
	Higher social safety nets	Decline in social safety nets
ii) Tipping points	Manufacturing no longer a major element in the employment system – training issues now have to address the service economy	Low skill equilibrium – difficulty of becoming a high value-added manufacturing economy
	Private sector effectively non-unionized	Long-term decline in membership and in recognition of unions for collective bargaining
	Rapid expansion of student numbers – from elite to mass/plus elite higher education	Slow expansion of student numbers in early 1990s
	Dual-earner family now the norm – childcare plus some support for working parents on policy agenda	No policy for childcare or for more than minimum leave for working parents

FDI = foreign direct investment.

have identified within this framework in the UK model over the period since 1994, and more specifically since 1997 and the change to New Labour.

Changes to factors exogenous to the varieties of capitalism models

A key change in the UK model under New Labour is in the framework for macroeconomic policy. The Thatcher project involved the pursuit of a monetarist economic policy. This connection had already been broken under Major and has been further disentangled under the Blair/Brown governments. Instead it is continental Europe that has been forced to adopt the deflationary policies embedded in the regulations for the Euro zone. Two political decisions framed the new approach. The first was to remain outside the Euro zone, initially taken under the Conservatives but not reversed under New Labour, despite an initial period of rapprochement with the European vision. The second was to make the Bank of England independent, to insulate Labour against the charge of financial incompetence that had dogged it in the past. Both decisions allowed for a more expansionary policy, more favourable to smoothing cyclical fluctuations than the Euro regime, since the Bank is not only charged with restricting inflation but also guarding against deflation. According to the Bank of England website, 'inflation below the target of 2 per cent is judged to be just as bad as inflation above the target. The inflation target is therefore symmetrical'. Conscious that Euro zone rules might impinge on his ability to implement his key policies of improving public infrastructure and fighting child poverty, Brown as Chancellor also established his own 'golden rules' on debt financing that allowed for fiscal deficits to vary over the economic cycle and for flexibility in how to define the period of the business cycle. The outcome over the last decade has been relatively stable macroeconomic conditions, a high employment rate and consistent growth, even if at the cost of a relatively high exchange rate and continuing declines in manufacturing output.

These more favourable macroeconomic conditions from the late 1990s until 2007/08 provided the opportunity to re-embrace social expenditure, which in turn fuelled high and stable demand. The decade of growth also reduced the social tensions associated with restructuring and changing employment relations and smoothed the transition to a largely service-based and primarily non-union private sector economy.

Turning points

The UK in the 1980s was launched on a development path from which it was said there was to be 'no turning back' and based on a belief that there was 'no alternative' other than to reduce public expenditure. This approach continued through the first two years of New Labour (1997–1999) as it sought to establish itself as a safe pair of hands. It was not until 1999/2000 (Peston, 2005) that Labour broke with this approach, particularly with respect to expenditure on health and education. As Table 2.2 shows, expenditure in real

Table 2.2 Real expenditure on selected major areas of public spending, 1992/93 to 2006/07 (£ billions)

	1992–3	1996–7	1997–8	1998–9	1999–0	2000–1	2001–2	2002–3	2003–4	2004–05	2005–6	2006–7
Health	47.4	53.4	54.0	55.5	57.3	62.0	66.7	71.6	78.5	84.4	88.7	92.8
Education[1]	44.0	45.1	45.1	45.5	47.0	50.5	55.2	56.6	61.2	63.7	67.1	69.8
Social protection	125.7	140.2	138.3	135.7	142.1	146.4	152.7	156.6	163.1	167.4	171.1	172.9
Defence	32.9	27.5	26.2	28.8	29.0	29.3	28.3	29.2	30.2	30.6	30.7	31.6
Public order	19.6	20.2	20.4	20.9	21.0	22.9	25.4	26.4	27.8	28.9	29.3	29.8
Transport	14.9	11.8	10.5	9.2	9.1	10.3	12.6	16.0	17.0	16.3	16.9	19.2
Public sector debt interest	26.3	35.0	35.9	34.6	29.3	30.3	25.2	23.5	24.1	25.2	26.6	27.6
Total[2]	*378.2*	*392.7*	*389.9*	*391.1*	*395.7*	*412.6*	*433.2*	*454.1*	*477.7*	*501.0*	*523.4*	*538.8*

Source: HM Treasury (2007), Public Expenditure Statistical Analyses (PESA), April 2007, Table 4.3. Internet home page: http://www.hm-treasury.gov.uk/media (accessed February 2008)
Note 1 Excluding training.
Note 2 The total refers to 'total managed expenditure' and includes any other items of expenditure not listed in the table here.

terms on health rose by £36 billion between 2000 and 2007 compared to an increase of only £10 billion over the seven years prior to the 1999/2000 turning point. Similarly, spending on education rose by £23 billion in the seven years after the turning point compared to £3 billion in the earlier period. The sharp change in public spending is evident in the rise in health spending from an average of just 5.4 per cent of GDP during the 1990s to 7.3 per cent by 2006/07; and a parallel rise in education spending from an average of 4.8 per cent during the 1990s to 5.5 per cent in 2006/07.

The outcome has been a steady increase in public sector employment, reversing the year-on-year downward trend during the 1990s. Numbers employed dropped from 5.9 to 5.2 million between 1992 and 1998, but increased to 5.8 million by 2005. The share of public sector employment in fact has been relatively stable at around 20 per cent since 1999 (following a decline from 25 per cent in 1990). This is explained in part by rising overall employment but also by the growing share of expenditures channelled to private sector firms to provide public services (see below). Indeed, outsourcing of public services, as well as the increased use of private sector firms in the direct provision of public services, has made an important contribution to the expansion of the private business services sector. Edmonds and Glynn (2005) estimate that around 550,000 private sector jobs were created as a direct result of increased public spending between 2000 and 2003, concluding in fact that net growth in UK employment during 2000–2003 was due to higher public expenditure. Coutts et al. (2006) have further estimated that the impact of public spending was particularly strong in the north, accounting for some closing of the North-South divide under New Labour, not just through boosting employment in public services and associated private sectors such as construction, but also through revitalizing cities of the north as attractive places for businesses to locate. The significance of these developments, where much of the growth in employment has come from the public sector, is put into perspective by the 1994 OECD Jobs Study that confidently stated that 'new jobs must certainly be generated by the private sector, because in nearly all countries budget deficits and resistance to tax increases rule out significant expansion of the public sector' (OECD, 1994, p. 33).

This change in direction can be considered to constitute a new turning point, comparable to that promoted by Thatcher in the 1980s to end the Keynesian consensus (Crouch and Keune, 2005); just as the City of London was waiting in the wings to embrace and facilitate the Thatcher vision, so too the Blair/Brown governments have been able to draw on widespread support for the provision of public services from an electorate that was critical of the neglect of the public space and the associated crumbling of the infrastructure over the previous two decades. This re-emergence of the role of the state indicates that the neoliberal view of the state as inefficient and unnecessary is much less firmly embedded in the UK than, for example, in the US political ideology.

The second associated turning point, the commitment to reduce and indeed eliminate child poverty, can be interpreted more as a personal commitment, particularly by Brown (both as Chancellor and as Prime Minister) than a response to electoral demands and opportunities. New money was made available to support all families with children but with particular efforts to help poor families, including lone parents. The result has been a decline in child poverty by a third, a development that is considered both a success – as it represents a significant decrease – but also a failure as it is expected to miss the target of a 50 per cent reduction by 2010 (HM Treasury, 2001; Palmer et al., 2006). Furthermore, in the UNICEF international comparison of children's welfare (UNICEF, 2007), the UK was still ranked 18th out of 21 countries on the score of 'material well-being'.

Both of these turning points were nevertheless linked to other aspects of the Blair/Brown project that could be considered to reinforce rather than reduce commitments to a neoliberal model. The expansion of public spending has become even more predicated on the opening up of public services provision to private providers (Crouch, 2003). Moreover, the establishment of the market state as a key principle in public services delivery is also being used to reopen and intensify debates over work organization and terms and conditions in the public sector (Grimshaw and Hebson, 2005; Dibben et al., 2007). Public sector unions have had some success in resisting these changes and in extending basic protection to employees of private sector contractors (especially in the National Health Service). Nevertheless, their success is patchy and subject to further revision as the opportunities for private sector involvement in public provision continue to multiply (see Grimshaw and Carroll, 2008).

Likewise, the commitment of resources to eliminate child poverty is linked to a work first policy involving a steady increase in pressure on welfare recipients, including lone parents, to seek work coupled with more generous support for those who do enter employment. The justification is that employment is held to provide the main way to escape poverty but the policy also allows the government to adjust the welfare system to fit the new flexible and often low-paid job opportunities; that is, it supports breadwinners in taking up low-wage jobs in preference to intervening to change and improve the conditions of work in the economy. The only exceptions to this stance have been the policies of introducing and upgrading the national minimum wage during the period 2001–2006, in part to reduce the costs of the in-work benefits to the state (see below).

There are at least two logics of change at work here that may be considered contradictory and paradoxical; at one and the same time we find evidence of the scope for political choice and of an increasing scope for international capital to shape policy. The role of international capital in pushing forward access for private capital to the expanding public sector market is undocumented and unclear but undoubtedly significant. The motivations for extending opportunities for private capital are likely to have been multiple: according to one media commentator, Brown's main motivation was to minimize pubic sector debt to satisfy the EU and the international community but Blair saw it as a necessary part of his personal commitment to deliver a continual revolution in working practices (Toynbee, 2005). Thus, while the changes to macroeconomic policy and the decisions to prioritize reducing child poverty and renewing health and education infrastructure do demonstrate the potential for independent national action, driven by political will, this reaffirmation of the scope for public choice is tempered by an unwillingness to depart from major elements of the neoliberal model, including the policy of limited intervention in the labour market (see below) and reinforcement of the opening up of the public procurement market to international capital through Private Finance Initiatives (PFI)[1] and other forms of public private partnership and outsourcing.

Continuity in the UK model
Reinforcement of distinctive characteristics

Many of the developments in the UK model over the last decade have reinforced rather than modified or weakened its distinctive characteristics. The strength of the City in financial markets was reinforced, as it benefited from a less 'heavy' regulatory regime than that which prevails in the US since the passing of the 2002 Sarbanes-Oxley regulations to address the conflict of interests in auditing revealed by the Enron fraud scandal (Balls, 2006). The further opening of the UK economy to international markets and capital over the past decade has occurred both in public sector and private markets. While penetration of public sector markets represents a relatively new development, the general increase in internationalization is more an intensification of one of the UK model's most distinctive characteristics. Even as all economies internationalize, the UK has still stayed 'ahead of the game' (Hirst and Thompson, 2000). The rhetoric of policymakers still refers to adjusting to or keeping up with globalization but in reality the UK has been at the forefront of the development of globalization. In this deepening of the UK's already high exposure to internationalization, measured by both inward and outward investment and through the internationalization of production chains, dominated by large UK retailers, the role of capital in driving change is explicitly evident (Hirst and Thompson, 2000).

The distinctiveness of the UK as a low regulated economy has also been reinforced. Not only has it retained its position as the most deregulated economy since 1998 (although now sharing first place with Australia) despite further trend decline in the regulatory index in most economies but also, according to the OECD, it is the only country with a liberal approach in all three policy areas, namely state control, barriers to entrepreneurship and barriers to trade and investment (the US is a less open economy but the

UK has more state control) (Conway et al., 2005). While some of the inputs into the product market regulation index – including openness to trade and FDI and low administrative barriers to setting up new firms – are clearly associated with the rapid growth of the UK service economy, some fruits of deregulation are beginning to be recognized as negative for business: for example, the inefficient and underprovided transport infrastructure that is associated with privatization is identified as a factor causing the UK to slip down the rankings of countries by their attractiveness for FDI (EIU, 2006). The 2008 financial crisis has also amply demonstrated the costs of a too relaxed regulatory approach in financial markets.

A further development that can be considered more a deepening than a reorientation of the UK model is the continued and expanded contribution of consumer and housing credit to domestic demand. While these characteristics were present in the 1980s and early 1990s, their importance has intensified. The massive growth in consumer credit, particularly since 2000, has been largely secured against housing assets such that the ratio of housing debt to assets has remained remarkably stable even though housing assets doubled in value from 1999 to 2006 (Halifax plc, 2007). The UK's economic growth over the last decade or so has relied on enormous consumer debt and what has proved to be an unsustainable housing boom as the cost of housing has become misaligned with the level of salaries. Even before the 2007/08 credit crunch more young people were staying at home longer, unable to afford their first homes. Housing shortages are at best only a partial explanation of the price boom; more important are concerns over the security of alternative investments – for example in the stock market – and the strong long-term record of housing in delivering wealth to the middle classes, combined with a limited rental market. Also important has been the role of the banking sector in a deregulated market; much of the instability is associated with the provision of unsustainable mortgages, through low fixed-term rates or even loans in excess of the value of the property.

Two more tendencies towards reinforcement of characteristic features are worth noting. First, there has been a reinforcement of the welfare system as a strongly targeted system based on household means-testing. The UK has only ever partially implemented an earnings-related welfare benefit system and even this partial system was removed under Thatcher. With the exception of education and health, higher benefits are expected to be funded by employers or individuals and while benefits are long term, they are directly linked to need. The improvement of social safety nets under New Labour has greatly expanded the range of households affected by means-testing. This has caused problems of poverty traps (or low-wage traps) as the households on means-tested in-work benefits face disincentives to increase earnings (OECD, 2005, Chapter 3). Furthermore, the pensions policy of providing an improved but still means-tested safety net has run into two kinds of problems. Firstly, the means-tested element reduces incentives to save and secondly, many employers have decided to close occupational defined benefit pension systems to new entrants, thereby increasing the future share of the population potentially dependent upon state benefits. These are emerging problems that have not yet been fully resolved and may lead to further modifications of the model.

The second reinforcing trend is towards yet higher levels of inequality, at least at the top end of the distribution. Explanations of widening inequality that stress skill-biased technical change are unconvincing in the UK, which already had one of the widest distributions of income in the 1980s and 1990s. The City is certainly linked to the widening earnings distribution, and indeed to the development of an elite layer, now known as the super-rich. Expectations of higher salaries have infected all areas of employment for higher-level staff, even if the gap with the super-rich has still widened.

Re-evaluation of distinctive characteristics

The changing social and economic environment has also resulted in some key features of the UK model taking on greater salience. One such example is the ability to absorb higher numbers of graduates (Elias and Purcell, 2003). Due to the weak linkage in the UK between subject studied, qualifications and job matching, graduates are able to search for jobs for which they are not specifically qualified. This weak linkage has been a longstanding feature of the UK system as educational achievement is taken primarily to be an indication of general ability, rather than a means of developing specific skills. This aspect of the flexible labour market comes at the cost of potential loss of productive potential for the economy and a risk for graduates that they will not earn a significant wage premium. Nevertheless, it has enabled the UK to base its system of skill development for a service economy primarily on the expansion of higher education.

Another core feature of the UK model – the English language – has also taken on greater importance for comparative advantage; the growth in trade in services, the greater importance of knowledge and information as sources of competitive advantage and the development of the worldwide internet and communications technology have all led to a reinforcement of the dominance of the English language.[2]

Incremental change in the UK model

Modifications to the UK model

Since the early 1990s there have been a number of changes that have moderated the distinctiveness of the UK model through incremental change without as yet fundamentally changing its character.

The first is in its shareholder finance system. While the focus on shareholder value strengthened in the 1980s, following the selling-off of public utilities and the development of shareholder value metrics by UK consultancy firms, Pendleton and Gospel (2005) argue that the increase in the institutional investors' share of UK-owned shares, from 60 per cent in 1981 to 73 per cent in 2001 (Pendleton and Gospel, 2005, Table 3.1) has reduced options for investment funds, particularly the large pension funds. As they become locked in to both the market and the individual firms in which they hold stakes (Deakin, 2005), investors have worked increasingly closely with companies. Shareholder commitment nevertheless remains contingent; when operating problems and profitability become really serious, these closer ties provide shareholders with leverage to impose rapid downsizing on the company and the workforce. The UK is thus far from developing 'patient capital', but nor is capital simply floating free on the market.

Two modifications can be identified in employment relations. The first is the implementation of the set of EU directives related to employment rights from which the UK was excluded when it negotiated its opt out from the social chapter of the 1992 Maastricht summit. When New Labour waived the opt out it committed itself to implement a raft of EU employment legislation, together with some domestically oriented legislation, as fulfilment of promises to the unions in the build up to the 1997 election, most notably the introduction of a national minimum wage. The consequence has been the establishment of a floor of legal employment rights, which is at odds with both the traditional voluntarist system in the UK and the deregulationist position of Thatcher. However, these rights remain minimal, with the UK taking advantage of the maximum concessions from the EU in its implementation, for example in its use of the voluntary opt out from the working time directive. Furthermore, since implementing the social chapter legislation it has opposed almost all further legislation from the EU, including recently negotiating an opt out from the EU charter of fundamental rights, while on the domestic front limiting new initiatives to some relatively weak work-life balance measures (see below).[3] These new employment rights have had relatively little impact as there is a lack of both awareness of rights and of effective enforcement mechanisms in workplaces without a union presence.

The most important element in the new floor of employment rights is the national minimum wage (NMW). Introduced in 1999, the NMW has probably had the most impact and has the highest profile. It was introduced at a low level and declined relative to median earnings during its first two years but is now at a moderate level compared to other OECD minimum wages (13th out of 21 in relative terms at 35 per cent of average wages [Immervoll, 2007]). However, wages are becoming compressed around the minimum and case study research suggests there are few routes to improved earnings and careers sufficient to bring the working poor out of poverty (Lloyd et al., 2008).

The second modification is the halt to the trend under the Conservatives towards decentralization of wage bargaining in the public sector. This was reversed both to control public sector wage costs and to allow for new unified pay systems to address issues of equal pay for work of equal value. However, the government would favour decentralization if public sector unions would accept variable pay by region. In the meantime the push for private sector outsourcing is in part to secure the benefits of lower regional wages. Moreover, while centralized wage structures are found in health, education and local government, decentralized pay systems are still the norm across the various agencies of central government.

The third modification identified is the raising of social safety nets under New Labour. There have been significant improvements to guaranteed minimum income levels for pensioners and families with children, in addition to the introduction of the NMW. This is an important reversal to the long-term trend decline in minimum income guarantees. But, as we have already discussed, the guarantees are based on systems of household means-testing that have proved complex to implement, leading to low take-up and problems of under and overpayment. Furthermore, access to benefits is increasingly conditional on active search for work with few options to refuse on grounds of care responsibilities or inconvenient working hours, travel times or low pay.

From incremental change to tipping points

By 2008 we can identify four areas where long-term incremental changes have resulted in such significant change that questions posed earlier with respect to the UK model appear no longer relevant. These trends were already present in the early 1990s in each of these four areas but their significance is, as historians well know, best appreciated through hindsight.

The significance of incremental change is first of all evident when we consider the starting point for the 1994 paper by Rubery, which is how to turn the UK into a high value-added manufacturing economy. By 2008 this question has much less purchase; it is the success of services rather than the decline of manufacturing that dominates the economic assessment. The critique that the UK was only an assembly plant using low-cost labour for the enlarged European market (Elger and Smith, 2005) lost its force as the UK became overwhelmingly dominated by services. The retail sector no longer promotes low-cost consumer manufacturing in the UK as it has largely switched orders from the UK to Asia and other developing countries. The UK has some traditional strengths in high-end manufacturing, mainly defence and pharmaceuticals, but has notably failed to expand its research and development (R&D) expenditure to provide a basis for future development (Bulli, 2008). Public and business R&D spending lags behind the US and Germany; at 1.9 per cent of GDP invested in R&D (HMT et al., 2004) the UK is unlikely to meet the government target of 2.5 per cent by 2014, let alone the more ambitious Lisbon 2010 target of 3 per cent of GDP. Manufacturing has continued to shed jobs; 1.8 million were lost between 1984 and 2004, in addition to the haemorrhaging of 1.6 million between 1980 and 1984. Growth in employment in services outstripped the loss of 850,000 more manufacturing jobs between 1997 and 2004. Thus the economy and employment have grown despite further and seemingly irreversible deindustrialization.

The UK, along with the US, has been categorized by Castells (1996; 2000) as a service economy model that prioritizes capital management services over producer services – in contrast to Japan and Germany. This type of model is said to 'emphasize an entirely new employment structure where the differentiation among service activities becomes the key element to analyse social structure' (Castells, 2000, p. 245). This service economy model is increasingly integrated into the international economic system, along with more traditional production models. The UK is in fact both an importer and exporter of service work. In 2002/03, it was second only to the USA in the offshoring of call centres, back-office processing work and IT (UNCTAD, 2004), including the movement of call handling work to India where the persistence of higher education in English has facilitated such developments. And it was also the second most important destination for export-oriented FDI projects after India, more than China and significantly more than any other EU country. The sustainability of these recent favourable employment trends remains open to question, not least because there is still a paucity of research on what factors are significant in developing and maintaining a successful service economy model.

The second tipping point is the final emergence of a virtually non-union private sector where by 2004 only 16 per cent of workplaces with ten or more employees recognized unions and only 11 per cent engaged in any collective bargaining (Kersley et al., 2005) compared to 17 per cent in 1998. This decline in union coverage and collective bargaining has been in process since the late 1970s and has not been halted by New Labour. Trade unions and collective bargaining are now effectively confined to the public sector where union recognition rates and collective bargaining coverage remain strong.[4] There are factors that could lead to some reversal of this trend; for example, trade union efforts to organize staff in the private companies contracted to provide public services. The implementation of the new information and consultation directive from the EU should also strengthen employee voice and could act as a stimulus to union organization (Hall, 2005). For the moment, however, the private sector of the UK economy can be considered to be effectively unorganized.

The third tipping point is the now established dominance of higher education as the route to skill development. There has been a gradual change from the traditional elite to a mass higher education system (albeit retaining an elite element). The expansion of student numbers in education has reinforced the UK's traditional preference for education over vocational qualifications as the screening device for securing access to employment.

Participation in higher education is currently 42 per cent and is targeted to be 50 per cent by 2010. This expansion of higher education has been in part funded by the ending of student grants and the introduction of fees. But state support for higher education remains high as these funding changes have been introduced through a system of state-subsidized loans with fees to be paid out of future earnings rather than paid upfront. In part, this dominance of higher education has come about because there has been very limited vocational training in services (unlike in Germany).

However, the focus on higher education has left a vacuum for the remaining 50 per cent of young generations and even higher shares of older generations. The continuation of the low-skills equilibrium phenomenon in all sectors is evident in the extraordinarily low shares of the workforce that managers regard as skilled (see Table 2.3). New Labour has been reluctant to require organizations to train, although training requirements are now built into some contracting arrangements with the private sector. This policy is thus unlikely to reverse trends towards polarization of skills. Yet another

Table 2.3 Proportion of skilled employees among the non-managerial workforce in the workplace, by sector

	Percentage of workplaces with			
	no skilled employees	*1–25% skilled employees*	*26–50% skilled employees*	*>50% skilled employees*
Manufacturing	4	40	20	37
Electricity, gas and water	2	8	21	68
Construction	19	12	14	54
Wholesale and retail	40	38	10	12
Hotels and restaurants	40	38	10	12
Transport and communications	33	42	9	15
Transport and communications	33	42	9	15
Financial services	57	23	13	7
Other business services	12	18	23	47
Public administration	27	31	13	29
Education	0	2	42	55
Health	22	33	23	22
Other community services	17	36	16	31
All workplaces	19	31	20	30

Source: Adapted from Cully et al. (1999, Table 3.4)

report on Britain's skill problems (HM Treasury, 2006) concluded that major efforts are needed to raise skill levels and recommended a raft of measures aimed at ensuring all young people are in either education or training up to age 18, a recommendation that appears to have been accepted by the government. However, the report also stresses the need to build skills among the adult population and suggests doing this in part through partnership between employers and higher education in an effort to overcome the widespread prejudice against training and vocational qualifications in the UK. Those who participate in training courses have, according to popular prejudice, failed to be selected either for higher education or for a proper job (Ashton, 1988). Plans are now developing for employers to work with universities in accrediting education and training programmes for degree status.

The fourth persistent but incremental change that can no longer be ignored by policymakers is the increased participation of women in employment and the associated growth of dual-earner households. The UK's welfare system has traditionally been characterized as a strong male-breadwinner society[5] (Lewis, 1992) with a high gender pay gap, a lack of support for working mothers – whether in the form of paid leave or childcare – and a continued dependence of women on their partners' pension entitlements. Despite this lack of support, women's employment rate has risen to one of the highest in the EU, fuelled by the growth of employment in the service sector. Much of this work has been low-paid and part-time and state policy has been by and large to allow women to be segregated into low-paid and flexible work with few prospects for career development, despite the rising education levels of women.

Under New Labour, public policy has begun to reflect the new reality of dual-earner households. Policies introduced to support working parents include: (i) a national childcare strategy to increase availability of childcare; (ii) a child tax credit to help with childcare costs; (iii) lengthening of maternity leave and improvements in pay (and proposals to allow some part of paid maternity leave to be transferred to fathers[6]); and (iv) a new right for parents of children under six and carers of adults to request employers to allow them to work flexibly. Compared to a Scandinavian model of support for working parents, these measures are weak; leave is either unpaid or paid at a low rate, childcare remains effectively unplanned and is expensive even with the child tax credits, and rights to request flexible working are much weaker than rights to reduce hours. However, significant changes are taking place. For example, many women returning to the labour market after having children have traditionally had to accept lower-level jobs in order to be able to work part-time or flexibly. Between 2002 and 2005 the share of women who changed employer on returning to work dropped from 41 per cent to 20 per cent (Smeaton and Marsh, 2006). This suggests that fewer women will be forced to give up their career jobs in order to continue in employment in the future.

The UK as a model for Europe?

Returning to the debate on how the UK over the last decade managed to reposition itself as a potential role model for Europe, we should note first of all that the debates on national models in the early 1990s still focused primarily on prospects for manufacturing. The poor prognosis for the UK model in 1994 (Rubery, 1994) reflected the identification of interlocking systems of buyer-driven production, low-quality, low-price consumer preferences, low-trust employment and industrial relations systems, low-status training provision and a public policy focused on undercutting European countries and fostering low-tech jobs. These underlying patterns and problems have been found to be still present but their salience for the effectiveness of the UK model is less strong for two main reasons. First, the experience of the New Labour decade has highlighted the importance of macroeconomic policy, and with it public expenditure, in shaping economic and performance outcomes. Second, the UK is now firmly a service-based economy, with manufacturing only accounting for 11 per cent of employment. Future prospects thus depend more on what sustains a successful service-based economy. In practice we are still rather ignorant as to what those ingredients might be – that is, what the precise linkages are between services and other sectors (including manufacturing), both national and international; what economic and institutional conditions underpin these linkages; and what the contributions of services are to improving living standards, productivity and innovation. The focus on services now even applies to the balance of payments; the need to correct the balance of payments was the main reason for policy attention on manufacturing but the UK now offsets the rising net imports of manufactures through increased exports of services and returns on overseas investments. Nevertheless, the sustainability of this method of balancing the trade account remains in question (Coutts et al., 2006).

The New Labour decade clearly built upon both the strengths and the weaknesses of the UK economy, and its position as a leader in the globalization of services and in the promotion of internationalized production chains was further strengthened. Furthermore, it extended its investment in higher education to fill the skills gap, arguably a safer bet than developing the vocational training route given the low value attached to vocational qualifications by UK employers. However, inequality and segmentation remain inherent features of the labour market, even if there has been more jobs and higher basic employment standards. The largest research project into investigating the future of work in the UK summarizes recent trends thus: 'The fastest growing areas of employment expansion are in caring and domestic services .... Like the United States we are witnessing the emergence of an hourglass economy in the UK that has been pump-primed by the largess of highly paid, two adult earner families on the one hand, and the growth of an under-class of wage labourers willing to undertake tasks that would have been familiar one hundred years ago' (Nolan, 2004, p. 4).

The consequences of segmentation are in part low productivity. The UK has reduced the productivity gap with Germany and to some extent the US over recent years (Broadberry and O'Mahony, 2004) but this is primarily due to higher labour input. Much labour has thus been expended to achieve relative success in employment and growth tables. The UK is still failing to develop widespread opportunities for decent work, as measured by quality of employment, although just enough may have been done to make the labour market system acceptable to the electorate; ready availability of work in tight labour markets has been combined with higher minimum wages and income guarantees.

The overall judgement on recent trends with respect to the prospects for job quality must, however, be mixed. While there has been no return – until the 2008 crisis – to the high levels of unemployment that characterized the 1980s, and even the share of workless households has declined somewhat,[7] the problems of a segmented and deregulated labour market have remained and may intensify if the public sector is further opened up to new providers. Further threats to the generation of decent work lie in the continued process of increasing profit-making opportunities for international capital and reducing the power of the unions in their remaining stronghold, the public sector.

These were the problems identified before the credit crisis in 2007/08 where the talk of the emergence of a new and revitalized model for the UK was clearly revealed to be premature. The prosperity of the UK is fragile. Its fragility relates both to its over-reliance on credit, which is now drying up, and its dependency on expansion of public expenditure, now threatened both by the costs of the bank bailout and by a potential swing of the political pendulum. Even before the current crisis it was clear that if the increased expenditure on public services was not seen by the electorate to have delivered high volume and quality, the next phase of the political cycle might see retrenchment and a return to lower growth and public expenditure. The current method of financing the expansion of the public sector also raises the spectrum of future generations paying far too high a price to the private sector for its current investment (Shaoul, 2005).

Inconsistencies in the model can be clearly identified. The commitment to reduce poverty has been predicated on the belief that getting people into work would solve problems of disadvantage but this policy has in part shifted the problem to poverty among the working population. More needs to be done to create pathways out of low-paid employment if poverty and social exclusion are really to be tackled (Palmer et al., 2006). Similarly, the efficacy of the development of higher but targeted benefits is not yet proven. As tax credits have proved complex and subject to technical breakdown, so there is also increasing awareness of the disincentive effects of tax credits on the participation of second-income earners and on saving for retirement. Furthermore, the opting out of employers from decent pension provision constitutes an unanticipated development that has not yet been fully addressed in current reforms of the UK welfare model. Much has therefore been done to reform the model but the verdict is still out on its sustainability and efficacy with respect to its stated objectives of reducing poverty while increasing incentives to work and to save that are the hallmarks of a liberal welfare model.

The overall assessment is that even though the UK model did deliver prosperity and high employment over a sustained period, it has not provided a model that either could or should be emulated as a model for the modernization of Europe. That it could not be easily emulated is because the UK's long-term, historically developed comparative advantage in services, particularly financial, is not easy to transfer – although the sustainability of this advantage post-credit crunch is now also in doubt. Additionally, the model should not be emulated first because of its shaky foundations of expanded personal credits and public sector expansion that is generating high levels of future servicing costs, and second because it is characterized by very high levels of inequality by class, gender and generation (Goos and Manning, 2003; Hills, 2004). Poverty in the UK may have declined but there is a growth in the working poor (Palmer et al., 2006); a continuing under-employment of labour, particularly women (Grant et al., 2005); a lack of employee voice, particularly in the private sector; and a continuous change agenda in the public sector that heralds further deterioration in work conditions. The rediscovery of the public space has set the UK apart from the US but this commitment is to a market state, not a public production model. As such, the UK could still be the Trojan horse that undermines European social models, even though the market state policy has been pushed through on the basis of a renewed commitment to social provision.

To conclude, the UK model performed better than expected during the New Labour decade, but the upturn was not based on solid foundations. The UK's long-term comparative advantage in the global services sector provided structural support to the model but this foundation was contaminated by the excesses of the banking system in the UK and worldwide. The future economic prospects for the UK thus remain highly uncertain. Moreover, while the collapse of the deregulated financial markets could provide an opportunity for the UK model to be revitalized through re-regulation and a reinforced commitment to the social dimension, the fact that any protest against the government by the electorate is likely to bring a Conservative government to power makes a regulatory turn less likely.

Notes

1. The PFI scheme operates throughout the public sector and involves private sector investment, rather than the traditional state-financed capital spending. Under PFI a consortium of private sector companies (typically a management consultancy, a construction firm or IT firm, a bank and a business services firm) pays for the building or refurbishment of public assets and recoups the money through a

charge on services it provides (for example, IT services, cleaning or maintenance services) or charges to individuals (for example, toll bridges).
2. Brown has identified education as potentially one of Britain's lead exports, predicting a possible increase of over 300 per cent by 2020 in students taught abroad (Brown, 2005).
3. The promotion of employment legislation has adopted the language of promoting business efficiency and best practice; the outcome may have been to promote fairness and equality but that outcome is now always subject to a business case test (Dickens and Hall, 2005).
4. Union membership for 2006 in the public sector was 58.8 per cent, compared to just 16.6 per cent in the private sector (Grainger and Crowther, 2007, Table 3).
5. Taxation is individualized in the UK but benefits are almost always based on household means-testing. Women often have earnings too low for them to build up their own entitlements to benefits.
6. The term 'maternity leave' continues to be used instead of 'parental leave' which is only available on an unpaid basis.
7. The overall proportion of workless households declined from a peak in 1996 of 19.1 per cent to 15.8 per cent in 2006 (ONS, 2006) with a much steeper decline in lone parent workless households from 52.1 per cent in 1996, to 50.3 per cent in 1997, to 39.4 per cent in 2006.

References

Ashton, D. (1988), 'Youth and the Labour Market', in D. Gallie (ed.), *Employment in Britain*, Oxford: Blackwell.
Balls, E. (2006), Speech by Economic Secretary to the Treasury, Ed Balls MP, at Bloomberg HM Treasury Press Release. http://www.hm-treasury.gov.uk/newsroom_and_speeches/press/2006/press_42_06.cfm
Broadberry, S. and O'Mahony, M. (2004), 'Britain's Productivity Gap with the United States and Europe: A Historical Perspective', *National Institute Economic Review* 189 (2004): 72–85.
Brown, G. (2005), Speech by the Rt Hon Gordon Brown MP, Chancellor of the Exchequer at the Academy of Social Science, Beijing, China, 21 February. http://www.hm-treasury.gov.uk/newsroom_and_speeches/press/2005/press_20_05.cfm
Bulli, S. (2008), 'Business Innovation Investment in the UK', Science and Innovation Analysis, DIUS. http://www.dius.gov.uk/publications/DIUS-RR-08-13.pdf
Burchell, B., Ladipo, D. and Wilkinson, F. (eds) (2001), *Job Security and Work Intensification*, London: Routledge.
Castells, M. (1996, 2nd edition 2000), *The Rise of the Network Society*, Oxford: Blackwell.
Conway, P., Janod, V. and Nicoletti, G. (2005), 'Product Market Regulation in OECD Countries: 1998 to 2003', *Economics Department Working Papers*, No. 419, Paris: OECD.
Coutts, C., Glyn, A. and Rowthorn, B. (2006), *Structural Change Under New Labour*, Department Of Economics, Discussion Paper Series, Oxford University. http://www.economics.ox.ac.uk/Research/wp/pdf/paper312.pdf
Crouch, C. (2003), *Commercialisation or Citizenship: Education Policy and the Future of Public Services*, London: Fabian Society.
Crouch, C. and Keune, M. (2005), 'Changing Dominant Practice: Making Use of Institutional Diversity in Hungary and the United Kingdom', pp. 83–102 in W. Streeck and K. Thelen, *Beyond Continuity*, Oxford: Oxford University Press.

Cully, M., Woodland, S., O'Reilly, A. and Dix, G. (1999), *Britain at Work: As Depicted by the 1998 Workplace Employee Relations Survey*, London: Routledge.

Deakin, S. (2005), 'The Coming Transformation of Shareholder Value', *Corporate Governance: an International Review* 13(1): 11–8.

Dibben, P., James, P., Roper, I. and Wood, G. (eds) (2007), *Modernising Work in Public Services: Redefining Roles and Relationships in Britain's Changing Workplace*, Basingstoke: Palgrave Macmillan.

Dickens, L. and Hall, M. (2005), 'Review of Research into the Impact of Employment Relations Legislation', DTI Employment Relations Research, Series no. 45.

Edmonds, J. and Glyn, A. (2005), 'Public Spending Explains Britain's Jobs Growth', *Financial Times*, 29 June.

EIU (Economist Intelligence Unit) (2006), 'The UK Slips Down The Global Business Environment Rankings', 27 March 2006. http://store.eiu.com/index.asp?layout=pr_story&press_id=1010001901&ref=pr_list

Elger, T. and Smith, C. (2005), *Assembling Work: Remaking Factory Regimes in Japanese Multinationals in Britain*, New York: Oxford University Press.

Elias, P. and Purcell, K. (2003), 'Measuring Change in the Graduate Labour Market', Research paper No. 1, Bristol: Economic and Social Research Council (ESRC) and the Higher Education Careers Advisory Service (HECSU). http://www.uwe.ac.uk/bbs/research/esru/rp1.pdf

Esping-Anderson, G. (1990), *The Three Worlds of Welfare Capitalism*, Cambridge: Polity Press.

Finegold, D. and Soskice, D. (1988), 'The Failure of Training in Britain: Analysis and Prescription', *Oxford Review of Economic Policy* 4(1988): 21–53.

Goos, M. and Manning, A. (2003), 'McJobs and MacJobs: The Growing Polarisation of Jobs in the UK', in R. Dickens, P. Gregg and J. Wadsworth (eds), *The Labour Market Under New Labour: The State of Working Britain*, Basingstoke: Palgrave Macmillan.

Grainger, H. and Crowther, M. (2007), *Trade Union Membership 2006*, Employment Market Analysis and Research, London: Department for Trade and Industry.

Grant, L., Yeandle, S. and Buckner, L. (2005), 'Working Below Potential: Women and Part-Time Work', EOC Working Paper Series No. 40, Manchester: Equal Opportunities Commission.

Grimshaw, D. and Carroll, M. (2008), 'Improving the Position of Low-wage Workers through New Coordinating Institutions: The Case of Public Hospitals', in C. Lloyd, G. Mason, and K. Mayhew (eds), *Low Wage Employment in the UK*, New York: Russell Sage Foundation.

Grimshaw, D. and Hebson, G. (2005), 'Public Private Contracting: Performance, Power and Change at Work', in M. Marchington, D. Grimshaw, J. Rubery and H. Willmott (eds), *Fragmenting Work: Blurring Organizational Boundaries and Disordering Hierarchies*, Oxford: Oxford University Press.

Halifax plc (2007), 'UK Private Housing Stock Worth £3.8 Trillion'. http://www.hbosplc.com/economy/includes/150107ukprivatehousingstock.doc

Hall, M. (2005), 'Assessing the Information and Consultation of Employees Regulations', *Industrial Law Journal* 34(2): 103–26.

Hall, P. A. and Soskice, D. (eds) (2001), *Varieties of Capitalism: The Institutional Foundations of Comparative Advantage*, Oxford: Oxford University Press.

Hills, J. (2004), *Inequality and the State*, Oxford: Oxford University Press.

Hirst, P. and Thompson, G. (2000), 'Globalisation in One Country: The Peculiarities of the British', *Economy and Society* 29(3): 335–56.

HM Treasury (2001), 'Tackling Child Poverty: Giving Every Child the Best Possible Start in Life'. http://www.hm-treasury.gov.uk

HM Treasury (2006), 'Prosperity for All in the Global Economy – World Class Skills', Final report of the Leitch Review of Skills, December 2006. http://www.hm-treasury.gov.uk/independent_reviews/leitch_review/review_leitch_index.cfm

HM Treasury (2007), Public Expenditure Statistical Analyses (PESA), April. http://www.hm-treasury.gov.uk/media

HMT (HM Treasury), DTI (Department of Trade and Industry) and DfES (Department for Education and Skills) (2004), 'Science & Innovation Investment Framework 2004–14', HMSO. http://www.hm-treasury.gov.uk/media/33A/AB/spend04_sciencedoc_1_090704.pdf

Immervoll, H. (2007), 'Minimum Wages, Minimum Labour Costs and the Tax Treatment of Low-Wage Employment', OECD Social, Employment And Migration, Working Papers no. 46. http://www.oecd.org/dataoecd/30/34/37930738.pdf

Kersley, B., Alpin, C., Forth, J., Bryson, A., Bewley, H., Dix, G. and Oxenbridge, S. (2005), *Inside the Workplace: First Findings from the 2004 Workplace Employment Relations Survey*. http://www.routledge.com/textbooks/0415378133/firstfindings/default.asp

Lewis, J. (1992), *Women in Britain since 1945: Women, Family, Work and the State in the Post-war Years*, Oxford: Blackwell Publishing.

Lloyd, C., Mason, G. and Mayhew, K. (eds) (2008), *Low-wage Work in the UK*, New York: Russell Sage Foundation.

Morgan Stanley (2007), 'Credit Crunch Fallout – UK Remains More Exposed than Most' (29 October), London: Morgan Stanley. http://www.morganstanley.com/views/gef/archive/2007/20071129-Thu.html

Nolan, P. (2004), 'Back to the Future of Work', ESRC programme on the future of work, University of Leeds. http://www.leeds.ac.uk/esrcfutureofwork/downloads/events/colloquium_2004/nolan_paper_0904.pdf

OECD (1994), *Jobs Study*, Paris: OECD.

OECD (2005), *Employment Outlook*, Paris: OECD.

ONS (Office of National Statistics) (2006), 'First Release: Work and Worklessness among Households, July 2006', 26 July. http://www.statistics.gov.uk/pdfdir/wwhh0706.pdf

Palmer, G., MacInnes, T. and Kenway, P. (2006), *Monitoring Poverty and Social Exclusion 2006'*, York: New Policy Institute and Joseph Rowntree Foundation. http://www.poverty.org.uk/reports/mpse%202006.pdf

Pendleton, A. and Gospel, H. (2005), 'Markets and Relationships: Finance, Governance and Labour in the UK', in H. Gospel and A. Pendleton (eds), *Corporate Governance and Labour Management: an International Comparison*, Oxford: Oxford University Press.

Peston, R. (2005), *Brown's Britain*, London: Short Books.

Rubery, J. (1994), 'The British Production Regime: A Societal-specific System?', *Economy and Society* 23(3): 335–54. Reprinted in S. Ackroyd and S. Fleetwood (eds) (2000), *Realist Perspectives in Management and Organizations*, Routledge and in D. Coates (ed.) (2003), *Models of Capitalism: Debating Strengths and Weaknesses*, Edward Elgar.

Shaoul, J. (2005), 'A Critical Financial Analysis of the Private Finance Initiative: Selecting a Financing Method or Reallocating Economic Wealth?', *Critical Perspectives on Accounting* 16 (2005): 441–71.

Smeaton, D. and Marsh, A. (2006), 'Maternity and Paternity Rights and Benefits: Survey of Parents 2005', DTI Employment Relations Survey No. 50, March. http://www.dti.gov.uk/files/file27446.pdf?pubpdfdload=06%2F836

Streeck, W. and Thelen, K. (eds) (2005), *Beyond Continuity*, Oxford: Oxford University Press.

Toynbee, P. (2005), 'Breathless Charioteer', *The Guardian*, 2 September 2005.
UNCTAD (2004), *World Investment Report 2004: The Shift Towards Services*, New York and Geneva: United Nations.
UNICEF (2007), 'Child Poverty in Perspective: an Overview of Child Well-Being in Rich Countries', Unicef Innocenti Research Centre, Report Card 7.
Wickham, J. (2005), 'The End of the European Social Model – Before it Began?', Employment Research Centre, Trinity College Dublin. http://www.iatge.de/aktuell/veroeff/2005/dynamo10.pdf

3
The Swedish Model: Revival after the Turbulent 1990s?

Dominique Anxo and Harald Niklasson

Introduction

The main objective of this paper is to analyse the major transformations of the Swedish model, its welfare regime, employment and production systems. Until the end of the 1980s Sweden was remarkably successful in combining low unemployment with high and growing employment rates and also with a high degree of income equality and small gender disparities. However, most economists and many policymakers were aware that the unprecedented activity level and the extreme labour market tightness during the second half of the 1980s were not sustainable in the long run. For many years inflation had been alarmingly high and in 1990 it reached 11 per cent, presaging a crisis that became dramatic. In just three years, from 1990 to 1993, the rate of employment fell by 10.5 percentage points and the rate of open unemployment quintupled from less than two to more than 8 per cent of the labour force.[1] Furthermore, the annual government deficit reached 14 per cent of gross domestic product (GDP), in spite of repeated 'reform packages' aimed at reducing public expenditure and increasing government revenues. The cutbacks in public spending, which principally took the form of lowering income replacement rates in various social insurance systems and reducing public sector employment, were considered by many citizens as a painful 'rolling-back of the welfare state'.

Some have argued that what the country endured in the early 1990s demonstrated that the original Swedish model had become obsolete or 'time inconsistent' in the sense that it gave rise to developments incompatible with its long-term sustainability. However, such interpretations raise some critical questions. Is it true that the traditional model initiated during the 1950s has been superseded and that a fundamentally different, more coherent and sustainable model has emerged? What are the main differences between the current national model, the original model and the one that prevailed during the period 1975–1990?

We argue here that the current model appears to *be in line* with the three core components of the original Swedish model developed during the 1950s. In our view, it is the period 1975–1991 that represents a clear deviation from the original model, a departure that culminated in the most severe crisis that Sweden has experienced since the 1930s. Since this period of turbulence the Swedish economy has experienced a particularly favourable period of development. From the second half of the 1990s, GDP growth rates have returned to early 1970s levels; unemployment has been cut by half; there have been large balance-of-trade surpluses; and public finances have improved substantially, posting a positive balance of 1 per cent of GDP in 2004. During the last ten years, in strong contrast to the 1980s, the Swedish economy has also experienced low inflation.

The changes in economic policy towards a more restrictive and anti-inflationary macro-economic policy, the reorientation of active labour market policies towards supply-oriented measures and the structural reforms undertaken in the tax and pension systems during the 1990s suggest a *revival and renaissance of the traditional Swedish model*. The modifications in industrial relations, in particular the clear trend towards a re-coordination of collective bargaining, have also played a vital role in the recovery.

The various reforms of the social protection system undertaken during the 1990s have essentially taken the form of a temporary reduction of income replacement rates and, with the notable exception of the restructured tax and pension system, have left the welfare state almost intact. The Swedish welfare state remains, by international standards, universal and inclusive in nature and still enjoys a high level of across-the-board political and public support. The reshaping of the pension and tax systems aimed at strengthening work incentives is also clearly in line with the general philosophy of the original Swedish model favouring integrative transitions instead of passive support and social exclusion. In our view, these developments reinforce the coherence of the Swedish model and the robustness of its social cohesion.

The origin, rise and decline of the Swedish model

The 'traditional model'

From its creation in the early 1950s until the mid-1970s the traditional Swedish model was based on three fundamental components. First there was a restrictive fiscal and monetary policy aimed at curbing inflation in a regime of fixed exchange rates. This anti-inflationary policy was complemented by the second and third components designed to preserve 'full and productive employment'. The second was a policy of wage moderation exercised by the two sides of industry, involving a centralized and coordinated wage bargaining system and the application of a wage norm – the so-called *solidaristic wage policy* – based on fairness, equity (equal pay for equal work) and efficiency (that is, fostering rationalization at company level and promoting productivity-enhancing structural changes through closure of unproductive plants). The third component involved the implementation of an ambitious counter-cyclical active labour market policy (ALMP) favouring occupational and geographical mobility and enhancing employment opportunities for those with reduced work capacity.

It goes without saying that the overall macroeconomic policies, while being restrictive enough to prevent inflationary pressures, were at the same time expansionary enough to secure both employment growth and a low unemployment rate. Although the solidarity wage policy might lead firms with relatively low productivity to decline or close, low unemployment was secured mainly by ALMP programmes favouring a reallocation of the labour force from the declining parts of the economy towards the expanding ones.

Such a model or policy strategy, often referred as 'the *Rehn-Meidner model*' (named after the Swedish economists Gösta Rehn and Rudolf Meidner), presupposed the existence of powerful and autonomous workers' and employers' organizations and a high degree of consensus/cooperation between them, as well as between the two sides of industry and the government. The main reasons why the Rehn-Meidner division of tasks and responsibilities[2] was widely accepted in the 1950s lie in the inheritance from the past. The Swedish trade union movement was strong and united. The coverage of collective agreements and union density was – by international standards – very high. The social democrats dominated the political arena and the cooperation between them and the trade unions as represented by LO (the Swedish Trade Union Confederation, that is the central organization of blue-collar unions) rested firmly on egalitarian ideals. However, without the support of the Swedish Employers' Confederation, SAF, it would have been impossible for LO alone to achieve the centralized and coordinated bargaining system necessary for the successful implementation of its solidaristic wage policy and the corresponding top-down coordination of wages across industries and sectors. For the employers a centralized and coordinated wage-setting system was a way of achieving a low degree of wage competition between firms and cost control in industries exposed to international competition.[3] The *solidaristic wage policy* involved not only the application of the principle of 'equal pay for equal work' (irrespective of individual firms' profitability, sectors or regions), it also became an instrument for reducing wage differentials within and between jobs, that is for promoting a more compressed wage structure.

The policies pursued, based on strong political commitment to the goal of full employment and to egalitarian ideals and on the above-mentioned division of tasks and responsibilities, resulted in remarkably low unemployment. Furthermore, by international standards Sweden was also successful in terms of labour market participation, gender equal opportunity, egalitarian income distribution and – disregarding the period from the mid-1970s to the early 1980s – sustained economic growth. To a considerable extent the good employment record during this period was also related to the expansion of public-sector employment and the creation of a modern welfare state. This implied strong government involvement in the financing and provision of healthcare, social care and education.

Early warnings: The crisis of the late 1970s and deviations from the original model

The Swedish economy started to show serious signs of weakness long before the dramatic economic downturn and the employment crisis of the early 1990s. In fact, from the mid-1970s, the country's macroeconomic performance deteriorated in the wake of the two oil crises, a restrictive economic policy in major OECD countries and intensified competition from Japan, the Republic of Korea and the Newly Industrialized Countries (NICs). This situation was addressed by means of extraordinary policy interventions, notably devaluations of the Swedish currency, implying apparent *deviations* from the policies prescribed by the model *per se*. The repeated devaluations carried out in the late 1970s and early 1980s reflected the inability of the social partners to achieve a wage development compatible with preserving the macroeconomic balance and maintaining the international competitiveness of Swedish companies in a regime of fixed exchange rates. Given that the maintenance of low wage inflation was regarded as an integral part of the model, the acceleration of wage inflation during the 1970s and the use of devaluation to restore the competitiveness of Swedish enterprises and to preserve full employment can be regarded as reflecting apparent policy failures and a departure from the original model.

The severe crisis of the mid and late 1970s did not lead, however, to major structural reforms. The successive devaluations could be justified as necessary 'extraordinary' policy responses to sudden and unexpected (imported) macroeconomic shocks: the 'oil crises' and the international 'stagflation' of the 1970s. It may be that the traditional model was unable to handle the consequences of such exceptional *exogenous* shocks, but this did not lead to the conclusion that the model *per se* had to be abandoned or profoundly and permanently restructured.

However, for full employment to be preserved and the temporary crisis to be overcome, the model had to be supplemented, for some time, by 'extraordinary' policies, including devaluations. In the mid and late 1970s, in the wake of international turbulence, the two sides of industry failed, in spite of the centralized bargaining system, to exercise the wage restraint required to prevent a severe cost crisis. Massive plant closures in Swedish manufacturing industry, particularly in the shipyards and textile industries, greatly unsettled the labour market and incited the policymakers to intervene to 'rescue the jobs' and restore 'full employment'. In addition to ALMP programmes oriented to labour demand, such as relief work and wage subsidies, massive industrial subsidy programmes were launched, stockpiling was stimulated and – not to be forgotten – public-sector employment was expanded. As a consequence the crisis also became a 'deficit crisis' involving large current account and public budget deficits. In the political arena the social democrats lost office in 1976 after 44 years of unbroken rule. The new centre-right government devalued the Swedish currency twice in 1976 (after 25 years of constant exchange rates) and again in 1977 and 1981, but it did not abandon the extensive use of industrial subsidies and ALMP schemes. When the social democrats returned to power in 1982 they devalued the currency yet again, actually creating an undervalued Krona. This devaluation, together with the relative wage restraint now exercised by the two sides of industry (at that time highly crisis-conscious), gave the exposed tradable sector a major expansionary boost which was fuelled by an international economic recovery. The 'cost crisis' was overcome and the current account and public budget deficits were eliminated by the early 1980s.

Despite the large decrease in employment in manufacturing that took place from the mid-1970s until the early 1980s, the rate of unemployment never exceeded (on a yearly basis) 3.5 per cent. The employment rate never fell below the 77 per cent reported for 1975 and from 1979 it was above 79 per cent. For men it fell from 87.2 per cent in 1975 to its minimum level at 83 per cent in 1983, but for women it increased, in the same period, from 66.5 per cent to 74.8 per cent. This reflected the loss of jobs in manufacturing and the simultaneous creation of jobs in services, notably in the public sector. Thus, the cost, deficit and structural crises of the late 1970s were never translated into a severe employment crisis, due in particular to the massive expansion of employment in the public sector. Furthermore, the emergency policies pursued did not include any substantial rolling-back of the welfare state. The social insurance systems remained intact and the public (especially the municipal) provision of health and social care was in fact expanded.

The crisis of the early 1990s

By contrast, the crisis of the early 1990s took the form of a dramatic employment crisis. Why was this allowed to happen and what were the main factors explaining the sharp increase in unemployment? Why was the emerging cost crisis, which was clearly observable well before 1990, not met by devaluation policies similar to those implemented during the previous decades?

The use of an accommodative monetary policy, that is devaluation as a means of combating excessive 'home-made' inflation (11 per cent in 1990), was unanimously rejected. The common understanding was that the country could not afford a repetition of what happened in the late 1970s and early 1980s but the main problem for the government and the central bank was to convince the actors in international financial markets that the devaluations of the previous decades would not be repeated. The central bank's main instrument, made possible by deregulation of the financial market, was to increase – sometimes very dramatically – its own interest rates, thereby influencing domestic interest rates in the same direction. Both the social democratic government in power in 1991 and the subsequent centre-right government of 1991–1994 tried to counteract the devaluation expectations by means of a restrictive fiscal policy involving substantial reductions in public spending. This commonality of approach begs a fundamental question: why did the policymakers involved fail to foresee the consequences of this consensus? The policies, in combination with the original cost crisis and the high interest rates, resulted in fact in soaring unemployment, decreasing public revenues and – in spite of the cutbacks in public expenditure – a rapidly increasing budget deficit. Apparently, many actors in the international financial markets came to the conclusion that Sweden would, as in the past, soon devalue. The attempts to defend the currency had thus resulted in reinforcing devaluation expectations such that in November 1992 the central bank had to allow the Swedish Krona to float. It immediately depreciated by about 20 per cent.

Needless to say, the policy failures behind the crisis of the early 1990s were extremely costly for the Swedish people. Between 1990 and 1993 GDP decreased by 5 per cent. The consequences were especially painful for vulnerable groups hit by unemployment and/or by the reductions in social benefits and public commitments that became elements of the emergency measures carried out.

The recovery since 1994

Since 1994 the macroeconomic and labour market conditions have improved in many ways. On the whole, the central bank has been quite successful in holding down inflation and maintaining its independence and autonomy vis-à-vis the government and parliament. By early 2001 the budget deficit had turned into a surplus. Between 1993 and 2000 the annual GDP growth rate was an average of 3.2 per cent. This relatively rapid growth reflects a substantial increase in exports, fostered by currency depreciation and wage moderation. Unemployment remained above 8 per cent until 1997 but by 2002 it had declined to about 4 per cent. We believe that developments since 1990 would have been significantly more favourable if a macroeconomic strategy, consistent with the unavoidable deregulation of the financial sector, had been established in the late 1980s, so that the futile and costly attempts to defend the currency could have been avoided. This is not to say, however, that it would have been possible to preserve the level of employment reached in the late 1980s or to avoid reforms perceived by a majority of Swedish citizens as involving 'rising inequality' and 'decreasing security'.

Recent transformations of the Swedish model

Reorientation of macroeconomic policy

In our view the devaluations in the late 1970s and early 1980s, and the deep crisis of the early 1990s, demonstrate that the policies pursued, in particular the lack of an institutionalized anti-inflationary mechanism, involved strong elements of time inconsistency. According to the traditional model developed in the 1950s, restrictive macroeconomic policies should be used to keep inflation at a level consistent with a fixed foreign exchange rate regime.

The reorientation of monetary and fiscal policy started in 1993 with the establishment of an inflation target as the main objective of the autonomous central bank policy.[4] Furthermore, the Swedish currency was allowed to float. In this context, the expectation was established that the autonomous and independent central bank would react to inflationary fiscal policies or excessive wage increases by raising its interest rates, leading to higher market interest rates and/or an appreciation of the Swedish Krona and thus, in the longer run, to decreasing employment. This new division of roles and responsibilities between the government and the central bank means that the anti-inflationary policies prescribed by the Rehn-Meidner model have been institutionalized in a way that precludes the kind of inflation-generating policy failures observed in the late 1970s and late 1980s. These new developments represent, we believe, a *strengthening* of, rather than a deviation from, the traditional Swedish model.

In our view the ability of the national economy to reach and maintain full employment in the coming years will depend heavily on the functioning of the wage-setting system. According to the analysis by Iversen (1999), in a context of an independent central bank pursuing a non-accommodating monetary policy, a bargaining system characterized by an intermediate degree of centralization and coordination (involving both a continuing important role for collective agreements at industry level, but also allowing for negotiations at local level) will be 'optimal' in terms of its capability to result in relatively low 'equilibrium unemployment'. This may give rise to some optimism since it is in this direction that the Swedish bargaining system has moved in recent years. We will come back to this in the section analyzing the recent transformations of the industrial relations system. Before that, however, we want to deal with another prominent element of the traditional and the current Swedish model: the extensive use of ALMP means and programmes.

Active labour market policies

Sweden's excellent record on employment and unemployment has often been ascribed to a particularly ambitious active labour market policy. This has played a vital role in stabilization policies since the late 1950s and constitutes, as mentioned previously, one of the cornerstones of the Swedish model. ALMP programmes have been used not only to promote an efficient allocation of resources and to facilitate transitions from unemployment to employment, but also to favour the integration of marginal workers, for example the disabled, who without public intervention would have been excluded from the labour force. The social partners' support for this policy reflects their desire to foster the integration of unemployed workers instead of relying on unemployment benefits. The system is also characterized by real decentralization and flexible management. In our view this decentralized infrastructure has created a favourable institutional framework for a flexible and efficient labour market policy (see Anxo et al., 2000). Hence, two key and distinctive features of Swedish employment policy may be identified: on the one hand the integration of unemployed workers instead of the provision of passive support; and on the other hand the key role played by the two sides of industry in ALMP programmes, thus ensuring their social legitimacy.

As already described, the early 1990s were notable for a sharp deterioration in the employment situation. The government responded by gradually putting more and more people on employment programmes, such that in 1994 beneficiaries accounted for almost 6 per cent of the active population, a figure never previously reached. However, with the gradual improvement in the employment situation the number of participants in ALMP programmes was gradually reduced. Moreover, the labour-demand related measures (for example temporary public employment schemes [relief works] and recruitment subsidies) that predominated in previous economic downturns (particularly from 1975 to 1983) were not used to the same extent in the early 1990s when the ALMP programme was reoriented to emphasize matching efficiency and labour mobility. The number of participants on vocational training programmes and/or practical insertion courses rose quickly, while traditional measures focusing on labour demand remained at a much lower level than during previous recessions (Anxo and Erhel, 1998).[5]

The growing role of vocational training in the ALMP indicates the importance that the government and the social partners give to occupational mobility and the development of skills over the life course. The employment crisis of the early 1990s hit low-skilled workers particularly hard. During the period 1993–2003 around 600,000 unskilled and low-paid jobs were lost in Sweden. The reorientation of active labour market policy towards traditional labour market training and adult education can therefore be considered as an attempt to upgrade the skill content of the labour force in face of the major restructuring that the Swedish economy experienced during the 1990s. In the same vein, when the youth labour market deteriorated in the early 1990s, the educational enrolment rate was also increased, with a significant expansion in the number of university places, which had fallen continuously during the previous decade.[6]

In our view the reorientation in the early 1990s of ALMP towards more supply-oriented programmes can be considered as a return to the initial conception of ALMP interventions designed to meet the increasing demand for skill upgrading and occupational mobility. Indeed the primacy of labour-demand oriented measures during the 1970s and early 1980s can be viewed as a deviation from the original ALMP strategy of the late 1950s. Hence, the extensive and institutionalized use of ALMP remains a major component of the present Swedish model.

Recent transformations of the industrial relations and wage formation systems

While the conjunction of several factors (namely the reorientation of monetary, fiscal and active labour market policy) explains the 'Swedish success story', there is no doubt that recent changes in industrial relations, notably important changes in the regulation of collective bargaining and wage formation, have played an important role in this development.

For more than 25 years (1955–1982) one of the three important components of the traditional model was a wage formation process based on a centralized and coordinated bargaining system (see Anxo, 1993). In 1983, however, the Engineering Employers' Organization concluded a separate agreement with the Metal Workers' Union, breaking up centralized economy-wide bargaining. The combination of the abandonment of inter-professional agreements, the erosion of the Swedish model of industrial relations (particularly the weakening of mechanisms for coordinating collective bargaining) and the resurgence of industrial disputes during the 1980s led the government and the social partners to formulate new strategies in the early 1990s. The three main trade unions[7] in the sector exposed to international competition asked their employer counterparts to consider the possibility of setting up a new collective bargaining system that fostered industrial peace and wage increases that guaranteed balanced growth and a return to full employment. These talks culminated in a signed agreement on Cooperation on Industrial Development and Salary Formation (*Samarbetavtal om Industriell Utveckling och Lönebildning, Industriavtal*) on 18 March 1997. This new agreement, covering about 600,000 workers (approximately 17 per cent of the gainfully employed population), may justifiably be compared with the historical compromise concluded at Saltjöbaden in 1938[8] (Elvander, 2000).

The main innovatory element of the Agreement on Industry, apart from the tendency to re-coordinate collective bargaining, was the establishment of explicit rules concerning the regulation of negotiations and the resolution of disputes. The main objectives of the Negotiating Agreement are to create a constructive climate that is favourable to the conclusion of collective agreements compatible with balanced growth and to avoid industrial disputes (see Anxo and Niklasson, 2006). Retrospectively, we can say that the last rounds of negotiation passed off without industrial disputes. By and large, negotiated wage increases have kept pace with the rest of the European Union. Negotiated pay rises within the industrial agreement affected other bargaining areas, thereby *re-establishing the normative pacesetting role* of the sector exposed to international competition. Also notable is that the agreement led to a sensible increase in real wages, in contrast to the situation in the 1980s which was characterized by stagnation in real wages.

As has already been emphasized, the period 1980–1995 was characterized by a clear tendency towards the decentralization of collective bargaining and a weakening of coordination mechanisms. Following the abandonment of inter-professional national agreements in 1983, collective bargaining was carried out at two levels: industry and enterprise. This decentralization was also accompanied by a marked tendency towards differentiation and individualization of wages and terms and conditions of employment. The questioning of egalitarian *solidaristic* wage policy both by the employers and by some trade unions – including the Engineering Federation (Metall) – that were influential inside the Swedish Confederation of Trade Unions led to a wider dispersion of wages and to an acceptance of a more individualized type of wage formation, based on individual skills and performance, and no longer only on job characteristics. Two main reasons may be advanced for this shift. First, solidarity mechanisms and the general raising of low pay that characterized the LO wage strategy during the 1970s ran out of steam as growth slackened and imbalances linked to economic recession in the late 1970s increased (Anxo, 1993). The second reason concerns major changes in work organization and the gradual abandonment of Taylorian modes of production. The acceptance of greater wage differentiation by the trade union federations also responded to a fear among LO affiliates that they might lose members to the white-collar confederations, which were traditionally more prone to accept wage differentiation.

The employers' more recent change of attitude regarding the strategy that was initiated during the 1980s of decentralizing collective bargaining to enterprise level, and therefore their acceptance of a re-coordination of collective bargaining at industry level, is certainly linked to an awareness of the cost incurred by the resurgence of industrial disputes, and to the transaction costs associated with the absence of coordination mechanisms. These developments since the mid-1990s may therefore be interpreted as the emergence of a new type of agreement in which the employers accept a degree of coordination in exchange for a guarantee of industrial peace. Clearly, in a situation where trade union density remains at 75–80 per cent and collective bargaining coverage at 90 per cent, and where there is limited government interference in the field of pay determination, coordination of negotiations at industry level ensures a certain degree of industrial peace (Sheldon and Thornthwaite, 1999).

Given the structural changes that Sweden has undergone in the last two decades, the recent developments in industrial relations augur well for a revival of the Swedish model of industrial relations. Indeed even though the two sides of industry are nowadays prone to accept a re-coordination of industry-wide agreements and give the traded goods sector a leadership role in wage determination, it would be erroneous to interpret these new tendencies as a weakening of enterprise-level bargaining. In fact, industry-wide agreements leave ample scope for enterprise-level negotiations, particularly regarding the distribution of the individualized part of the wage increase negotiated and concluded at industry level. Strong trade union organization and high union density at company level ensure the implementation of negotiated forms of individualization and differentiation. In our view this two-tier system provides an institutional and legal framework that is favourable to the emergence of *negotiated flexibility*.

These new developments therefore appear to respond to a three-pronged objective: ensuring industrial peace; limiting transaction costs and ensuring against the impact of uncontrolled wage drift on employment and firm competitiveness; and guaranteeing a *principle of subsidiarity*, making it possible to adapt the provisions contained in industry-wide agreements to the productive and competitive constraints of Swedish companies.

The developments in industrial relations in Sweden during the last ten years may justifiably be seen as the emergence of a new historic compromise combining employers' demands for greater productive flexibility with the trade union movement's desire for sustained growth in employment and in household real incomes. In other words these developments confirm the impact that changes in the conditions of competition and production have had on the system of industrial relations. Two further challenges should be mentioned, however. First, the reform launched by the new centre-right government of the financing of the unemployment benefit system is leading to a slight decline in trade union membership, due in part to an increase in the self-financing of unemployment insurance and the subsequent increase in trade union fees. Nevertheless, by international standards Sweden remains among the countries with the highest union density. Second, the surprise ruling in relation to the Laval case (see EIRO, 2008) in December 2007 by the European Court of Justice, in contradiction of the earlier opinion of the advocate general, could in principle call into question the right of Swedish trade unions to use industrial action to force compliance with sectoral collective agreements, opening the way for so-called 'social dumping' in Sweden. However, steps may still be taken within Sweden – even though the revisions of the EU's Posted Worker Directive to ensure that collective agreements on minimum pay do have to be observed. While these are significant challenges, the strength of the social partnership is such that they are unlikely to undermine the role of the partners in regulating the labour market, including wage and employment conditions, even in a context of more open international borders.

Institutional and structural reforms

Main characteristic of the Swedish welfare state and employment regimes

The Swedish model is based on a strong political commitment not only to the goals of full employment and price stability but also to egalitarian ideals. Often presented as the ideal type of the so called Nordic social democratic regimes, the Swedish welfare state emphasizes the principles of egalitarianism, decommodification and individualization. The latter has been a key part of the Swedish universal welfare state: the basic principle of the institutional model is entitlement based on citizenship/residence. The individual, and not the family, has for many years been the unit used both for taxation and for entitlement to social benefits. However, the individualization of Swedish social policy is strikingly illustrated by the lack of social benefits awarded to women on the basis of their status as wives.

Sweden stands out as providing one type of societal system based on a high incidence of two-earner households; high employment rates at the two ends of the age spectrum, with a small gender gap; extensive and generous family policy; strong welfare support systems both for childcare and parental leave; and egalitarian wage structures, including low gender wage inequality. To a considerable extent the good employment records experienced by the Swedish economy during the post-war period are clearly linked to the creation of a modern welfare state, strong public involvement in the financing and provision of healthcare, social care and education, and the related expansion of public-sector employment. The high union density and the relatively high degree of centralization and coordination of collective bargaining produce a rather low dispersion of working time and a high concentration of dependent employees around the standard full-time norm (40 hours). Some gender differences persist, with a relatively large share of women working part-time, but in contrast to other EU member states with high part-time rates, such as the United Kingdom or The Netherlands, many women in Sweden work long part-time hours and receive income compensation as paid parental leave when working less than full-time. Part-time work in Sweden must be considered more as an historical transition from married women's inactivity towards a strategy – largely initiated by labour market and political institutions – to strengthen women's labour market commitments. While 47 per cent of Swedish women worked part-time in 1981, the share had dropped to 35 per cent in 2005. The parental leave system allows for an income-compensated temporary reduction in working time, thereby reinforcing women's bargaining power and status as significant breadwinners even when they are temporarily not participating on a full-time basis in the labour market. The overall political context characterized by gender mainstreaming and high female involvement in the political process (government bodies, parliament and labour market organizations) creates a favourable institutional context for a more balanced gender division of labour and responsibilities over the life course.

As already mentioned, Sweden is characterized by high employment continuity over the life course, and relatively low gender disparities in labour market integration. Neither marriage nor family formation affect women's employment rates. Family formation is in fact positively related to female labour market participation, and having children has (compared to other EU member states) no lasting effects on female labour supply. The main impact is a temporary reduction in working hours to long part-time hours while children are of pre-school age. Women's working time then increases steadily as the children grow, eventually attaining a level similar to their male counterparts at the end of working life.

While Sweden has been very successful in integrating women, the elderly and the handicapped, Sweden has been singularly less successful in integrating immigrants into the labour market. Despite some improvement in the labour market situation during the second half of the 1990s, the extent of labour market integration of the foreign-born population, in particular among immigrants born outside Europe, remains very low. At the beginning of the new millennium the employment rate among foreign-born citizens was 22 per cent lower and their labour income 33 per cent lower than native Swedes. Several explanations have been put forward for the decline in labour market integration of immigrants in Sweden. First, in spite of the strengthened legislation against discrimination, a shift in the composition of the foreign-born population towards a larger share of immigrants from outside Europe may have entailed a tendency towards greater discrimination from authorities, employers and employees. Second, the large structural changes experienced by the Swedish economy, in particular the shift towards a service-oriented and knowledge-based economy and the related demands of qualifications and skills, may have been detrimental to the labour market integration of non-natives.

The growing awareness among politicians of the marginalization process at play has led the various Swedish governments to take specific measures in order to ease the entry of immigrants and refugees into the labour market. The active labour market measures targeted towards immigrants, introduced in the early 2000s, are promising and the few evaluations performed so far suggest that they are having beneficial impacts on the integration of immigrants. While these specific measures go in the right direction, there are reasons to believe that the goal of integrating immigrants to roughly the same extent as the native population will not be achieved in the near future and that discrepancies will remain, implying a need for further political efforts to sustain the process of labour market integration of the foreign-born population.

Social protection system: Structure and evolution

A knowledge of the reforms to Sweden's institutional structures and policies undertaken over recent decades is crucial to an understanding of the country's employment system, particularly the high employment rates and gender employment profiles. These reforms aimed explicitly at encouraging high and continuous labour force participation of men and women, narrowing the gender employment gap and ensuring similar patterns of employment over the life course. The following institutional features appear to be determinant: the generous and flexible leave of absence; the expansion of subsidized and high-quality childcare; and the reforms of the benefits, taxation and pension system.

Parental leave

The Swedish parental leave programme, introduced in 1974 (replacing the maternity leave legislation), has plainly sustained the growth of female labour participation and contributed to the changes in women's behaviour in the labour market. Since 1974 there has been a marked reduction in the frequency with which women withdraw from the labour market compared to the 1960s and the employment rate of mothers of children under age seven is among the highest in the OECD countries. The change of name (from 'maternity' to 'parental') also reflects a desire to influence the division of labour between men and women and to favour gender equal opportunities.

The length of parental leave was initially six months and was gradually extended to 16 months (480 days) in the 1990s, with full job security on return. The level of compensation is 80 per cent of gross earnings for the first 390 days. For the remaining 90 days parents receive a flat rate of SEK60. Parental leave offers considerable flexibility in that part of the time can be taken over a longer period by working a shorter week with wage compensation. Generally speaking, the parental leave schemes offer considerable scope for re-arranging working time. Parents may use their leave at any time from the child's birth or adoption until its eighth birthday.[9] In order to favour a more equal gender distribution of absence, a first non-transferable month for each parent was introduced in 1993 and a second in 2002. Fathers thus have a strong incentive to use their rights to parental leave for at least 60 days. The gender division of parental leave remains, however, unevenly distributed, since in 2005 81 per cent of the total number of compensated days were taken by mothers. Nevertheless, the incidence of fathers' parental leave and the average duration of fathers' absence have risen continuously, from 1 per cent of compensated days in the mid-1970s to almost 20 per cent in 2004 (about 50 days of absence).

Even though the extent of universalism and the degree of decommodification of the Swedish welfare state are high, the level of income compensation in the parental leave system is not independent of individual work history. The amount of income-related benefit is based on earnings during the six months immediately preceding the birth of the first child; this constitutes a strong economic incentive for parents to be gainfully employed and to work full-time prior to childbirth. The benefit system has therefore had a great influence on working-time patterns for prospective parents. Typically, Swedish women work full-time before childbirth, take parental leave, return to employment on a part-time basis and increase working time as the children grow up. Paid leave is also available to care for a sick child or adult relative.

Public childcare

The public childcare system has substantially improved over the last three decades. In 1995, municipalities were made responsible for providing, without unreasonable delay, pre-school programmes and leisure-time activities for all schoolchildren from ages one to 12 whose parents are gainfully employed or are studying. The number of places in community childcare centres or community-sponsored homes has increased from about 12 per cent of children between age one and six in 1972 to almost 85 per cent in 2004. The Swedish system is specially designed to help working parents. The day care centres provide meals for children and are open until 6 pm. Between 2001 and 2003 further improvements were introduced, including the fixing of a maximum level of parental contribution. The main objective of these reforms, besides labour supply considerations, is to make childcare part of the general welfare system, available to all. The basic principle is that all children should have access to childcare and that no child should be excluded on the basis of cost.

Tax system

The tax policy has also contributed to the sharp increase in female participation in the labour force. The shift in 1972 from family-based to individual income tax treatment encouraged married women to enter the labour force. The development of public-sector employment during this period, together with generous social benefits and transfer systems for income redistribution, increased government spending, which led to increased tax pressures and a sharp increase of marginal tax. The system of individualized taxation in a context of high average and marginal tax rates has also reinforced the dual breadwinner model.

Many Swedish economists have stressed the detrimental impact of high taxes on work incentives, on investment in human capital (educational attendance and attainment) and on entrepreneurship. These negative effects may, however, be determined by the tax (and transfer) structure rather than by the overall tax rate. Such considerations led to a comprehensive tax reform in 1991, aimed primarily at reducing the total tax level rather than reforming the tax structure. The measures reduced marginal tax rates on earned income, widened the tax base and introduced a more uniform taxation of capital.[10] Despite this reform Sweden remains a high-tax country and the reduction of total tax pressures in terms of GDP has been limited.[11] The tax reforms of the 1980s and early 1990s might also be a factor explaining the increase in average working time, particularly for women, over the past ten years. The gender gap in working hours has in fact narrowed, from over nine hours in 1963 to less than five hours in 2004.

Reform of the pension system

The old benefit-defined 'pay as you go' pension system introduced in the early 1960s combined a flat universal benefit (*Folkpension*) with a supplement based on previous earnings (ATP). Full earnings-related benefit could be obtained with 30 years of employment at age 65, calculated on an average of the best 15 years – the so-called 15–30 years rule (Palmer, 2000). During the 1980s this system became increasingly underfinanced and it was clear that the problem would become more serious. In June 1994 parliament passed legislation replacing the old benefit-defined system (DB) with a mandatory defined contribution (DC) scheme. The old state pension system was converted into two defined contribution pillars: a *pay-as-you-go notionally defined contribution system* (NDC) and a *financially defined* (FD) *contribution system*. These two earnings-related components are both based on contributions from lifetime earnings and the total contribution amounts to 18.5 per cent of earnings.[12] The two mandatory defined contribution schemes were also supplemented by a *guaranteed minimum pension* for those on low income or no income from work, designed to protect the lifetime poor.

This new system is the result of a broad political consensus[13] and an awareness among all politicians of the urgency to reshape the pension system in order to secure its long-term sustainability. The NDC is based on lifetime earnings and the initiators of the reform were aware that the life income principle could affect individuals' earning during retirement quite differently, depending on the distribution of risks concerning career and employment disruptions between socio-economic groups. Hence, the reform of the pension system had to consider the diversity in the patterns of labour market integration over the life course and the uneven distribution of risks by limiting the cost of necessary work interruptions linked to parenting, care activities or involuntary employment disruptions such as unemployment, disability or sickness. While one important motive in the pension reform was to increase the labour supply and lengthen the time devoted to paid work over the life course, the time that workers devote to higher education, to care of small children or to national military service, as well as absence due to unemployment and sickness, also gives entitlement to pension rights.

Adjustments to sickness pay

Health insurance was extended to all in Sweden in 1955. The system is not directly linked to working life and there are no legal thresholds concerning working time that affect coverage. Sickness benefits are also available to all gainfully employed people; it is paid for an unlimited period and is subject to income tax, with the level of benefit related to actual income. Expenditure on sick pay is seen as a major cost of the welfare system; from 1997 to 2003 spending on sickness benefits increased from less than SEK15 billion to more than SEK43 billion. Since then sick leave has decreased somewhat but remains at a high level, while early retirement for medical reasons has continued to increase. The problem is greater among women and low-income earners, possibly reflecting harder and more demanding working conditions after the 1990s reforms, in particular in the female-dominated and relatively low-paid state care sector.

To curb the rapid growth of sick leave, in the early 1990s the replacement rate of sickness benefits was lowered from 90 per cent to 80 per cent of previous income and one waiting day was introduced. Various rehabilitation and 'return to work' programmes have also been launched during the last ten years.

The Swedish production system

Sweden entered the post-war period with an undamaged production apparatus, and up to the early 1970s its rate of economic growth was among the highest in the world. From the mid-1970s to the early 1990s, however, the annual growth of industrial production in Sweden averaged about one percentage point below that for EU-15. The beginning as well as the end of that period was marked by deep economic crises involving significant decreases in industrial employment and production. In the following period, from 1993 to 2001, the rate of growth in industrial production reached on average about 5 per cent per year, well above the OECD average. After decreasing in the recession of 2001/02 it is once more among the highest in the European Union. The continuous structural transformation of manufacturing industry towards more knowledge-intensive and less labour-intensive production has in recent years manifested itself in rapid productivity growth. For example, the share of the electronics and telecommunications sector in manufacturing industry's total value added rose from 6 per cent in 1990 to 20 per cent in 2006.

Between 1965 and 2005 manufacturing's *share of total employment* fell from 30 to 16 per cent, although it stabilized at around 20 per cent between 1992 and 2000. The subsequent decline reflects remarkably large increases in industrial productivity. In 1965 the *public sector* (excluding state-owned companies) accounted for 15 per cent and *private services* for 43 per cent of total employment. In 2005 the corresponding figures were

34 and 48 per cent respectively. An increasingly large number of employees in the service sector are, however, providing services to manufacturing companies ('business to business services') as a result of a growth of outsourcing, including of knowledge-intensive services. Only 1 per cent of companies or corporate groups in Sweden have more than 200 employees but together they account for 60 per cent of total employment in the private sector. This makes Sweden one of the countries with the heaviest *dependence on large companies*. However, the proportion of employees working in small to medium-sized enterprises has gradually increased over the last ten years. The larger companies are, to an increasing extent, focusing on their core activities and as a consequence many service units have been transformed into – outsourced to – separate companies.

For their long-term survival the large enterprises depend on their ability to continuously develop their products and methods of production. This is one of the main factors behind the relatively high level of research and development (R&D) spending in Sweden. Swedish multinationals are among the most R&D-intensive in the world. Since 1989 average R&D investments have increased by more than 10 per cent per year and in 2001 they corresponded to almost 4 per cent of GDP. This share seems to be larger for Sweden than for any other industrialized country. Private industrial companies – mainly multinationals in the pharmaceutical, heavy engineering, automotive, aerospace and IT sectors – account for about 75 per cent of these investments. Between 1990 and 2002 the average annual growth of knowledge-intensive production was 6 per cent. The service share of Swedish exports has also increased notably in recent decades. In 1980 it was 14 per cent and in 2003 about 23 per cent.

Since the late 1980s large parts of the service sector in the Swedish economy have been subject to different forms of *deregulation and/or privatization*. Prominent examples are the deregulation of the financial markets (in the mid and late 1980s), railways (1988), taxi services (1990), domestic aviation (1992), postal services (1993), telecommunications (1993) and electricity (1996). The implementation of these and other reforms has involved the dismantling of detailed – although not overall – public governance. The recognition of competition as promoting economic efficiency and growth has also led to intensified efforts on the part of the governmental Competition Authority to prevent illegal competition and to enforce EU directives and rules on competition.

Household-related services accounting for a large share of female labour market participation – notably schooling, higher education, childcare, healthcare and social care for the elderly and the disabled – are still mainly provided by the public sector. In recent years, however, tendering and outsourcing to private providers have gained some ground, although on the basis of *retained overall public governance and financing*. In 2002 private entrepreneurs took care of about 12 per cent of all children enrolled in day care or pre-school activities organized and supervised by the municipalities. In care of the elderly the corresponding share was about the same, but in schooling it was significantly smaller at about six to seven per cent. In the healthcare sector the provision of private hospital services has been held back by existing regulations.

Maintaining full employment?

In view of the quite favourable developments in the Swedish economy since the mid-1990s, including the high level of R&D investment, it is paradoxical that these improvements have not yet involved more substantial changes in total *employment*. With regard to R&D and the switch to more knowledge-intensive production, it should be observed, however, that while the *development* of new products and methods of production offers new job opportunities, the *implementation* of such innovations in large-scale production often requires a rather limited amount of labour per unit produced. As for labour-intensive production, a more profitable alternative might be to relocate mass production to countries where labour costs are considerably lower than in Sweden. Up to now direct *re-localization* from Sweden to other countries has been limited but the preservation of internationally competitive industry in Sweden has largely been based on labour-saving rationalization. Furthermore, the total *number* of job opportunities in R&D-intensive activities will probably remain limited, particularly as many of these jobs require highly educated workers.

In the aftermath of the crisis of the early 1990s the scope for *counter-cyclical variations* in public investment and employment has become rather narrow. Since a significant further increase in the already high regular public employment is unattainable, the re-establishment of the 1980s levels of employment and unemployment might imply the creation of new job opportunities primarily in the *private service sector*.

The reduction of wage dispersion during the 1970s combined with a growing tax wedge may explain the comparatively low employment growth in the labour-intensive part of the private service sector, particularly household-related services. The centre-right government elected in 2006 has proposed to discontinue employers' contributions for parts of the service sector and has allowed a tax deduction on household-related services in order to promote the development of domestic services. This plan to stimulate domestic services comes alongside a tax reform – the so-called job deduction – aimed at reducing threshold and marginal effects for low and medium earners. The average tax rate for labour income has been reduced by 1.5 percentage points, with a reduction in the marginal rate for low earners of 3 percentage points. Another change, following the significant fall in unemployment during the last two years, has been to toughen entitlement rules for unemployment insurance and reduce its income replacement level and to cutback active labour market policies. There is still a major question, however, over whether the new government actions will constitute a major break with the Swedish model or whether the outcome may be a reinforcement of supply-oriented labour market policy measures and improved matching of job-seekers with vacancies, still much in line with the basic philosophy of the Swedish model.

Sweden may in fact be regarded as standing at a crossroads: *either* it will pursue its high-road strategy based on low wage dispersion, a continuous upgrading of skills (ALMP and lifelong learning), high investment in R&D and the development of a knowledge-based service economy, together with employment-promoting structural and institutional reforms; *or* it will develop policies aimed at increasing wage dispersion and earnings inequality, drastically reducing the tax wedge and the provision of public services, and favouring the development of a low-skill/low-paid labour-intensive private service sector. Recent political developments indicate that the second scenario seems to be favoured, at least to some extent, by the new centre-right government, but it is too early to say whether the recent measures will profoundly alter the Swedish model.

Conclusion

The present Swedish model, in our view, appears today more in line with the three core components of the original model developed and implemented during the 1950s and 1960s. The period 1975–1991 represents a clear deviation from the original Swedish model, a departure that culminated in the most severe crisis that the country has experienced since the 1930s. The recent changes in economic policy towards a more restrictive and anti-inflationary macroeconomic policy, the reorientation of active labour market policies towards supply-oriented measures, and the structural reforms undertaken in the wage formation, tax and social protection systems suggest a revival and renaissance of the traditional Swedish model.

After a period of turbulence in the early 1990s, for the last ten years the economy has experienced a particularly favourable development. Unemployment has been cut by half, inflation has been curbed and the country appears to have recovered from the deep economic crisis of the early 1990s. Besides the reorientation of macroeconomic and employment policy, the recent modifications in industrial relations, in particular the clear tendency to a re-coordination of wage bargaining, have without doubt played a vital role in the Swedish recovery. These new developments reflect a desire on the two sides of industry to re-coordinate collective bargaining at industry level and to restore the leading role of the traded good sectors in wage formation.

Hence, the tendency towards a re-coordination of collective bargaining coexists with a marked tendency to a decentralization, differentiation and individualization of wage setting and working conditions. Although contradictory at first sight, these tendencies should not be interpreted as a weakening of the Swedish collective bargaining tradition, but rather be considered as a recomposition and adaptation of the industrial relations system in face of the major transformations in work organization and production processes during recent decades. In our view these developments do not question the basic foundation of the Swedish model, namely a strong contractual tradition based on the existence of powerful social partners who enjoy considerable autonomy from the public authorities. Instead they reflect a transition and adjustment of the Swedish model to the new challenges posed by post-industrial societies. Sweden's various bipartite cooperation agreements concluded during the late 1990s may be interpreted as a new historic compromise combining employers' demands for greater flexibility with a desire on the part of the trade union movement to restore full employment and sustained income growth.

The various reforms of the Swedish social protection system undertaken during recent decades have essentially taken the form of a temporary reduction in the level of income compensation. With the notable exception of the fundamental restructuring of the tax and pension system, the reforms have left the welfare state almost intact. The social protection system is still clearly universal and inclusive in nature and it still enjoys a high level of across-the-board political and public support. Important structural reforms were undertaken in the tax and benefit system, particularly the reshaping of the pension system and the tax reform initiated in the early 1990s aimed at strengthening work incentives and fostering investment in human capital. These measures were also clearly in line with the general philosophy of the original Swedish model favouring integrative transitions instead of passive support and social exclusion. In our view the social protection system constitutes an integrated and coherent system of time and income management over the life course. In fact, the large palette of individual reversible working time options in Sweden, backed by a complete employment guarantee, generous income replacement rates and extended childcare facilities, gives considerable opportunities for households to adapt their labour supply to various situations and commitments over the life course without significant income loss. However, even though the gender employment gap has narrowed significantly in recent years, gender inequalities in time allocation and income over the life course still persist. The bulk of unpaid housework and care activities are still predominantly carried out by women, even though the male share of household and caring tasks has increased. Further efforts have to be made in order to reduce the gender gap in the division of unpaid work in order to favour a more even distribution of time and income over the life course. A gradual individualization of the parental leave system, further reduction of the prevailing gender wage gap and gender occupational segregation appear to be good policy instruments to cope with the remaining disparities and foster gender equal opportunity.

Last but not least, the third main element of the Rehn-Meidner model, the overall *policy of activation*, still occupies a central role in Swedish stabilization policy. Indeed its reorientation towards supply-oriented measures (occupational and geographical mobility, active search programmes and so on) in many respects accords with the strategy initiated in the 1950s.

Overall, the recent modifications of the Swedish model constitute an interesting advance, creating an institutional framework favourable to the emergence of negotiated flexibility and a return towards balanced economic and employment growth. In our view these developments reinforce the coherence of the Swedish model and the robustness of its social cohesion.

Notes

1. The data referred to in this paper are from Statistics Sweden, unless stated otherwise. Also 1 SEK = 0.107 Euro, 1 Euro = 9.38 SEK in May 2008.
2. The government was responsible for macroeconomic policy (price stability) and the implementation of the ALMP to ensure both an efficient allocation of resources and the preservation of full employment, while the two sides of industry were mainly responsible for regulation of the labour market and wage formation without government intervention.
3. Initially the LO was actually more reluctant than SAF to fully accept a system of centralized wage bargaining, only supporting nationally coordinated wage bargaining in 1961.
4. The inflation target is a 2 per cent per year rise in the consumer price index, plus or minus 1 per cent.
5. Unemployed job-seekers have the right to be enrolled in ALMP schemes after an unemployment period of 6 months (3 months for young people 20–4 years old), limiting the development of long-term unemployment. Since the early 1990s, expenditure on training programmes has exceeded that on job creation measures and subsidies, accounting for 42 per cent of expenditure on ALMPs, compared to EU and OECD averages of 27 and 29 per cent respectively. The 1992 and 1993 measures, such as temporary trainee replacement schemes, youth training and work experience programmes, are also mixed programmes combining temporary employment and training, rather than pure job-creation (see Anxo and Erhel, 1998).
6. Sweden has a higher educational attainment than most OECD countries; by 2000 more than 50 per cent of the adult population had upper secondary education and more than 30 per cent tertiary education. During the academic year 2003/04 almost 45 per cent of 19–26 year olds were enrolled in tertiary education.
7. The Swedish Federation of Blue-Collar Workers in the Engineering Industry (Svenska Metallindustriarbetareförbundet, Metall), which is affiliated to the LO Confederation, the Swedish Federation of White-Collar Workers in Industry (Svenska Industritjänstemannaförbundet, SIF), which is affiliated to the TCO Confederation, and the Swedish Association of Graduate Engineers (Sveriges Civilingenjörförbundet, CF), which is affiliated to the SACO Confederation.

8. The Saltsjöbaden Agreement, which was signed by the LO-S General Confederation of Labour and the Swedish Employers' Confederation, the SAF, put an end to the frequent labour disputes of the 1930s and had a decisive influence on the development of peaceful industrial relations. It also established a series of regulations covering the roles of the various actors in the labour market and accorded the social partners considerable manoeuvring room in respect to wage policy. The agreement also influenced the organization and functioning of negotiations and regulated industrial disputes by demanding prior agreement with the two confederations in the case of disputes affecting more than 3 per cent of the workforce, thus guaranteeing industrial peace as soon as the collective agreements were concluded.
9. Parental leave is one of the few social rights that is not fully individualized and the issue of whether the system of leave of absence should be fully individualized is currently widely debated.
10. The current income tax is composed of a municipal tax rate ranging from 26 to 35 per cent, depending on the municipality, and a national income tax of 20 per cent for income above SEK 252,000 and 25 per cent for income above SEK 390,000. The highest marginal tax is therefore 55 per cent compared to over 80 per cent during the 1990s. All capital income is taxed at 30 per cent regardless of the amount.
11. According to the OECD, in 2005 Swedish tax revenues amounted to 50.6 per cent of GDP. The corresponding figures for the 15 EU member countries, the OECD countries, and the United States were 40.5, 36.9 and 28.9 per cent respectively. The new centre-right government, elected in October 2006, has also started to implement a major reform of income taxation: wealth tax has already been abolished and the tax ratio has fallen from 49.8 per cent of GDP in 2006 to 47.7 per cent of GDP in 2007.
12. Half is an employer contribution, half an employee contribution. For people covered fully by the new rules 16 percentage points will go to the NDC pay-as-you-go component of the system and 2.5 percentage points to the mandatory funded component (FD).
13. The new system is the result of a broad political consensus among five of the seven parliamentary parties in 1994, representing 80 per cent of voters.

References

Anxo, D. (1993), 'Les années 1990 où la fin du modèle suédois', pp. 221–9 in B. Gazier (ed.), *Trajectoire de l'Emploi*, Paris: Economica.

Anxo, D. and Erhel, C. (1998), 'La politique de l'emploi en Suède: Nature et évolution', pp. 35–75 in J. Gautie and J.-C. Barbier (eds), *Les politiques de l'emploi en Europe et aux Etats-Unis*, Paris: Presse Universitaire de France.

Anxo, D. and Niklasson, H. (2006), 'The Swedish Model in Turbulent Times: Decline or Renaissance?', *International Labour Review* 145(4): 339–71.

Anxo, D., Carcillo, S. and Erhel, C. (2000), 'Aggregate Impact Analysis of Active Labour Market Policy in France and Sweden: A Regional Approach', pp. 49–76 in J. de Koning and H. Mosley (eds), *Labour Market Policy and Unemployment*, Cheltenham: Edward Elgar.

EIRO (2008), 'Unions Fear ECJ Ruling in Laval Case Could Lead to Social Dumping', European Industrial Relations Observatory. http://www.eurofound.europa.eu/eiro/2008/01/articles/eu0801019i.htm

Elvander, N. (2000), *The Industrial Agreement: an Analysis of its Idea and Performance*, Stockholm: Almega.

Iversen, T. (1999), *Contested Economic Institutions: The Politics of Macroeconomics and Wage Bargaining in Advanced Democracies*, Cambridge: Cambridge University Press.

Palmer, E. (2000), 'The Swedish Pension Reform Model: Framework and Issues', SP Discussion Paper Nr. 0012, Washington DC: World Bank, June.

Sheldon, P. and Thornthwaite, L. (1999), 'Swedish Engineering Employers: The Search for Industrial Peace in the Absence of Centralised Collective Bargaining', *Industrial Relations Journal* 30(5): 514–32.

Statistics Sweden (SCB), *Labour Force Surveys*, various years, Stockholm.

4
From the 'Sick Man' to the 'Overhauled Engine' of Europe? Upheaval in the German Model

Steffen Lehndorff, Gerhard Bosch, Thomas Haipeter and Erich Latniak

Introduction

For most of the 1960s–80s the Federal Republic of Germany was regarded both at home and abroad as one of the countries that had been particularly successful in combining economic growth and social equality. For many economists and social scientists Germany was the exemplar of 'Rhenish capitalism' (Albert, 1992) which, by virtue of the 'beneficial constraints' (Streeck, 1997) imposed on German capital by strong labour unions and institutions, fostered long-term corporate strategies and an environment of trust relationships, not only within capital but also between the strong associations representing capital and labour. It was under these conditions that a system of high-quality and export-oriented production was developed, which in turn powered the entire employment system.

According to these analyses the essence of the 'German model' ultimately lies – or lay – in the fact that the high value added generated by the country's high-skill, high-quality manufacturing (and exporting) sector benefits the whole of German society by being redistributed through generalizing institutions such as the collective bargaining system, labour law and the welfare state. It was only through this interaction that the German model's characteristic combination of economic dynamism and low social inequality could be achieved.

However, after the historic turning point of 1989/90 when, in the aftermath of the unification of the West German Federal Republic and the German Democratic Republic (GDR; East Germany), the unemployment rate rose to new highs, opinions on the German employment model began to diverge. Significant contributions in the Anglo-Saxon literature in particular continued to emphasize the 'coordinated' nature of German capitalism as the basis of the country's 'comparative institutional advantages' (Hall and Soskice, 2001). Some German authors, on the other hand, maintained that the system was geared to stagnation. A prominent economist, especially popular among journalists, regarded Germany as the 'sick man of Europe' and raised the question 'can Germany be saved?' (Sinn, 2003). In particular, it was the design of the welfare state that started to attract criticism, for allegedly driving up labour costs and hence impeding employment growth in the service sector, particularly in the low-wage sectors (Streeck and Trampusch, 2005).

Some three to four years later, as the German export machine regained its momentum and unemployment figures began to drop, this line of critical argument lost much of the public prominence it once had. '"Sick man" is picture of health' was the diagnosis of the *Financial Times,* which added: 'Overhauled: Why Germany is Again the Engine of Europe' (*Financial Times,* 2007). However, it is also fair to assume that when the current (2008) financial crisis recedes and the state is no longer widely regarded as the anchor of last resort, if economic growth continues to decline or stagnate, these critical and pessimistic views will be back at the forefront of the debates on the German model. In fact, we share the assessment that the German employment model is in upheaval. For a better understanding of the reasons, however, we suggest it is necessary to go beyond the prevailing approaches in several respects. First, our analysis is not confined to manufacturing, unlike most of the investigations into the German employment model to date. Services need to be included, not only because they account for the greater share of activity but also because the significance of the welfare state cannot be fully revealed without examining the employment model in its entirety. Second, and unlike most analyses of institutional change, we place the role of politics and policy at the heart of our analysis. Far from strengthening the existing institutions, the economic and employment policies adopted by governments of various stripes and other influential actors have served only to undermine them through a combination of deregulation and a restrictive budgetary policy. The political and economic conditions under which Germany was united have had a decisive influence in this regard. This is why, thirdly, we put particular emphasis on the impact of unification both on the fortunes of East Germany and on the macro-economic strategies and social reforms that have contributed to the development of a new German employment model.

Thus, the question is no longer to what extent the 'old' West German model will be re-established after overcoming its crisis. Rather, almost two decades after unification the more appropriate challenge for socio-economic analysis is to identify the major new features that are emerging from the current upheaval of the German socio-economic model.

Prime years and crisis

The main pillars of the model

The numerous contributions to the extensive international literature on the German employment model vary in their emphasis. Some authors concentrate on analysing the long-term relationships between companies and their banks, others on work organization and the vocational training system and yet others on industrial relations. Despite these considerable differences of emphasis they reach the same conclusion, namely that strong institutions served to establish relationships of trust among the key actors, which in turn provided the foundation for long-term corporate strategies. This long-term approach paid off in an economy that specialized in high-quality products and at the same time had high levels of productivity. This created the economic basis for a system of social equalization through high wages and good social security on which German corporatism was based. Most of these analyses were carried out in the 1980s and reflect the situation of the time. Since much, though not everything, has changed since then, we use the past tense to describe the German model in its prime. In our view the following institutions constituted the main pillars of the German model at the beginning of the 1980s.

The structure of corporate governance: Unlike in the English-speaking world, the ownership of German companies used not to be subject to frequent change. Most shares were held by other joint stock companies or the house banks. Only 25 per cent of shares were held by diverse shareholders (Höpner, 2003), which gave companies protection from takeovers. The banks concentrated on maximizing long-term earnings and German tax legislation made short-term investment banking unattractive. Another important aspect was the so-called *Mittelstand*, the small and medium-sized companies that have been described as the 'hidden champions' or the innovative backbone of the German economy (Simon, 1996). Just as the major private banks financed larger companies, so the local savings banks made 'patient capital' (Hall and Soskice, 2001) available to small and medium-sized companies.

Vocational training and work organization: In the German 'skill machine' (Culpepper and Finegold, 1999) around two-thirds of young people were trained in the dual system of vocational training (that is, below graduate level), which combined workplace training with theoretical knowledge acquired in vocational schools. In contrast to school-based training systems this provided for a close link with the labour market, drawing on the involvement of the social partners in the development of vocational training. The pay grades in collective agreements largely paralleled the training system, thus restricting the importance of seniority in determining pay levels. Since the dual system also opened up opportunities for promotion to the middle echelons of the management hierarchy, it was also attractive to young people leaving secondary school, which explains the relatively low share of university graduates. The broad base of operational skills facilitated productivity advantages through specialization in high-quality, high-value products. Finegold and Soskice (1988) use the term 'high-skill equilibrium' to denote this virtuous circle. The deployment of skills in the workplace was generally embedded in organizational structures characterized by a clearly defined division of labour between individual occupations, multi-level hierarchies and a strict demarcation between company functions, such as research and development (R&D), production and sales.

The industrial relations system: Sector-wide collective agreements (mostly at regional levels) that were concluded between strong trade unions and employers' associations and which covered the vast majority of companies in a given industry took wages out of market competition. As a result the only way firms, including the export-oriented manufacturing sector, could obtain competitive advantages was by improving quality and efficiency. For this reason specialization in high-quality, high-value products became a question of survival at an early stage. The member unions of the German trade union confederation and the employers' associations, gathered together under the umbrella of the national federation of employers' associations, worked very closely with each other on coordinating their collective bargaining policy. Works councils provided a separate channel of workers' interest representation, based on general elections within establishments. Works councils have codetermination rights with regard to hiring, dismissals, training or overtime work and have the right to bargain except on those matters that are usually covered by collective agreements. The division of labour between works councils and unions is intended to take conflict out of the workplace. Müller-Jentsch (1991) coined the term 'conflictual partnership' to characterize the two-way recognition of interests involved.

The welfare state: Most dependent employees (with the exception of marginal part-time workers) were insured against major risks through compulsory health, unemployment and old-age insurance schemes. These schemes were funded on a joint basis by employers and employees through contributions, the level of which was linked to individual wages. The level of wage replacement benefits for the unemployed was relatively high, as were pensions which were automatically uprated in line with the general rise in wages. Health insurance schemes generally paid the full costs of treatment.

Labour law and labour market policy: A high level of dismissal protection was another key instrument in the decommodification of labour (Polanyi, 1978). As a side-effect firms were encouraged to adopt a long-term human resource strategy. Thus, the internal labour markets were at the same time occupational labour markets, which enabled firms to rely on a high level of functional flexibility. When unemployment began to rise sharply in the 1970s and 1980s important further training efforts were made to reintegrate the unemployed into occupational labour markets. Pressure from high unemployment on the prevailing collectively agreed wages rates was reduced by the payment of high unemployment benefits and provisions that protected unemployed skilled workers from pressure to take lower-skilled jobs.

From an historical perspective it is clear that many of the institutions, such as codetermination for example, emerged out of fierce disputes and had not been put in place according to any plan. Other institutions went through serious crises and were put back on their feet again. Consequently, a functionalist view of the German employment model is inappropriate (cf. Coates, 2005 for a discussion) as it might obscure the contradictions and shortcomings within the employment model, which although still largely hidden in the 1980s have come to the surface in more recent years.

Arguably, it is the bias towards manufacturing that is a major source of functionalist tendencies in analyses of the German employment model as it gives a one-sided view of the German productive system. The institutions in the manufacturing sector are assumed to represent the whole of the system, although they actually constitute only one segment of the economy as a whole. True, the implicit assumption that the institutions and configurations of actors observed in manufacturing were typical of the system as a whole did have a certain validity until well into the 1980s. This becomes clear if the economy is divided into three segments, which can be designated 'production' (including manufacturing, construction, R&D, financial and other business services), 'consumption and distribution' (including trade, hotels and restaurants, transport, telecommunications) and 'provision' (including public administration, utilities, education, health and other social services) respectively. The links between these segments, and within each of them, were particularly strong (see Figure 4.1).

Service industries and activities located within the production segment were to a large extent subject to the same governance structures as manufacturing itself and were included in the same type of collective bargaining system. In the consumption and distribution and provision segments, publicly-owned companies played a major role: the railways, post office, public transport and electricity and water supplies were in public ownership, as were most schools, kindergartens, universities and hospitals. Trade union density in state-owned enterprises was above average and, with political support, the unions were able to obtain actual rights to codetermination that exceeded those enjoyed by workers in most other sectors.

In sectors in which trade union density was low, in the consumption segment for example, collectively agreed minimum pay rates were extended by the federal government in conjunction with the social partners and thus generalized. The dual vocational training system was not confined to manufacturing occupations: there were also occupational profiles and promotion paths in the other two employment segments. Labour law and social security arrangements applied equally to all sectors of the economy. As with collective bargaining and vocational training policies, the driving force behind the development of the welfare state and employment benefits such as sick pay also often originated in the manufacturing sector.

Area of regulation	Segments		
	Production	Consumption and distribution	Provision
Governance	Stable ownership by banks /'Patient capital'	State ownership of public transport and utilities	State ownership or strong regulation by he state
Industrial Relations	Industry-wide collective bargaining Co-determination laws Extension of collective agreements Pattern wage agreements Predominance of collectively agreed sector standards over firm-level agreements		
Training	Dual system of vocational training		
Employment	Decommodification through employment protection in labour law Labour market policy and public tenders respected collectively agreed wages High unemployment benefits, active labour market policy concentrated on retraining and work creation schemes		
Welfare system	Decommodification through mandatory welfare system (health, old age, accident, unemployment) Welfare system oriented to male breadwinner (income splitting taxation, subsidies for marginal part-time jobs, derived entitlements in health and old age insurance schemes, half-day school and cash benefits for children instead of childcare provision)		

Figure 4.1 Regulation of the segments of the German employment model in the 1980s
Source: Own representation

Looking back at the prime years of the German employment system, its highly gendered nature appears to be of particular importance. It was very much oriented to the single male breadwinner and, through arrangements such as derived social security entitlement for married women, the joint taxation of married couples (income splitting) and the priority given to financial benefits for households with children over the provision of childcare, the effect was to subsidize married women, who either took a marginal part-time job or withdrew from the labour market altogether.

It was this gender bias in particular that was the reason for critical assessments of the German welfare state (Esping-Andersen, 1990), in contrast to the more favourable assessments of other pillars of the German employment model. Remarkably enough, these contrasting pictures did not attract a great deal of attention. In our view, however, the reluctance to modernize the welfare state, combined with the effects of persistent unemployment, has proved to be one of the most significant barriers to employment growth and undermines the vitality of the employment system in Germany. It is the crisis in that system to which we now turn.

The crisis

The first cracks in the German employment model became visible at the end of the 'golden age' of post-war capitalism. Like many other developed countries Germany began to rub its eyes after the 'short-lived dream of everlasting prosperity' (Lutz, 1984). In the first half of the 1980s, registered unemployment rose from 3.8 to 9.3 per cent; by the end of the decade it was still at 7.9 per cent, despite a revival of economic growth (BA, 2008). In key areas of manufacturing, growth prospects were increasingly restricted by the intense competition in world markets, in particular from Japan, where quality and diversity were delivered at much lower cost than in Germany. The need to respond through radical innovations in work organization designed to make better use of the potential of skilled workers was widely neglected, thus turning the earlier virtuous circle of 'diversified quality production' into a vicious circle of technology fixation/lack of shop-floor involvement/high labour costs within the production model (Jürgens, 2003). What made things even worse was the delay in developing the service sector as a counterweight to the diminishing potential for employment growth in manufacturing.

As in many other Western industrialized countries there emerged influential calls for a radical market or liberal approach.[1] Although the neoliberal critics of the German employment system were unable to achieve welfare state cutbacks on the scale they were demanding, at the same time its defenders were equally unable to initiate a new wave of reforms that could have brought the known strengths of the German system into play more effectively. It was not until German unification that the balance of power changed substantially.

The economic integration of East Germany into the enlarged Federal Republic of Germany began with the 1:1 conversion of the East German currency into Deutschmarks, which equated to a revaluation of roughly 300 per cent and made large swathes of the East German economy uncompetitive overnight. A process of extensive deindustrialization got under way within a very short period of time. Between 1989 and 1991 East German gross domestic product (GDP) dropped by more than 40 per cent; by 1992 manufacturing output had fallen by 70 per cent and by 1993 employment had decreased by 40 per cent (Hickel and Priewe, 1994, p. 21). Given the high level of unemployment East Germany turned into a 'dependency' or 'transfer economy' (Hickel and Priewe, 1994) as transfer payments from western Germany continued to fund more than one quarter of aggregate demand in eastern Germany (Ragnitz, 2005). These transfer payments had important repercussions on the German economy. The share of social security contributions in GDP rose from 15 per cent in 1990 to 18.5 per cent in 1997 and the public debt relative to GDP rose from 41 per cent in 1989 to 63 per cent in 1998 (Bofinger, 2005, p. 67). It was this rapidly increasing strain on public and social security budgets that sparked the public debate on the viability of the German social security system (see below).

Today, more than 15 years after the currency union, within an overall stronger economic environment, the economic catch-up process in eastern Germany has stalled; apart from a few urban growth centres GDP per capita is stagnating at 60 per cent of the level in the western part. The skill base of the workforce is underutilized and regional unemployment rates have stuck at an average of little less than 17 per cent, twice the western German level (8.4 per cent in 2007; BA, 2008). While the birth rate, which had more than halved in the early 1990s, is gradually recovering and converging with the (notoriously low) west German level, there is still a great deal of east–west migration of skilled workers, particularly young women (Rehberg, 2006).

Besides its economic effects, the manner of German unification had equally important political and institutional repercussions on the German model. The economic and welfare state structures that had previously been the targets of increasing criticism were quickly exported to eastern Germany. As a result of this 'colonization' a model in need of reform was kept alive and applied to the whole of the country. This 'institutional conservatism' (Wiesenthal, 2004) was also reflected in the absence of any interest in institutions that had been established in the GDR and could have been used in the enlarged Federal Republic. These included the system of comprehensive schools (a contrast to the divided and selective education system in the former West Germany) and the combining of vocational and academic education in the polytechnics, as well as the polyclinic and public childcare systems.

Interestingly, the only institution whose transfer failed was the collective bargaining system. While it was initially introduced very quickly into the East German *Länder* it soon became abundantly clear that there was a world of difference between bureaucratic transfer of an institution and the embedding of an institution in the social model (Ritter, 2006). In the course of the rapid privatization process it became obvious that this crucial element of the old German model had not taken root in the eastern part of the country. While it was primarily the large West German manufacturing companies that stuck to industry-level bargaining, these were small in number compared to the small and medium-sized West German outsourced subsidiaries and home-grown small East German firms, the bulk of which either left the employers' associations or did not join them in the first place (Schmidt et al., 2003).

Arguably, the importance of 1990 as a turning point for the German employment model can best be characterized by what did *not* happen. As Hickel and Priewe (1994, p. 41) have it: 'There was probably no situation in Germany's post-war history in which there was greater need for economic and political coordination between societal groups and the key state institutions than in this one. Market failure was further compounded by blatant political failure'. In other words, what was most striking was the *absence* of what might have been expected given the widely celebrated features of German corporatism and coordinated capitalism.

Thus, the shock of German unification and its economic and political consequences triggered a rapid change in the political climate. The political and economic elites, along with key opinion formers, now shared the belief that the only way of solving Germany's problems was to adopt the harsh prescriptions of neoliberalism. These were held to include restricting the earnings of the vast majority of workers, cutting back on welfare state benefits and government expenditure as a share of GDP and deregulating the labour market, giving priority to company-level arrangements geared to undercut industry-wide collective agreements. The principal actors in politics, the media and interest groups began to distance themselves from the German employment model. Its recognized strengths, which were once the object of a broad societal consensus, no longer constituted a positive reference point. The prevailing wisdom among mainstream politicians – more or less explicitly stated – was that its main pillars, and in particular the welfare state and the 'conflictual partnership' of the industrial relations system, had to be weakened if the economic dynamic was to be strengthened and employment increased. Both institutions were criticized for no longer being in touch with the imperatives of globalization, but connections between these growing difficulties and the process of German unification were simply not made.

Macroeconomic policy played a crucial role in creating a supportive background for this turn of the tide. In conjunction with the policy pursued by the European Central Bank with the strong support of successive German governments, the country was pushed into a vicious circle of high real interest rates, weak growth and high unemployment. Consequently, receipts from social security contributions declined and budget deficits rose.

In response, and with reference to the Maastricht criteria, which Germany was instrumental in drawing up, politicians 'declared the victim guilty' (Bofinger, 2005, p. 67) and pursued their efforts to drive down the share of government expenditure in GDP. In particular, the SPD-Green coalition government tried to '*save* rather than *grow* their way out of debt' (Horn, 2005, p. 158) while cutting back on the benefits paid out by the social insurance system and simultaneously trying to boost economic growth by introducing a series of tax reductions for companies and private households. The combined share of taxes and social security contributions (total tax revenue according to OECD criteria) fell from 37.2 per cent in 1995 to 34.7 per cent in 2005, now below the UK and also the EU average (OECD, 2007a). This strategy proved to be particularly harmful for public investments, whose share in GDP dropped from 4.8 per cent in 1970 to an all-time low of 1.7 per cent in 2004 (Mosebach, 2005, p. 167; Välilä et al., 2005).

The turn of the political tide proved to be particularly harmful for the trade unions. They lost significant numbers of members and a considerable part of their influence, which drove trade union density from about 29 per cent in 1995 to roughly 20 per cent in 2004, which is below the EU-25 average (European Commission, 2006, p. 25). Within a very short period of time the unions found themselves cornered. On the one hand the government and central bank refused to countenance any expansionary macroeconomic strategy to address high unemployment rates and sluggish growth in both parts of the country. On the other hand they also faced an onslaught on their control in the workplace, with a fierce cost-cutting approach from big business intent on regaining their international export leadership and an increasingly beleaguered system of collective bargaining in both parts of the country. Symptomatically, from 1997 to 2006 real compensation per employee rose by no more than 0.7 per cent per year, which is among the lowest rates in the EU (European Economy, 2007).

This certainly helped to reduce unit wage costs and considerably strengthened the international price competitiveness of the German economy, but German successes in export markets have far from compensated for the lack of domestic demand. Apart from its negative short-term impacts on growth and employment, it is the long-term implications of this policy for the financial basis of the welfare state which have to be taken into account. The state's inability to provide for crucial infrastructure investments has contributed substantially to the current upheaval in the institutions of the German employment model, to which we now turn.

The upheaval

As already noted, it was implicitly assumed in earlier analyses of the German employment model – albeit not without some degree of justification – that the manufacturing sector, and the structures and configurations of actors

Table 4.1 Quantitative shifts in employment between and within employment segments, 1985–2004*

Employment segments	1985	1995	2006
Production	50.8	47.5	44.1
Of which:			
Manufacturing industry	35.6	27.6	25.5
Business services	7.6	10.2	12.4
Consumption/distribution	24.0	24.3	24.1
Provision	25.1	28.3	31.8
Of which:			
Education	4.4	5.3	6.2
Health	5.4	8.9	11.5

Source: European Labour Force Survey, special tabulation.
*Share of employees in the various segments and sectors in total dependent employment (%).

observed therein, could be taken to represent the entire system. The grounds for this assumption were already shaky in the 1980s, and today they have largely disintegrated. The declining importance of manufacturing industry within the employment system is clear from the quantitative shifts that have taken place between and within the three employment segments (see Table 4.1).

Moreover, the shifts in quantitative importance have been accompanied by institutional changes. The links and interdependencies that held the system together in its prime years have been substantially weakened (see Figure 4.2).

We will now examine in greater detail the changes in the most important elements of the German employment model shown in the synoptic overview above.

Capital becomes impatient

The long-term strategic planning and cooperation that marked the old 'Germany plc' and which were key characteristics of the entire German employment system are being pushed back by a concern with short-term returns. The change in corporate governance is being driven by two developments in particular: the increasing importance of the financial markets and shareholder value in the production segment; and the privatization of publicly-owned enterprises and their organizational principles in the consumption and provision segments.

The trend towards 'financial market capitalism' (Windolf, 2005) is attributable to at least three factors (Vitols, 2005). First, the major private banks have shifted their strategies towards investment banking, a change that is linked with their withdrawal from both the long-term financing of manufacturing

	Production	Consumption and distribution	Provision
Governance	Changes in ownership structures and role of banking system and increasing importance of shareholder value orientation Challenges to links between high- and low-added-value segments of the production chain Outsourcing of business services into areas with weaker regulatory standards	Privatization of post/telecoms and parts of public transport German Railways AG (plc) floated on stock market Increasing importance of tendering in local transport Pressure on labour costs through low-price competition in distributive services	Privatization trend in health and elderly care Cost-cutting pressures in health and elderly care in conjunction with governance strategies borrowed from private businesses Staffing cutbacks in public services and clash over collective agreements
Industrial relations	Industry-wide collective bargaining in manufacturing maintained but traded against decentralization and growing number of derogations Agreement on fundamental reform of status and pay in metal and engineering sector East–West gap in coverage and binding character of collective bargaining Challenges to predominance of collectively agreed sector standards over firm-level agreements in various manufacturing and service industries Demise of extension of collective agreements except for construction	Industry-wide bargaining in largest private service industry (retail trade) 'on the point of collapse'	Break-up of association of public employers Major reform of pay and employee status structures in public services

Training	Dual System of vocational training modernized but increasing reluctance to provide vocational training among employers in some industries
Employment	Persistent decommodification of labour through employment protection in labour law but blurring of standards at fringes of labour market Improved opportunities for electing works councils in smaller establishments Labour market reforms drive jobseekers into low wage jobs far below collectively agreed wages Public tenders do not always respect collectively agreed wage rates
Welfare system	Persistent decommodification of labour through extensive social security coverage but cuts in benefits Continuing male breadwinner orientation of tax / social security system in spite of gradually improved child care provision and modernized parental allowance Subsidies for marginal part-time work extended

Figure 4.2 Changes in the German employment model by employment segments
Source: Own representation

firms (no longer regarded as lucrative) and their monitoring and control functions on supervisory boards. Second, since the mid-1990s the previously high levels of taxation on capital gains have been reduced. The consequence of both changes was the break-up of the traditional interlocking structures that used to characterize 'Germany plc'. Third, and finally, a market for the control, purchase and sale of companies has emerged.

In the course of these changes the ownership structure of German big business has been largely internationalized: in 2007 53 per cent of the shares of the Dax 30 companies were owned by foreign investors, as compared to 10 per cent only ten years before (*Handelsblatt*, 2007). Even if stock market listing still falls short of UK or US levels, and there are still moves by many companies to remain independent from short-term stock market volatility, share prices and shareholder expectations now influence companies' investment decisions to an extent hitherto unknown in Germany and are called on to legitimate make-or-buy decisions. As a consequence, when the bursting of the financial bubble in the USA sent shock waves across the Atlantic, large parts of the German banking and stock market systems proved to be as vulnerable as their counterparts in many other European countries.

Under these circumstances collective agreements can be called into question, as can the obligation to invest in vocational training, hitherto considered a behavioural norm. The pressures have also extended to small and medium-sized enterprises (SMEs), which are not normally quoted on the stock exchange. New lending regulations have induced the banks to pay greater attention to borrowers' creditworthiness as the profits achievable in financial markets turned SMEs into less attractive customers for major banks. In contrast, private equity funds started to explore the SME market as an area of restructuring and short-term profit-making.

The change in corporate governance also affects the consumption and provision segments. Here the privatization of government and public services, initiated by EU regulations but also desired by successive German governments, acts as the functional equivalent of the 'financialization' (Kädtler, 2003) of corporate governance in the production segment. Privatizations to date have primarily concerned postal and telecommunications services, together with energy and water companies and public transport. There is also a trend towards privatization in the provision segment, particularly in care of the elderly and health services which are under considerable financial pressure. These changes in ownership and governance structures in the consumption and provision segments of the employment system add to the destabilizing effects on the German employment model.

Modernizing the production model

Germany's high-quality productive system was based on a functional and hierarchical form of company and work organization that was able to rely on specialist skilled workers. This organizational form proved to be too inflexible to react quickly to changes in customer requirements. The Japanese lean production system was being adopted across the world as a new organizational paradigm that was to replace traditional mass production. In the 1990s many German companies, firstly in manufacturing and then in the service sector, were completely reorganized.

The model for this change can be described as a German variant of lean production as it differs from the US, French and British variants in retaining a high share of skilled workers. The use of various forms of flexible working time to adjust staffing to match order levels is more widespread than in other European countries (Schief, 2006). Despite sharp fluctuations in orders and flexible production it has been possible to maintain a strikingly high level of job tenure (Auer and Cazes, 2000; Erlinghagen, 2008) by combining high internal functional flexibility with numerical flexibility in working time. The marked shift within organizations and among employees towards greater flexibility and customer orientation has set new standards for many parts of the private and public service sector.

As in other countries, process-oriented 'slimming-down measures' have been taken with a view to reducing or eliminating entire levels of the management hierarchy and central services and to reorganizing production departments by market or product area (Latniak, 2006). Supply chains have been reorganized and activities have been outsourced so that internally generated value added as a share of turnover has declined considerably in large and medium-sized German companies. While the high share of skilled workers employed by German suppliers has encouraged outsourcing geared to exploiting the advantages of specialization, uncomplicated service activities have been outsourced from industries with high levels of coverage by collective agreement to sectors with low levels of coverage. At the same time the new EU member states and, more recently, China and India are increasingly the focus of German direct investment. It is true that tapping new markets is also an important motivation here, but at the same time this direct investment also serves to reduce wage costs in labour-intensive stages of production processes in particular.

Interestingly, the radical *process* innovation that helped German manufacturing regain its leading position in export markets was accompanied by a strategy of *product* innovation, which closely followed the established pattern of incremental innovation and across-the-board diffusion of advanced technology. As the expert report for the federal government notes (BMBF, 2007), in 2004 the German economy recorded the biggest export surplus per capita in R&D-intensive goods of all OECD countries. In fact most of this was based on 'advanced technology', in contrast to 'cutting-edge technology' products where the trade balance was close to zero. As Lane (2000, p. 223) has it, the German innovation system is unlikely to make a complete transition from its focus on high-value goods to a concentration on high-technology goods, but 'it has proven more viable than many critics have allowed for'.

Along with the process innovations, the vocational training system came under considerable pressure to innovate. In fact the social partners have created many new occupations since the mid-1990s, particularly in the service sector. Existing occupations have been comprehensively modernized to fit them for modern forms of work organization and flexible careers and have been combined to form basic occupations with broadly based skill profiles (Bosch and Charest, 2008). In this way vocational training, from being a laggard, has become a driving force in corporate reorganization, particularly in those companies that are still organized along traditional lines (Schumann, 2002).

Nevertheless, the dual system still faces considerable problems. The first cause is the increasing reluctance of firms to offer training. The long-term approach to the development of human capital that is inherent in the dual system clearly runs increasingly counter to the short-termism that now dominates corporate thinking. The share of companies providing training places fell from 34.3 per cent in 1985 to 24.3 per cent in 2002; in eastern Germany the share was only 19.5 per cent (BMBF, 2004). In 2004 proposed legislation on the introduction of a training place levy, which would have ensured that firms not providing training contributed to the costs of vocational training, was withdrawn because of strong resistance from business associations (Bosch, 2004).

The second reason for the problems facing the dual system is deficiencies in the school system, which is still structured on a tripartite basis (lower secondary schools, intermediate secondary schools and grammar schools). Lower secondary schools in large urban areas in particular are becoming 'sink schools' for the children of immigrant families living in difficult circumstances. As highlighted in the PISA studies (OECD, 2007c), the German school system has apparently been less successful than those in other countries in compensating for the disadvantages associated with social class. Many school-leavers no longer have the basic skills and knowledge required to learn a trade where skill requirements have increased. The share of people under age 34 without a secondary school leaving qualification has risen in the last decade from around 30 per cent to 60 per cent of the OECD average. Thus the federal government (BMBF, 2006a) is justified in speaking of 'cracks in the foundation' of an economy that relies primarily on skills.

To summarize, within its high value-added approach, business has shifted emphasis markedly towards labour cost reduction and price competitiveness. The traditional high value-high wage link enshrined in the German production model has been weakened. This observation points to the importance of changes in the industrial relations system, to which we now turn.

Industrial relations in the process of fragmentation

Despite some important innovations (major reforms of the pay grading and remuneration systems in the public service and in the metal industry, for example) by far the dominant trends within the German industrial relations system are those leading to its erosion. The associations representing capital and labour, and with them the institutions responsible for sustaining the industry-wide collective agreement system, are under increasing pressure from the financialization of corporate governance, the systematization of inter-site competition and, not least, the low growth rates in the German economy. The state is also playing an important role in this regard. The public sector, once a haven of stable industrial relations, is now a contributor to the destabilization of the system as a result of budget restructuring and privatization. Significant numbers of employers in both the private and public sectors are inclined to abandon the traditional 'conflictual partnership' and to exploit their increased power in the labour market in order to establish decentralized concession bargaining. The trade unions have lost much of their previous status as an influential and shaping force and are increasingly confining themselves to defending existing labour standards.

The most striking indicator of the upheavals in the industrial relations system is the decline in coverage by collective agreements, triggered by the declining membership of the employers' associations which is indissolubly linked with the haemorrhaging of members from the trade unions. In 2006 63 per cent of German employees were covered by collective agreements, out of which 54 per cent were industry-wide and 9 per cent firm-level agreements. From 1998 to 2006 the share of employees covered by collective agreements dropped from 76 per cent to 65 per cent in western Germany and from 63 per cent to 54 per cent in eastern Germany. As small firms are under-represented in the employers' associations, the shares of firms covered by collective agreements in 2006 are much lower, namely 40 per cent in western and 24 per cent in eastern Germany (Bispinck, 2008). In consequence, from 1992 to 2004 labour costs in establishments with 500 and more employees rose at twice the rate of costs than in establishments with ten to 50 employees (Bosch and Kalina, 2008).

It is not only coverage by collective agreements that is diminishing but also their power to shape the regulation of working conditions (Haipeter, 2006). Decentralized bargaining, which in the prime years of the German model used to yield extra pay beyond industry standards, has crossed the divide and is now leading to the payment of wage increases below those agreed at sector level. As trade unions have recently taken major efforts to increase internal coordination and to intensify their activity in the work place, the momentum of decentralized concession bargaining has slowed down while the overall erosion of the collective bargaining system has not so far been stopped.

Differences in pay and working conditions between industries and segments are growing. Union influence is highest in industries exposed to globalization pressures but much weaker in industries dependent solely on the internal market or public budgets. While the collective bargaining actors in the core manufacturing industries have managed to agree wage increases slightly above inflation rates, real wages in large areas of the public and private service sectors are stagnating or even falling, due largely to the blocking of negotiations over long periods, for example in retail. Moreover, in growing low-wage sectors, such as food processing, there are virtually no associations on either side in a position to negotiate, and powerful capital groups in outsourcing markets, such as call centres and former monopoly markets such as mail services, are actively fostering competition based on low wages (Bispinck, 2008). Between 1996 and 2004 average labour costs in the private service sector dropped from 83 per cent to 78 per cent of those in manufacturing, which is the largest gap among EU countries (Horn et al., 2007). With real wages stagnating in manufacturing and falling in parts of the service sector, both the wage moderation in core areas of the collective bargaining system and the crisis of that system in large areas of the service sector contributed to the decline in Germany's unit labour costs relative to the Euro area by almost 10 per cent between 1999 and 2006, as computed by the ECB (2007, p. 64).

Given the crisis affecting both the trade unions and the employers' associations, the lack of institutional defences in the German industrial relations systems against outsiders intent on undercutting collectively agreed labour standards becomes decisive. Even worse, the scant defences that once existed have been demolished by political intervention. First, at the instigation of the employers' associations, the state has virtually given up using its power to declare collective pay agreements generally binding. Second, the privatization of publicly owned companies and competitive tendering for public services have given rise to competition between companies bound by collective agreements and those not so bound. Third, as a result of budgetary pressures, bargaining structures in the remaining areas of the public sector are becoming fragmented. It is only recently and in a very limited number of industries that minimum wages have been extended by the Federal Ministry of Labour, while the introduction of a general statutory minimum wage remains, for the time being, a highly controversial issue in public debates. In consequence, wage dispersion in Germany, which had started to increase in the 1980s at the upper end of the wage scale, increased at the lower end in the course of the 1990s and is now above the EU average and approaching the UK rate (OECD, 2007b).

Labour market reforms in need of reform

Major structural changes have taken place in the labour market as a result of persistently high levels of unemployment. As in many other countries, precarious employment relationships such as agency and temporary work and fixed-term employment have increased over the fairly long term. One German particularity, however, is the boom in marginal part-time jobs for which the German tax and social security system offers considerable incentives (so-called mini-jobs). This segment now accounts for around one-fifth of all employees and has made a considerable contribution in recent years to the development of a low-wage sector (Bosch and Kalina, 2008).

The increase in precarious employment relationships and the dynamic of the low-wage sector were given a decisive boost by the labour market reforms introduced by the SPD-Green coalition government. Originally, their main intention was to modernize job placement services. It was not long, however, before there was a shift of focus towards the introduction of new labour market policy instruments, the purpose of which was to increase the pressure on the unemployed to accept job offers. This was to be achieved by simultaneously reducing benefit levels and strengthening controls and sanctions. Moreover, vocational training and further training became less of a priority in German labour market policy: between 2003 and 2005 participation in publicly funded further vocational training programmes fell by 47 per cent (BMBF, 2006b, p. 249).

This same shift of emphasis applies to the centrepiece of these labour market reforms, namely the restriction of entitlement to unemployment benefit to one year. Anyone remaining unemployed for more than a year now receives a means-tested flat-rate benefit roughly equivalent to what used to be known as social assistance. As there is no entitlement to this flat-rate benefit until personal savings above a defined threshold have been spent, people who may have paid insurance contributions for 30 or even 40 years will lose the bulk of their savings as a result. Thus, for the long-term unemployed the income-linkage principle of the German unemployment regime has been replaced by a means-tested poverty relief principle, which represents a paradigmatic shift within the German welfare regime (Knuth, 2007).

In addition, the pressure on recipients of the flat-rate unemployment benefit to accept any job irrespective of their level of qualification has been considerably increased. Moreover, wages up to 30 per cent below the collectively agreed rate are now considered reasonable. This regulation has done much to encourage the development of a low-wage sector and at the same time is undermining the system of industry-wide collective agreements.

For the large central segment of the German labour market, made up of workers with vocational qualifications, these labour market reforms point the way towards a downward spiral of social relegation. They are perhaps the most far-reaching repudiation yet of the social protection for the middle classes that had been built up over decades and was a fundamental element of the German employment system.

Welfare state and institutional conservatism

The 'welfare state reforms' that have been pursued in Germany for some years, to applause from the OECD and other international organizations, arise out of the government's drive to consolidate the national budget and reduce non-wage labour costs. Unemployment is causing the number of benefit recipients to rise relative to the number of people paying contributions, the austerity policy is reducing the scope for benefits funded out of taxation and the reductions in social security contributions that are regarded as a necessary part of economic policy mean that revenue flows are also reduced. One example of this approach was the pension reform introduced by the SPD-Green government which cut pension benefits while fostering individual savings.

Despite the financial squeeze, the welfare state continues to give financial support to the single (male) breadwinner model. Next to incentives in the social security system, the income-splitting system used in the taxation of married couples amounts to around EUR21 billion per year, to which must be added the tax advantages associated with 'mini-jobs' (Spangenberg, 2005). At the same time, the insufficient provision of childcare facilities continues to hamper women's career prospects, in particular in western Germany (OECD, 2007d).[2] In consequence, the female employment rate in full-time equivalents has stagnated over the past ten years (cf. Chapter 1 of the present volume).

Politicians are now beginning to pay more attention to these problems. More resources – albeit in limited quantities – are being made available for the development of nurseries and all-day schools. Moreover, the current grand coalition government has introduced a Scandinavian-style parental allowance in the form of an income replacement scheme that is intended to increase take-up rates among men and reduce career interruptions among women. The latter objective, however, makes the conflicting paradigms within the German welfare state all the more evident: it is hard to imagine how the subsidies for the traditional family model can continue alongside a modern infrastructure for the reconciliation of family responsibilities and women's career prospects. The failure to make a choice between these two options is undermining the financial foundations of the welfare state as a whole and is weakening what used to be a strong pillar of the German employment model.

Export championship amidst institutional and social fragmentation

Until the 1980s, on the verge of its prime years, the essence of the German model could be characterized as a combination of economic dynamism and low social inequality. The high-value approach adopted by German manufacturing industry, fostered by long-term relationships within capital and between capital and labour, benefited the wider German society through generalizing institutions such as the collective bargaining system, labour law and the welfare state. Twenty years later, the German model, after more than a decade of turmoil, could be characterized by economic recovery amidst institutional and social disintegration. Important elements of its core institutions have either been changed gradually but substantially or are suffering a lack of support from major actors and are subject to controversy. Government policy has fostered 'a hardening of the division between the core labour system in the advanced sector of the economy and the "outsider" labour system with a less supportive welfare state and weaker protective labour market institutions in low skill sectors' (Carlin and Soskice, 2007, p. 3). However, the dualism goes far beyond *sectors*: it includes fragmentations *within* sectors, including the export industries, and increases job insecurity within the core labour system itself.

The nature of the changes in the German employment model can no longer be captured by focusing solely on the export-driven manufacturing industries. However, German companies' success in their export markets, which is reflected in the all-time record net contribution exports now make to GDP, has brought the contradictory nature of the new German employment model increasingly under the spotlight. The high-skill, high-quality productive system at the heart of the German employment system has exhibited impressive regenerative capacities. The development of a German form of lean production, which has benefited from the specialist qualifications of large parts of the labour force, and the restructuring and internationalization of the value-added chain have contributed to this revitalization of the export machine.

Whether or not the process of corporate 'slimming down' is sustainable in the long run remains to be seen, given its inherent risks for human resources, flexibility and innovation potentials. What has become obvious already, however, are that the ways in which the export machine – embedded in the other expanding sectors of the economy – have changed markedly. One key aspect here is the pressure on labour costs, on which business attention is increasingly focused. The radical restructuring of the production model has been closely intertwined with the exploitation of increasingly fragmented labour relations. The labour input to high-value production has become heterogeneous and now includes larger shares of precarious labour. The labour market reforms of past years have added to the rise in social inequality and to a widespread perception of job insecurity, while tax reforms have limited government's capacities to compensate for the weakening of employment growth potential beyond the export machine.

This fragmentation, in turn, has become the Achilles heel of the employment model as a whole. In contrast to the prime years of the German model, the basic mechanisms for disseminating the benefits of export success throughout the wider economy and society, which were rooted in the industrial relations system and the welfare state, have been damaged or partially dismantled. Stagnating wages and increasing shares of low-wage and precarious employment provide a weak basis for domestic growth. The dependence on the success of the export industry ties economic fortunes more than ever to the volatilities of export markets, whereas the emphasis regarding the factors behind export success has changed: the focus is increasingly on driving down labour costs and not on the development of workers' capabilities as assets for the whole of society.

The trend towards the 'financialization' of capitalism is squeezing out 'patient capital'. This change in the economic structure has created a strategic challenge for policymakers; the less corporate governance structures encourage the leading actors to adopt behaviour oriented to the long term, the more important counterweights in labour market and welfare state institutions become, at national and, above all, supranational level.

However, German policymakers, far from meeting this challenge, have instead contributed to the undermining of an employment model that drew its strength from its human resources. The underinvestment in education and training, from the inadequate provision of care for younger children to cutbacks in further vocational training, is also a reaction to budget deficits, which increased sharply in the 1990s. German unification and its implementation, both economically and politically, was a decisive factor that helped to trigger a vicious circle of low economic growth rates and austerity. The government's room for manoeuvre has been further restricted by its own tax-cutting policy. High levels of unemployment continue to undermine the financial and political basis of the institutional structure. European Economic and Monetary Union (EMU) stability criteria and, especially, the policy adopted by the European Central Bank have proven to be beneficial for German business, which has taken advantage of an actual 'devaluation' within the Euro zone, but have also served to constrain German policymakers. As the latter group fought actively for this system, it has turned out to be a self-made straitjacket.

The vicious circle of a weak domestic market, stagnant or falling incomes for service-sector employees, increased precariousness in the labour market and the break-up of institutional links between the various areas of the economy has not only become an obstacle to Germany's economic development but is also an indication of the lack of a German model for the service society. This is not a new problem as Germany has long been a service society, at least as measured by the number of service-sector employees, but there is now a more urgent need for a vision for its future development. In order to boost employment growth and decent work in the service sector, there needs to be an increase in both investment and demand, the impetus for which, beyond the manufacturing sector, would have to come from German consumers as well as from government investment.

German policymakers are faced with challenges that are difficult to meet. Is the state to invest more heavily in social services and, in doing so, will it, as regulator and employer, establish the basic conditions determining the extent and quality of provision or will they seek to gain public acceptance for a growing polarization in provision between good services for the few and poor services and poor working conditions for the many? If the collective bargaining system becomes fragile and the associations themselves lack the power to renew the system on a countrywide basis, is the state to introduce a national minimum wage, or leave it to the self-regenerating forces of the actors in collective bargaining to prevent an even further expansion of the low-wage sector entailing a boost in poor relief?

In the face of these unresolved questions social dislocation and political conflicts are increasing. The German employment model has become contested terrain.

Notes

1. Most prominently the memorandum written by the then Minister for Economic Affairs (Lambsdorff, 1982).
2. While the East German childcare service was partly dismantled after unification, the coverage rate is still higher than in the western part of the country (Konsortium Bildungsberichterstattung, 2006, p. 34). However, attitudes have remained different. Compared to their West German counterparts, more East German women want to continue working full-time after the birth of their children, and more East German husbands are ready to support this (Familienbericht, 2006, p. 125). However, due to higher unemployment in the east than in the west, job insecurity in the east is much higher for both women and men.

References

Albert, M. (1992), *Kapitalismus contra Kapitalismus*, Frankfurt/Main: Campus Verlag.

Auer, P. and Cazes, S. (2000), 'The Resilience of the Long-term Employment Relationship: Evidence from the Industrialized Countries', *International Labour Review* 4 (2000): 379–409.

Bundesagentur für Arbeit (BA) (2008), 'Statistik der Bundesagentur für Arbeit, Arbeitsmarkt in Zahlen, Zeitreihen für Arbeitslose', Nürnberg.

Bispinck, R. (2008), 'Das deutsche Tarifmodell im Umbruch', *Wirtschaftsdienst* 88(1): 7–11.

BMBF (2004), 'Berufsbildungsbericht 2004', Berlin: Bundesministerium für Bildung und Forschung.

BMBF (2006a), 'Bericht zur technologischen Leistungsfähigkeit Deutschlands 2006', Berlin: Bundesministerium für Bildung und Forschung.

BMBF (2006b), 'Berufsbildungsbericht 2006', Berlin: Bundesministerium für Bildung und Forschung.

BMBF (2007), 'Report on the Technological Performance of Germany 2007. Summary', Berlin: Bundesministerium für Bildung und Forschung.

Bofinger, P. (2005), *Wir sind besser als wir glauben: Wohlstand für alle*, München: Pearson Studium.

Bosch, G. (2004), 'Brauchen wir eine Ausbildungsplatzabgabe?', pp. 217–33 in D. Haubner, E. Mezger and H. Schwengel (eds), *Wissensgesellschaft, Verteilungskonflikte und strategische Akteure*, Marburg: Metropolis-Verlag.

Bosch, G. and Charest, J. (2008), 'Vocational Training and the Labour Market in Liberal and Coordinated Economies', *Industrial Relations Journal* 39(5): 428–47.

Bosch, G. and Kalina, T. (2008), 'Low-wage Work in Germany: An Overview', pp. 19–112 in G. Bosch and C. Weinkopf (eds), *Low-wage Work in Germany*, New York: Russell Sage Foundation.

Carlin, W. and Soskice, D. (2007), 'Reforms, Macroeconomic Policy and Economic Performance in Germany', International Macroeconomics, Discussion Paper Series No. 6415, Centre for Economic Policy Research.

Coates, D. (ed.) (2005), *Varieties of Capitalism, Varieties of Approaches*, Houndmills, Basingstoke: Palgrave Macmillan.

Culpepper, P. D. and Finegold, D. (eds) (1999), *The German Skills Machine: Sustaining Comparative Advantage in a Global Economy*, New York, Oxford: Berghahn Books.

ECB (2007), 'European Central Bank, Monthly Bulletin', 02/2007, Frankfurt am Main.

Erlinghagen, M. (2008), 'Self-Perceived Job Insecurity and Social Context: A Multi-Level Analysis of 17 European Countries', *European Sociological Review* 24(2): 183–97.

Esping-Andersen, G. (1990), *The Three Worlds of Welfare Capitalism*, London: Polity Press.

European Commission (2006), 'Industrial Relations in Europe 2006', Luxemburg.

European Economy (2007), 'European Economy, Statistical Annex, Autumn 2007'. Luxemburg.

Familienbericht (2006), 'Siebter Familienbericht. Familie zwischen Flexibilität und Verlässigkeit', Bundesministerium für Familien, Senioren, Frauen und Jugend, Berlin.

Financial Times, 11 December 2006 and 30 March 2007.

Finegold, D. and Soskice, D. (1988), 'The Failure of Training in Britain: Analysis and Prescription', *Oxford Review of Economic Policy*, 4(1988): 21–53.

Haipeter, T. (2006), 'Can Norms Survive Market Pressures? The Practical Effectiveness of News Forms of Working Time Regulation in a Changing German Economy', pp. 319–41 in J-Y. Boulin, M. Lallement, J. C. Messenger and F. Michon (eds), *Decent Working Time: New Trends, New Issues*, Geneva: International Labour Office.

Hall, P. A., and Soskice, D. (2001), 'An Introduction to Varieties of Capitalism', pp. 1–71 in P. A. Hall and D. Soskice (eds), *Varieties of Capitalism: The Institutional Foundations of Comparative Advantage*, New York: Oxford University Press.

Handelsblatt, 17 December 2007.

Hickel, R. and Priewe, J. (1994), *Nach dem Fehlstart. Ökonomische Perspektiven der deutschen Einigung*, Frankfurt am Main: Fischer.

Höpner, M. (2003), *Wer beherrscht die Unternehmen? Shareholder Value, Managerherrschaft und Mitbestimmung in Deutschland*, Frankfurt/Main, New York: Campus Verlag.

Horn, G. (2005), *Die deutsche Krankheit – Sparwut und Sozialabbau: Thesen gegen eine verfehlte Wirtschaftspolitik*, München: Carl Hanser Verlag.

Horn, G. A., Logeay, C., Stephan, S. and Zwiener, R. (2007), 'Preiswerte Arbeit in Deutschland. Auswertung der aktuellen Eurostat Arbeitskostenstatistik', Düsseldorf: IMK Report Nr. 22.

Jürgens, U. (2003), 'Transformation and Interaction: Japanese, U.S., and German Production Models in the 1990s', pp. 212–39 in K. Yamamura and W. Streeck (eds), *The End of Diversity? Prospects for German and Japanese Capitalism*, Ithaca, London: Cornell University Press.

Kädtler, J. (2003), 'Globalisierung und Finanzialisierung: Zur Entstehung eines neuen Begründungskontextes für ökonomisches Handeln', pp. 227–49 in K. Dörre and B. Röttger (eds.), *Das neue Marktregime: Konturen eines nachfordistischen Produktionsmodells*, Hamburg: VSA.

Knuth, M. (2007), 'Implementing the New Basic Allowance for Job Seekers in Germany', Discussion Paper, Peer Review Programme of the European Employment Strategy. IAQ, University of Duisburg-Essen. http://pdf.mutual-learning-employment.net/pdf/DE%2007/discussionpaper_DE_07.pdf

Konsortium Bildungsberichterstattung (eds) (2006), *Bildung in Deutschland: Ein indikatorengestützter Bericht mit einer Analyse zu Bildung und Migration*, Bielefeld: W. Bertelsmann-Verlag.

Lambsdorff, O. Graf (1982), 'Konzept für eine Politik zur Überwindung der Wachstumsschwäche und zur Bekämpfung der Arbeitslosigkeit', Friedrich Naumann Stiftung, Archiv des Liberalismus. http://admin.fnst.org/uploads/644/Lambsdorffpapier_1.pdf.

Lane, C. (2000), 'Globalization and the German Model of Capitalism – Erosion or Survival?', *British Journal of Sociology* 51(2): 207–34.

Latniak, E. (2006), 'Auf der Suche nach Verteilungs- und Gestaltungsspielräumen: eine Bilanz der Organisationsveränderungen seit den 90er Jahren', pp. 34–70 in S. Lehndorff (ed.), *Das Politische in der Arbeitspolitik: Ansatzpunkte für eine nachhaltige Arbeits – und Arbeitszeitgestaltung*, Berlin: Edition Sigma.

Lutz, B. (1984), *Der kurze Traum immerwährender Prosperität: Eine Neuinterpretation der industriell-kapitalistischen Entwicklung im Europa des 20. Jahrhunderts*, Frankfurt, New York: Campus.

Mosebach, K. (2005), 'Erosion of the Tax Basis: Fiscal Policy and International Tax Competition', pp. 157–78 in S. Beck, F. Klobes and C. Scherrer (eds), *Surviving Globalization? Perspectives for the German Economic Model*, Dordrecht: Springer.

Müller-Jentsch, W. (1991), *Konfliktpartnerschaft: Akteure und Institutionen der industriellen Beziehungen*, München, Mering: Rainer Hampp Verlag.

OECD (2007a), 'Revenue Statistics 2007', Paris.

OECD (2007b), 'Employment Outlook', Paris.

OECD (2007c), 'PISA 2006', Paris.

OECD (2007d), 'Babies and Bosses – Policies towards Reconciling Work and Family Life', Paris.

Polanyi, K. (1978), *The Great Transformation: Politische und ökonomische Ursprünge von Gesellschaften und Wirtschaftsystemen*, Frankfurt/Main: Suhrkamp.

Ragnitz, J. (2005), 'Originäre Wirtschaftskraft der neuen Länder noch schwächer als bislang angenommen', IWH-Pressemitteilung 20/2005, Halle: Institut für Wirtschaftsforschung.

Rehberg, K-S. (2006), 'Ost – West', pp. 209–33 in S. Lessenich and F. Nullmeier (eds), *Deutschland – eine gespaltene Gesellschaft*, Frankfurt/New York: Campus.

Ritter, G. A. (2006), *Der Preis der deutschen Einheit. Die Wiedervereinigung und die Krise des Sozialstaats*, München: Beck.

Schief, S. (2006), 'Nationale oder unternehmensspezifische Muster der Flexibilität?', pp. 228–48 in S. Lehndorff (ed.), *Das Politische in der Arbeitspolitik. Ansatzpunkte für eine nachhaltige Arbeits- und Arbeitszeitgestaltung*, Berlin: Edition Sigma.

Schmidt, R., Röbenack, S. and Hinke, R. (2003), 'Prekarisierung des kollektiven Tarifsystems am Beispiel der ostdeutschen Metallindustrie', *Industrielle Beziehungen* 10(2): 220–49.

Schumann, M. (2002), 'Struktureller Wandel und Entwicklung der Qualifikationsanforderungen', Vortrag auf dem 4, BiBB-Fachkongress 2002, Berlin, 23–25 October 2002.

Simon, H. (1996), *Die heimlichen Gewinner. Erfolgsstrategien unbekannter Weltmarktführer*, Frankfurt, New York: Campus.

Sinn, H.-W. (2003), *Ist Deutschland noch zu retten?*, München: Econ.
Spangenberg, U. (2005), 'Neuorientierung der Ehebesteuerung: Ehegattensplitting und Lohnsteuerverfahren', Düsseldorf: Gutachten, gefördert durch die Hans-Böckler-Stiftung (Ms.).
Streeck, W. (1997), 'Beneficial Constraints: On the Economic Limits of Rational Voluntarism', pp. 197–219 in J. R. Hollingsworth and R. Boyer (eds), *Contemporary Capitalism: The Embeddedness of Institutions*, Cambridge: Cambridge University Press.
Streek, W. and Trampusch, C. (2005), 'Economic Reform and the Political Economy of the German Welfare State', *German Politics* 14(2005): 174–95.
Välilä, T., Kozluk, T. and Mehrotra, A. (2005), 'Roads on a downhill? Trends in EU Infrastructure Investment', *EIB Papers* 1(2005): 18–38.
Vitols, S. (2005), 'German Corporate Governance in Transition: Implications of Bank Exit from Monitoring and Control', *International Journal of Disclosure and Governance* 2(4): 357–67.
Wiesenthal, H. (2004), 'German Unification and ‚Model Germany': An Adventure in Institutional Conservatism', pp. 37–58 in H. Kitschelt and W. Streeck (eds), *Germany: Beyond the Stable State*, London, Portland: Frank Cass.
Windolf, P. (ed.) (2005), *Finanzmarkt-Kapitalismus: Analysen zum Wandel von Produktionsregimen*, Sonderheft 45 der Kölner Zeitschrift für Soziologie und Sozialpsychologie, Wiesbaden: VS Verlag für Sozialwissenschaften.

5
Is Institutional Continuity Masking a Creeping Paradigm Shift in the Austrian Social Model?

Christoph Hermann and Jörg Flecker

Introduction

The 'varieties of capitalism' literature focuses on large (Western European and North American) countries. Depending on the authors, the literature differentiates between two (Albert, 1993; Hall and Soskice, 2001), three (Coates, 2000) and five models (Amable, 2005). Small and economically less powerful countries such as Austria are hardly mentioned in the debate. On the other hand there is a body of literature that discusses the periodically stunning economic and labour market successes of small countries, sometimes presented even as role models for the rest of Europe (Katzenstein, 1985; Auer, 2000). A common weakness of the 'varieties of capitalism' literature is that it does not take into account the interdependence between different models, in particular between large and small countries. The relationship between Austria and its ten times larger northern neighbour Germany is a case in point. Many German companies have subsidiaries in Austria. The relative dependence on German capital has an important impact on the Austrian model and limits the choices of domestic actors (the same is true for the new European member states with even larger proportions of foreign direct investments [FDI]). On the other hand small states tend to adjust faster to new challenges and have opportunities that are blocked for large countries. Wage restraint and export-orientation may work for Austria but not for a reunified Germany in an enlarged Europe (see Chapter 4, this volume). At the same time the example of Austria, which as a result of EU enlargement into Central and Eastern Europe (CEE) has itself become a net capital exporter, also shows the advantages of economic power over other countries.

Related to the question of interdependency, a second weakness of the debate is the problem of coherence. Much of the literature assumes that institutions are complementary and models are coherent – or at least that they have been at some point in history (Hall and Soskice, 2001, p. 17–8; Amable, 2005, pp. 82–3). An often cited example is the complementarities between high levels of job protection, sector-wide bargaining and the system of vocational training in Germany. However, although some institutions may indeed be complementary, such assumptions underestimate the contradictions and tensions and overestimate continuity in actual national models. Austrian social partnership, for example, can hardly be understood without taking into account the traumatic experiences of a short civil war in the 1930s and the following decade of fascist dictatorship. Of similar importance was the reintegration of Austria in the Western capitalist system through the Marshall plan that promoted the expansion of basic industries at the expense of final production facilities. Rather than being complementary, institutions often reflect structural constraints and social compromises. In this respect Austria stands out by combining many features of a 'coordinated market economy' with levels of sector-based wage inequality typical of 'liberal market economies'. In addition, coherence may also be disturbed by changes induced by shifts and cracks in the underlying social and political compromises.

This brings us to a third difficulty: the pace and extent of change. Much of the literature has searched for fundamental breaks and structural shifts. As these are relatively rare in history the emphasis is on continuity and path-dependency rather than on change (which, to some degree, seems to be a general bias of the institutionalist approach). Yet the reason may be that change occurs slowly, developing over several decades and affecting only parts of the model while others remain unaffected. Change, in other words, may not only be path-breaking and eruptive but selective and incremental. Incremental change, as Streeck and Thelen (2005, pp. 8–9) note, may nevertheless be transformative through the accumulation of small, often seemingly insignificant adjustments, leading the observer to underestimate the cumulative effect and thereby 'miss the tree for the forest' (Albo, 2005, p. 81). In Austria radical changes such as the privatization of public companies took place over a period of two decades. Furthermore, while key institutional settings continue to exist, they still may be 'redirected to new goals, functions, or purposes' (Streeck and Thelen, 2005, p. 26). The result may be institutional continuity, coupled with radical changes in policies. The latter seems to be a particular apt description of the Austrian situation. In sum we argue that the accumulation of changes over the last 20 years has indeed significantly altered the Austrian model. In this process Austria has not only abandoned several of its key post-war characteristics, such a large state-owned sector and extensive market regulation, thereby adjusting to what may be described as European mainstream, but has also introduced features that are commonly attributed to a (neo)liberal form of capitalism, such as budgetary austerity.

The chapter is structured in three parts. The first gives an overview of the basic features of the Austrian social model in the post-war period up to the late 1970s. The second describes the main changes in the 1980s and 1990s that, cumulatively, resulted in a significant change of the national model. The third discusses aspects of continuity in the changing social model. The chapter ends with a brief conclusion and outlook.

The Austrian model of the post-war decades

Alongside the aforementioned characteristics of state ownership and extensive market regulation, the Austrian model of the post-war decades is also characterized by social partnership. As such it without doubt presents a variation of what Albert (1993) called 'Rhenish Capitalism' and Hall and Soskice (2001) describe as 'coordinated market economies'. In contrast to 'liberal market economies' this type of capitalism is characterized by the dominance of collaborative relationships and non-market forms of coordination (Hall and Soskice, 2001, p. 8). Although the Austrian economy certainly was not released from markets and competition, they played a significantly less prevailing role in the post-war period compared to other countries and compared to today's situation. In particular capital markets were subjected to numerous restrictions. Telling in this regard is the story of the Vienna stock market which, after decades of virtual insignificance, experienced a strong revival in the late 1980s.

In a different typology Coates (2000, p. 10) emphasizes worker rights and the role of organized labour in industrial decision-making processes, resulting in what he labels 'negotiated or consensual capitalisms'. Austria, with its extraordinarily high degree of coordination and its propensity to reach comprehensive consensus, institutionalized in various mechanisms and arenas commonly referred to as 'Austrian social partnership' (Tálos, 2005a), can be regarded as a role model of 'consensual capitalism'. It is no accident that Austria stands out for having one of the lowest strike rates in Western Europe during the post-war decades. With few exceptions private sector employers are mandatory members of the Chamber of Economy which represents the interests of capital and negotiates most private sector collective agreements. On the other side workers are organized in sector-wide single unions (with the exception of the Private Employee Union which represents white-collar workers across sectors), with the Austrian Trade Union Federation acting as an intersectoral umbrella organization. Although union density is not much higher than 40 per cent, collective agreements apply to all employees in the sector or company, with the effect that 95 per cent of the workforce is covered by sector agreements and another 3 per cent by company agreements (Traxler and Behrens, 2002). In industrial relations literature 'Austro-coporatism' frequently serves as a blueprint for 'neo-corporatist' arrangements (Lehmbruch and Schmitter, 1982).

In addition, worker interests are also represented by the Chamber of Labour which, like the Chamber of Economy, is a statutory body with extensive consultation rights in law-making processes. For many years trade unionists and employer representatives have been elected members of the federal parliament, adding to the influence of the social partners on parliamentary decision-making processes. The main fields of social partner activity included economic, social and labour market policies – with this last category including the administration of the Employment Service and the system of vocational training. As a result workers still enjoy a comprehensive system of labour protection based on law and collective agreements as well as substantial co-determination rights at the company level.

Despite the role of social partnership, Austria has never been as clear a case of 'negotiated capitalism' as it might look at first sight. According to Coates (2000, p. 10) 'negotiated capitalisms' are characterized by a small degree of direct state regulation of capital accumulation, in contrast to what Coates labels 'state-led capitalisms' where the state plays a dominant role in structuring the relationship between the economic actors. In these cases, including most notably France and Japan, accumulation decisions 'are invariably taken only after close liaison with public agencies, and are often indirectly determined through administrative guidance and bank leadership' (Coates, 2000, p. 10).

However, in Austria the state played an extraordinarily important role in organising capital accumulation in the post-war period. In the 1970s about a quarter of Austria's gross domestic product (GDP) was produced by publicly-owned firms and the state owned almost a third of registered capital, including assets in mining, basic industries and major banks (Beer et al., 1991). Although final production was officially exempted from the nationalization law, the state-owned banks held shares in a number of non-financial corporations, thereby creating a second layer of indirectly state-owned enterprises, some of which were final producers. In 1985 the nationalized industries together accounted for about a quarter of turnover and almost 17 per cent of employment of the country's industrial sector (Butschek, 2004, p. 177). Hence, as Aiginger (1999) notes, 'while public ownership in infrastructure had long been a common feature of European economies, maintaining a large public ownership in manufacturing up to the 1990s was an Austrian speciality among Western market economies.'[1] Thus, the state not only supported the growth of employment through tax incentives, infrastructure and training policies, but actively created jobs through ownership and investments. In this regard the Austrian state very much acted as an 'entrepreneurial state' and by doing so developed strong similarities to the French case – although in a less coordinated manner than the French planning system (see Chapter 7, this volume).

The role of the state sector as a reservoir of stable and relatively well-paid jobs became particularly evident in the mid-1980s when the post-war-crisis finally reached Austria. While private companies quickly cut jobs and reduced investments, state-owned firms maintained high levels of employment, even at the cost of mounting corporate debts (which in the long run increased the pressure for privatization). However, the state sector not only created employment but also subsidized privately-owned companies by providing raw materials below world market prices and by lending money to the private sector through state-owned banks. Hence, although the nationalized sector was exceptionally large, there was a broad political consensus that the nationalized sector served the interests of the private sector, rather than competing with it. In addition, the state-owned firms supported the dual system of vocational education by providing more apprenticeship positions than needed to meet their own skill requirements.

While the nationalized banks and industries were one essential element in the Austrian post-war model, another was a high proportion of foreign direct investments mainly originating from Germany. Several large German industrial enterprises founded subsidiaries in Austria, often as final assembly divisions, in order to take advantage of the comparatively cheap but highly skilled labour force. In Austria not only were wages significantly lower than in Germany but working hours in the metal industry were also longer. Trade unions were very well aware of the 'comparative advantage' of Austrian production sites. Working hours rarely fell below 38.5 hours per week (compared to 35 hours in the German metal sector). On the other hand German owners were not averse to trade union representation and co-determination. Tax incentives may also have played an important role, but geographical proximity, language and cultural affinities certainly were strong pull factors for German investors. Of course Austria itself also had a substantial share of domestic private industries but not to the same extent as countries such as Sweden and The Netherlands, and only a few internationally significant companies had foreign subsidiaries. The concentration of public investments in basic industries and the relative weakness of domestic private capital resulted in a deficit in high-tech production and a comparatively low share of expenditure in research and development (Mayer, 2003).

The industrial sector was complemented by a large number of small and medium-sized firms, some of which were active in the production sector. Here, Taylorization and de-skilling never reached the level commonly associated with Fordist mass production systems. Workers retained comparatively high skills that were perpetuated through a comprehensive apprenticeship system. Again there are strong similarities to Germany and perhaps this production segment comes closest to what in the literature is considered German 'diversified quality production' (Streeck, 1991; Bosch et al., 2005). Many of these firms, however, were suppliers for car manufacturers and other mass production industries. As several of them were located outside Austria – to some degree Austria's role as supplier to big German car manufacturers was already laid down in the specific application of European Recovery Programme Funds – economic dependence did not only stem from foreign direct investments but also from the particular importance of trade, especially with Germany but also with other neighbouring countries.

However, the scope of Austrian 'diversified quality production' has always been limited. New forms of work organization in production, such as semi-autonomous working groups, remained rare in Austria. There were hardly any political initiatives to support such organizational innovations. Repetitive work with short cycle times continues to dominate medium and large manufacturing plants in spite of the sometimes high proportions of workers with vocational qualifications. Thus, the organization of production did not necessarily match the skill base. Instead skilled workers trained in the small and medium enterprise (SME) sector frequently took up jobs as semi-skilled workers in larger and/or nationalized companies because of the higher wages paid – even at the cost of working shift work. Hence, apart from building on its highly skilled workforce, de-skilling and the maintenance of a substantial 'skill reserve' should also be considered as essential parts of the traditional Austrian production model.

Austria, furthermore, was also home to a large segment of small and medium-sized companies providing less favourable employment and working conditions and significantly lower wages. High levels of labour turnover and repeated periods of unemployment are other characteristics of these labour market segments. Such conditions also prevailed in tourism, construction and the clothing industry. Not by accident these sectors employed a high proportion of migrants, actively recruited since the 1960s as 'guest workers', and, with the exception of construction, women. Much of the employment in tourism and construction was seasonal, adding to an already flexible labour market where workers frequently changed jobs. As a result the Austrian model has always been characterized by highly segmented labour markets and by a high degree of sectoral wage inequality, including a large gender pay-gap. In 2005 the mean gross income in the high-wage mineral/oil industry was more than three times that in the tourist industry (Guger and Marterbauer, 2007, p. 7). Measured according to sectoral wage distribution, Austria in fact is more similar to the Anglo-Saxon model than to the continental European, let alone the Nordic model (Rowthorn, 1992, p. 508; Guger, 1993, p. 236). Although the Austrian trade unions officially pursued a 'solidaristic wage policy', the aim was never to put pressure on the less efficient segments of the economy in order to promote economic change. And it was not until the late 1980s that the trade union movement, pressured by female union leaders, adopted an intersectoral minimum wage policy (Hermann, 2006).

High levels of income inequality persisted despite the development of a comprehensive and relatively generous welfare state. The roots of the Austrian welfare system reach back to the 19th century. After completion of post-war reconstruction in the mid-1950s a comprehensive insurance system was introduced protecting citizens from risks associated with sickness, old age, unemployment and long-term inability to work. In the 1960s and 1970s the benefit system was further improved in quantitative and qualitative terms (Tálos, 2005b). As a result the vast majority of the population is covered by mandatory social insurance. Additional benefits were introduced to cope with specific risks such as poverty. However, since eligibility for and, in some cases, even the level of benefits depends on previous contributions arising from work-dependent income, the social security system tends to reinforce inequalities created by unequal access to and participation in paid employment.

Among those disadvantaged are women who reduce their hours of employment or stay at home to take care of young children or parents who need assistance. The system whereby women's social security was derived from their husbands has been criticized as following a 'male breadwinner model' (Mairhuber, 2000). In Austria the 'male breadwinner model' was promoted by special tax incentives for sole-earner families and by a widespread lack of childcare facilities and full-time schools. The flip-side of this model was a large quantity of unpaid work provided by women within families, a low female employment rate and a concentration of women in the lower-paying and precarious sectors of the labour market (Angelo et al., 2006; Mairhuber, 2006). In 2005 the female employment rate in Austria was 62 per cent, up from 59 per cent in 1995 and about 50 per cent in 1975. However, calculated in full-time equivalents the female employment rate has actually decreased since the mid-1990s, which is (apart from Germany) highly exceptional in the European context (European Commission, 1998 and 2006). Its contribution-based social security system and its support for the 'male bread-winner model' makes Austria a country with a 'conservative welfare state regime' (Esping-Andersen, 1990, p. 27). Likewise, the Austrian 'care regime' is characterized by a lack of institutional support and high levels of informal work (Bettio and Plantenga, 2004). However, welfare state provisions have also been used to facilitate economic change. Unemployment is kept low by deliberate use of early retirement schemes, particularly for public sector workers (Unger, 2001). This has resulted in a comparatively low employment rate for older people and mounting debts in the social security system fuelling pressure for reform.

Despite its heterogeneity and the relative dependence on foreign capital and trade, the Austrian model of the post-war years generated extraordinarily high levels of growth and decades of full employment up until the mid-1980s. These exceptional growth rates during the post-war period stabilized the social partner system of comprehensive interest mediation. As a result of what Hwaletz (1990) has described as 'catching-up Fordism', GDP per capita reached the level of the richest Western European nations in the late 1970s and exceeded the Western European average in the early 1980s (Butschek, 2004, p. 103). Growth was stabilized by a mixture of demand-side deficit spending and hard-currency policy (through the linkage of the Austrian schilling to the German mark), also known as 'Austro-Keynesianism' (Unger, 1999). The model proved particularly viable for navigating the country through the economically rather stormy period of the 1970s and first half of the 1980s. It was not until the mid-1980s that Austria dipped into a severe economic recession accompanied by rapidly rising unemployment. By that time, however, the political consensus behind the post-war model had shifted, symbolized by the end of the social democratic majority government in 1983, opening up the way for restructuring.

Dynamics of change

As in other societies, Austria has experienced a number of secular changes over the last 30 years, including a shift from production to services, an increase in female employment and rising educational levels. The focus here is on the more specific changes and challenges to the Austrian model. By the mid-1980s the model had run into a severe crisis – both economically and politically. The maintenance of employment through the state-owned industries had resulted in mounting corporate debts weighing on the federal budget, while early retirement schemes and increasing unemployment had put growing pressure on the national social security system. Yet there were also external forces at play, including the change in international interest rate policy and the subsequent rise in interest rates in the early 1980s. Clearly, the maintenance of a national development path had become increasingly difficult. At the same time Austria, highly dependent on external trade with the EU, risked being sidelined through the 'single market' project which was launched in the mid-1980s. Consequently, the elites of both major political camps – conservatives and social democrats – opted for an opening-up of the economy and further integration into the European and international economy. In 1987 the social democrats and the people's party formed a 'grand coalition' which in the early 1990s decided to join the European Union. The accession to the EU in 1995 and the related external demand for adaptation in the model facilitated a number of subsequent changes – including stronger competition, especially in the traditionally sheltered sectors, budgetary and fiscal austerity, and the liberalization of public services.[2]

Privatization is the main driver of change in the Austrian model. This not only altered the role of the state but also led to further increases in the proportion of foreign-owned capital and to a transformation of the principles of corporate governance. In addition to inflowing FDI, the internationalization of the economy was further enhanced by outflowing FDI into neighbouring CEE countries, thus mitigating Austria's position of relative dependence in the international capitalist system. Privatization, internationalization and EU membership, together with an increasing acceptance of the neoliberal policy agenda, clearly had repercussions on the model of production, the system of vocational training, the labour market and welfare policies. In the following paragraphs we outline these changes before discussing the continuities within the Austrian model.

Privatization and shareholder value

One of the most dramatic departures from the post-war model was the privatization of state-owned industries and banks. In order to tackle the mounting deficit the 'grand coalition' decided to privatize some selected state-owned companies, yet initially only up to a share of 49 per cent. In 1993 the scope of the privatization project was significantly broadened with the adoption of a bill mandating the selling-off of the state's majority holdings in all industrial enterprises. In the late 1990s the government also sold some of its banking stocks (after a wave of mergers in the Austrian banking sector). However, until the end of the 1990s the state still kept a minority control stock in most companies. It was only the right-wing government that came to power in 2000 that decided to sell off the remaining stocks, arguing that the former state-owned companies were better off with private shareholders. Hence, a third wave of privatization began and reached a preliminary peak with the sale of the last asset in the prestigious and historically significant steel producer VOEST-Alpine in the summer of 2003 – some 15 years after the start of the privatization endeavour.

This privatization programme not only raised money to lower the federal budget deficit but also revived the Vienna stock market; enterprises of the state holding company (ÖIAG) accounted for 45 per cent of new issues in 1992–1995, and 30 per cent of the Vienna stock exchange turnover in 1995 was attributable to shares of privatized enterprises (Nowotny, 1996, p. 395). Following the state-owned industries and banks, public services next became a new source of privatization revenues. After parts of the federal electricity supplier Verbund AG and of Austrian Airlines were sold in the 1990s, Telekom Austria shares were publicly offered on the Vienna stock market in 2000, followed by Post AG shares in 2006. With the privatization of the postal services Austria has actually become a privatization-forerunner in the European Union. Apart from important material effects, the privatization campaign and the revival of the stock market also took on a crucial symbolic character: the fortification of the role of private capital and the diffusion of shareholder-value orientation.

A survey of the balance sheets of 324 joint stock corporations over the ten years up to 2008 shows that dividends have increased faster than output, with shareholders not only receiving back their investments but also another 71 per cent in profit, whereas personnel costs increased significantly more slowly than output (Kraus, 2003). The same survey also shows that the presence of foreign investors exacerbated these redistributions of revenue, with higher profits and yet lower personnel costs (Kraus, 2003). An outstanding example of growing shareholder-value orientation is the behaviour of the previously state- and now foreign-owned Bank Austria Creditanstalt. Despite record-high profits management abandoned the existing employee-friendly collective agreement for savings banks and instead switched to the cheaper agreement for commercial banks. Hence, although Austria has an exceptionally high coverage of collective agreements, the large sector-specific differences present a strong incentive for employers to switch agreements. This is particularly appealing in the newly liberalized and privatized industries and services, but also in those branches where employees have acquired particularly beneficial employment conditions, such as in parts of the banking sector.

Less visible consequences of privatization include a weakening of trade unions, reduced employment security and changing training policies. In manufacturing the unions had operated *de facto* closed shops in nationalized companies. Not only was union density high but works councils were also able to influence management decisions in large companies because of the direct access to the government they enjoyed. Privatization contributed to the decrease in union density and to a weakening and role change for works councils. While the nationalized sector had offered high levels of job security and had been used to keeping unemployment low in the 1970s and early 1980s, jobs became increasingly insecure in the 1990s. In public services mass layoffs occurred as companies were prepared for privatization (Atzmüller and Hermann, 2004). Paradigm shifts in company policies and increasing short-term profit orientation can also be seen in the decreasing willingness of firms to invest in training and to provide for apprenticeship positions. The consequences of these changes affected the national employment system as a whole: the nationalized sector had not only provided vocational training beyond its own need for skilled labour but had also had the effect of raising employment and working conditions in private companies in the same industries and regions.

Internationalization and shifting dependence

Although banks still play a vital role in the Austrian model, capital markets have become increasingly important in financing corporate investments over the last two decades. With the liberalization of capital markets the already high share of FDI has increased even further. Furthermore, EU accession in 1995 led to the abolition of the few remaining tariffs and quotas (causing, among other things, substantial job losses and a major restructuring in the Austrian food industry and logistics business). As a result the Austrian economy became even more firmly entrenched in the European and worldwide economy. Increasing internationalization also led to a higher rate of mergers and takeovers, which had been rather low during the post-war decades.

Apart from accession to the European Union, the most significant single development impacting on the Austrian economy in the last 20 years has been the lifting of the 'iron curtain' and the EU expansion into central and eastern Europe. This had two major effects: on the one hand some of the final assembly divisions of international companies were relocated to CEE countries, resulting in significant job losses (Beer, 2005); and on the other hand Austrian capital gained immensely from its geographical proximity to the emerging markets and from historical ties to the former communist countries. Although Austria was firmly integrated in Western European capitalism with the Marshall plan, trade with its eastern neighbours endured after 1945, giving Austria as a non-allied country a privileged position in East–West trade relations during the Cold War. In 1975 about 20 per cent of Austrian exports went to Eastern Europe, making Austria the country with the highest share of trade with the Council for Mutual Economic Assistance (COMECON) (Butschek, 2004, p. 128). Here, once more, historical legacy becomes apparent. Trade relations further intensified after 1989. While several international companies opened regional headquarters in and around Vienna, Austrian companies bought up existing corporations and created new subsidiaries in the new member states, with the result that Austria not only reached a balanced trade account but, since 2004, also became a net exporter of capital (Nationalbank, 2005; Aiginger et al., 2006, p. 17). Also the balance of foreign direct investments in Austria has shifted, with outbound FDI surpassing inbound FDI after 2000. While inbound FDI has doubled since the 1990s, outbound FDI has quadrupled,[3] with an increasing share destined for the new CEE member states. As a side-effect of this development some of the former state-owned companies have become important international players.

Since 2003 strong growth rates in the new member states have partly compensated for sluggish growth at home. Austrian firms took advantage of the cheap labour costs in the former communist countries by shifting certain activities eastward. This not only concerned low-skilled blue-collar jobs but also highly skilled white-collar work such as IT. Companies set up subsidiaries in neighbouring CEE countries partly as an alternative to shifting programming work to India (Flecker and Kirschenhofer, 2002). The case of Siemens is particularly telling in this respect: the German multinational set up a software company in Austria in the 1960s and 1970s to tap into Austria's comparatively cheap pool of high-skilled labour. By the 1990s the company had grown significantly to reach some 3000 employees. In the second half of the 1990s it established subsidiaries in Hungary, Slovakia, the Czech Republic and Croatia to make use of lower personnel costs in order to remain competitive. Within five years employment in the CEE countries reached half that in Austria and the number employed has continued to increase while the number in Austria has started to fall in recent years. The case is particularly illustrative of the international position of the Austrian economy: at the outset its dependent position vis-à-vis Germany led to the establishment of the Austrian subsidiary; in the 1990s the experience of such 'nearshoring' was used in the further move to CEE, sometimes referred to as 'India at the doorstep'.

However, as a result of the eastward expansion Austria clearly improved its position in the international division of production and labour. As Altzinger

(2006, p. 13) notes: 'The remarkable profitability of Austrian affiliates in CEE confirms the widely-held impression that the opening-up of CEE economies has helped to improve the overall competitiveness of the Austrian firms considerably. The strong increase of Austrian outward FDI due to the opening up of the transition economies produced ... many winners and losers .... Only the aggregated net effect seems to be rather favourable for the Austrian economy'. The banks in particular have repatriated substantial profits from their CEE operations for the benefit of their Austrian shareholders. Whether Austria will be able to maintain this position is far from clear. In the long run, low-cost competition and restrictive immigration policies in Austria may tempt international capital to shift their headquarters even further east.

Production: Between internal flexibility and outsourcing

The opening-up of the economy, increased competition, privatization and shareholder-value orientation are all increasing pressures on companies and establishments to innovate, to cut costs and to raise profitability. While changes in the production model were thus expected, the issue is whether the Austrian economy would follow a path-dependent evolution, capitalizing on its particular institutional strengths, or adopt international 'best practice', even when at odds with traditional country-specific organizational forms. The last two decades actually saw a series of innovations in production and work organization (Flecker, 1997), many of them related to the introduction of the workflow principle in production and, in some industries, to the establishment of team-working. Multinationals in the automobile industry were among the forerunners of change in traditional forms of production and work organization. A common aim was to increase functional flexibility based on the principle that workers, including skilled maintenance workers, should be able and willing to carry out different production jobs according to need. Case study evidence suggests that companies have been able to adopt new forms of production organization and human resource policies, outside of the traditions of Austrian manufacturing (Flecker, 1997). However, there has been no general trend towards post-Fordist work organization: traditional forms of division of labour persist and repetitive work is to be found in new plants as well. Survey data show that adverse working conditions associated with industrial work, far from diminishing as might have been expected, became even more widespread during the 1990s (Fasching, 2000).

Privatization and changes to corporate governance principles have had consequences for companies' investments in their skill base. Large companies, in particular in the former nationalized industry, abandoned the tradition of offering training opportunities beyond their needs. Cost-cutting even led to a shortage of apprenticeship positions, in particular in manufacturing, that, with a time-lag, resulted in a shortage of skilled labour. To overcome the shortage, in 2007 the government agreed to issue additional work permits for skilled workers from abroad. If this turns out to be a viable solution the move may further reduce the incentives for companies to invest in apprenticeships.

Company restructuring has also led to outsourcing in many industries, with many companies determined to concentrate on core activities and seeking to outsource activities or business functions that could be carried out more cheaply externally or placed with specialized companies that find it easier to keep up to date with new knowledge. A good example is the banking industry, which accelerated the outsourcing of IT because of the spread of Internet use and the fast-changing technology, and also outsourced facility management, cleaning, logistics, human resources and other business functions. A recent survey of works councils showed that over the last three years some 40 per cent of Austrian companies have outsourced support activities, 28 per cent outsourcing typical white-collar work and 26 per cent production work (Hornung et al., 2005). The outsourcing of low-skilled service sector jobs, together with the liberalization of shop opening hours (even if still rather strict in international terms), has fuelled the use of non-standard forms of employment.

Company restructuring has also been aimed at making systems more responsive to markets and competition. Examples of this internalization of markets include the creation of cost and profit centres and the increasing use of benchmarks to compare different production sites (Haipeter et al., 2005). Among white-collar workers, especially in knowledge-intensive services, project organization has become a widespread pattern of work organization. However, the results are not altogether positive as highly skilled workers have suffered from increasing pressure caused by ever-tighter project deadlines and growing customer demands. Overall, changes in production and work organization have led to a substantial increase in productivity and, as economists point out, in competitiveness. Yet they have also increased work-related strains, making it particularly difficult for older workers to stay in employment and thereby undermining labour market policy attempts to increase their employment rate.

Labour market flexibilization

The restructuring of the post-war economy had major effects on labour markets. Although the Austrian labour market has always been characterized by high segmentation, this tendency has been reinforced and expanded over the last three decades with outsourcing and the privatization of the former state-owned companies. As a result of growing competition, cost-cutting, 24-hour production and flexibilization of shop opening hours the number of part-time jobs has increased more than three times since the mid-1970s and has more than doubled since 1990. The share of part-time employees in total employment has increased from 6 per cent in 1974 to more than 20 per cent in 2005 (40 per cent of female employment). This increase can also be explained by labour supply: the gender contract in Austria and the legacy of the conservative 'male breadwinner model' make part-time employment the only feasible possibility for many women with care obligations. The increase in female employment since the mid-1990s can almost entirely be ascribed to the rise in part-time employment, while the number of women working in full-time jobs has stagnated or even slightly fallen. Yet part-time employees suffer from a number of disadvantages. Part-time jobs are concentrated in certain sectors associated with female work, with the result that part-time workers on average earn less than full-timers. Moreover, workers on marginal part-time hours, which accounts for 6 per cent of total employment, are not necessarily included in the mandatory social insurance system. The bulk of part-time work in Austria is concentrated in a few sectors, including wholesale and retail trade and manufacturing (Angelo et al., 2006). While in retail trade a large proportion of employees works very short hours, in industrial companies women often work 35 hours, which in other countries would result in a full-time contract. Another major form of atypical work is self-employment: overall self-employment still accounts for somewhat less than 10 per cent of employment but in certain sectors new forms of self-employment, such as dependent self-employment or freelancing, are on the increase. In parts of the call centre industry, for example, quasi-freelancers represent a majority of the workforce. Further examples of non-standard work include fixed-term contracts and agency work which are both still relatively marginal but have increased rapidly since 1990.

Interestingly, the flexibilization of labour markets was not so much the result of active deregulation. Instead changes in employment legislation, including the introduction of a special category of freelancers for whom employers have to pay social security contributions (with the exception of unemployment insurance), were passive reactions to shifting employer practices and primarily driven by the need to allocate additional funds for the social security system. The process of flexibilization and in particular the increase in self- and marginal employment can therefore also be described as a flight from employment and social security legislation (Tálos, 1999, p. 227). Similarly, a new law attempted to regulate rather than promote the use of agency workers. In both cases, however, the new statutory regulations did not prevent employers from using even more atypical workers. Recent Austrian labour market experiences hence show that it is not enough to focus on institutions; one has also to take into account changes in company practices that take place regardless or because of official regulations.

The flexibilization of labour markets was accompanied by a shift from 'passive' to 'active' labour market policies. While in the post-war decades resources from unemployment insurance were mainly used to compensate for lost income, since the second half of the 1980s resources are increasingly deployed to reintegrate workers into labour markets through various retraining schemes and through financial support for employers. Since

1996 the number of unemployed workers undergoing training courses has increased continuously and in 2003 accounted for 17 per cent of those officially registered as unemployed (Zauner, 2006, p. 209). Yet, in contrast to the Nordic countries, 'activation' expenses per unemployed have actually decreased between 2000 and 2005 (Fink, 2006, p. 177). This points to a strong 'workfarist' touch in the reforms, especially as the shift from 'passive' to 'active' labour market policies was linked to a lowering of benefits and to a restriction of entitlement rights – including the repeated widening of the criteria used to assess whether a job offer is reasonable and must therefore be taken up by a person on unemployment benefits (Dimmel, 2000; Fink, 2006, p. 177). However, with regard to the number of long-term unemployed workers, the effects of the 'activation policies' have been moderate at best (Bock-Schappelwein, 2005).

Austerity policy and welfare state restructuring

Cutbacks in benefits and restrictions on entitlement rights were justified with rising costs, caused not least by the still looming unemployment problem (even if unemployment remained low by European standards). Since the late 1980s the government has struggled to reduce the federal budget deficit by delivering repeated austerity packages – indeed the effects were not always those that were hoped for. Since the mid-1990s austerity policy has increasingly been justified by the accession to the European Union and subsequently to the EU Economic and Monetary Union (EMU). However, by declaring a balanced budget – publicly promoted as 'zero deficit' – to be the most important objective of budgetary policy, the right-wing coalition that came into power in 2000 took the austerity policy to a new level (Marterbauer, 2006). One of the main focuses of the reforms has been the pension system. While early retirement schemes had initially been used to lower the unemployment rate of older workers, since the late 1980s there have been numerous and mainly restrictive pension reforms that have reduced benefit levels and limited access to early retirement.

The last comprehensive pension reform took place in 2003. As losses for pensioners would have amounted to 30 per cent of the previous benefits, hundreds of thousands of workers went onto the streets to protest against the proposed changes. The result was a less dramatic but still far-reaching reform (Obinger and Tálos, 2006). One major objective of the pension reform was to increase the employment rate of older workers. While in this respect the effects were moderate at best – Austria has still one of the lowest employment rates of older workers in Europe – the reform clearly succeeded in encouraging workers to invest in an additional private pension scheme for which the government provided strong financial incentives. The growing size of private pension funds is linked to the revitalization of the stock market which has become an increasingly important source of finance for corporate debt (although in absolute terms traditional bank credits are still much more important). Hence, welfare state reform appears connected to the liberalization of financial markets and to the reinforcement of the power of private capital over the lives of ordinary citizens. Among the main 'losers' of the reform are women on lower wages and discontinuous careers for whom it is now even more difficult to achieve an adequate level of income after retirement (Mairhuber, 2006).

Successive tax reforms aimed at reducing the tax burden on high-income earners and private investors have pushed in the same direction. Contrary to the previous tendency to use taxes in part for redistribution, corporate taxes have been lowered significantly in recent years and Austria is now among those with the lowest corporate tax rates in Europe. In addition, the government introduced a unique tax model in Europe allowing groups of companies to offset losses made outside Austria against domestic profits. According to Eurostat (2003, p. 97) Austria experienced one of the sharpest drops in implicit tax rates on capital income in the European Union between 1995 and 2001, surpassed only by Sweden. Hence, some authors have asserted a shift in economic policy from 'Austro-Keynesianism' to 'Austro-neoliberalism' (Unger, 1999). The Austrian state has clearly abandoned its role as a creator of employment and instead is putting increasing effort into the creation of an investor-friendly environment in order to attract international capital. The question is how sustainable this policy is in the face of the fierce competition from the new EU member states that have even lower corporate tax rates.

Dynamics of continuity

In 2003 the protest against the pension reform and a strike of railway workers against the liberalization of the railway sector led to an unprecedented increase in strike activity in Austria's post-war history. With around 800,000 participants and more than ten million hours lost, strike activity recorded in one year exceeded the sum of the previous ten years (Tálos, 2005a). At the same time, under the right-wing government of 2000–2006, 'social partnership' suffered as labour representatives were continuously sidelined in parliamentary decision-making processes – the 'social partners' influence on social and economic policy has changed from being the rule to being the exception' (Tálos, 2005a). Under the new grand coalition government social partnership has partly been restored as the government repeatedly called on the employers' association and the unions to develop major policy initiatives and even to prepare legislation.

Even greater continuity exists at the level of collective bargaining, where the social partners have been highly successful in avoiding industrial conflict. In fact, and against the trend in other countries including neighbouring Germany, the sector-wide bargaining system has been surprisingly stable (Flecker and Hermann, 2005). The system benefits from favourable statutory regulations that include the mandatory membership of private employers in the Chamber of Economy, which makes it difficult for private companies to escape existing collective agreements. As a result the Austrian minimum wage system, which is based on collectively agreed sector-specific minimum wages, is still relatively effective, while the trade unions oppose the introduction of a statutory minimum wage (Hermann, 2006). Furthermore, in order to make use of the leeway for flexibilization provided by the 1997 working time law, employers have to reach agreement with unions on the sector level. Flexibilization as a result has taken place in a rather coordinated way (Traxler, 1998).

The stability and effectiveness of the bargaining system can also be seen in the fact that the social partners even reached new agreements in the few remaining sectors that have so far not been covered by a collective agreement. Apart from social services and agency workers (who receive basically the same pay and working time conditions as permanent staff in the same workplace), this includes also the IT sector which many observers believed to be notoriously anti-union (Hermann and Flecker, 2006). This, again, distinguishes Austria from other countries including Germany. The stability of the bargaining system does not mean that there are no conflicts: apart from the traditionally rather moderate wage demands, unions had to make major concessions, especially with respect to working time flexibility, in order to reach new agreements (Hermann and Flecker, 2006). Furthermore, enterprises exert strong pressure to shift the bargaining arena from the sector to the company level. According to recent employers' proposals, not only working hours but also wage increases above compensation for increases in inflation should be negotiated between management and staff representatives. And while the sector-level bargaining system is still relatively stable and effective, the number of elected work councils has decreased over recent decades, resulting in a growing 'representation gap' at the company level (Flecker et al., 2006). Another tendency towards erosion of the bargaining system is evident in some of the newly liberalized and privatized public services. Contrary to the general trend, increasing fragmentation of the bargaining system can be observed, with several collective agreements applying to similar categories of staff in the same companies and with a growing number of – for Austria – highly unusual company-level collective agreements (Atzmüller and Hermann, 2004; Flecker and Hermann, 2005, pp. 45–50). Overall, however, Austria still belongs to the category of 'negotiated capitalisms', although given that the social-democratic dominated trade union movement has accepted and defended successive 'austerity packages' under the 'grand coalition' of the 1980s and 1990s, the focus has shifted from 'demand-side' to 'supply-side corporatism' (Traxler, 1993). This seems to be an illustrative example of how an institution that has hardly been altered in a formal sense has taken on a radically new meaning.

Another persistent feature of the Austrian model is its heterogeneity. Despite the far-reaching structural changes there are still a number of large internationally significant and technologically advanced companies that provide their employees with comparably decent employment conditions. There is also a large sector with small and medium-sized enterprises that have successfully specialized in high-quality niche production. These companies employ a comparatively highly skilled workforce and are willing to invest in human resources by providing apprenticeship positions. However, Austria also still has substantial areas that provide for less favourable employment conditions. Tourism is still very important and while the clothing industry almost disappeared due to low-cost competition from eastern Europe and Asia, the retail sector has gained in importance in recent years and is one of the major sources of part-time and marginal employment.

Consequently, as a reflection of its heterogeneity and its highly segmented labour markets, Austria is still characterized by a high level of inequality. In fact, inequality and polarization have even increased as a result of economic restructuring, labour market flexibilization and successive welfare state reforms (Guger and Marterbauer, 2004). This is also true of the gender wage-gap which has widened again since the mid-1990s. However, even though atypical employment has increased over recent decades as a result of a 'silent deregulation' of labour markets, the standard employment relationship still prevails as the most popular form of employment. In some cases, such as parts of the call centre business, campaigning by the trade unions and pressure from social security institutions has even caused some customer service providers who typically employ quasi-freelancers to switch to standard employment relationships.

Furthermore, and despite decades of struggle by social-democratic and liberal feminists, the conservative Austrian welfare system still favours a family model in which one family member, usually the mother, reduces paid work to take care of children or other dependent family members. A widely welcomed long-term care benefit introduced in the mid-1990s had exactly this effect because it was provided in cash rather than in services. The money created a strong incentive for women to stay at home and take care of disabled parents while the expansion of elderly-care services would have created new opportunities for paid employment (Hammer and Österle, 2003). In the same way the introduction of a three-year childcare allowance in 2002, benefiting all parents regardless of their employment status, has created increasing problems for women to return to work after their 'child break'. The period of benefit entitlement was extended to 36 months after the birth of the child (30 months if only one of the two parents applies for the benefit) but the right to return to the job was still limited to 24 months. Not surprisingly, after 30 months the share of women in dependent employment has fallen by 7 per cent compared to the previous regulation and the ratio of unemployed women has risen by almost 40 per cent (Mairhuber,

2006, p. 31). While, as a result, the unequal distribution of paid and unpaid work has hardly changed over the last three decades, the dominant family model has changed from the 'male breadwinner' to the 'one-and-a-half earner model' with an increasing number of single-parent mothers. And although the number of jobs in health and education has increased quite substantially since the mid-1990s, at least in the care sector the number of formal jobs still lags behind those existing in Sweden and other Nordic countries. The Swedish elderly-care sector, for example, employs more than eight times more workers than the Austrian equivalent, although total population in Sweden is only slightly higher than in Austria.

Conclusions

Looking at the development of Austria over the 20 years since 1988 we can clearly see that the Austrian model has lost a number of the key features that were characteristic of the model of the post-war decades. Above all this includes the high share of public ownership in industries and banks, but also extensive market regulations that sheltered businesses from international competition. Instead, much of what happened during the last two decades has been intended to create an environment that is attractive to foreign capital and to make native capital more competitive. Subsequent measures included the liberalization of trade and capital flows and the reduction of corporate taxes. Lower tax revenues aggravated budgetary problems and demands for budgetary austerity and cuts in the welfare system. While previously economic and social policy was directed towards sharing the gains from the post-war boom, and in the 1970s increasingly also towards stimulating growth through public investments and progressive fiscal and interest policies, in the 1990s a great deal has become subordinated to the overall objective of improving profitability. Many of the changes were facilitated through Austria's accession to the EU in the mid-1990s, which in turn led to a further Europeanization and internationalization of the Austrian economy. On the other hand Austrian capital also profited immensely from the EU's eastward enlargement. Yet while profitability soared as a result of outsourcing, increasing productivity, shareholder-value orientation and eastward expansion, unemployment remained high compared to the post-war decades. In terms of economic policy – though not relating to the institutional setting – Austria has come much closer to what may be called a neoliberal mainstream. As *The Wall Street Journal* noted on the eve of the last Austrian general election, thanks to 'free-market' reform and tax cuts 'the once sleepy, corporatist economy has changed into one of Europe's most competitive.'[4]

What is remarkable, however, is that this shift took place slowly, developing over several decades: the first 'austerity package' was introduced in 1987 while the last major welfare cuts took place in 2003. In a similar way the privatization process started in the late 1980s but was still not completed by 2007 (although the new 'grand coalition' seems to have put a halt on it after massive privatizations by the previous government). Hence, as Unger asserts with respect to changes in economic policy, the 'departure ... took place so slowly that the actors themselves often did not realize the change in paradigm' (Unger, 1999, p. 174). Yet although changes have been slow, the results are nevertheless impressive: while the share of wages as a proportion of GDP increased from 63 to 80 per cent from the mid-1950s to the end of the 1970s, it has since fallen back to 70 per cent. Conversely, profits and other non-wage incomes, especially from financial assets, have increased substantially in the 30 year-period since the late 1970s (Guger and Marterbauer, 2004, pp. 4 ff.).

From an institutional perspective things look different, however. What we see here is the prevalence of institutional continuity. In some cases institutions have been reformed in order to continue to fulfil certain functions. In Austria this is certainly true for the conservative welfare state, which despite certain reforms continues to disadvantage women, and the collective bargaining system that has been extended to new sectors in the economy. In other cases institutions have not changed, yet they have lost part of their regulatory capacity. Austrian labour market regulation and the flight from employment legislation is a case in point. Streeck and Thelen (2005) have found similar developments in other countries. Following their typology of institutional change (Streeck and Thelen, 2005, p. 31) the adaptation of the Austrian conservative welfare state can be described as 'layering', while some tendencies of hollowing out the Austrian labour market regulation qualifies for what the authors call 'drift'. A third major form of institutional change is what they have termed 'conversion'. Here old institutions are redeployed to new purposes (Streeck and Thelen, 2005). This seems to be a particularly apt description of the development of Austrian social partnership. Although social partnership continued to have a major impact on Austrian economic and social policies – at least until the installation of a right-wing government in 2000 – it was increasingly used to defend the adoption of unsocial policies, which was described as a shift from 'demand-side' to 'supply-side corporatism' (Traxler, 1993). Both the employer organizations and the trade unions supported the accession to the EU and the subsequent introduction of austerity measures – at least until the 2003 pension reform that was openly rejected by the unions. Hence, political and social change in Austria was actually facilitated through institutional continuity. On the other hand the mass demonstrations and the subsequent rejection of the pension reform, as well as the successful resistance against repeated attempts to flexibilize employment legislation, are proof that the unions still have the ability to defend their primary interests.

While the paradigm shift towards neoliberal economic policies occurred under a remarkable stability in institutions, interest groups and political actors seem to have prevented Austria from adopting a fully-fledged liberal model. But rather than classifying the country case according to the extreme types of the variety of capitalism models, we should try to account for the changes on the grey scales between them (Höpner, 2003). In this respect we can clearly see an expansion of the market both for capital, corporate control and for products and services. However, this expansion of the market is not accompanied by a far-reaching deregulation but rather by a modest and 'organized' flexibilization of the labour market. As a result of path dependencies and the complex dialectics of institutions and political struggles, Austria, in spite of some rapprochement with the model of liberal market economies, remains a coordinated market economy with a fairly regulated national employment model.

Notes

1. Public ownership in the nationalized industries and banks is based on two nationalization acts adopted in 1946 and 1947. At the time there was a broad political consensus in favour of nationalization, especially of German property which otherwise was threatened with confiscation by the four allied powers as compensation for the war expenses.
2. As one of the first measures after accession the government adopted two consecutive austerity packages in 1995 and 1996.
3. Due to considerable yearly fluctuations, yearly averages of 1992–1998 are compared with yearly averages for 2000–2006. Data were taken from the Austrian National Bank's database accessible through its website (www.oenb.at).
4. *The Wall Street Journal*, 29 October 2006, p. 10.

References

Aiginger, K. (1999), 'The Privatisation Experiment', *Austrian Economic Quarterly* 4 (1999): 261–70.
Aiginger, K., Tichy, G., and Walterskirchen, E. (eds) (2006), *WIFO-Weißbuch: Mehr Beschäftigung durch Wachstum auf Basis von Innovation und Qualifikation*, Vienna: Austrian Institute of Economic Research.
Albert, M. (1993), *Capitalism vs. Capitalism. How America's Obsession with Individual Achievement and Short-term Profit Has led it To the Brink of Collapse*, New York: Four Walls Eight Windows.
Albo, G. (2005), 'Contesting the "New Capitalism"', pp. 63–82 in D. Coates (ed.), *Varieties of Capitalism, Varieties of Approaches*, Houndmills, Basingstoke, Hampshire und NY: Palgrave Macmillan.
Altzinger, Wilfried (2006), 'Distributional Implications of Austrian FDI in CEE', Paper presented at the 12th workshop on Alternative Economic Policy in Europe of the EuroMemorandum Group, Brussels: 29 September–1 October 2006.
Amable, B. (2005), *Les cinq capitalisms. Diversité des systèms économiques et sociax dans la mondialisation*, Paris: Éditions du Seuil.
Angelo, S., Moritz, I., Pirklbauer, S., Schlager, C., Woltran, I. and Zuckerstätter, S. (2006), *AK Frauenbericht*, Vienna: Chamber of Labour.

Atzmüller, R. and Hermann, C. (2004), 'Veränderung öffentlicher Beschäftigung im Prozess der Liberalisierung und Privatisierung', *Österreichische Zeitschrift für Soziologie* 29 (4): 30–48.

Auer, P. (2000), *Employment Revival in Europe. Labour Market Success in Austria, Denmark, Ireland and the Netherlands*, Geneva: International Labour Office.

Beer, E. (2005), 'Der Wirtschaftsstandort Österreich im Wettbewerb', pp. 87–93 in Arbeiterkammer Wien (ed.), *Ein Jahr EU-Erweiterung – Trends und Fakten*, Vienna: Chamber of Labour.

Beer, E., Ederer, B., Goldmann, W. et al. (1991), *Wem gehört Österreichs Wirtschaft wirklich?*, Vienna: Orac Verlag.

Bettio, F. and Plantenga, J. (2004), 'Comparing Care Regimes in Europe', *Feminist Economics* 10 (1): 85–113.

Bock-Schappelwein, J. (2005), 'Entwicklung und Formen der Arbeitslosigkeit in Österreich seit 1990', *WIFO Monatsberichte* 7 (2005): 499–510.

Bosch, G., Haipeter, T., Latniak, E. et al. (2005), *Changes in the System or Change of the System? The National Employment Model of Germany*, DYNAMO mimeo. From www.dynamoproject.eu

Butschek, F. (2004), *Vom Staatsvertrag zur EU. Österreichische Wirtschaftsgeschichte von 1955 bis zur Gegenwart*, Vienna: Böhlau Verlag.

Coates, D. (2000), *Models of Capitalism. Growth and Stagnation in the Modern Era*, Cambridge: Polity Press.

Dimmel, N. (2000), *Gemeinnützige Zwangsarbeit – Arbeitsmarktintegration zwischen Arbeitspflicht und innovativen Beschäftigungsmaßnahmen*, Vienna: Chamber of Labour.

Esping-Andersen, G. (1990), *The Three Worlds of Welfare Capitalism*, Princeton: Princeton University Press.

European Commission (1998), *Employment in Europe 1998*, Luxembourg: Office for Official Publications of the European Communities.

European Commission (2006), *Employment in Europe 2006*, Luxembourg: Office for Official Publications of the European Communities.

Eurostat (2003), *Structure of Taxation Systems in the European Union 1995–2001*, Luxembourg: Eurostat.

Fasching, M. (2000), 'Arbeitsbedingungen – Hauptergebnisse', *Statistische Nachrichten* 55 11 (2000): 866–75.

Fink, M. (2006), 'Zwischen "Beschäftigungsrekord" und "Rekordarbeitslosigkeit": Arbeitsmarkt und Arbeitsmarktpolitik unter Schwarz-Blau/Orange', pp. 170–87 in E. Tálos (ed.), *Schwarz-Blau. Eine Bilanz 'Neu-Regierens'*, Vienna and Münster: LIT Verlag.

Flecker, J. (1997), 'Zwischen Anpassung und Abkopplung. Arbeitsgestaltung und gesellschaftliche Institutionen im internationalen Standortwettbewerb', pp. 13–42 in J. Flecker (ed.), *Jenseits der Sachzwanglogik. Arbeitspolitik zwischen Anpassungsdruck und Gestaltungschancen*, Berlin: Edition Sigma.

Flecker, J. and Hermann, C. (2005), 'Geliehene Stabilität. Zur Funktionsfähigkeit des dualen Systems der Arbeitsbeziehungen in Österreich', pp. 37–56 in F. Karlhofer and E. Tálos (eds), *Sozialpartnerschaft. Österreichische und Europäische Perspektiven*, Münster and Vienna: LIT-Verlag.

Flecker, J. and Kirschenhofer, S. (2002), *Jobs on the Move: European Case Studies in Relocating Work*, Brighton: Institute for Employment Studies.

Flecker, J., Hermann, C. and Schmid, A. (2006), 'Betriebe ohne Betriebsrat in Österreich – wachsende Lücken und alternative Vertretungsstrategien', pp. 291–308 in I. Artus, S. Böhm, S. Lücking and R. Trinczek (eds), *Betriebe ohne Betriebsrat. Informelle Interessenvertretung in Unternehmen*, Frankfurt a. M.: Campus Verlag.

Guger, A. (1993), 'Lohnpolitik und Sozialpartnerschaft', pp. 227–42 in E. Tálos (ed.), *Sozialpartnerschaft. Kontinuität und Wandel eines Modells*, Vienna: Verlag für Gesellschaftskritik.

Guger, A. and Marterbauer, M. (2004), *Die langfristige Entwicklung der Einkommensverteilung in Österreich*, Vienna: Austrian Institute of Economic Research.

Guger, A. and Marterbauer, M. (2007), *Langfristige Tendenzen der Einkommensverteilung in Österreich – ein Update*, Vienna: Austrian Institute of Economic Research.

Haipeter, T., Lehndorff, S. and Voss-Dahm, D. (2005), *Internalising the Market within Organisations – Towards an Erosion of National Employment Models?*, DYNAMO mimeo. From www.dynamoproject.eu

Hall, P. and Soskice, D. (2001), 'An Introduction to Varieties of Capitalism', pp. 1–70 in P. Hall and D. Soskice (eds), *Varieties of Capitalism. The Institutional Foundations of Comparative Advantage*, Oxford: Oxford University Press.

Hammer, E. and Österle A. (2003), 'Welfare State Policy and Informal Long-Term Care Giving in Austria: Old Gender Divisions and New Stratification Processes', *Journal of Social Policy* 32 (2003): 37–53.

Hermann, C. (2006), 'Mindestlöhne in Österreich', pp. 246–68 in T. Schulten, R. Bispinck and C. Schäfer (eds), *Mindestlöhne in Europa*, Hamburg: VSA Verlag.

Hermann, C. and Flecker, J. (2006), 'Neue Flächentarifverträge in neuen Branchen – Erfahrungen aus Österreich', *WSI Mitteilungen* 7 (2006): 396–402.

Höpner, M. (2003), *Wer beherrscht die Unternehmen? Shareholder Value, Managerherrschaft und Mitbestimmung in Deutschland*, Frankfurt a. M.: Campus Verlag.

Hornung, A., Leitsmüller, H. and Samsinger, R. (2005), *Die Auswirkungen von Umstrukturierungen auf Beschäftigte und Mitbestimmung*, Vienna: Chamber of Labour.

Hwaletz, O. (1990), *Über den Prozess von Akkumulation und Kapitalverwertung in Österreich*, Vienna: Böhlau Verlag.

Katzenstein, P. J. (1985), *Small States in World Markets. Industrial Policy in Europe*, Ithaca: Cornell University Press.

Kraus, A. (2003), *Von Arbeit zu Kapital. Umverteilung in Industrie und Handel*, Vienna: Chamber of Labour.

Lehmbruch, G. and Schmitter, P. (1982), *Patterns of Corporatist Policy-Making*, London: Sage Publications.

Mairhuber, I. (2000), *Die Regulierung des Geschlechterverhältnisses im Sozialstaat Österreich*, Frankfurt a. M.: Peter Lang Verlag.

Mairhuber, I. (2006), *Regulierung und Absicherung von Übergängen im weiblichen und männlichen Lebenserwerbsverlauf in Österreich*, FORBA-Schriftenreihe 4/2006.

Marterbauer, M. (2006), 'Interessenpolitik und ihre Grenzen – sechs Jahre rechtsliberale Wirtschaftpolitik in Österreich', *Interventionen* 3 (1): 51–8.

Mayer, K. (2003), 'Running After the International Trend: Keynesian Power Balances and the Sustainable Repulsion of the Innovation Paradigm in Austria', pp. 157–88 in P. Biegelbauer and S. Borrás, (eds), *Innovation Policies in Europe and the US: The New Agenda*, Aldershot: Ashgate Publishing.

Nationalbank (2005), *Finanzmarkt Stabilitätsbericht*, Vienna: Austrian National Bank.

Nowotny, E. (1996), 'Privatisation in Austria. Causes and Consequences', *Annals of Public and Cooperative Economics* 67 (3): 387–401.

Obinger, H. and Tálos, E. (2006), Sozialstaat Österreich zwischen Kontinuität und Umbau. Bilanz der ÖVP/FPÖ/BZÖ-Koalition, Wiesbaden: Verlag für Sozialwissenschaften.

Rowthorn, R. (1992), 'Centralisation, Employment and Wage Dispersion', *The Economic Journal* 102 (1992): 506–23.

Streeck, W. (1991), 'On the Institutional Conditions of Diversified Quality Production', pp. 21–61 in E. Matzner and W. Streeck (eds), *Beyond Keynesianism. The Socio-Economics of Production and Employment*, London: Edward Elgar.

Streeck, W. and Thelen, K. (2005), 'Introduction: Institutional Change in Advanced Political Economies', pp. 1–39 in W. Streeck and K. Thelen (eds), *Beyond Continuity: Institutional Change in Advanced Political Economies*, Oxford: Oxford University Press.

Tálos, E. (1999), 'Atypische Beschäftigung in Österreich', pp. 252–84 in E. Tálos (ed.), *Atypische Beschäftigung. Internationale Trends und sozialstaatliche Regelungen*, Vienna: Manz Verlag.

Tálos, E. (2005a), 'Vom Vorzeige- zum Auslaufmodell? Österreichs Sozialpartnerschaft 1945 bis 2005', pp. 185–216 in F. Karlhofer and E. Tálos (eds), *Sozialpartnerschaft. Österreichische und Europäische Perspektiven*, Münster and Vienna: LIT-Verlag.

Tálos, E. (2005b), *Vom Siegeszug zum Rückzug. Sozialstaat Österreich 1945–2005*, Innsbruck: Studienverlag.

Traxler, F. (1993), 'Vom Nachfrage- zum Angebotskorporatismus', pp. 103–16 in E. Tálos (ed.), *Sozialpartnerschaft – Kontinuität und Wandel eines Modells*, Vienna: Verlag für Gesellschaftskritik.

Traxler, F. (1998), 'Austria: Still the Country of Corporatism', pp. 239–61 in A. Ferner and R. Hyman (eds), *Changing Industrial Relations in Europe*, Oxford: Blackwell.

Traxler, F. and Behrens, M. (2002), *Collective Bargaining Coverage and Extension Procedures*, European Industrial Relations Obeservatory. www.eiro.eurofound.ie/2002/12/study/tn0212102s.html

Unger, B. (1999), 'Österreichs Wirtschaftspolitik: Vom Austro-Keynesianismus zum Austro-Neoliberalismus?', pp. 165–90 in F. Karlhofer and E. Tálos, (eds), *Zukunft der Sozialpartnerschaft – Veränderungsdynamik und Reformbedarf*, Vienna: Signum Verlag.

Unger, B. (2001), 'Österreichs Beschäftigungs- und Sozialpolitik von 1970 bis 2000', *Zeitschrift für Sozialreform* 47 (4): 340–61.

Zauner, H. (2006), 'Entwicklungen und Maßnahmen der aktiven Arbeitsmarktpolitik in Österreich', pp. 204–16 in C. Stelzer-Orthofer (ed.), *Arbeitsmarktpolitik im Aufbruch*, Vienna: Verlag Mandelbaum.

6
Crisis of the Post-Transition Hungarian Model

László Neumann and András Tóth

Introduction

It is a common wisdom to say that Hungary has faced two historical challenges since 1988: first, the so-called 'regime change' which took place in 1989/90 when the state socialist system collapsed and gave way to democratization and a market economy based on private ownership; and second, joining the European Union which formally took place on 1 May 2004. The former involved far-reaching changes in politics, economy and society, and at the same time represented a real break with the past in many fields. The latter on the other hand involved a relatively smooth transition with incremental changes. No wonder that a huge body of literature across political science, economics, sociology, anthropology and even psychology deals with the 'post-communist' transition/transformation (the choice between the two terms is also addressed by many writings). In contrast, the enlargement of the EU has been addressed by highly specialized papers only, characterized by a limited focus, mainly on administrative, legal, economic and technical aspects.

Despite the huge differences between these two major changes in recent Hungarian history, what they seem to have in common is a belief that they constitute a sort of 'catching up with the developed world', a belief prevalent both in 1989/90 and around 2004 in Hungary. This dominated not only the politicians' speeches and the public discourse but the whole population also nurtured a sort of expectation of economic advancement and increasing wealth. This is quite understandable in a relatively poor country, which during the 40 years of communism became a backward part of Europe, and whose historical identity of being on the periphery of Europe also dates back to the Middle Ages. That is why economic growth and catching up with the core European countries have become such focal issues, just as in the majority of developing countries. This explains why the underlying concept of this paper is to describe the country's recent economic history in terms of 'development paths' and to present the different policies that underpinned various development strategies.

Since 1988 Hungary has managed to break with the state-socialist system and develop a market economy which is well integrated in European and global markets. This transformation required both enormous institution-building efforts and the restructuring of the inherited backward industries. Institutional reforms began in the mid-1980s and then accelerated with the political changes. The main driving force of the changes was fast and far-reaching privatization and the attraction of foreign direct investment (FDI). Contrary to initial expectations the 'transition recession' was deeper in economic terms than the Great Depression: it involved a 20 per cent drop in gross domestic product (GDP) and an even sharper decline in industrial output and investments as well as the collapse of a large share of productive capacities. The 'social cost' was also enormous: real wages dropped by almost 20 per cent and unemployment rose dramatically due to a mass-scale loss of jobs. The employment rate has been persistently low ever since as a result of various forms of withdrawal from the labour market. Popular support for market reforms could have been maintained by preserving the provisions of the welfare state and by introducing – from the outset – generous unemployment insurance and various active labour market policies (ALMP). From the mid-1990s, however, the welfare regime underwent piecemeal reforms; not only were criteria for unemployment benefit gradually tightened, but changes were made several times to pension systems, family allowances and welfare transfers in order to alleviate poverty. By the end of the 1990s Hungary had recovered from the 'transition recession', due mainly to FDI-driven restructuring and stringent macro-economic policy. Today this post-socialist model is facing new challenges: decreasing FDI inflow coupled with fiscal problems stemming from subsequent governments' neo-Keynesian style policies between 2000 and 2006 have resulted in major budget imbalances and finally in the adoption of new austerity measures and reform initiatives affecting mainly the public sector and welfare provisions.

Given the abundant 'transitology' literature, what this paper seeks to add to the existing knowledge on post-communist countries is partly information about the specificities of Hungarian development, and partly understanding of the dynamics of change by tracing the series of economic, societal and policy changes over the whole period since the transition began.

Transition from state socialism to democracy and an open market economy

From the mid-1960s the planned economy underwent half-hearted economic reforms to enhance efficiency and to increase trade with the world on the other side of the Iron Curtain. Hungary achieved substantial progress in establishing a basic legal and institutional framework for a market economy by the late 1980s. Companies had developed a number of contacts with Western markets and small private businesses were burgeoning. Thus, the initial conditions for the transition to a market economy were arguably more favourable than in other Eastern European countries, save the even more open Slovenia.

Following the political changes of 1990 the country faced a severe economic crisis related to the collapse of the state-socialist economic model and the former Soviet bloc's Council for Mutual Economic Assistance (COMECON) market, as well as the global recession of 1991–2004. Also, the heavy debt service cost compelled successive governments to implement a rapid privatization programme and to open up the country to inward foreign direct investment, which proved to be the key condition for industrial renewal in Hungary.

As a result of deep economic restructuring, the direction and composition of foreign trade has changed dramatically. In the 1980s Hungary exported mainly low-tech manufacturing goods to the COMECON market, especially to the Soviet Union. Nowadays, Hungary's major trade partners are EU member states, with about 76 per cent of Hungarian exports directed towards the EU and 65 per cent towards older (EU-15) member states. Hungary's major partner is Germany, which alone accounts for 30 per cent of Hungarian exports. Russia, the former main trading partner, only receives 1.9 per cent of Hungarian exports. The first half of the 1990s was characterized by the survival of the stop-go cycles 'inherited' from the 1980s, namely looser and stricter economic policies alternating with each other. First, Hungary fell into a deep recession within the first years of the transition, with GDP contracting by 17 per cent between 1990 and 1993. The early years also saw a period of high inflation, reaching a rate of 22.5 per cent in 1993. In March 1995 the government introduced a stabilization programme aimed at avoiding a Mexican-style financial meltdown and putting the economy on a sustainable path of low-inflationary growth. The austerity programme (the 'Bokros-package' named after the finance minister of the era) included currency devaluation, a new, predictable exchange-rate mechanism, a tight wage policy in the public sector and fiscal measures to enhance revenues (through temporary extra taxation on imports) and cuts in expenditure, including some welfare provisions. Real gross wages dropped by 8.9 per cent in 1995 and 2.6 per cent in 1996. The contraction in aggregate demand that followed this fiscal tightening resulted in slow GDP growth in 1995 and 1996. The implementation of the austerity measures, however, produced successful stabilization and by 1998 Hungary had paid back the inherited foreign debts. Sustained economic growth began from 1997 onwards. It is important to note that Hungary is still a relatively poor country. In 2004 the per capita GDP measured by parity effective demand was 56.2 per cent of the EU-15 average. It is also worth noting that the relatively rapid increase in GDP and real wages was accompanied by a relatively slow growth of employment of not more than 0.2 to 0.5 per cent annually.

The year 2000 was the turning point in macroeconomic policy. In the context of increasing dominance of populist political discourse in Hungary, the then governing right-wing government gave up the neo-conservative economic policy pursued since 1995. The new neo-Keynesian style policy facilitated growth through government spending and government measures increasing real wages. In 2000 the conservative government led by the Alliance of Young Democrats – Hungarian Civic Party (Fiatal Demokraták Szövetsége – Magyar Polgári Párt: FIDESZ-MPP) unilaterally doubled the minimum wage and introduced generous subsidies for home construction. In 2002 the Hungarian Socialist Party (Magyar Szocialista Párt: MSZP), the leading party of the opposition, claimed that the policy of FIDESZ only favoured the middle class, and in its election campaign promised to spread the dividends of economic growth across the whole society through measures in social policy, and to build up a fully-fledged welfare state. Having won the 2002 election, MSZP carried out its generous programme of increasing public sector wages, pensions and social transfers. By 2005/06 this had resulted in serious macroeconomic imbalances.

The new neo-Keynesian style economic policy also had controversial impacts on the economy. On the one hand labour costs increased by 15 per cent in the period 2001/02, putting enormous pressure on export-oriented companies and speeding up the eastward relocation process from Hungary. On the other hand both the current deficit and the accumulated public debt increased. At the same time Hungary became a net capital exporter as FDI inflow slowed down, while the outflow grew as a result of profit repatriation and capital flight. From summer 2003 the Hungarian currency went through a series of crises. There was a widespread view that the government needed to redress the economy's imbalances but that it was afraid of a political backlash in response to any restrictive policy measures it might take.

Hungary's EU accession implied a further pressure on the government. The criteria to join the 'Euro-zone' in the future posed new difficulties for the governing socialist-liberal coalition. Many commentators agreed that the fierce 'populist-style' electoral competition between the left- and right-wing conservative political camps was the major reason for an inability on the part of the government to introduce and carry out thorough economic reforms.

Finally, the second socialist-liberal government had to tackle the problems arising from the extravagant budgetary policy of previous governments. In June 2006 the re-elected government immediately announced a comprehensive package of austerity measures and reform proposals to redress budget imbalances and to ensure that the country could meet the strict macroeconomic conditions for joining the 'Euro-zone'. The measures included withdrawal of the state from price subsidies and cuts in public institutions' budgets and staff. It also affected welfare provisions, with social policies in general shifting from universal towards means-tested provisions. A wide range of taxes have increased and household energy and transport costs have also risen. The expected macroeconomic figures of the new strategic plan were disclosed on 1 September 2006 when the government submitted a revised convergence programme to the European Union showing how it envisages the country meeting the Maastricht criteria. This plan not only further postponed the introduction of the Euro as the national currency, but also failed to set a definite deadline for joining the Euro-zone. The major impact of this macroeconomic U-turn on the country's development path, however, has been the slowing down of economic growth and a lack of job creation. In addition, decreasing subsidies to education, research and development might be detrimental to achieving the 'knowledge-based society' targets set earlier, in line with the Lisbon objectives (see Figure 6.1).

2006 also saw unprecedented political tensions, partly due to the government's austerity and reform package, but due also to fierce competition between the political parties in which right-wing opposition parties continuously questioned the legitimacy of the government coalition, especially that of the prime minister. The series of street fights was shocking in a country where 17 years ago the transition from state-socialism went peacefully, in a 'negotiated way'. Alongside the political conflict, the austerity and reform steps also translated into industrial action in the public sector.

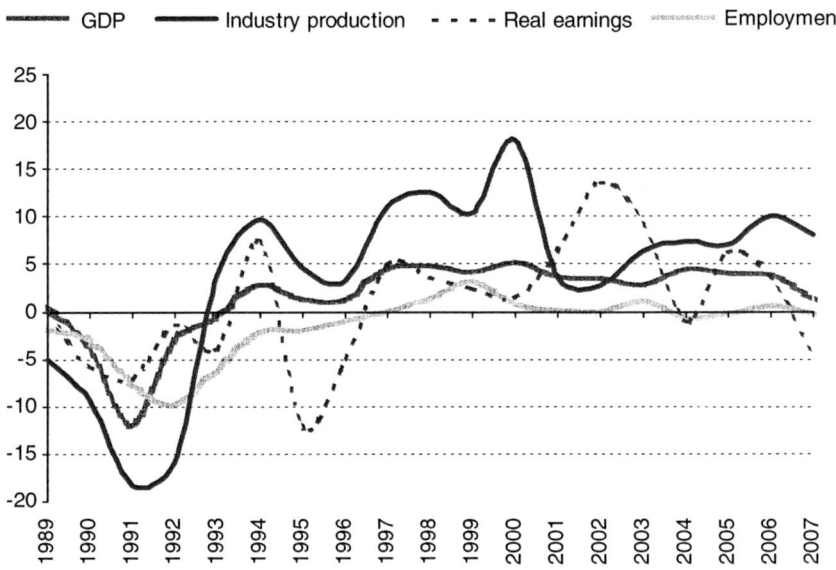

Figure 6.1 Annual changes of basic economic indicators
Source: Hungarian Statistical Office (KSH)

Changes in production model

Privatization

Prior to 1988 the state-socialist industrial model was based on less than 2000 large state-owned companies. In the 1990s economic policy under a number of post-transition governments focused on a rapid privatization of manufacturing based on direct sales at market rates, deregulation and liberalization of the economy, and the stabilization of budgetary deficits. Privatization was conducted in four phases: between 1990 and 1992 the major manufacturing companies – the so-called crown jewels – were sold to strategic foreign investors; between 1992 and 1994 the main emphasis was on selling medium-sized state-owned enterprises, and various schemes were set up to facilitate their acquisition by domestic investors, including managers and employees; and in 1995/6 the major public utility companies, including the telecommunication and electricity companies, were sold to strategic foreign investors. Privatization of manufacturing industries and major commercial banks was more or less completed by the end of 1997. Privatization went hand-in-hand with decentralization and liquidation, and practically resulted in the dismantling of the sector of former large state-owned manufacturing companies and, *inter alia*, of the well-knit network of supply chains among state-owned and cooperative firms.

Corporate governance is not a highlighted issue in Hungary as in the prevailing two-tiered system the law provides shareholders with a relatively strong controlling position over company boards. On the other hand protection of minority shareholders' (with less then 25 per cent of shares) rights is relatively weak, employees' board representation in quite formal and employee ownership is rare. So far, the major debated issue has been the government's influence on privatized companies. In earlier privatizations veto power was ensured through 'golden shares' owned by the state, but this was eliminated due to incompatibility with the anti-protectionist nature of EU legislation.

Emergence of the private small and medium-sized company sector

The socialist regime limited private entrepreneurship to small-scale crafts and retail shops. These limits were gradually lifted in the 1980s and various forms of small-scale private undertakings burgeoned.

The number of undertakings between 1990 and 1994 doubled to reach one million. Most of this increase was due to an increase in the small and medium-sized enterprise (SME) sector. As a consequence of the start-ups and rapid decentralization of state companies, the average company size in Hungary is currently well below the European average, and SMEs provided 51.8 per cent of employment in 2003. Since 2002 the creation of jobs has slowed in the sector, arguably due to the rapid increase in the minimum wage level.

There are three distinct segments to the SME sector. One is the traditional micro-enterprise sector, where the face-to-face relationship translates into traditional informal patterns of employment practices, which are in many cases different from legally stipulated forms of employment relationship. A second grouping involves businesses that make use of modern technologies and human relations and quality management practices, especially in that part of the medium-sized manufacturing sector which is integrated into the supply network of major multinational companies. In many cases these specialized medium-sized companies are fully or partially owned by strategic foreign investors. A third grouping concerns a growing number of medium-sized companies that in recent years have embraced modern forms of human resource practices, teamwork and quality management. Yet the SME sector is still characterized by a widespread use of traditional practices, particularly when it comes to domestic companies. This translates into lagging efficiency and a lack of product innovation. According to the statistics, in 2001 only 19 per cent of innovations were introduced by small enterprises and 38 per cent of innovations came from medium-sized companies. This low level of innovation makes the Hungarian SME sector similar to that in Portugal or Spain. The sector is also known as the major source of illegal and unregistered employment, especially in the construction industry and service sector. Thus, public discussion focuses on how to control tax evasion and illicit employment practices in the SME sector.

Foreign direct investment

Between 1990 and 2005 EUR53 billion of foreign direct investment flew into Hungary, the country recording the highest per capita ratio of FDI in the region (EUR5.265). About 80 per cent of inward FDI came from EU countries, 30 per cent from Germany alone.

In the early 1990s the main form of FDI was the acquisition of state-owned companies. In this period the major goal of investors was to obtain a foothold in the local market and to acquire those manufacturing capabilities which could act as springboards for launching export-oriented manufacturing. Running parallel with privatization, 'green-field' investments were also very important sources of FDI inflow. While for the most part it was mainly low-tech assembly plants that were established, already in the early 1990s important 'green-field' projects such as the Audi and GM engine plants were launched. Both produce mainly large batches of car components (engines) which are shipped to assembly factories.

These investments underpinned the export-driven economic development of Hungary. As early as 1995 51 per cent of Hungarian exports were produced by firms with at least 10 per cent foreign equity. Nevertheless, these firms operated in this period as 'cathedrals in the desert', that is without any major domestic supplier background. At that time the Hungarian economy was characterized as 'double-layered', a highly efficient segment of foreign firms producing primarily to export but with no connection whatsoever to the domestically-owned companies producing primarily for the local market.

In the mid-1990s Hungary experienced a smooth shift in its main FDI focus, from privatization to green-field investments. As a result, by the end of the decade the Hungarian private economy became dominated by foreign investors. Firms with foreign participation produced about 32 per cent of Hungarian GDP, 72 per cent of Hungary's gross export, 45 per cent of manufacturing value-added, and employed 25 per cent of private sector workers.

From the second half of the 1990s onwards, reinvested profits of foreign-owned firms outperformed FDI inflow. This kind of capital formation became a key factor in the constant enlarging and upgrading of Hungary's manufacturing capabilities. Beyond increasing output and manufacturing depth, another important process gradually began: relocation of various activities with higher value added into Hungary, such as research and development, design, process engineering, and control and management functions to accompany manufacturing investments. Thus, the former dual-layered Hungarian economy evolved into a three-layered one, with a new segment of companies emerging in the supplier chains of major original equipment manufacturing firms, both domestic and foreign-owned SMEs.

The period beginning in 2000 represented a new stage in the development of FDI. In the context of a Europe-wide recession and the increasing opening up of Romania, Bulgaria, Ukraine and even China to FDI, the increase in labour costs resulted in relocation of low-technology, labour-intensive, assembly-line style manufacturing from Hungary to cheaper locations, especially in textile, clothing, shoe-making and electronics industries. On the other hand there was a marked increase of inward FDI into technology-intensive, export-oriented manufacturing industries. This investment process further strengthened the dependence of the Hungarian economy on foreign-owned firms, which accounted for 80 per cent of exports in 2003.

Following the rapid development of infrastructure, especially that of the road network, Hungary began to emerge as one of the regional logistical centres. Another important trend, which gained momentum from 2003 onwards, has been the partial or full relocation of European or central and eastern European countries' regional business and management centres into Hungary. General Electric's Consumer & Industries Division, for example, relocated its European headquarters into Budapest.

Research and Development

Hungary lags far behind the EU average in terms of information and communication technology (ICT) penetration, research and development (R&D) expenditures and, in general, of indicators of transition towards a knowledge-based society. Hungary spends around 1 per cent of GDP on R&D, some way off the 3 per cent level specified in the Lisbon strategy. Moreover, the share of business expenditures is about 30 per cent instead of the 70 per cent target figure. The proportion of researchers within the Hungarian population is half the EU average, while their average age is relatively high. The number of graduates in technical and natural sciences within the age group 20–29 is one-third that of the EU-15 average. Despite earlier efforts by government, the penetration of personal computers, broadband Internet access and use of ICT tools and services is weak among both domestic households and businesses.

Changes in human resource management practices and work organization

The opening up of the economy was accompanied by a rapid adoption of modern management techniques and efficient work organization practices. 'Organizational learning' by management was facilitated by the inflow of strategic foreign investors and the integration of Hungarian companies into the supplier networks of major multinational companies. Case studies carried out on Hungarian subsidiaries of multinational enterprises found that many companies introduced cost-saving and flexible organizational methods (such as 'just-in-time' production, the Kaizen philosophy, teamwork, job rotation, 'total quality management', flat hierarchies, new pay systems linked to the introduction of appraisal systems, and new forms of employee involvement). These were not only transplanted from parent companies but in some cases a more efficient, up-to-the-minute system was established even earlier than in existing plants of the same companies in their home country.

The development of new practices was to a certain extent facilitated by the fact that the unionization rate is fairly low within export-oriented manufacturing enterprises in Hungary, where the pressure is most apparent for a highly efficient and flexible work organization. Collective agreements, if they exist in these companies at all, typically do not include stipulations on specific changes in shop-floor work organization, or procedures for negotiating them. More important to note, however, is that Hungarian unions lack a tradition of 'job-control' style trade unionism and craft divisions. This implies that the detailed regulation of job descriptions, wage tariffs and work rules are outside collective agreements.

Transformation of the industrial relations system in the wake of transition

Legislation in 1988/89 ensured the legal conditions for lawful strikes and the freedom of association. In 1992 the new Labour Code further qualified the operation of trade unions and employers' associations. However, the negotiated nature of the transition made it possible to make continuous reforms, to preserve organizational continuity as well as old practices and procedural routines, and to continuously adapt to the new environment rather than to break totally with the past.

On the unions' side a pluralistic structure developed involving grassroots organizations and new unions arising out of the reform and fragmentation of the old trade union centre. In the period between 1988 and 1990 three new union confederations were founded, a combination of groups of 'activists' with strong politico-social commitments and of workplace level unions emerging from local conflicts. In March 1990 the old trade union centre split into four successor organizations, based on groupings of existing industrial federations. All seven union confederations were recognized in 1990 as nationally representative and were invited by the government to participate in the national tripartite council.

Organizational plurality went hand in hand with decentralization of the union structure. The former 19 sectoral federations broke up into smaller industrial sub-associations; these are loose voluntary associations of company union structures. The basic building block in the new union structure remained the company union section as legal entities with the right to freely choose adherence to any confederation, federation or sub-sectoral association. The outcome is that the Hungarian union movement is fragmented and organizationally weak, with union density dropping from 84 per cent in 1990 to 17 per cent by 2004.

In 1989 and 1990 the socialist company associations with compulsory membership reformed themselves into voluntary employers' associations. The seven major successor organizations, however, retained a profile inherited from the socialist past, invariably representing companies of the same sector (that is, agricultural businesses, manufacturing and commercial enterprises, SMEs, cooperatives). Additionally, two more employers' associations were founded by newly established private companies. Altogether nine employers' associations of national importance were set up and were offered a seat in the national tripartite forum in 1990.

The common characteristic of all the employers' associations is that they have a rather limited role as bargaining partners of unions. Typically, employers' associations do not hold the authorization of their members to conclude a collective agreement on the terms and conditions of employment, but draft agreements concluded by the associations are subject to approval of their members. Invariably, employers' associations also perform the role of business associations, providing various business services as well as acting as lobbying organizations.

The national tripartite forum, currently called the National Interest Reconciliation Council (OÉT), is a central element of the Hungarian industrial relations system. It has been operating since 1990 and, despite various reorganization efforts, has changed very little in terms of members and agenda. The OÉT discusses practically all major issues related to labour market development and regulation, including the pension system and the development of education. As far as economic policy issues are concerned the most important function of the OÉT is to set the minimum wage and make a recommendation on wage increase for the coming year.

Following the abolition of governmental wage regulation inherited from the socialist system, a three-layer wage bargaining system was developed, involving the above-mentioned national tripartite negotiations, multi-employer (sectoral and sub-sectoral, company-group with ownership ties) agreements, and workplace bargaining.

However, the main arena for the social regulation of wages is still the company level wage bargaining. In a few industries sectoral bargaining plays a supplementary role by setting minimum wages for broad categories of employees (for example unskilled, semi-skilled and skilled) at levels only slightly higher than the national minimum wage. The coverage of sectoral bargaining is low, so that in 2004 only 10.1 per cent of employees were covered. These agreements are not able to regulate wages in whole sectors and do not provide a safety net for employees working in companies outside these agreements. Thus, an increasingly larger share of employees are exposed to individualized wage settings.

Nonetheless, the overall coverage of different agreements has shrunk drastically over recent years; in 2004 only 39.5 per cent of employees were covered in the competitive sphere of the economy, in contrast to 45.2 per cent in 1998 (data provided by the Ministry of Employment and Labour, which runs the registry of agreements). A recent study on the clothing industry found that in many workplaces unions are no longer able to conclude local collective agreements and that there is a shift from collective bargaining to consultation and *ad-hoc* problem solving. A further sign of the weakness of unions is that there have been hardly any genuine strike actions particularly in the private sector. Recently the public sector has been an exception where industrial actions have been triggered by the government's public sector reform initiatives, which include substantial staff reductions.

The Labour Code of 1992 institutionalized works councils, mainly with information and consultation rights. Setting up a works council became mandatory for companies with more than 50 employees. Researchers seem to agree that works councils are mainly operating in companies where a union organization is in place. The coexistence of parallel structures (that is of works councils and union representation) of employee representation with overlapping information and consultation rights, however, has led to a controversial situation in many workplaces, while in others it has reinforced the role of enterprise-level union organizations.

Changes in the employment system

Labour market changes in the transition period and the building of new labour market institutions

Departure from the full-employment model of the state-socialist system began in the mid-1980s when the first signs of job-shedding at state-owned companies appeared. Open unemployment became politically accepted and registration of the unemployed was introduced in 1986. Redundancies became more frequent following the 1989 amendment of the Labour Code, which made it possible to terminate an employment contract for economic reasons. In the same year, on the demand of trade unions, mandatory severance pay was introduced. The first redundancies hit the Roma especially hard, the biggest ethnic minority group in Hungary that makes up 5 to 6 per cent of the entire population. While in the 1970s 85 per cent of Roma men were active earners and 75 per cent of them employees, in 1993 the same figures were 28 per cent and 18 per cent respectively. Basically, their labour market position has not improved in the intervening years. Welfare transfers as well as undeclared work done on a casual basis are of special importance in providing for the livelihood of Roma families (Kemény and Janky, 2003).

At a time of still low unemployment the first freely elected government introduced a generous unemployment insurance and active labour market policy measures. ALMPs of the early transformation period were focused mainly on collective redundancies and crisis situations in regions hit hard by plant closures. The first government built up the national network of Public Employment Service and involved social partners in decision-making on the management of the Labour Market Fund, financed mainly by employer and employee contributions.

During the 'transitional recession' between 1990 and 1994 Hungary lost almost 1.2 million jobs, practically one quarter of all jobs. The unemployment rate grew steeply, reaching a record 13 per cent, about 700,000 unemployed, in 1993. Nevertheless, another 800,000 chose to withdraw from the labour market in some other way: many opted for a pension (early retirement or disability pension), younger women chose childcare support (the government maintained the maximum three-year period and extended it for mothers with three or more children), young people postponed their entry into the labour market, and many others simply gave up the job search and engaged (or not) in some informal activity to make a living. The changes in the economic structure played a highly significant role in the life-cycles of middle-aged or older generations. The collapse of the socialist economy and the privatization of state companies terminated the careers of many or forced them to change their living strategies (for example through becoming 'forced entrepreneurs'). The informal or illegal economy certainly grew in this period, estimated to have accounted for 18 per cent of GDP (Lackó, 2000).

The share of the inactive population remained high, even when unemployment was falling substantially. Another constant feature of the labour market is significant regional differences, largely coinciding with inequalities in economic development: the capital and north-western counties have the lowest unemployment rates, while those in the north-east have the highest rates.

During the transition period, the more unemployed who applied for the dole, the stricter the eligibility criteria became because of financial constraints. The rules changed several times: the period of payment shortened and the income compensation rate (the benefit/wage ratio) decreased. In the meantime various governments tried different ALMPs; as commentators noted, 'there is no type of programme that cannot be found in Hungarian practice'. In 1994 the number of the participants in ALMPs was 218,000, while the number of registered unemployed was 568,000. Major changes in the unemployment compensation system occurred in 1999 under the right-wing government. Although unemployment had stagnated at around 6.5 per cent since 1997, the eligibility criteria were tightened again and the dole period was shortened considerably. Moreover, income support for those who exhausted the unemployment insurance period was replaced by a means-tested assistance which required recipients to actively search for jobs and spend at least 30 days in public work. The objective was to trigger a 'welfare-to-work' style change, but the reform proved to be a failure: it reduced the number of benefit claimants significantly but without raising non-subsidized private-sector employment (Fazekas, 2002).

What several researchers agree on is that wages are remarkably elastic. Compared to estimates from elsewhere, Hungarian wages appear to be responsive to market conditions. Demand elasticities, albeit falling over time, compare not unfavourably with those of other European countries (Köllő and Nacsa, 2005). Comparative statistical studies of central and eastern European countries show that as early as 1988 wages were the most differentiated in Hungary throughout the region. In the transition period the purchasing power of wages declined in all of these countries and inequalities grew, with Hungary leading the list for the latter development. The Gini coefficient, measuring inequality, was 0.27 in Hungary in 1988 while it ranged between 0.16 and 0.22 in the rest of the region; in 1993 it rose to 0.30 in Hungary and to 0.22 to 0.27 in the other countries (Rutkowski, 1996).

Post-socialist welfare regime and reforms

After the 1960s the state-socialist regime made healthcare, pensions and childbearing provisions almost universal. In the case of family policy these measures were driven by concerns about the shrinking reproduction of the population/workforce and eventually resulted in an unprecedented expansion of female employment. Institutional family support, in its full development in the 1980s, included the following pillars: cash support (family allowance, which was due for each child under 18, maternity support on a flat-rate basis, and proportional to income for up to three years); in-kind transfers (nursery and day-care institutions); and housing subsidies.

All in all, a 'maternalist' welfare state developed during the socialist period, whereby women's needs as mothers were separated from those of other social groups, and motherhood itself became a major entitlement to welfare (Haney, 2002; Koistinen et al., 2006; Glass and Fodor, 2007). After 1990 frequent and significant modifications occurred in the family policy system so that the whole system became unpredictable for the would-be beneficiaries. For a long time the real value of family allowances decreased continuously, but in 2004 it rose sharply again. This was the result of an institutional change, namely the abolition of the family tax break system, introduced in 1998 to benefit tax-paying earners at the same time. These changes were mainly due to the changing concepts of different successive governments: the right-wing coalition favoured middle-class families by universal provisions and tax breaks, while the left-wing coalition strengthened targeted and means-tested measures (Spéder, 2004). The number of available spaces in childcare institutions fell dramatically, primarily because of the elimination of 'factory nurseries'. Housing subsidies were dramatically cut back and the new preferential loan schemes were also exposed to political twists and turns.

The restructured labour market today allows less room for reconciling work and family needs than in the pre-1990 period, including the return to the workplace for women after giving birth. Even though it is enacted in legislation that after maternity leave mothers must be re-employed, at least for three months, this regulation often fails to guarantee the mother's reintegration into the workplace. The existence and number of children also play decisive roles in the dynamic transformation of labour market positions, in that they increase the risk of withdrawal from the labour market and decrease the chances of reintegration. Growing poverty risks for families having an increasing number of children have become a permanent statistical phenomenon (Spéder and Kapitány, 2005).

In the early phase of transition Hungarian economist János Kornai coined the expression 'premature welfare state' because, in his view, 'Hungary can vie with the most developed Scandinavian countries in the range of codified entitlements to benefits and in the proportion of GDP laid out on social spending' (Kornai, 1996, p. 944; cited by Ferge, 1996). While the metaphor of the early-born child became popular among reformers, their views on the reforms implemented to effectively mitigate the social cost of the 'transition recession' have remained widely varied. One typical assertion was that a liberal model of the welfare state had been formed, often inspired by international financial institutions (Barr, 1994; Ferge, 1996; Vaughan-Whitehead, 2003). For instance, Zsuzsa Ferge (1996) identifies the following trends in Hungary in the early 1990s: (1) most universal benefits and universal public services had been abolished and were transformed either into means-tested schemes or into insurance; (2) the standards of benefits (pension, sick pay, health services) were continuously lowered, and eligibility criteria were toughened (unemployment insurance); (3) the legitimacy of public insurance schemes was undermined, thereby paving the way for alternative, particularly private/privatized solutions while the state in its role of owner, financing agent and service deliverer was slowly (or rapidly) withdrawing from the welfare sector; (4) the spreading of market or near-market solutions excluded certain groups from access and/or two-tier systems were created that reinforced inequalities. On the other hand several authors have pointed out that liberal reforms have been implemented only partially, while new areas of state intervention (like assistance for the unemployed) have developed since the beginning of transition. Major reforms (such as in healthcare) have been postponed by successive governments or have resulted in dubious institutions (like mandatory private pension funds, which in Hungary produce very low returns on individual accounts). They view the considerable drop in social welfare performance a kind of 'back to normality' process whereby the levels of welfare provision have been adjusted to the actual economic capacity during the first years of the transformation (Kovács, 2004). As far as mitigating the social cost of the 'transition recession' is concerned, various forms of early retirement have been of vital importance. To avoid the social and political tensions arising out of the radical contraction of the labour market and the wholesale elimination of workplaces, the new political leadership made it possible, through a variety of methods, for older people whose workplace was eliminated to go into retirement. The most preferred method of 'mass retirement' was claiming a disability pension, submitted on the basis of some official medical justification. An extraordinarily high number of people receiving various kinds of retirement payments before reaching official retirement age is a crucial feature of post-transition society in Hungary. In January 2006, of the little over ten million residents of Hungary, over three million were receiving 'pensions, allowances or other pension-like transfers' and of this number some 700,000–800,000 had not yet reached the official age for retirement.

Recent labour market developments and debates in light of the Lisbon objectives

So far the EU's single market for labour has not resulted in serious changes in the Hungarian labour market. The 2004 Accession Treaty included transition clauses ensuring that the EU-15 countries may uphold restrictive regimes for seven years. Although some of the countries have already waived the restriction, with the exception of certain labour market segments (for instance healthcare professionals), there is no considerable outward migration. On the other hand immigration of ethnic Hungarians from neighbouring countries is not a new phenomenon at all, and given the mostly illegal nature of these movements, it contributes to maintaining the high share of the hidden economy.

Clearly, the main problem with the Hungarian labour market is the low employment rate, more than eight percentage points below the EU-15 average and 11 per cent for people over 55. Labour economics research has found that the key determinant of labour market changes has been the revaluation of education and work experience since the beginning of transition. There has been a growing demand for educated labour and – at least in part – this has caused the persistent low level of employment. The latest (2001) census data show that the proportion of lower-educated people in the Hungarian population is larger than the EU-15 average and that their employment opportunities are worse than elsewhere in the EU. Between 1985 and 2000 at least 20 per cent of each cohort entered the labour market without any qualification. A continuation of this trend will have harmful consequences for the labour market for at least another 30 years (Kertesi and Varga, 2005). The policy implication of these research findings is that to increase the employment rate profound reforms in the Hungarian primary education system are needed. Tackling dropout rates among and discrimination against the children of the Roma minority are the most crucial tasks.

These conclusions are underpinned by statistical information on the output quality of the education system. The rate of pupils not completing eighth grade primary education by the age of 16 (the age limit for compulsory schooling) has been stable at about 5 per cent in recent years, and 4–5 per cent of those completing primary school do not enter secondary education in the following year. In the traditional vocational schools the drop-out rate was above 20 per cent in the 1990s but rose to 35 per cent in the early 2000s. The results of the PISA survey in 2003 showed that Hungary is one of the countries where the education system most fails to offset inequalities stemming from family background (Kertesi and Varga, 2005).

The mismatch between labour market supply and demand in terms of educational attainment highlights other dysfunctions of the educational system. Employer/business organizations often complain about the obsolete vocational training system. The reason for the shortage of skilled workers, however, is a complex one. After the political transition a lot of manual jobs were eliminated which devalued the overall prestige of manual labour. To make matters worse it also became increasingly difficult for vocational schools to offer traineeships/internships as the big companies that formerly operated training workshops were eliminated and newly formed companies were reluctant to offer similar opportunities. By 2000 a significant part of vocational training had thus become the kind of training in which disadvantaged young people (the underprivileged, of Roma ethnicity, or with learning handicaps) took part until reaching the end of the compulsory education period, with no real chance of attaining employment subsequently.

Traditional vocational schools have lost pupils to upper secondary education establishments (providing school-leavers with a certificate required for higher educational studies) which started to expand rapidly in the second half of the 1980s. The real expansion in education took place in higher education; between 1990 and 2002 the number of full-time students admitted to higher education tripled. In 1990 they made up 8.5 per cent of the 18–22 age group, and 25 per cent in 2002 (Lannert, 2005). Nevertheless, the evaluation of the higher education boom is controversial. Labour economists highlight the rapid increase in 'returns to education'. With massive restructuring of the economy, more and more modern jobs were created and the demand for educated workers grew. As a result wage premiums for the young and better-educated workers were considerably hiked and the labour market experience of older workers was devalued. Despite the palpable reconfiguration of jobs filled by university graduates, the sustainable wage premium justified the higher education boom and the economy absorbed the extra number of degree holders and rewarded their knowledge.

The mainstream view of labour economists in Hungary stresses the strong correlation between employment rates and education and training. They are convinced that increasing investments in human resources offers the way out from the present crisis. This is not because they are stubborn believers in supply-side theories; it is more the case that statistical evidence from the 1990s (high returns on education and the extremely low employment rate of the under-educated) has proved that the labour market could absorb school-leavers with up-to-date skills (Galasi, 2005).

Other researchers, however, incline more towards a demand-side approach in evaluating increasing retention rates, akin to job-competition models. In their view the higher education boom is not necessarily a welcome development. They claim that a country's economic development and the extent of higher education should be strongly correlated, and that a well-structured education system must produce qualifications to meet employers' demand; otherwise public and private resources are wasted, graduates squeeze out lower educated job applicants and cause growing unemployment, and the over-educated are dissatisfied and tend to be exposed to brain-drain. Given the current trend in higher education enrolment rates, by 2015 every third employee in Hungary will have a higher education degree – which would match the rate in the UK or Sweden – while economic development will still be lagging behind (Kővári and Polonyi, 2005). As to the policy implications, these authors call for coherent state policy and planning based on long-term forecasts. Nowadays the self-interest of the universities and the pressure from would-be students seem to set enrolment quotas. As far as the students and their parents are concerned, their demand is a consequence of the post-socialist societal change; that is, a university diploma is perceived as a precondition to upward mobility, and universities are fashionable because they are part of the life-style of the middle-class youth.

The socialist-liberal government during its first term introduced a number of new active labour market measures in order to get more of the inactive into work. In 2004 targeted ALMPs were introduced to increase the employment rate among the Roma. Another measure involved targeted cuts in employers' social contributions: employers may pay only half the social security contribution if they hire young job-seekers, women returning to work from parental leave and long-term unemployed aged over 50. During the current term of the government, piecemeal reforms continue to focus on 'making work pay', mainly through extending ongoing programmes and enhancing assistance for job-seekers by modernizing the Public Employment Service. In November 2005 the unemployment compensation system was reformed as well. The dole was renamed as 'job search benefit' and active job searching became a precondition for entitlement. To encourage job searching the amount of benefit decreases over the maximum 270-day eligibility period. In 2006 a sort of 'in-work benefit' was also introduced, under which certain jobseekers are allowed to work on a casual basis while they are eligible for a minimum level allowance. Another measure aims to assist those receiving disability pension; the government envisages their re-entry into the labour market through the overhaul of the disability pension system, together with the provision of suitable rehabilitation services. Thus, EU policies (and especially the model of the UK) have had an enormous impact on Hungarian employment policymakers.

As far as the 'active ageing' objective is concerned, the measures introduced in Hungary have proved controversial. On the one hand these included a gradual rise in the retirement age (1997–2010), a tightening of control on disability pensions together with more 'rehabilitation' programmes, and a special programme for long-term unemployed over 50s aimed at extending working life. On the other hand, in 2005 a pre-retirement part-time employment scheme ('Premium Years' Programme) was reinstated for streamlining public administration, and in 2007 immediate changes in the pension system (a decreasing pension to wage ratio and a policy of suspending the pension for those engaging in paid work over the minimum wage for those retiring later) encouraged many to retire as soon as possible.

Most of the new measures, however, are in line with the targets of the EU's Lisbon strategy, which was adopted first by the National Employment Plan and submitted to the EU by the Hungarian government in the autumn of 2004, following several years of cooperation between the EU and Hungary in the field of labour market policies. Given the low level of employment, in 2004 the Hungarian government set ambitious targets regarding employment, aiming at a level of 63 per cent by 2010 (see Table 6.1). However, in view of the 2006 austerity measures these targets had to be scaled down (Hungarian Government, 2006).

All in all, the Lisbon process is of paramount importance for Hungary. As the main challenge is the low employment rate, policies tackling how to 'activate' the inactive population and crack down on illegal employment are a major focus. Given the crisis of the post-socialist development path, 'upskilling' the labour force is also a highlighted issue (the Human Resource Development Operational Programme of the National Development Plan is devoted to educational programmes and ALMPs.) And last but not least, the National Development Plan ensures access to EU structural funds for human

Table 6.1 Lisbon employment targets of Hungary (2004, 2006)

Employment rate	EU-15 objectives		Hungary baseline	National objectives (set in 2004)		Hungary baseline	Revised national objectives (set in 2006)	
	2005	2010	2003	2003	2010	2005	2008	2010
Total	67	70	57.0	59	63	56.9	57	58.7
Women	57	60	50.9	53	57	51.0	51.8	53.2
55+	–	50	29.0	33	37	33.0	33.3	34.8

Source: Hungarian Government (2006)

resource, environmental and rural development, investments in infrastructure and improving companies' competitiveness. The government expects the EU funding to amount to 3.0–3.5 per cent of GDP by 2010/11. At the same time, in the context of the U-turn of economic policy from 2006 onwards, labour market policies and government initiatives to foster a transition towards a knowledge-based society increasingly seem to be dependent on a stringent macroeconomic regime.

Conclusion

In this conclusion we would like to address the question as to whether the evolving new Hungarian model is closer to the liberal market economy or belongs to the group of coordinated market economies (to use the Hall-Soskice terminology for variants of capitalism). There are clear-cut factors pushing Hungary towards the liberal market model. Weak unions, weak employers' associations and the gradual erosion of welfare provisions imply that these institutions are all but unable to create an appropriate framework for a proper functioning of the Rhenish model. The lack of powerful domestic manufacturing companies means that the economy is dependent on foreign investors. Thus, the all-important positive attitude of major business towards locality and the national system is missing. Instead, pure efficiency calculations and global benchmarking exercises are driving the most important sectors of the economy. Among domestic actors, business circles and employer organizations are the protagonists for economic policy. External factors are also pushing Hungary towards a liberal model. Hungary is located in a region where governments have entered into fierce 'regime-competition' for investment and jobs through lowering of taxes and pursuing liberal regulatory policies. Last but not least, the criteria of the European Stability Pact for monetary integration are powerful factors pushing towards a neo-conservative economic policy and Anglo-Saxon style of institutional environment.

However, alongside the forces pushing for a liberal model there are other counterbalancing factors driving Hungary towards a Rhenish model. Many characteristics of the institutional arrangements of the former regime, which were carried over into the post-socialist system, are akin to the Rhenish model. These include the highly institutionalized system of state administration, the importance of the nation state in guiding economic development, widespread universal welfare services and a dense network of catch-all institutions. Historically and culturally Hungary is also influenced by the role-models of neighbouring Austria and Germany. Also important is the influence of the European social model, particularly the policy approaches favoured by the EU bureaucracies that are promoting the model. Many domestic actors are in favour of a coordinated market economy. The population, as a whole, would prefer a European-style welfare model, one which provides stability, security and relative income equality. Many large state-owned business organizations and domestic entrepreneurs who are well interconnected with local political elites and who hold somewhat paternalistic attitudes would also prefer such a model. Obviously, trade unions are protagonists for a Rhenish model, independent of their political affiliations.

Escaping from the straitjacket of the state-socialist system, the 'model search' has always been a subject of intensive political infighting, twisting and turning in one or other direction. The relative weakness of the state's administrative capacity allowed many variations, depending on the local balance of power, and thus has not facilitated a consolidation of a coherent system. The complex and sometimes contradictory processes of 'regime-shopping' and innovations in institution building has not helped the development of a cohesive national system either. In this respect the impact of existing institutions and the behaviour and attitude of the actors involved, inherited from the socialist regime, are also contributory factors. Contrary to the simple 'path dependency' theory, many scholars studying the transformation process stated that these complex processes resulted in a 'bricolage' of institutions and policies (Andor et al., 1994; Stark and Bruszt, 1998).

'Bricolage' is certainly a useful conceptual term to understand the complexity of the system, and explains the difficulty of placing Hungary firmly into one or other model of the variants of capitalism. Nevertheless, as far as model-building efforts are concerned, we argue that there have been two distinct periods since 1989, in each of which a dominant political will and corresponding institution-building push towards one definite model can be observed. While the first phase, from 1989 to 2000, was the period representing development towards a liberal market economy, between 2000 and 2006 there was a policy turn towards the Rhenish model. The first phase was very successful in creating a competitive export-oriented market economy, but it created enormous tensions in

Hungarian society. Instability, increasing inequality and disenchantment with the market economy facilitated a shift towards a new phase. Then, fuelled by widespread disillusionment, major political parties across the board adopted programmes promising extension of the welfare state and rapid increases in wages. The year 2000 represented a clear-cut policy change towards a neo-Keynesian style economic policy. Since then governments and opposition parties alike have competed in terms of welfare promises. Between 2002 and 2006 the socialist-liberal government not only extended the welfare system but also facilitated the institutional development of social dialogue to strengthen the social component of the Rhenish model.

2006 represented a new turning point again. It became clear that the neo-Keynesian budget policy had resulted in steeply increasing budget deficit and indebtedness. The success of competing neighbouring countries for investment and jobs, especially that of Slovakia, had a powerful demonstration effect, showing that something was amiss with Hungarian economic policy. The launch of excessive deficit procedure against Hungary forced the government to rethink its economic policy and to submit a new convergence programme to Brussels; this provides for reductions in state budget expenditures and for major structural reforms in the area of public services. The U-turn and the ensuing economic slowdown suddenly highlighted the structural problems of the economy and society, which previously had been masked by economic successes.

Nowadays (in spring 2008) there is an emerging consensus among economists that it is necessary to seek a new model. They seem to agree that generous welfare state provisions and high-level tax burdens on employment are the major obstacles to increasing employment levels, as they provide incentives for work in the informal sphere of the economy only or to combine legal employment at the minimum wage level and employers' undeclared extra payment. At the same time steep increases in the minimum wage have forced low-wage industries to flee into lower-wage countries. This view states that the key problem is the low labour market participation rate, which has been sustained by bad policy decisions in the past. The emerging consensus among economists suggests a need for a policy turn towards a liberal model, which would reinvigorate labour markets through cuts in the welfare state provisions and reduction of tax level on employment.

Despite the consensus among leading economists, political parties are still undecided whether to accept such a strategic turn. Between 2006 and 2007 the socialist-liberal coalition government intended to introduce certain policy reforms – reforms that were heavily contested by the right-wing opposition parties as well as by trade unions, and which met with fierce rejection by the populace. Faced with a huge loss of popular support the Hungarian Socialist Party has backtracked and now clearly states that it is impossible to introduce any major reform. The right-wing opposition party FIDESZ (Hungarian Civic Union), having rejected all reform initiatives of the government, keeps on demanding policy measures to increase living standards. At the same time it also states that once it has gained an overwhelming majority at the next general election, it will develop a 'strong state' in order to carry out a policy of rapid economic development.

In the meantime the general public is against any reform initiatives and, according to opinion polls, overwhelmingly supports the opposition. In essence, it supports the policy of rejecting the reforms in favour of a new phase of development. This is a 'Catch-22' situation, a real regime crisis. Quite suddenly, Hungary has become a performance laggard in the region, one whose economic regime is unable to provide the conditions for further harmonization with the EU-15. The convergence programme foresees major structural reforms and a very conservative approach to state budget expenditures. Everybody knows there is a need for major structural reforms. Such reforms, however, will hurt Hungarian society, and society is not ready to take the pain. Political parties meanwhile are unable to develop a consensus on the necessary measures. The ensuing period will see which way the pendulum swings.

References

Andor, M., Kuczi, T. and Swain, N. (1994), 'Rural Employment and Rural Regeneration in Post-Socialist Central Europe', University of Liverpool, Centre for Central and Eastern European Studies, Working Paper No. 39.

Barr, N. (ed.) (1994), *Labor Markets and Social Policy in Central and Eastern Europe*, New York: Oxford University Press.

Fazekas, K. (2002), 'Local Government Practices of Providing Income Support and Public Works for the Working Age Unemployed', pp. 254–63 in K. Fazekas and J. Koltay (eds), *The Hungarian Labour Market 2002*, Budapest: Institute of Economics, HAS, Hungarian Employment Foundation.

Ferge, Zs. (1996), 'The Perils of the Welfare State's Withdrawal', *Social Research* 64: 1381–402.

Galasi, P. (2005), 'Reallocation of Workers with the Higher Education Diploma, 1994–2002', pp. 44–50 in K. Fazekas and J. Koltay (eds), *The Hungarian Labour Market 2004*, Budapest: Institute of Economics, HAS, Hungarian Employment Foundation.

Glass, C. and Fodor, E. (2007), 'From Public to Private Maternalism? Gender and Welfare in Poland and Hungary after 1989', *Social Politics. International Studies in Gender, State & Society* 14 (3): 323–50.

Haney, L. (2002), *Inventing the Needy. Gender and the Politics of Welfare in Hungary*, Berkley, California: University of California Press.

Hungarian Government (2006), 'Revised National Lisbon Action Programme for Growth and Employment', Budapest: Hungarian Government.

Kemény, I. and Janky, B. (2003), 'A cigányok foglalkoztatottságáról és jövedelmi viszonyairól' [About employment and income of the Roma], *Esély* 6: 58–73.

Kertesi, G. and Varga, J. (2005), 'Foglalkoztatás és iskolázottság Magyarországon' ['Employment and Educational Attainment in Hungary'], *Közgazdasági Szemle* 52 (7–8): 633–62. (In Hungarian.)

Koistinen, P., Roivas, S. and Neumann, L. (2006), 'Policies Promoting Employment and Gender Equality in the Knowledge Based Society', pp. 229–60 in L. Mósesdóttir, S. Pascual and C. Remery (eds), *Moving Europe towards the Knowledge-based Society and Gender Equality. Policies and Performances*, Brussels: ETUI-REHS.

Köllő, J. and Nacsa, B. (2005), *Flexibility and Security in the Labour Market; Hungary's Experience*, Budapest: ILO-CEET.

Kornai, J. (1996), 'Paying the Bill for Goulash-Communism. Hungarian Development and Macro Stabilization in a Political-Economy Perspective', *Social Research* 63 (4): 943–1040.

Kovács, J. M. (2004), 'Approaching the EU and Reaching the US? Transforming Welfare Regimes in East-Central Europe. Rival Narratives', *West European Politics* 25 (2): 175–204.

Kővári, G. and Polonyi, I. (2005), 'A felsőfokú képzés és a gazdaság szakemberigényének összehangolási lehetőségei' ['Possibilities to Harmonise Higher Education and the Economy's Needs for Professionals']. (Manuscript, in Hungarian.)

Lackó, M. (2000), 'Hidden Economy – an Unknown Quantity? Comparative Analysis of Hidden Economies in Transition Countries, 1989–95', *Economics of Transition* 8 (1): 117–49.

Lannert, J. (2005), 'Facts on Expansion of Education', pp. 50–5 in K. Fazekas and J. Koltay (eds), *The Hungarian Labour Market 2005*, Budapest: Institute of Economics, HAS, Hungarian Employment Foundation.

Rutkowski, M. (1996), 'Changes in the Wage Structure during Economic Transition in Central and Eastern Europe', World Bank Technical Paper No. 340, Washington: World Bank.

Spéder, Zs. (2004), 'Fertility decline, changes in partnership formation and their linkages', in T. Kolosi, I. G. Tóth and G. Vukovich (eds.), *Social Report 2004*, Budapest: TÁRKI, 117–131. http://www.tarki.hu/adatbank-h/kutjel/pdf/a726.pdf

Spéder, Zs. and Kapitány, B. (2005), 'Poverty and Deprivation. Assessing Demographic and Social Structural Factors', Working Papers on Population, Family and Welfare No. 8, Budapest: Demographic Research Institute.

Stark, D. and Bruszt, L. (1998), *Postsocialist Pathways. Transforming Politics and Property in East Central Europe*, New York and Cambridge: Cambridge University Press.

Vaughan-Whitehead, D. C. (2003), *EU Enlargement versus Social Europe? The Uncertain Future of the European Social Model*, Cheltenham: Edward Elgar.

7
Capitalizing on Variety: Risks and Opportunities in a New French Social Model

Isabelle Berrebi-Hoffmann, Florence Jany-Catrice, Michel Lallement and Thierry Ribault

Introduction

Researchers who endeavour to draw up comparative typologies of national models, always experience difficulties in classifying France relative to other developed countries.[1] Indeed, whether they focus on production, employment or welfare regimes as a whole, or on the specific components of such regimes such as management systems, corporate governance, social protection, gender contracts, industrial relations or various combinations of these aspects, France is often placed in an ambiguous position reflecting the complexity of its system and the institutional layering that characterizes its political structure.

A difficulty of this kind is clearly evident, for example, in Hall and Soskice's (2001) currently much-cited study of the varieties of capitalism, which draws on the combinatory principle in order to identify two ideal types of capitalism (the liberal and coordinated market economies). In an attempt to go beyond this dichotomy, Schmidt (2003) argues that France, along with countries such as Spain and Italy, provide illustrations of a third variety in which the state has always played a central role in contrast to its weaker role in both market capitalism, as exemplified by the UK, and managed capitalism, as exemplified by Germany. Moreover, while the UK, Schmidt argues, has reinforced its market orientation such that its economy is now driven by financial markets and private firms, and Germany has moved to a mixed position where it has adopted some neoliberal principles but retains a role for social actors as well as firms in managing its evolution, France for its part has moved from 'state-led' to 'state-enhanced' capitalism. That is to say, France has developed a form of capitalism in which firms and the state are both the main drivers of change.

More recently, Hall (2007) has suggested that France, in responding to the challenges of globalization of production and financial systems and the strengthening of the supranational European Union since Maastricht, has adopted a paradoxical set of policies that operate at right angles to each other.

Successive French governments have reinforced market coordination while at the same time strengthening state-subsidized employment and social policies (through the so-called 'emplois aidés', subsidized jobs targeted primarily at certain groups such as young people and those excluded from the labour market). Unable to eradicate endemic unemployment, such contradictory options have reinforced social stratification, particularly in the labour market.

While our argument agrees with the general thrust of the conclusions to these studies, in which the role of the state is still significant but evolving in often quite contradictory ways, our approach emphasizes four factors. Firstly, we will give priority to a dynamic analysis. Secondly, we pay greater attention to the new kinds of interactions that have developed between the various economic, politic and social actors. This way of looking at social change helps to shed light on the unexpected effects and tensions that characterize the new French social model. Thirdly, we will argue that France's state-enhanced capitalism is less the product of radical overall change than the fruit of incremental and unequal developments. The timing of the changes has been different in the various segments of French capitalism, and to some extent each segment also has its own dynamic of change, even though there are also considerable interdependence effects. Fourthly, as Hall (2007) also notes, the EU is increasingly driving change and therefore has to be included within the overall framework if we are fully to understand the changes, the strategies adopted in France and the country's doubts and hesitations.

In the first part we describe the main pillars of state-led French capitalism. This model, which was dominant during the 1970s, has been put under pressure by profound changes in the economic, social and political environment. The second part develops the argument that there is a close link between structural change and the reconfiguration of actors. In the third part and in the final section we examine what the multiple consequences of the changes outlined previously entail for the French model.

The pillars of the old French national model

The employment regime in the French 'statist' model

To describe the model that prevailed in France during the three decades after the Second World War, we can usefully draw on the work of Maurice et al. (1982). In a free interpretation of their theory, the employment regime can be said to consist of four interrelated elements: the education and training system, the labour market, corporate governance and the division of labour and the industrial relations system. We will analyse each of these elements in succession.

Until the 1970s the French educational system was a mixture of general and vocational training. However, the former was more highly developed and enjoyed greater esteem, including symbolical esteem, than the latter.

Levels of education and training in France had certainly risen since the end of the Second World War under the influence of a dual phenomenon: a widening of access to the various levels of the education system on the one hand, and on the other a tendency among all social classes to extend the period spent in education and training. In secondary education the *lycées* were still the most prestigious institutions, while in higher education the *grandes écoles* continued to produce the country's future political and business elites, with the universities and their extensive range of subjects and options educating the rest of the student population.

In the 1970s the labour market – the second element of the employment regime – was characterized, firstly, by the existence of a minimum wage and, secondly, by the predominance of internal markets. The minimum wage, a truly centralized labour market institution since its level is set by central government, was introduced in France in 1950, first as the SMIG (*salaire minimum interprofessionnel garanti*) and then as the SMIC (*salaire minimum interprofessionnel de croissance*). The greatest increases in the level of the minimum wage were recorded throughout the 1970s and up to 1983. The French state's objective in deploying this instrument was to increase the purchasing power of the poorest households. In so doing it hoped to stimulate economic development (Direction de la prévision, 2004a). At the beginning of the 1980s about ten per cent of wage-earners were paid the minimum wage (Direction de la prévision, 2004b, p. 3). For their part the internal labour markets used by large companies were based on two main pillars (Gautié, 2003). The first was a set of rules, implicit or otherwise, that were designed to protect jobs. Dismissal, for example, was a more difficult procedure to implement than in many comparable countries. The second pillar consisted of the wage-setting institutions. These were the product of rules negotiated by means of collective agreements and set in stone in the collectively agreed pay scales. However, since the education and training system was segmented and the determinants of pay could vary considerably depending on occupational status and industry, even within companies wages for comparable qualification levels were far from homogeneous.

With respect to work organization the French system was characterized, in accordance with Taylorist and bureaucratic rationales, by the use of large numbers of middle managers. The organizational dynamic of French firms was based on a close link between individuals and their work positions and by the 'defence of each individual's territory and the centralized management of everybody' (Silvestre, 1990).

The French industrial relations system, the final constituent element of the employment regime, has been constructed over a long period of time by successive social strata (peasants, then craftsmen). As a result the French working class can be considered as both heterogeneous and proletarian, a characteristic which has not facilitated the development of a homogeneous labour movement based on just a small number of large trade union organizations.

Furthermore, following the Second World War the state played a leading role in the industrial relations system. During this period economic growth and industrial harmony were more crucial than dealing with the challenge of competitiveness or employment issues (Touraine, 1990). The state's action in this sphere had three objectives: the defence of national identity, the promotion of technological progress and the rebirth of trade unions. In such a framework characterized by a desire to modernize industrial democracy, the division of labour was the object of a tacit compromise. While employers concentrated on labour rationalization in order to obtain productivity gains, the trade unions gave priority to wages without challenging the system as a whole, which was rather efficient at generating profits. Such a system led to a situation in which a large minority of workers were unionized (union density was about 25 per cent at the beginning of the 1970s) and the industry level was regarded as the most pertinent collective bargaining level.

The French welfare state

The general principles underlying the constitution and operation of a welfare state 'à la française' were firmly established as early as 1945. As Palier (2007) notes, the French welfare regime was based on four pillars that supported the model until well into the 1980s at least: the eligibility criteria for social protection were based on the protection of workers, social benefits were considered as a deferred wage and social insurance contributions determined individual rights to social protection as well as the legitimacy of collective actors to be actively involved. In such a system both the decision-making and the management and control processes denied the state a dominant role. Rather than just the welfare state alone it was the social protection apparatus as a whole that constituted a system in the 1970s. Until the beginning of the 1980s France's conservative-corporatist regime (Esping-Andersen, 1990) was characterized by the important role played by occupational status in the acquisition of welfare rights. The social security system was funded by contributions based on wages. Its primary purpose was to provide wage-earners with resources in periods when they were not working, in other words in case of sickness, unemployment or retirement (Gautié, 2003). The French model could be described as 'conservative' because the head of the family occupied a dominant position within it. Welfare rights were derived from work and not individual citizenship. In a system of this kind spouses and children had the status of indirect beneficiaries.

However, the state's role in the employment and social system was not merely protective. Indeed in the 1970s it was a major actor in the socio-economic system. During this Fordist period it strengthened the wage-labour nexus in at least two ways. Firstly, it was a large provider of jobs. In the 1970s the public sector accounted for 18 per cent of all jobs. Secondly, the French State owned the most important firms in key industrial sectors (gas and electricity, transport, postal and telecommunications services, automotive) and was the initiator of macroeconomic policies which, especially during the 1970s, gave priority to investment and, more generally, to Keynesian policies. At the beginning of the 1980s, with the election of a Socialist president, the state became an even more important player following several waves of nationalization in both the manufacturing and financial sectors (including the leading French banks).

This link between the state and the economy was especially strong since the largest companies, including the major banks, had extremely close relations with the state, not least due to the manner in which their leaders were selected.[2] Thus, decisive action taken by the political/administrative elites is one of the main features of the French mode of governance. To a greater extent than in other countries the top graduates of the prestigious *grandes écoles* (Ecole Polytechnique, Ena and so on) are able to move freely between the world of business and the upper reaches of the political/administrative system. These characteristics, combined with the high level of public spending on industrial policies and the institutionalization of state intervention in the economy through the economic planning system (which includes subsidies for firms and industries), are the reasons why France is often classified in typologies of capitalism as a 'statist country' or a 'dirigist state'.

Structural changes and new actor configurations

A paradigm shift brought about by a process of 'sedimentation'

It was in 1983 that monetarist considerations took over the Keynesian-Colbertist precepts that had hitherto underpinned economic coordination. The deflation strategy ordered in 1983 by François Mitterand exemplifies this strategic turning point, with the socialist government doing an about-turn after having tried to revive the economy by boosting demand immediately on coming to power. This strategy was presented both as a response to an exogenous shock and as the result of the increasingly constraining pressure exerted by European institutions. As government experts of the time noted, not to have given way to this pressure would have plunged the indicators into the red, aggravating the budget deficit and increasing government debt at a time when the international economic situation was bleak. The rhetoric accompanying the policy U-turn focused on the need for competitive deflation. From the point of view of employment policy this major change meant that priority was henceforth given to the supply side. The lowering of social insurance contributions to drive down overall labour costs was soon to become a lever favoured almost as a matter of course by governments of both right and left. This turning point is further illustrated by the marked slowdown in the growth of the purchasing power of the minimum wage (SMIC) from 1983 onwards, which has never again reached its previous level (Direction de la prévision, 2004b).

In the second phase it was social policy that was affected. The objective was to strike a balance between maintaining a system of social protection (to which French citizens are much attached) and controlling direct and indirect labour costs. A compromise was found through the gradual separation of occupational and national solidarity, a split that grew wider from the second half of the 1980s onwards. The introduction of the *revenu minimum d'insertion* (RMI) in 1988,[3] of the *contribution sociale généralisée/generalized social contribution* (CSG) in 1991 and of the anti-exclusion legislation in 1998 all adhere to the same principle, whereby the state takes responsibility for the poorest members of society but is required to refocus its action on the most impoverished, in order to contain what Castel (1995) calls the new 'mass vulnerability'. This shift towards a more welfare-based form of social solidarity, a shift we could also describe as a hybridization of the Bismarckian French welfare regime, has taken place through a process of 'sedimentation', that is a series of incremental changes rather than a sudden break with the past. The social safety nets already existed in France before the 1980s. It was partly as a result of the gradual cutting back of unemployment insurance benefits that a large number of people were transferred to welfare benefits. Finally, it should be noted that the new balance between occupational and national solidarity has benefited from a policy that encourages young people to remain dependent on their parents for a longer period (for example encouragement of young people to stay longer and longer in education in order that the vast majority of any one generation can obtain the baccalauréat). In this respect the French family has acted, and continues to act, as a social shock absorber that cushions young people from the difficulties they experience in obtaining a permanent foothold in the labour market.

The political/administrative elite at the heart of the split

Jobert and Théret (1994) show that the French political elite was converted to neoliberalism even before it was adopted by the left-wing government that came to power in the early 1980s. Initially, Europe was used as a resource by national actors already won over by the idea of neoliberal reforms. Exchanges between the French and European elites then intensified and shared values and ideas gradually emerged, which undoubtedly had some influence on the attempts to reform social protection during the 1990s. Thus, it was in the name of Europe and of European integration that many unpopular policies were pursued in France. The Maastricht Treaty finally put the seal on this declared dependency between national economic policies and the European project, since from then on politicians were to refer incessantly to the stability pact when attempting to push through neoliberal reforms.

Indeed, responsibility for the 1983 break with the past cannot be attributed to employers' associations, for example the Centre National du Patronat Français who up until the end of the twentieth century have had a low profile in the promotion of neoliberalism. However, the trade union actors have also remained divided and weak (about 8 per cent of French employees now belong to a trade union, and the figure in the private sector is only 5 per cent). The hardening of economic and social policies has undoubtedly increased the historical fragmentation of the trade union movement and blurred the established divisions in the political landscape. The fact remains that the legitimacy of the trade unions is weaker than ever before. Three indicators (among others) bear witness to this: the decline of the traditional trade unions' activist and membership base, the emergence of new actors (independent [non-confederated] trade unions, NGOs, associations for the unemployed, coordinating committees, informal economy) and, finally, the reduced involvement of the major trade union confederations in economic and social decision-making at national level in favour of increasingly decentralizing bargaining to industry and company level. Moreover, in the 2000s the renamed Mouvement des Entreprises de France (formerly CNPF) became a source of new ideas and demands for change. For example, one of its highest-profile initiatives in the 2000s (Lallement and Mériaux, 2003) has been to promote individualized pay management and a competence-based approach in human resource management to complement the increasing contractualization of industrial relations.

The state's new personas

In line with the changed economic philosophy the reduction of public expenditure has been a constant and omnipresent objective since the mid-1980s. What are the actual implications of this? The first one is that the state's role as an entrepreneur has faded away over the years. The Commission for the National Plan, and with it the very idea of economic planning, had already lost any influence it once had before the agency was abolished at the end of 2005. In fact industrial policy quickly went out of fashion after the left came to power at the beginning of the 1980s. The ambitions once associated with the interventionist state were scaled back drastically as the *'grands projets'* strategy inherited from the Gaullist period ran out of steam and the national champions were privatized. The two major waves of privatization completed the withdrawal of the state from its role as shareholder. Does this mean the end of any intervention by the French state in industrial matters? This is certainly not the case and we will show that state intervention continued, albeit in new ways, as at the time of major mergers in the manufacturing and banking sectors. State-funded research has also undergone many decisive changes. One of the most spectacular recent reforms paves the way for the gradual replacement of a model embodied by the *Centre National de la Recherche Scientifique*, which employs full-time researchers with the status of civil servants, with a system which combines a funding agency (*Agence Nationale de la Recherche*) and incentives for the expansion of private research.

Over the last two decades the state has tended to reposition itself as an actor in the realm of public action; at the same time the modes of coordination between the state and the other actors have undergone a gradual change which 'assured that large firms were able to construct a novel institutional environment for their own adjustment and then induce other relevant actors – the state, labour unions, the workforce, other companies, and the financial world – to act according to their preferences' (Hancké, 2001, p. 333). The 'hard core shareholders' policy[4] adopted by Prime Minister Edouard Balladur in 1993 clearly illustrates the way in which the state can intervene on specific occasions in order to defend a Gaullist vision of the economy while at the same time continuing to play the neoliberal card. After all, the intention behind the 'cross holdings' strategy was to preserve a national form of capitalism based on captains of industry while at the same time allowing the state gradually to withdraw from its position as shareholder in the large industrial groups. The consequence is that certain elites have been in a stronger position than ever to influence the future of the large firms and hence that of many employees' jobs. At the end of the 1990s 45 per cent of the members of the board of directors of CAC 40[5] companies were drawn from the senior branches of the civil service (the so-called *grands corps*), 10 per cent of directors held 35 per cent of the seats and of the 12 directors who held the most seats, ten were graduates of the *Ecole Polytechnique*. In recent years, however, the elites' predominance has been tempered by the rise of new actors in the wake of financial globalization, with international shareholders such as investment funds gaining seats on management boards and outside consultants implementing reforms.

When it comes to social policy the state has adopted yet another persona, that of driving force or prime mover (Donzelot and Estèbe, 1994). This persona of the state as prime mover has emerged at a time when two major trends are transforming public action: decentralization and territorialization. Decentralization, firstly, denotes the transfer of competences to elected local bodies that used to be the preserve of the legislative and executive branches of central government. In two separate waves of decentralization (Decentralization Acts I and II of 1984 and 2004 respectively) the *conseils généraux* (roughly equivalent to the English county councils) have been given virtually full responsibility for the management of social welfare (including the RMI) and for the implementation of social programmes. The overall planning of vocational training and the provision of continuing vocational training for the unemployed (both young people and adults) was also decentralized between 1984 and 2004.

The territorialization of public policies brings into play another mechanism for mobilizing local actors, this time within the state itself (Gaudin, 1999). The aim here is to take account of local realities in the implementation of public policies by giving the local representatives of central government considerable room for manoeuvre when it comes to the targeting and distribution of budgets. This applies, for example, to the management of labour market integration measures aimed at individuals. The last institutional innovation in this area was the introduction of so-called territorial plans. These are plans drawn up by local actors who come together in order to build a development strategy based on a common diagnosis. Regional authorities are encouraged by law to enter into contracts with actors in their territories on the basis of their development projects.

Between new governance and social fragmentation

Unlike the Nordic countries France has never been fertile ground for neo-corporatism, a system commonly defined as a political architecture within which the state grants just a few actors the legitimacy of representing the main interest groups in a given area. In the world of work this leads to 'political exchanges' that encourage the negotiation of compromises that commit both trade unions and employers. The social history of France since the end of the Second World War clearly reveals the obstacles to adopting such a model and the reluctance of the actors to do so. Thus, it is no paradox that, even today, the state is still the prime mover in certain spheres. Should negotiations break down it is the state that, as a last resort, imposes its views and instruments. In several areas, nevertheless, the traditional actors in industrial relations, especially the state itself, have lost ground to market rationales. This has had a direct impact on employment in a number of different ways. Between 1985 and 2000 employment in public firms was dramatically reduced. As a result of its privatizations the state lost its control over strategic firms and its 'hard core shareholders' strategy has been challenged by foreign capital flows. Financial markets are playing an increasing role, while large companies are concentrating on their core activities in order to improve their share value. However, the model of governance that is emerging is not totally new. It would be more accurate to talk of a sliding effect because, in spite of some significant changes, neoliberal pressure is actually strengthening some classic features of French capitalism, such as the increasing exclusion of employees from decision procedures and the central role of management in the training process (Culpepper et al., 2006).

Such an outcome, rather than confirming the radical rupture hypothesis, encourages us to reconsider the evolution of French capitalism and of its employment regime in terms of fragmentation. This is particularly true in the case of industrial relations, since it is a field in which there are sectors and spaces regulated in ways that diverge from the dominant features of the French model. There is very little similarity, for example, between sectors that have no tradition of social dialogue, in which the actors are not organized and precarious employment is widespread (for example retailing), closed labour markets in which the trade unions play an important role in the management of employment (for example banking), and major sectors (such as the metalworking industry) that have powerful actors and are often at the forefront of innovation in bargaining. Not only is the French industrial relations system heterogeneous, it also includes neo-corporatist spaces that still flourish today. This is the case in the field of vocational training and the management of social insurance schemes (unemployment, sickness and so on). It is thus these new configurations of actors that have shaped the dynamics of the French employment model over the past 25 years.

Transformations of the French model

Economic growth: Paradoxical symptoms, paradoxical analyses

The evolution of the French economy is marked by a number of tensions. First, the crisis in the French growth model has been primarily characterized by a single, more or less permanent feature, namely a high unemployment rate that has persisted since the mid-1980s (see Figure 7.1). Second, sustained gains were achieved in the 1980s, particularly in many service activities such as retailing or banking. This growth was even more spectacular when the French performance in this area is compared with that of other developed countries. The early 1990s marked a clear break, since it was during this period that the lowest hourly productivity gains were recorded (1.5 per cent per annum between 1990 and 1993, see Table 7.1). The slowdown was partially checked in the years that followed due to the introduction of the 35-hour week and the work intensification that occurred as a result (almost 2 per cent per year between 1999 and 2005).

The idea that growth no longer creates jobs is a received idea based on the notion that unemployment is linked to the growth in productivity gains. However, the slowdown in the increase in per capita productivity gains observed in the industrialized countries, from 4 per cent per annum between 1950 and 1979, then to 2 per cent per annum and even as low as

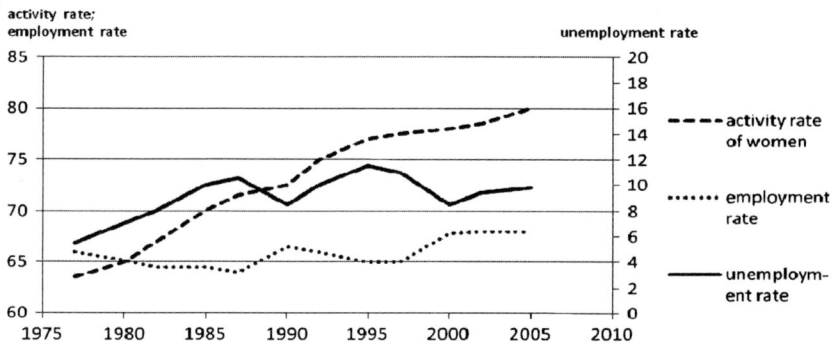

Figure 7.1 Activity rate, employment rate, unemployment rate in France, 1975–2006 (%)
Source: Eurostat and Enquêtes Emploi

Table 7.1 Labour productivity, 1987–2005

	Labour productivity	Hourly productivity
1987–90	2.3%	2.7%
1990–93	1.3%	1.5%
1993–96	1.1%	1.7%
1996–99	1.4%	2.0%
1999–2005	1.7%	1.9%

Sources: French national accounts (in full-time equivalents) for labour productivity; OECD, for hourly productivity

1 per cent in some countries, including France, means that, all other things being equal, growth has become twice as 'rich in jobs'. Whereas in the three decades following the Second World War growth of 4 per cent was required to increase employment in Europe, only a little more than 1 per cent is required today. Thus, the problem is more a lack of growth, particularly in the Euro zone.

Investments are a second area for paradoxical trends. France's international performance with regard to foreign direct investment (FDI) has for several decades now reflected the improvement in the attractiveness of the French economic system (5th in the world in 1990, 2nd in 2006). This attractiveness is not unconnected with the increases in price competitiveness resulting from the spectacular reduction in relative wage costs. But this attractiveness is also the result of high average living standards and the generally high quality of life associated with France's generous welfare state. In any case France has followed hard on the heels of many of its partners in opting for a policy of price and cost control. The real turning point came in the mid-1980s. However, it has often implemented the policy even more rigorously than its partners, as the following graph (Figure 7.2) shows.

This has been reflected in a strong desire to keep interest rates relatively high, a policy given fresh impetus by the Central European Bank, in the name of the fight against inflation. Inflation has indeed been held in check spectacularly in France over the last two decades (see Table 7.2), albeit at the cost of a relatively low level of investment in a 'structurally recessionary' context. Thus, the dynamism of FDI contrasts with the low levels of investment by French companies, particularly in new technologies.

Third, France's economic performance, as reflected in the evolution of the balance of trade, has been variable. The 1980s were a period of deficit, with trade being particularly sensitive to fluctuations in the price of oil. The improvement in the balance of trade from 1991 onwards reflected the increased competitiveness of French firms; however, this competitiveness weakened from the end of the 1990s as a result of the combined effects of the Asian and Russian crises and the weakening of the dollar. The turning point of

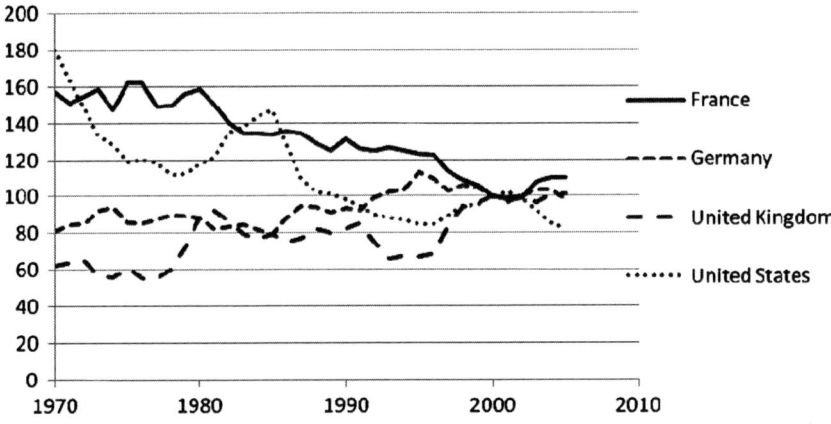

Figure 7.2 Relative unit labour costs in manufacturing, 1970–2005 (year 2000 = 100)
Source: OECD data base

the beginning of the new century is reported to have been the direct consequence of the Euro's strength *vis-à-vis* its major international partners. It is indeed a competitive burden for the country's large tourist industry (Chevillon and Timbeau, 2006). Finally, public investment as a share of gross domestic product (GDP) has declined sharply over the last decade. Between 1960 and 1991 the share was 3.5 per cent per annum on average; since 1991 it has stabilized at a low level of 1.2 per cent per annum on average (Camdessus, 2004). It is the public tools that the state is dispensing with, which also shows how, within a few years, a Keynesian economic policy has given way to a neoliberal policy, validated by the process of European integration.

Despite recurring changes of government a political consensus has been forged around an economic ideology – and diffused in a similar way by the principal elites – the main thrust of which is that the French economy has had to adapt to an open market economy that has become increasingly financialized (Aglietta and Rebérioux, 2004).

Only occasionally has France succeeded in emerging from this long-lasting crisis, at least from the point of view of job creation and economic growth. The 1997–2001 revival, during which economic growth was greater than in Europe as a whole, most certainly benefited from the cumulative effect of the introduction of the 35-hour week and of an international global economic upturn. France performed better than average when the Jospin government shifted (slightly) towards more expansionary policies while at the same time forcing companies to increase efficiency (via the 35-hour week). After the double setback of an international downturn and the Socialists' failure in the 2002 polls, the relatively short-lived period of success seemed to end rapidly.

Table 7.2 Annual variation in the French consumer price index, 1981–2005

1981–85	1986–90	1991–95	1996–2000	2001–05
9.6	3.1	2.2	1.3	2.0

Source: Institut national de la statistique et des études économiques (INSEE)

Over the period between 1997 and 2001 1.8 million jobs were created (of which 500,000 were permanent contracts concluded between March 2000 and March 2001) and unemployment fell by one million and the unemployment rate by 30 per cent. In fact, this surge in employment was driven by household consumption. Concurrently with the introduction of the 35-hour week, the positive evolution of purchasing power – real wages per capita were increasing at at least the same rate as productivity – and several budgetary measures helped to increase households' disposable income. It is also true that the Euro was weak enough at the time not to have an excessively negative impact on France's trade surplus and that the reduction in interest rates encouraged both consumption and investment. During this period, therefore, France can be said to have adopted a truly Keynesian reflationary policy in favour of full employment which, moreover, was accompanied by a shrinking of the budget deficit.

The partial recovery in growth, which extended beyond 2001, hardly had a lasting positive impact on employment. The 2008/9 crisis has destroyed the fragile progress made after the end of 2005 in reducing unemployment. France has not yet found an efficient way of dealing with its main economic and social concern: unemployment. Until now France has attempted to retain the broad principles underpinning its social model while at the same time striving to create jobs, sometimes at any price. This twofold ambition is no guarantee of coherence or consistency. This is why many tensions and contradictions have been stirred up in recent years in the very heart of the employment regime.

Current tensions in the productive and employment systems

The state: Welfare provider, employer, shareholder or strategist?

Aware of the major perceived weakness of the national model, the French state has increased its intervention in the labour market as mass unemployment has become entrenched in French society. It is against this background that we need to understand one of the significant tensions specific to the French regime. Between 1973 and 2005, and directly contrary to what the dominant neoliberal rhetoric would have us believe, public expenditure on employment soared from less than 1 per cent of GDP in the 1970s to its present share of almost 4.8 per cent of GDP. This reflected the need to develop new intermediate modes of regulation as the state consolidated its intervention in employment policy. Moreovoer, as the workfare approach has become ever more firmly established, the structure of this expenditure has changed significantly: from a fairly low level in the mid-1980s, active expenditure now accounts for 48 per cent of total expenditure on employment. The elements of this total expenditure that have increased the most are the costs of the general reductions in social insurance contributions for the low-paid and, although showing more cyclical trends, those policies for supporting the reduction in working time. Overall, the share of these tax and social security reliefs in GDP rose from 0.58 per cent in 1997 to 1.03 per cent in 2003, equivalent to 800,000 full-time minimum-wage jobs. While public spending on industrial policies almost vanished, social expenditure increased dramatically over the same period, making France's social budget close to those of the Nordic countries.

Active public policy has also reinforced the state's direct presence. Particularly since the mid-1980s, governments have very clearly committed themselves to the development of non-market jobs (subsidized jobs, mainly in the public sector and targeted at young people) and have turned them into an instrument of labour market integration. This change in the structure of public expenditure has been accompanied by a radical change in the state's analysis of the causes of unemployment. The introduction of the RMI in 1988 and its substitution by the *revenu de solidarité active* (RSA) in 2009 is symptomatic in this regard: the benefit offered to individuals without a job is combined with a so-called integration contract that potentially affords them access to the labour market. From this point of view the state has undoubtedly given in to the siren calls of workfare (Astier, 2007). At the same time active public policy has also encouraged the development of market-oriented local services (personal and domestic services such as non-public childcare), of business services and of the hotel and catering industry. The tools used for this purpose are the so-called service cheques and tax reliefs for employers for the first type of services (personal and domestic services), reductions in social insurance contributions for part-time jobs and low-paid jobs for the second type.

The French state still leaves its imprint directly on the labour market through a steady increase in employment in the public service. In 2005 it was still the largest employer in France, with a workforce that varies, depending on the agreements, between 5.2 and 5.9 million people, that is between 21 and 24 per cent of total employment (Ministère du budget, 2007). In this particular segment of the labour market employment grew by 24 per cent between 1982 and 2004, with the public service in the regions accounting for a large share of the increase (+38 per cent). Over the same period total employment in France rose by only 13 per cent (Raynaud, 2003).

The changes in state policy have also had a direct impact on corporate governance. The mid-1980s are the key period in this regard. They mark the beginning of the state's withdrawal from its role as corporate shareholder as a result of two waves of large-scale privatizations, the first in 1986, the second in 1993. The last public monopolies – electricity generation and distribution (EDF), the railways (SNCF) and postal services (La Poste) – were not dismantled but opened up to competition as a direct result of European directives. Until the crisis of 2008 no government, of either left or right, has undertaken any new nationalizations since 1982. In this respect France today is in a similar situation to its European partners.

Furthermore, the globalization of financial markets has quickened the pace of mergers and acquisitions and led to a new level of concentration and restructuring. This is particularly true in manufacturing industry (automotive industry, life sciences, chemicals) and increasingly so in the service sector (telecommunications, large-scale retailing, hotels, IT). In contrast to earlier periods the strategic decisions of large multinational firms, including employment policies, are now no longer strongly influenced by the state. Moreover, the new national champions, such as Cap Gemini (the leading European IT service firm), have developed without benefiting from the French economic planning system. With their origins in the strictly French tradition of economic planning put in place after the Second World War, the five-year plans were finally abolished in 1993.

At the same time, however, the role of small and medium-sized firms has never before been lauded to quite the same extent by the authorities, as is shown by the recurrent waves of policy initiatives intended to encourage new start-ups. Another area of state activity is revealed if we examine more closely the alarms regularly sounded about corporate relocation and deindustrialization. Public concern with these issues has led to different initiatives, such as the establishment in 2005 of an industrial innovation agency and the funding of regional competitiveness clusters (*pôles territoriaux de compétitivité*). In this indirect way the state is still seeking to influence broad economic strategies. It also still intervenes more directly by accelerating or blocking planned mergers or acquisitions. This was the case with Arcelor and Mittal (steel making) and the long-mooted merger between Suez and Gaz de France. True, these interventions are the object of hard negotiations with the European supranational authority. Nevertheless, the state is always very active in a number of different and sometimes contradictory ways, depending on the particular area of intervention.

An employment regime under pressure from unemployment

Since the mid-1980s the unemployment rate in France has always been very high, regardless of the government in power; it has never been lower than 8 per cent as shown in Figure 7.1 above. There has been virtually no period of respite in the labour market, with the exception of the slight improvement between 1997 and 2001, in contrast to the experience of most other European countries.

Such high labour market disequilibrium constitutes a real tension and impacts on the overall labour market situation. It impacts first on financial balances as the welfare system has remained overall relatively generous over time. Funding unemployment insurance and social policy have become key financial issues. Social issues have also concerned the way to deal with the exclusion from the labour market and the relative impoverishment of a growing segment of the population. Indeed since 1992, apart from time-sharing, efforts to deal with this structural unemployment have focused on reducing labour costs.

The most important development in this respect is undoubtedly the policy of wage moderation that has been in place permanently since the mid-1980s. In any event one of the specificities of the French model is still the difficulty of producing a balanced wage compromise in which productivity gains are accompanied by simultaneous guarantees of stable wages.

The reduction of labour costs has also been on the agenda of successive governments, which have displayed a remarkably consistent concern with driving down employer's social insurance contributions, particularly for low-paid jobs, in order to create employment: between 1996 and 2004 they fell from 44 per cent to 32 per cent. One of the notable effects of this policy is the increase in the number of people employed in minimum-wage jobs. Thus, between 1994 and 2002 the share of workers receiving the minimum wage increased from 8 per cent to 14 per cent (Direction de la prévision, 2004b). This phenomenon is due in part to substitution effects: employers are being encouraged to use low-paid labour rather than workers that cost more. However, this development can also be explained by regular upratings of the minimum wage.

The focus on labour cost reductions has contributed to persistent overall economic inequalities in France. According to the most recent studies there was a turning point in the mid-90s, with the richest 1 per cent of households experiencing a 20 per cent increase in income between 1998 and 2005. The top 0.1 per cent or 0.01 per cent of wealthy people have gained even more: 32 per cent and 43 per cent respectively over the last eight years. This is in sharp contrast to what happened to 90 per cent of households, who gained less than 5 per cent over the same period (Landais, 2007). More generally, high unemployment rates and the implementation of policies aimed at reducing labour costs have had the effect of increasing segmentation, as the large number of workers who are either unemployed or in insecure jobs have been marginalized.

Against a background of persistent unemployment, how is the employment regime reconstituting itself? Social dynamics in general and those of employment in particular cannot be described without reference to the profound changes in productive activity and workers' profiles. As far the latter are concerned, over the long run it is the steady inflow of large numbers of women into the labour market since the beginning of the 1960s that emerges first as one of the most distinctive characteristics of the evolution of employment in France. Thus, the female participation rate rose from 51 per cent in the mid-1970s to 64 per cent in 2006. Since the unemployment rate remains high and unevenly distributed between the genders, the female employment rate is significantly lower (58 per cent in 2006). Moreover, contrary to the French tradition of combining a relatively high female labour market participation and high fertility rates, recent governments have shifted their 'family policy' towards greater incentives for women to reduce their labour market participation after giving birth to a first or second child. In the past these incentives applied only to women with three children or more.

Although the average employment rate for the 25–50 age group is quite close to the European standard, lower employment rates are to be found at the extremes of the age spectrum. The evolution of participation rates among the under-25s is characterized by a very significant reduction up until the beginning of the twenty-first century: this is the simultaneous effect of a high youth unemployment rate and a national standard that tends to delay young people's exit from the education system. With an unemployment rate of the order of 23 per cent in 2006, the 15–24 age group has gradually become a true adjustment variable in the labour market (Givord, 2005). Among older workers the evolution of participation rates differs by gender. The constant increase in participation rates among women aged over 50 contrasts with the more varied evolution of the male participation rate, which declined significantly for men aged over 50 during the 1980s and then remained stable until 1995 before beginning to rise quite significantly again. The year 2000 seems to have marked an important turning point, however. After 20 consecutive years of decline in the share of young people and older workers in employment, that share began to rise, particularly among older male workers. However, this development, which is consistent with the Lisbon goals, has not had a lasting effect on the national unemployment rate, which remained above 9 per cent between 2000 and 2005.

From employment conditions to working and training conditions

With respect to work organization the French productive system essentially combines organizational modes of the 'lean production' type, in which workers' autonomy is restricted and closely controlled, with organizational modes of the 'learning' type, in which workers enjoy considerable autonomy and are subject to fewer constraints in the workplace. Taylorism has not disappeared but it now plays a minor role (Lorenz and Valeyre, 2004). The trend towards concentration among financial groups, which are playing an increasingly important role in structuring the division of labour, is in fact favouring an expansion of organizations that adopt simple organizational structures. Over and above the constraints associated with performance targets or work intensification, the advent of a service economy based on such jobs has been accompanied by a worsening of working conditions for a significant proportion of wage workers (increase in part-time working, absence of regulations in some areas of the domestic and personal services sector). The expansion of the service sector, and more specifically of activities based on service relations, has also disrupted the ways in which skills and pay levels are defined. The previous institutionalized grading structures combining work content, job and pay level are being replaced by new ways of recognizing employees' worth (classification criteria, competence criterion). To this must be added the explosion since 1994 of unskilled jobs, which were wrongly thought to have been eliminated by the advent of the knowledge and information society (Gadrey et al., 2004). This strong increase is directly linked to the generous tax reductions granted to firms hiring low-paid workers.

It is perhaps in the rigidities of education and training that path dependency is most pronounced. On the one hand a system that values strong formal links between training and employment persists, with formal qualifications continuing to play a key role in recruitment. On the other hand these same links are being called into question, particularly as a result of the emergence of new needs (for example the banking industry, as well as in elderly care services or hotel and restaurant services) demanding new forms of certification. At the point where these two trends meet, therefore, life-long training is beginning to play an increasingly important role. It started with the alternating contracts introduced in the mid-1980s. Similarly, the 2004 Continuing Training Act is the legislative embodiment of an intersectoral agreement signed by all the social partners. It introduced 'upskilling contracts' (*contrats de professionnalization*) and an individualized right to training. Nevertheless, these measures are often regarded as inadequate given the scale of the challenges to be met. We would concur with Verdier (2001) that these multifarious changes in the employment and productive systems have not affected the education and training regime in any predictable way. Despite the establishment of mass education on an unprecedented scale, the selection, filtering and exclusion mechanisms continue to operate.

Working time, finally, has been a political issue in France for the last 15 years (since 2003), with the aim always of finding ways of reducing unemployment. It is still dependent on state action, as is illustrated by two major shifts: the increase encouraged by the state in part-time work since the beginning of the 1980s (from 6 per cent in 1972, to 9 per cent in 1983 and up to 17 per cent in 2006) and the move to the 35-hour week at the end of the 1990s, under the provisions of the two so-called Aubry Acts. Although the state remains active in this area, encouraging work-sharing through either of these two channels, firms enjoy considerable room for manoeuvre to negotiate the implementation of this individual or collective working-time reduction. Thus, the transition to the 35-hour week, which applies to approximately half of all employees, has been accompanied by an increase in production plant utilization, significant productivity increases and a consequent reconfiguration of employees' working and living conditions (Lallement, 2003).

Towards a segmented welfare regime

Each of the welfare regime pillars mentioned earlier has been under pressure and has changed as a result. Again, the persistence of high unemployment at the beginning of the 1990s led to major changes in the funding of unemployment benefit, in particular an increase in social insurance contributions through extension of the contributions period and a sliding scale of benefits depending on age and duration. However, these major changes, although they have improved the social security accounts, will increase the number of long-term unemployed excluded from any state assistance.

Over and above the financing of unemployment benefit, the whole of the social protection system has been gradually reformed. The new forms of social precariousness and insecurity that have become widespread with the crisis have helped to confuse the relationship, in matters of social policy, between the assistance principle and the insurance principle. For a long time the assistance principle prevailed when it came to covering the risks of socially targeted populations incapable of working, because of handicap, sickness, age or family situation, while the insurance principle was applied to the most impoverished who could not be assisted because they were not suffering from any form of incapacity. Today there are two types of institutional arrangements aimed at employable people without jobs who find themselves in the expanding no man's land between assistance and insurance. Firstly, there is the national unemployment insurance scheme, which is administered by UNEDIC (*Union nationale pour l'emploi dans l'industrie et le commerce*). A significant change was negotiated in 1984 with the introduction of the ASS (*allocation de solidarité spécifique*/special solidarity allowance), which replaces unemployment benefit when entitlement has expired. Secondly, the state provides various forms of income support (of which there are now eight) which, with the notable exception of the RMI, are means tested. The RMI is an interesting case. This is a benefit whose principle is not far removed from that of an unconditional income; in its way – and starting as far back as the 1980s – this benefit is testament to the failure of employment policies and the increasing marginalization of populations that are employable but not in employment. Because of the tightening of the conditions for claiming unemployment benefits since the beginning of the 1990s, the number of people claiming the RMI has more than tripled, from 400,000 in 1990 to 1,256,000 in 2006.

The reforms of the French social protection system, by separating insurance and welfare, have had a dualizing effect at three levels (Palier, 2007). Firstly, the populations concerned have been segmented into two groups. On the one hand there are those people covered by insurance, that is those who have made sufficient contributions to claim social insurance benefits, social security itself and supplementary insurance benefits. On the other hand there are those whose only recourse is the solidarity or welfare regime and who can only claim means-tested benefits. Secondly, social protection is now provided through private as well as public organizations. People in the insurance regime are no longer covered by a single, unified public system, since private actors are playing an increasingly important role, particularly since the turn of the twenty-first century. Thirdly, mandatory social protection administered by the state is itself increasingly segmented into two subsectors. The first is made up of schemes based on the social insurance principle (retirement pensions and unemployment benefits, even though they include means-tested benefits for the poorest). The second is composed of schemes in which the non-contributory rationale is playing an ever greater role; these schemes are financed out of taxation and provide lump sum benefits (healthcare, family allowances and state social policy at national, regional and municipal level).

Conclusion

The current French employment model is the outcome both of continuities with the past, which may be linked to a certain individual and collective resistance to change, and of changes brought about by the increasing role of market coordination and the reconfiguration of actors and of their roles against a background of increasing European construction. Profound changes have taken place while the institutional framework has remained largely in place, maintaining and strengthening the minimum wage, high social protection and so on. In spheres as crucial as employment and social policy the role of social actors has been strengthened. In others, such as education policy or industrial relations, they have given way to new actors. Thus, the principal characteristic of the changes in the French employment regime lies less, as is often believed, in the important position that the state still occupies in economic and social life. Rather, it is the diverse configurations of actors involved in management of the changes, which as we have seen have taken place through a process of 'sedimentation' or incremental change. Overall the consequence of this process of incremental change is that France is better conceived of as a form of state-enhanced capitalism that is driven by both the state and firms, rather than as either a market-driven or a state-driven economy, let alone a neo-corporatist system.

The first consequence of these changes is the persistence of tensions, not to say contradictions, arising out of the coexistence of hybrid regulatory principles. However, the changes that have taken place in the last two decades have also had the effect of creating new risks, and even of multiplying them. Moreover, the distribution of risk across the different groups in French society has definitely changed.

Comparison of employment expectations over the life cycle in the last 25 years shows that the structure of men's and women's labour market participation rates is becoming increasingly convergent. However, if women are now more active in the labour market – in numbers well above the Lisbon target – it is at the price of a growing set of inequalities: wages, responsibilities and horizontal segmentation as a result of the feminization of certain sectors. Moreover, women tend to continue to work while birth rates remain higher than in most European countries and it is they who bear much of the burden of reconciling family life and working life.

Young people are also at risk. They have never been well integrated in France, first because they were excluded from the permanent core of the workforce during the period of growth and then because they have been used as an 'adjustment variable' during the crisis period. As a result, they are now trying to conquer a position that is still not theirs. Second, to be young in France is regarded as being dependent on family solidarity. In a context where seniority remains a determining factor for wages, older people are not as badly affected as young people by the impact of destabilized internal labour markets on unemployment.

Lastly, immigrant workers are also at risk. Selective immigration policies aimed at encouraging workers into sectors suffering from labour shortages are a new way of avoiding the growing pressure to acknowledge the skills of many low-paid service workers by increasing their pay levels. At a time when professionalization and upskilling have become watchwords in the drive to improve the quality of both work and services, the side effects of developing a growing low-wage, low-skill segment of the working population seems to be regarded as a necessary transitional period on the way to a better future. However, in a context of general crisis it might be that this transitional period will last too long, creating a circle that will be less virtuous than expected.

Notes

1. The authors gratefully acknowledge the contributions of F. Berton, F. X. Devetter, L. Lima, G. Lefevre and C. Nicole-Drancourt to previous versions of this chapter.
2. A special feature of French public life is the fact that 'five large state administrations recruited a total of forty young people in each generation, producing one third of the leading company heads in France, showed clearly that an essential part of the detection, selection and training of future industrial leaders was occurring within the nursery of the state' (Bauer and Bertin-Mourot, 1995, p. 50).
3. The RMI, a minimum welfare payment made to those not entitled to unemployment benefit, can be claimed by any person resident in France who has an income below a certain level (EUR440 for a single person), is over 25 years of age and is bringing up one or more children (already born or expected) and who undertakes to take part in programmes or activities decided on in agreement with the claimant and that will help him or her find employment or become better integrated into society.
4. The aim was to guarantee continuity in company policy by reserving a proportion of shares for a 'hard core' of shareholders who undertook to keep their shares for a minimum period before selling them again.
5. The CAC 40, which stands for *Cotation Assistée en Continu* (Continuous Assisted Quotation) is the most frequently used French stock exchange index.

References

Aglietta, M. and Rebérioux, A. (2004), *Dérives du capitalisme financier*, Paris: Albin Michel.
Astier, I. (2007), *Les nouvelles règles du social*, Paris: PUF.
Bauer, M. and Bertin-Mourot, B. (1995), 'La tyrannie du diplôme initial et la circulation des élites: la stabilité du modèle français', pp. 48–63 in E. Suleiman and H. Mendras (eds), *Le recrutement des élites en Europe*, Paris: La découverte.
Camdessus, M. (2004), 'Le sursaut – Vers une nouvelle croissance pour la France', Report for the Ministry of the Economy, Finance and Industry, Paris: La Documentation Française.
Castel, R. (1995), *Les métamorphoses de la question sociale*, Paris: Fayard.
Chevillon, G. and Timbeau, X. (2006), 'L'impact du taux de change sur le tourisme en France', *Revue de l'OFCE* 98 (2006): 167–81.
Culpepper, P., Hall, P. and Palier, B. (eds) (2006), *Changing France. The Politics that Markets Make*, New York: Palgrave Macmillan.
Direction de la prévision (2004a), 'Compétitivité et attractivité de l'économie française', *Analyses économiques* 36 (2004): 1–8.
Direction de la prévision (2004b), 'Le Smic en France, pouvoir d'achat et coût du travail sur longue période', *Analyse économique* 39 (2004): 1–6.
Donzelot, J. and Estèbe, P. (1994), *L'Etat animateur*, Paris: Esprit.
Esping-Andersen, G. (1990), *The Three Worlds of Welfare Capitalism*, Cambridge: Polity Press.
Gadrey, N., Jany-Catrice, F. and Pernod, M. (2004), 'Les non qualifiés qui sont-ils?', pp. 166–81 in D. Méda and F. Vennat (eds), *Le travail non qualifié, permanences et défis*, Paris: La découverte.
Gaudin, J. P. (1999), *Gouverner par contrat. L'action publique en question*, Paris: Presses de Sciences Po.
Gautié, J. (2003), 'Marché du travail et protection sociale: quelles voies pour l'après fordisme?', *Esprit*, Novembre (2003): 78–115.
Givord, P. (2005), 'Formes particulières d'emploi et insertion des jeunes', *Economie et Statistique* 388–9: 129–43.
Hall, P. (2007), 'The Politics of Social Change in France', pp.1–26 in P. D. Culpepper, P. A. Hall and B. Palier (eds), *Changing France. The Politics that Markets Make*, New York: Palgrave.
Hall, P. and Soskice, D. (eds) (2001), *Varieties of Capitalism*, Oxford: Oxford University Press.
Hancké, B. (2001), 'Revisiting the French Model: Coordination and Restructuring in French Industry', pp. 307–34 in P. Hall and D. Soskice (eds), *Varieties of Capitalism*, Oxford: Oxford University Press.
Jobert, B. and Théret, B. (1994), 'France: la consécration républicaine du néo-libéralisme', pp. 21–85 in B. Jobert (ed.), *Le tournant néo-libéral en Europe*, Paris: L'Harmattan.
Lallement, M. (2003), *Temps, travail et modes de vie*, Paris: PUF.
Lallement, M. and Mériaux, O. (2003), 'Status and Contracts in Industrial Relations. "La Refondation sociale", a New Bottle for an Old (French) Wine?', *Industrielle Beziehungen* 10(3): 418–37.
Landais, C. (2007), 'Les hauts revenus en France: 1998–2006', Ecole d'Economie de Paris.
Lima, L. and Nicole-Drancourt, C. (2006), 'For a Modern Social Protection System in Terms of Life Cycle. Where does France Stand?', Report for the Dynamo Project.

Lorenz, E. and Valeyre, A. (2004), *Les formes d'organisation du travail dans les pays de l'Union Européenne*, Dares, Ministère de l'emploi, Document de travail, 32.

Maurice, M., Sellier, F. and Silvestre, J. J. (1982), *Politiques d'éducation et organisation industrielle en France et en Allemagne*, Paris: PUF.

Ministère du budget, des comptes publics et de la fonction publique (2007), 'Rapport annuel sur l'état de la fonction publique 2006–2007'.

Palier, B. (2007), 'Des assurances de moins en moins sociales', pp. 855–71 in S. Paugam (ed.), *Repenser la solidarité*, Paris: PUF.

Raynaud, P. (2003), 'L'emploi public est tiré par la fonction publique territoriale', *Economie et Statistique* 369–70: 75–92.

Schmidt, V. A. (2003), 'French Capitalism Transformed, yet Still a Third Variety of Capitalism', *Economy and Society* 32 (4): 526–54.

Silvestre J. J. (1990), 'Systèmes hiérarchiques et analyse sociétale', *Revue française de gestion* 77 (1990): 107–15.

Touraine, A. (1990), 'La crise des systèmes de relations professionnelles', pp. 371–77 in J. D. Reynaud, F. Eyraud, C. Paradeise and J. Saglio (eds), *Les systèmes de relations professionnelles*, Paris: éditions du CNRS.

Verdier, E. (2001), 'La France a-t-elle changé de régime d'éducation et de formation?', *Formation Emploi* 76 (2001): 11–34.

8
Continuity and Change in the Italian Model

Annamaria Simonazzi, Paola Villa,
Federico Lucidi and Paolo Naticchioni

Introduction

The Italian model does not fit well with the existing classifications of production and welfare regimes. According to the varieties of capitalism approach, Italy is a 'deviant' case, characterized by 'a mix of logics, a high degree of institutional incoherence and an apparent absence of complementarities' (Molina and Rhodes, 2007, p. 223). A predominance of small, family firms, a large state-enterprise sector and a familistic welfare state place Italy firmly within the southern European model (Karamessini, 2008). However, in the industrial district economy of northern Italy a different dynamic interaction of economic, social, political and cultural factors is found that conforms more to the continental model of coordinated market economies (Becattini, 1987; Brusco, 1989). Two production systems are thus nested within the Italian production model. Over time the economic divide has trickled down to the social sphere so that two varieties of social services have been developed within the national familistic welfare system. This latter divide, evident in education, health and social care, is characterized by a northern model of local services, which for quality and quantity tends towards the continental model, and a southern model which is struggling with economic, structural and political difficulties. The North-South dualism of the production *and* social models is the most distinctive trait of the Italian model. These models, at the national and local level, are confronted by various challenges.

At the national level Italy has been required to make macroeconomic adjustments to meet not only the conditions for participation in the European Economic and Monetary Union (EMU) but also the challenge of globalization. The response so far has involved a wide programme of liberalization aimed at enhancing competition and efficiency. The piecemeal deregulation of the labour market which started in the 1980s has been extended to the product market through an ambitious privatization programme. The progress of reforms, however, has been hindered by a lack of consensus within politically weak coalitions subject to the veto power of various interests. The need to mediate between conflicting claims has opened the way to fragmented, often contradictory policy measures. The end result of these reforms has been an increased segmentation of the labour market – which has not been mitigated by a much-needed reform of the social protection system – and a process of privatization that, in spite of its size, has been unable to remedy the problems of inefficiency and rent seeking in the production of services and utilities.

Even stronger pressures for change have been experienced by the local productive systems. The northern and the southern production models have very different economic and political capabilities, and have responded in different ways to the increasing demands raised by changes in the demographic, social and production spheres. The industrial district model, and the pattern of specialization upon which its success was based, have been subjected to heavy pressure by the competition of low-cost countries in the far and near (European) East. The south, which risks being even more marginalized by the recent eastward enlargement of the European Union, has been unable to release itself from the grip of a pervasive underground, irregular economy. The end result does not suggest convergence between the two sub-systems: signs of a successful restructuring of the productive systems in the north, promoted by a resurgence of medium-sized firms operating *within* the prevailing pattern of specialization, coexist with signals suggesting the drift of the *Mezzogiorno* away from the north and towards a southern model no longer supported by generous transfers of funds from north to south by the central government.

In the following sections we briefly outline, first, the main features of the Italian social model, and second the main reforms of the labour and product markets. We then go on to argue that these reforms – although following to a significant extent the EU policy agenda that sets out the key areas for reform and modernization of national models – in practice have not tackled the structural weaknesses of the Italian model, namely its specialization pattern, the North-South divide and the dualism in social protection.

The making of the Italian social model

Up until the 1980s Italy's growth performance was good in comparative terms. The Italian pattern of specialization was based on a division of labour within the EU whereby Italy specialized in the production of consumption goods while continental/northern countries specialized in investment goods.

The peculiar structure of the Italian productive system allowed rapid economic growth because it was well suited to take advantage of the changes in the technological and market environment in the 1970s and 1980s that favoured flexible producers of semi-customized high-quality products (Piore and Sabel, 1984; Streeck, 1997). In the north-east of Italy a dense network of small firms, clustered in industrial districts, specialized in the manufacture of 'traditional' consumer goods; over the years these firms moved up the value chain into the manufacture of the machinery and equipment required to produce the consumer goods themselves (Brusco, 1989). At the same time the Italian share in sectors characterized by economies of scale (transport equipment) and/or high research and development (R&D) intensity was shrinking.

In the 1980s Italy had to defend its comparative advantage in the production of traditional goods by resorting to frequent devaluations of the lira. It is still an open question whether this exchange rate policy had the unintended effect of allowing procrastination in the adaptation of the Italian productive system to the changed conditions in global production and demand, thereby paving the way for the later decline in competitiveness.

The south of Italy only partially shared in this growth: the gap with respect to the north narrowed in the 1950s and 1960s but opened again in the 1970s and 1990s (having slightly narrowed in the 1980s). The search for the causes of the enduring *questione meridionale* (the southern question) produced an enormous body of literature. Among the explanations suggested were: geographical reasons, pointing to the south's distance from the core markets of continental Europe; cultural, sociological and institutional factors with their roots in a distant past (Cipolla, 1995) and resulting in a lack of social capital (Putnam, 1993); and the classical mechanisms of 'unequal exchange' between developed and less developed areas. Whatever the explanations the divide appeared impervious to public policy interventions, whether it was public investment in infrastructure, creation of state-owned enterprises or incentives to private firms to invest in the south. Disillusionment with the efficacy of public policies in promoting growth and employment, combined with the need to observe restrictive EU directives in the field of public subsidies, led to the abandonment of any direct policy in favour of the *Mezzogiorno*.

The years of high economic growth saw the enactment of several reforms that contributed to the construction of the so-called southern model of welfare (Ferrera, 1996). These reforms concerned employment and pension schemes, as well as education and health.[1] The regulatory framework of the labour market was established in the post-war period by gradually reinforcing the protection afforded to the 'standard worker'; that is, an employee working full-time on an open-ended contract. This development culminated in the approval of the Workers' Charter (*Statuto dei Lavoratori*, L. 30/1970) which laid down principles for the protection of workers and union activists at the workplace, as well as for the regulation of both industrial disputes and union organization. This law decreed that workers should be reinstated in cases of unfair dismissal in firms with at least 15 employees.[2] In 1975 two inter-confederal agreements reinforced the degree of protection granted by law. The first agreement modified the wage indexing system (*scala mobile*) and established full compensation against increases in the cost of living. The second agreement created the CIG (*Cassa Integrazione Guadagni*) for companies undergoing restructuring.[3] Protection against inflation was general (as it applied to all employees), while protection against industrial disruption (and collective dismissals) applied almost exclusively to workers employed in large firms. The combined effect of the state regulatory system (with distinct rules according to the size of firms) and differences in union power created an accentuated dualism between large and small firms. In large firms, where protection was high, unions were also able to improve working conditions through local collective bargaining; in small firms, where protection was lower, access to the CIG was much more limited, union organization was weaker, decentralized bargaining did not exist and management had greater scope for discretion.

The social protection system did not – and still does not – provide universal safety nets. The labour market system and the institutional schemes effectively grant protection to core workers, mostly prime-age men – heads of households – while tending to exclude the young, women and older workers. The income maintenance schemes, based on occupational status, display a high degree of dualism: peaks of generosity (pensions, CIG) are accompanied by large gaps in protection. There are no national minimum-income schemes for individuals and families with insufficient resources, no safeguards for workers employed in the irregular economy (a fairly large area of activity),[4] no benefits for first-time job-seekers and no safety nets in case of uninsured unemployment. In this dualistic system the way to protect oneself (and one's family members) is to gain access to what has been called the *cittadella del garantismo* (citadel of guarantees) (Ferrera, 1996, p. 20); that is, to secure a standard employment contract in the protected sectors – the public sector or large enterprises. The weak segments of the labour force must rely on their families for protection. However, in Italy there is no general state support for families in poverty and no universal guarantee of a minimum income for those outside the labour market. The lack of state support for families in poverty is only partly counterbalanced by an inefficient and unfair mix of policy tools at the national level (tax credits, tax allowances, family benefits) as well as by local authority safety net schemes, and by charities.[5]

Finally, social protection has been provided primarily through monetary transfers (especially pensions, but also disability benefits and CIG), while public services – not only childcare and elderly-care, but also public employment services – have been neglected. The focus on the family as the main care provider has had important consequences for both the product and the labour markets, namely the underdevelopment of the market for services, a lack of job opportunities for women and a correspondingly low female employment rate.

Changes and reforms

Over the past three decades the performance of the Italian economy has worsened substantially in terms of both growth and job creation (see Table 8.1). Poor job creation (a low and declining annual average rate of growth since the

Table 8.1 GDP, employment and unemployment in Italy, 1961–2006 (annual percentage change, unless otherwise stated)

	GDP (at 2000 market prices)	GDP per person employed (at 2000 market prices)	Adjusted wage share (% GDP at current factor cost)	Employment (national accounts)	Employment rate (% population)*			Unemployment rate (%LF)*	
					MF (15–64)	F (15–64)	MF (55–64)	MF (15–24)	MF (15–64)
1961–70	5.7	6.2	72.2	−0.5	na	na	na	na	na
1971–80	3.8	2.8	72.2	0.7	54.7	32.8	36.1	18.7	5.3
1981–90	2.4	1.8	68.7	0.6	53.6	34.8	34.1	25.9	8.0
1991–2000	1.6	1.6	64.6	0.2	52.1	36.8	29.3	31.4	10.7
2001–06	0.9	0.0	62.0	1.3	55.3	41.9	29.0	27.5	9.2

Source: For data on GDP, wage share, employment: European Economy, Statistical Annex (Spring 2007). For data on employment and unemployment rates (1977–2003): own computation on FGB-Istat-Cnr (1977–96) and Istat (RTFL 1993–2003)
*Average employment and unemployment rates refer to the following periods: 1977–80, 1981–90, 1991–2000, 2001–03; M = male, F = female.

mid-1970s) has translated into a low and stationary employment rate: 56 per cent in 2003 against 54.5 per cent in 1977 for the population aged 15–64.

The currency crisis of September 1992 and the ensuing severe recession[6] marked the watershed between two different economic policy scenarios. The macroeconomic context characterizing the pre-1992 period was one of instability: a tight monetary policy, aimed at accelerating the process of disinflation to keep Italy within the European Monetary System (EMS), slowed down growth, kept unemployment high and fed public deficits. The enduring inflation differential with the rest of Europe had to be compensated by frequent devaluations. With the decision to enter the EMU, monetary policy was no longer available as a policy tool. With fiscal policy restrained by the Stability and Growth Pact, and exchange rate adjustment precluded, labour and product market reforms were the only policy instruments left to the government to sustain competitiveness and growth.

Income policies: De-indexation and wage moderation

In the 1980s the persistence of inflation[7] and the difficulties faced by the economy were blamed on the labour market, namely wage indexation and labour market regulation. In the early 1990s a period of cooperative industrial relations (so-called *concertazione*) brought wage moderation and disinflation. Two inter-confederal tripartite agreements, signed in 1992 and 1993 in a context of emergency conditions in the economy, abolished the *scala mobile* (which had already been drastically reformed in 1984) to break the wage-price spiral and also reformed the bargaining system by setting two levels of bargaining: the national level was to be devoted to preserving the purchasing power of wages, and the firm level to distributing productivity gains.

Wage increases were linked to the government's inflation target, with ex-post adjustment in case of a gap between the actual and the target inflation rates, and were only to be negotiated at the end of the two-year national agreement. Thanks to the wage freeze, by 1997, the crucial year for Italy to qualify for the EMU, the inflation rate was brought down to 2 per cent. However, since the target inflation rate systematically underestimated actual inflation, and the second element (that envisaged pay increases linked to productivity) was only implemented to a very limited extent and only in medium to large firms (Naticchioni and Lucidi, 2006; Brandolini et al., 2007), the real wage in 2004 was 2.9 per cent lower than in 1992.

Finally, by drastically flattening the progression of pay with seniority, reform of the bargaining system introduced a new element of inequality between those who were employed before the agreements (and had already accumulated significant seniority pay) and those entering after the agreements, whose wage profiles remained flat at the lower entry wages.

A two-tiered labour market reform

The deregulation of the labour market started in a mild way in the mid-1980s but has progressed to a more thorough reform over the last decade.[8] Up until the end of the 1980s, in a context of a relatively even balance of power in industrial relations, reforms of labour market policies tended to proceed by consensus among government and social partners. Greater internal flexibility (in working hours, hiring practices, share of part-timers)[9] was exchanged for a limited extension of external flexibility by allowing for 'exceptions' to the standard employment contract for the hiring of youngsters and/or unemployed, so as to ease their access to employment. Thereafter, the deregulation of the labour market progressed in an erratic way, with no formal agreement with employers and unions. To avert the risk of conflict, flexibilization of the labour market was realized through the introduction of so-called non-standard employment contracts for particular groups, basically new entrants, while standard employment contracts (applying to the bulk of people already in employment) were left untouched.

As in other EU countries Italy implemented two-tiered reforms of employment protection: flexibility was increased 'at the margin' by changing the rules on hiring but leaving unchanged the rules on firing and income maintenance schemes for core workers. This policy was instrumental in the preservation of the basic framework of the Mediterranean welfare regime based on the male, prime-age breadwinner. The end result was a new segmentation among successive cohorts entering the labour market, with the latest cohorts experiencing both lower employment protection and lower income (Berloffa and Villa, 2007).

From 1995 to 2005 the share of employees with fixed-term contracts in total employment rose from 7.3 per cent to 12.3 per cent, but reached about 50 per cent among newly hired people in terms of flows. Other atypical contractual arrangements (such as collaborators and freelance workers) expanded as well. This process was accompanied by less security (in terms of future employment prospects), insufficient protection (against illness, unemployment, maternity) and lower earnings.[10] The compensating differentials theory (according to which temporary workers should command a risk premium to compensate for their higher employment instability) does not seem to hold. Available data indicate that, even after controlling for observed and unobserved personal characteristics, temporary workers earn less than their permanent counterparts, allowing firms to save on wage costs (Picchio, 2006). There is also evidence that entry wages are often below the poverty line. Increasingly precarious jobs thus command increasingly lower entry wages; hence the gap between entry wages and regular wages has widened (Rosolia and Torrini, 2007). With pay too low to guarantee economic independence, young people hired on these contracts often have to rely on their parents. This results in long cohabitation with the family and delayed formation of a new family (Facchini and Villa, 2005; Simonazzi and Villa, 2009).

The main argument in favour of deregulation of the labour market was that it would favour entry into employment of weaker segments of the workforce, primarily young people. The idea was that even a bad job is better than no job at all, because once in employment it would be easier to move to more stable jobs. Empirical studies finding partial evidence in favour of the 'stepping stones' hypothesis (Ichino et al., 2005) have been countered by other research showing that the risks of entrapment have increased for the younger cohorts (Barbieri and Scherer, 2005). There is agreement, however, that the turnover rates across various atypical jobs is far from equally distributed among young workers. Thus, temporary contracts may provide a stepping stone for the strongest segments of the young population while worsening the prospects for the weakest segments. Education, gender, geographical area and the business cycle affect the probability of transition, even if not always in the expected direction. The implications in terms of social equity are significant: those families that cannot afford to support their members while they search for a good job will be discriminated against, and their children will lack opportunities to transit to good jobs. Difficulties in transition to a regular job will result in an extended period of mobility, which means passing through extended spells of unemployment.

Demographic change and pension reforms

Italy is ageing rapidly as a result of a declining birth rate and an increase in life expectancy. By affecting the size of flows in and out of active life,[11] demographic factors may explain the recent parallel downward trends in youth employment and unemployment rates (Simonazzi and Villa, 2009). Indeed, despite favourable demographic trends and labour market reforms intended to favour the entry of young cohorts into the labour market, their employment rate remains very low. The reduction in youth unemployment rate since the mid-1990s (see Table 8.1) is due more to the fall in the numbers of young cohorts (resulting in a reduction of inflows into the labour force) than to the supposedly beneficial effects of deregulation policies.

Italy also has one of the lowest employment rates for older workers (Table 8.1), particularly for females. Access to generous early-retirement schemes (that is, earnings-related seniority pensions) has certainly played a role: workers in their 50s were allowed or even encouraged to exit the formal labour market, very often to re-enter the grey market, owing to legislation that restricted the possibility of having a dependent work contract once retired. However, the lower participation of older workers is also the result of choices made over the whole life cycle: first and foremost, for women, the life-cycle 'decision' of not participating in the labour market.

The combination of an ageing population and the generosity of the pension schemes developed in the years of high growth severely strained public finances. The pension reforms undertaken in the 1990s[12] aimed at curbing the share of pension expenditure in GDP relied on three factors: benefit computation rules (from earnings-related to contribution-related schemes); indexation rules (benefits no longer indexed to real wage growth but to GDP growth rate); and retirement age and eligibility criteria (modified on the basis of actuarial rules).

Pension reforms have reduced expectations concerning the future level of pension benefits. First, the replacement rate (that is, the ratio between the first pension benefit and last wage) has been significantly reduced, so that it is almost impossible for an atypical worker to provide for a decent state pension in retirement.[13] Second, the changes introduced in the indexation mechanism will lead to a progressive reduction in pension benefits after retirement.

But the implementation of the pension reforms has been gradual, with a very long transitional period. Hence, the reforms have created three different groups: senior employees, still enjoying not only earnings-related pension benefits but also the possibility of 'seniority pensions', allowing early retirement once they reach 35 years of contributions; prime-age employees with benefits computed partly on the old and partly on the new rules; and the young employees to whom only the new rules will apply. These three groups have been affected by the pension reforms to very different extents, not only with respect to contributions and payments but also pensionable ages.[14]

By interacting with the deregulation of the labour market the pension reform has superimposed yet another dualism on an already dualistic structure, affecting the younger generations in particular. The cohorts born in the 1940s and 1950s, the only ones to have fully benefited from the brief period of employment protection, must cope with the insecurity of their grown-up children caused by their present increased precariousness and their future meagre pensions, as well as with the increasing risk of skyrocketing costs of care in the case of loss of independence in their own old age. With no safety nets in place, greater vulnerability at these various levels – on the job, in family income and in the macroeconomy – affects future perspectives and can explain the widespread perception of increasing poverty and insecurity even among older generations.

Privatization and corporate governance

During the past 15 years (since 1993) the Italian economy has undergone a raft of privatizations (the largest in Europe in terms of total revenues) combined with gradual liberalization of public utilities' markets. Various factors have combined to trigger privatization plans: the need to reduce the national debt, the crisis of large firms, stringent European legislation in the areas of competition and state subsidies, and the search for greater efficiency and competitiveness. The creation of a National Antitrust Authority (AGCM) in 1990, significantly later than in most other European countries, is a landmark in the change of attitudes in favour of competition.

Deregulation and privatization are still ongoing. But after 15 years, market inefficiencies, prevalence of rent seeking and shortages in the supply of collective services have been widely denounced.[15] These massive reforms have created the *conditions* for a truly market-oriented capitalism but so far they have only marginally changed actors' expectations and behaviour (Barca, 2005). The impact of privatization on the productive system has been different in regulated sectors, operating under a natural monopoly regime, and in market sectors, where state-owned and private companies coexisted prior to privatization. In the former case, with the possible exception of telecommunications, privatization effectively transferred a dominant position from a public to a private enterprise, thus calling for effective regulation to prevent abuses, but which has only been partially implemented. In the latter case involving more traditional industries, the main outcome has been an increase in market concentration: privatized companies have been acquired by companies operating in the same sector in order to achieve economies of scale and expand market share.

Whether these reforms have generated greater efficiency is still an open question. Costi and Messori (2005) have passed a severe judgement on the entire process of privatization. They maintain that privatization provided the few remaining large private Italian firms with opportunities to enter protected sectors, where high rents could still be earned. The way in which privatizations were implemented produced three negative results: (1) it created a tight web of interests in favour of rent-seeking positions, thus reinforcing opposition to further liberalization of public utilities; (2) it diverted financial and organizational resources from the core businesses of the buying firms, thus reinforcing the negative trend in competitiveness in sectors open to international competition; and (3) it led to increased indebtedness of the newly privatized firms as a consequence of the debt used to finance the acquisitions. Privatized firms, which under the previous regime of state-owned enterprises had benefited from a 'soft budget constraint' and made up the core of the R&D activity, met their enormous indebtedness by cutting back on investment in innovation and moving to the more lucrative activity of service provision. Costi and Messori (2005) conclude that the privatization and liberalization process in Italy has destroyed positive externalities for the Italian productive system and resulted in a missed opportunity to introduce real innovation into the Italian productive structure.

The privatization process also affected financial markets. In particular it contributed to the development of the Italian stock market, from a very low base. In 1992 the value of listed companies was only 7.6 per cent of GDP, while in 2000, at the end of the main wave of divestments, it was 51.9 per cent; 60 per cent of this increase was related to the flotation of privatized companies (Mediobanca, 2000, Chapter 3). At the same time the number of savers investing in the stock exchange increased considerably, providing more opportunities for firms to finance themselves through equity. However, the privatization programme probably missed the chance to create 'public companies' on the Anglo-Saxon model. As regards the ownership structure, the privatization programme did not affect the peculiar features of Italian corporate governance: Italian companies maintained a high level of concentration of ownership and a limited separation between ownership and control, even in large firms.[16]

In addition, the modernization of financial markets – which unfolded during the 1990s with the aim of extending and liberalizing the role of financial intermediaries (in order to transpose EU directives into Italian law) and of strengthening the protection of investors and minority shareholders – did not significantly modify the corporate governance of Italian firms. The ownership structure of Italian firms has not changed greatly in the last decade: high levels of concentration, stability of control and intra-family portfolio swaps were still the norm (Giacomelli and Trento, 2005).

To sum up, since the 1980s the various components of the Italian social model have developed along different lines, converging at different speeds on the European model, as embodied in various elements of EU level policy. While convergence on legislative requirements and on macroeconomic policy has been almost mandatory, owing to the external constraints represented by European directives and the common currency, in other fields, namely the labour and product markets, reforms have often been 'at the margin' or have not substantially altered the Italian model.

Persisting challenges

Frozen specialization?

The structure of the Italian economy has evolved along the lines followed by most industrialized countries, with a reduction in the share of agriculture and manufacturing in favour of services.[17] Within manufacturing, however, the specialization pattern has not changed greatly over time, raising concerns about the ability of the Italian productive model to adjust to changes in the composition of world demand and to the increasing competition on traditional goods raised by developing countries.

All standard indicators seem to support the hypothesis of 'frozen specialization' in low-skill intensive sectors, marking a divergence from the dominant northern European productive structure, which has moved away from mature sectors (Bugamelli, 2001).[18] In spite of wage moderation since the 1990s a substantial slowdown in labour productivity growth has resulted in a sizeable increase in relative unit labour costs. Loss of competitiveness and industrial specialization are having an effect on Italy's share of world trade, which was down to 3.7 per cent in 2004 from a post-depreciation peak of 4.7 per cent in 1996. Table 8.2 summarizes the structure and the dynamics of Italy's export performance in recent years. Italy has lost market shares in high-growth sectors – characterized by economies of scale and high intensity

Table 8.2 Structure and dynamics of manufacturing exports in Italy and in the world, 1996 and 2002

Economic activities	Italian exports (% composition)		World exports (% composition)		Growth rates		Italian share (% of world exports)	
	1996	2002	1996	2002	Italy	World	1996	2002
Traditional manufacturing	44.9	42.7	31.9	28.5	−4.5	7.6	7.6	6.7
Textiles and clothes	*16.0*	*14.1*	*8.8*	*7.7*	*−11.5*	*5.9*	*9.8*	*8.2*
Economies of scale	22.3	23.0	28.9	29.7	3.4	23.9	4.2	3.5
Automobiles	*3.2*	*2.7*	*5.4*	*6.2*	*−15.1*	*38.2*	*3.2*	*2.0*
Specialized supply	22.4	21.7	15.5	14.4	−2.6	12.3	7.7	6.7
Machinery and equipment	*16.9*	*15.8*	*8.9*	*7.5*	*−6.0*	*2.6*	*10.3*	*9.4*
High intensity of R&D	10.4	12.6	23.7	27.3	22.0	39.0	2.4	2.1
ICT	*5.5*	*5.0*	*16.6*	*18.4*	*−9.9*	*33.4*	*1.8*	*1.2*
Pharmaceuticals	*1.8*	*3.7*	*1.7*	*3.0*	*108.6*	*112.8*	*5.5*	*5.4*
Total	100.0	100.0	100.0	100.0	0.4	20.5	5.4	4.5

Source: Istat (2005, Ch. 2).
ICT = information and communication technology.

of R&D – as well as in those sectors characterizing its specialization, namely traditional goods and specialized suppliers goods. Slower growth in world demand and increasing competition from low-cost countries have taken their toll, setting in motion a severe process of selection among the firms operating in these sectors. The relatively young clusters of firms in the south of Italy, formed from outsourcing by northern firms, have been among those most heavily damaged by the increasing competition (resulting in offshoring to neighbouring low-cost eastern European countries).

The view that the problem of Italian competitiveness lies in its specialization pattern calls into question the viability of the Italian productive system. The much-praised virtues of the industrial district economy – once regarded as a comparative advantage of the Italian production system – have come under severe scrutiny and are now mostly regarded as hindering growth.

The debate on the structural weaknesses of a productive system based on small firms dates back to the late 1970s, when the crisis of the large enterprise and the processes of downsizing, delocalization and outsourcing tilted the structure of Italian companies even more towards small size. It is now argued that the factors which favoured the growth of the small firm in the 1970s and 1980s (post-Fordist production techniques reducing the importance of firm-level scale economies, and changes in demand requiring increased flexibility in production) have been overpowered by the new forces of information technology and globalization. In the new environment, where R&D, ICT and human capital investment are crucial for competitiveness, medium and large enterprises perform better in terms of labour productivity, profitability and wages (Fabiani et al., 2003; Melitz and Ottaviano, 2005).

Delocalization to low-cost countries and the upgrading of production to higher stages of production (within the value chain or to new products) have been singled out as the only feasible defence strategies (Istat, 2005, Chapter 2). There is no agreement, however, on the extent of the upgrading process.[19] Standard indicators of innovativeness seem to support the pessimistic view. Italy's investment in R&D (1.1 per cent of GDP in 2004) is far below the European average and the Lisbon target of 3 per cent (by 2010). Italy's pattern of specialization and the prevalence of small firms explain the extremely low share of R&D undertaken by the private sector (48 per cent as against 63 per cent for the EU-25) (Istat, 2007, Chapter 2). Finally, data from the European Patent Office (EPO) show that in 2003 Italy submitted 87.3 patents per million inhabitants, against a EU-15 average of 160.6.

The relatively short supply of educated people[20] has been cited as an explanation for both the initial specialization of the Italian productive system in traditional sectors and its delay in undertaking innovative and R&D-based production paths (Faini and Sapir, 2005). This interpretation accords with the skill-biased technical change literature, which posits a causal relation from skills to specialization of production (Acemoglu, 1998). The implication is that a more rapid increase in the supply of skills may accelerate demand, with a consequent adaptation of the structure of supply. This approach lies behind the Lisbon strategy, which stresses the primary importance of education and lifelong learning policies for innovation and growth.

This interpretation is not fully convincing, however. It seems more plausible that, given the pattern of specialization, firms' demand for skills falls short of potential supply. Indeed, returns to education contradict what would be expected from a shortage in the supply of skilled labour. In Italy returns to tertiary education are much lower than in most other OECD countries, and they have been decreasing since the 1990s (Naticchioni et al., 2007). Scant demand for skills and low-wage premiums may discourage young people from attaining higher education. In this case policies acting only on the supply side by encouraging education and lifelong learning, though important *per se*, would not stimulate a change in the pattern of specialization. Structural policies which address both the demand and supply sides and focus on the complementarities between skilled workers and investment in high technologies and R&D would be more rewarding.

The 'rhetoric of decline'[21] has come under scrutiny, also in light of recent data on exports and profitability. The consensus view, it is argued, mistakenly equates a delay in reallocating manufacturing activities to high-skill intensive sectors with a lack of upgrading *within* the sectors of specialization. This error derives from overestimating the role of process innovation, cost reduction and price in long-term competitiveness, and correspondingly underrating product innovation. Sectors are thus ordered in a hierarchy that assumes an internal homogeneity. That is, there is no consideration of the fact that many high-value added, high-skilled stages and products are included in the so-called 'traditional' or 'mature' sectors, and many low-value added, low-skilled productions are widespread in 'high-tech'/research-intensive sectors (as proved by the high and rapidly increasing export share of low-cost countries in 'high-tech' industries) (Ginzburg and Simonazzi, 2005). R&D and patenting statistics are not necessarily good indicators of technological progress either. In many consumer sectors (and even more so in the case of small firms) most product innovations are not protected by patents and process innovation occurs through adoption of new technologies rather than through R&D expenditure. Finally, the role of 'tacit knowledge' has already been firmly established in the literature on innovation. A different assessment of the innovation performance of firms is obtained by addressing firms directly through surveys (see the Community Innovation Survey, Istat, 2006). Although confirming the overall weak performance of Italian firms, these surveys find that Italian small enterprises achieve better innovative performance, ranking higher than their UK and French counterparts. In short, there is evidence of the dynamic behaviour of Italian small firms.[22] The hypothesis that a process of upgrading is currently occurring within the pattern of specialization, with firms competing in market niches where quality rather than price matters, is supported by recent data on medium firms' performances (in terms of turnover, profits, exports) and by Italy's diverging pattern in market shares at current and constant prices. The constancy of the value index, compared with the fall in the quantity index, can be interpreted as an indicator of the price-setting capacity of Italian firms. These results seem to suggest that (at least some) Italian firms have been successful in upgrading their products and entering new, high-value markets.

The North-South divide

Lack of economic development in the *Mezzogiorno* is still the main structural weakness of the Italian economy and a source of economic and social inequalities. The economic divide between the rich north and the poor south has increased over time, as testified by all indicators on labour market conditions. In 2003 the employment rate in the south was 20 percentage points below that in the north (Table 8.3), the geographical gap having increased between 1977 and 2003. This is the combined effect of both a lower male employment rate and a much lower female employment rate which has been fuelled by a huge difference in the increase in female employment rates (only two percentage points in the south as against 15 in the north and in the centre of Italy).

The unemployment rate (8 per cent in 2004) broken down by age, gender and region confirms the extremely diversified situation that exists across each category: it ranges from 1.2 per cent for men aged over 35 resident in Trentino-Alto Adige, to 36.8 per cent for women aged 15–34 resident in Sicily (Istat, 2005, pp. 173–7).

Paradoxically, the labour market in southern Italy is far more flexible than in the centre-north. The pervasive presence of an underground, irregular,

Table 8.3 Employment rates by sex and geographical area, 1977–2003 (percentage of population aged 15–64)

	North	Centre	South and islands	Italy
MF				
1977	58.91	53.89	48.97	54.57
2003	64.12	59.08	44.11	55.99
Change 1977–2003	*+5.21*	*+5.20*	*−4.87*	*+1.43*
M				
1977	80.33	76.78	73.68	77.39
2003	74.61	71.42	61.40	69.31
Change 1977–2003	*−5.72*	*−5.36*	*−12.29*	*−8.08*
F				
1977	38.01	31.73	25.05	32.39
2003	53.44	46.92	27.08	42.68
Change 1977–2003	*+15.44*	*+15.18*	*2.03*	*+10.29*

Source: Own computation based on Istat, LFS data

often illegal economy has resulted in the debasing of job quality. Poor jobs, in terms of both pay and working conditions, in many sectors of the economy have been taken by an increasing flow of often illegal immigrants, while internal south-north migratory flows have resumed to such an extent that there are concerns about a brain-drain depriving the southern economy and society of its more skilled and able members.

Given the structure of social protection in Italy, with the family acting as a 'social clearing house' (Ferrera, 1996, p. 21), the key factor in fighting poverty and social exclusion is to have at least one member within the primary segment of the labour market. This is why employment conditions in the south make for a situation of real social emergency: the south has the largest shares of all the unemployed, of long-term unemployed and of families with unemployed heads of household, as well as a very low percentage of dual-earner families. No wonder that the south accounts for the largest proportion of families in poverty (Morlicchio and Pugliese, 2004, p. 191).

Following the recent eastward enlargement of the EU, and the need for the northern production system to follow the new markets in order to survive, the south is at risk of becoming even more marginalized. With stalled economic growth the devolution of government functions from the centre to the regions – which has implied higher financial autonomy and less generous transfers of funds – risks widening the gap in the quantity and quality of social services even further. These various elements raise concern about the drift of the *Mezzogiorno* further away from the north of the country, as well as from Europe.

The gender gap

Changes in gender roles are among the most important innovations in the Italian social model, one which unifies the north and south of the country. In the past three decades Italian women have closed the gender gap in education. Higher education has brought emancipation from traditional cultural values and higher aspirations with regard to work and lifestyles, shaping the identity of Italian women around waged work. Young women invest in education in order to secure good employment prospects, postpone motherhood till they have gained access to a decent job and enter employment with the intention of remaining in it for life.[23] Education also shapes the pattern of non-interruption over the childbearing interval: it is among the least-educated women that motherhood (as well as marriage) continues to have a marked negative impact on participation (Bettio and Villa, 1999). With education weakening the impact of motherhood, strong attachment to the labour market has been the feature of the new cohorts of women entering active life. In 2003 four out of ten women aged 15 or over were in employment as against only three in 1977 (Table 8.1).

However, gains in education have not been matched by equivalent gains in terms of employment or job quality. Italian women still encounter great difficulties, first in entering employment, then in balancing family responsibilities with paid work and in gaining access to good jobs (Simonazzi, 2006). With respect to young men, young women have a higher unemployment rate, they are over-represented in all types of atypical employment, are at higher risk of losing their jobs and receive systematically lower pay. The still extremely low female employment rate helps explain Italy's low overall employment rate, both in absolute terms and in comparison with other European countries.

Lack of reform of the welfare system is yet another obstacle to change in the Italian model. The need to reconcile care and paid work, in the absence of any adequate public support, has resulted in different solutions for the two polar cases: children and dependent elderly family members. Following the drastic fall in fertility rates, parents are now investing time and resources in what is now often their one and only child, mobilizing a complex network of family (grandparents), private and public kindergartens and private child-minders hired by the hour. The need to provide long-term care for an ageing population, on the other hand, has produced a new model which relies on large inflows of care migrants. In the new division of labour, family carers (mainly women) provide the coordination, the task of minding is entrusted to the female immigrant, while the more skilled and predominantly native care workers, in both the private and public sectors, take on paramedical tasks when necessary. A limited supply of specialized public services has thus been supplemented by an abundant supply of cheap, often irregular labour, giving rise to a complex segmentation of the care market along gender and ethnic lines and raising issues of social equity and long-term viability (Bettio et al., 2006; Simonazzi, 2009).

Modernization of the Italian model: An incomplete and skewed process

Changes in social patterns and in social policies have profoundly changed the Italian family and society. New technological and economic conditions have challenged the old pattern of production, employment and labour standards. Italy's response has been a 'limping reformism'. Macroeconomic and budget constraints, conflicts of interest and economic ideology have shaped the process of reform. At the macro level, the EMS first and then the EMU have provided the legitimacy of an external constraint for unpopular policy measures aimed at coping with structural disequilibria. Such reform as has taken place has encountered the difficulty of tackling deeply rooted features of the Italian society, of countering vested interests and reducing rent-seeking activities. We thus observe that selective reform of the labour market has not been accompanied by reform of the so-called 'shock absorber' systems (that is, unemployment benefit schemes), and reform of the product market has been limited to privatization unaccompanied by true liberalization.

Failure (or only partial implementation) of reforms in one area has shifted the cost to other areas. Hence, the failure of privatization to increase efficiency and to reduce rents has translated into a persistent inflation gap *vis-à-vis* Italy's main European competitors (especially Germany). The continuing emphasis on labour and product market deregulation, which reflects an unshakable confidence in the market mechanism, has diverted attention from the need to cope with the structural problems of the Italian model; those being the dualism of the Italian economy and the need to reshape the pattern of production and to upgrade skills. The inability (or unwillingness) of successive governments to constrain the growth of the informal economy has provided a further formidable obstacle to reform of the model. The large size of the underground economy (which expands and contracts with the political cycle) drastically reduces the tax base and thereby makes it impossible to finance a true income support system and social services.

The end result has been the exacerbation of old segmentations and the creation of new ones. While the northern production system seems to have managed to restructure, the south is still locked in to a low-efficiency and low-growth model. The level, coverage and effectiveness of income safety nets are still highly differentiated and unequal, which transfers the burden of flexibility to the most vulnerable sections of the labour force. Because of the interaction between working status and social rights, precarious or atypical arrangements in the labour market affect social citizenship. The result of the deficiencies in the Italian welfare regime is that families maintain an important role in shaping the life chances of individuals (Simonazzi and Villa, 2009).

These problems persist not because there has been no change. Indeed, reform of the Italian model has been taking place, under pressure from both external forces (EU recommendations, directives, constraints) and changing internal behaviour and patterns. This process of change is set to continue as the challenges are likely to strengthen rather than weaken. However, pursuit of the EU's 'modernization' agenda – including joining the EMU and undertaking product market and labour market reforms – has yielded only a partial, incomplete and incoherent set of reforms which has not provided a framework through which the key challenges of social citizenship, competitiveness and the entrenched dualisms can begin to be addressed.

Notes

1. The healthcare reform law of 1978 introduced tax-financed universal coverage, while pension benefits, computed on the basis of earnings (final salaries) since 1969, were gradually extended to various occupational groups.

2. The threshold of 15 employees is crucial in the case of Italy, given the large weight of small firms: about 30 per cent of all employees work for small firms (<15 employees).
3. The CIG is a national fund financed by the state and by contributions of employers and employees. In essence it is a system of subsidized labour hoarding: laid-off workers maintain their formal employment status and receive a generous wage subsidy. Large firms benefited from CIG more than small and medium-sized enterprises for two reasons. First, economic downturn and restructuring in the 1970s hit especially large manufacturing firms in capital intensive sectors (motor vehicle, steel, chemicals, textile and so on). Second, employers and trade unions of large firms had the bargaining power (through lobbying at the central level) to ask for the intervention of the CIG.
4. There is a significant underground economy in Italy. It is more widespread than in other European countries, accounting for 27 per cent of GDP and over 30 per cent of people in employment (Schneider and Enste, 2002, pp. 51–2). It is important to stress that it is a structural but non-homogeneous phenomenon: the underground economy in central and north Italy is mainly characterized by fiscal evasion; the one prevailing in the south, because of a lack of entrepreneurship, technology and infrastructures, absorbs substantial numbers of people working for low wages and without standard social benefits and protection. The question is whether the underground economy is the 'norm' of the south, thus impeding its growth, or rather a consequence of the south's underdevelopment.
5. The Italian welfare regime can be labelled as 'familialist' in the sense that it is assumed that state intervention covers only 'major' social risks, against which the family cannot protect itself (old age, health), while 'minor' individual social risks (for example, unemployment, insufficient income) are borne by the family (often by the extended family). This helps to explain the lack of national policies for families in poverty.
6. The drastic readjustment of the public budget that followed the 1992 currency crisis exacerbated the economic slowdown. GDP growth dropped to 0.8 per cent in 1992 and became negative, to −0.9 per cent, in 1993. The repercussions on the labour market were dramatic. The recession of the early 1990s was the most severe of the post-war period in terms of job losses (Brandolini et al., 2007, p. 31).
7. Following the second oil shock, in the early 1980s there was another burst of inflation above 20 per cent.
8. Labour policies aimed at favouring the entry of young cohorts into the labour market dated back to 1984, when work-and-training contracts for young people (allowing for a temporary contract at a discounted wage) were introduced. A weakening of the strict rules for fixed-term contracts was approved in 1987 (law 56/1987); thereafter these contracts were made more convenient for firms (law 451/1994; law 608/1996). New working arrangements such as collaborations and freelance relations grew exponentially after the 1995 pension reform, when INPS opened a new fund for the so-called '*parasubordinati*' (a special status of self-employment, mainly characterized by a close and continuous relation with a single company, as well as freelance relationships), enabling firms to 'hire' workers with no commitment and lower contributions. After a creeping process of deregulation, the 'big bang' arrived with the 'Legge Treu' (law 196/1997), which introduced a wide range of atypical contractual arrangements. In 2001 the regulation of fixed-term contracts was reformed (law 368/2001), making use of these contracts easier. Finally, the so-called 'Legge Biagi' (law 30/2003 and legislative decree 276/2003) enacted in 2003 further enlarged the variety of atypical contractual

arrangements, while establishing more stringent rules to curb the indiscriminate recourse to collaborations and freelance relations.
9. In Italy, part-time was introduced (and regulated by law) only in 1984. The late introduction of part-time work, with respect to the experience of other EU countries, resulted from strong opposition by trade unions. For a long time the unions limited the use of part-time contracts by setting relatively low upper limits for the share of part-timers in each firm in national collective agreements. Large firms in retail benefited from being able to use extensively part-time workers (with no upper limits) in order to meet peaks in demand (whether during the day, the week or the year).
10. Atypical workers (collaborators, to a larger extent) are not covered by employment protection legislation, and minimum contractual wages do not apply. Moreover, social security contributions and pension benefits are lower than those for standard employees, making their lifetime outlook even worse.
11. For the cohort of people aged 20 inflows into active life have fallen from about 800,000 per year up to the late 1970s to less than 600,000 in 2005.
12. The main normative interventions are: D. lgs. 30 December 1992, no. 503 (Riforma Amato) and the laws 24 December 1993, no. 537; 23 December 1994, no. 724; 8 August 1995, no. 335 (Riforma Dini); 27 December 1997, no. 449 (Riforma Prodi); law 23 August 2004, no. 243 (Riforma Maroni).
13. Under the earnings-related scheme (pre-1992 reform) a representative employee retiring at the age of 60 (with 37 years of contribution) was expected to have a replacement rate of around 75 per cent. Under the contribution-related scheme (post-1995 reform) the same individual is expected to have a replacement rate of around 58 per cent (if an employee) and 35 per cent (if self-employed) (Berloffa and Villa, 2007).
14. Workers with contributory records equal to or exceeding 18 years on 31 December 1995 have their pensions calculated with the old defined-benefit scheme; workers having entered the labour market before the end of 1995, but with less than 18 years of payments, have their pensions calculated in part with the old and in part with the new system; all new entrants from 1996 will have their pensions entirely computed according to the notional defined-contribution scheme. The legal retirement age differs accordingly. Under the new system retirement will be possible between the ages of 57 and 65. But at present, for workers still enjoying earnings-related pensions, entitlement to the old-age pension is acquired at age 65 for men and 60 for women; entitlement to the seniority pensions is acquired at age 57 with 35 years of contributions or at any age with 38 years of contributions. Recent estimates put the average retirement age at 60 years.
15. The Antitrust Authority (AGCM, 2005, p. 8) denounced former monopolists, in recently liberalized sectors, who still tend to 'refuse competitors access to essential infrastructures or prevent their entry into the market with predatory strategies'.
16. Historically, the main role in the ownership structure during the post-war period was played by 'families' and coalitions, while institutional investors and banks had only a marginal role in monitoring companies and exerted little influence on corporate governance.
17. From 1980–84 and 1999–2003 the share of services in value added rose from 64 to 68.1 per cent (from 53.2 to 65.5 per cent in terms of employment). Contributing mainly to this increase were financial intermediation and business services (from 19.8 to 25.4 per cent) while the share of other service activities (education, social

and personal services, public administration) decreased (from 20.7 to 18.5 per cent). Own computations on ISTAT national accounts data.
18. According to the Balassa index – defined as the ratio between a country's market share in a sector's world exports and its market share on total world exports – the specialization in office and electrical equipment, which was significantly positive in the 1970s, turned negative in the early 1980s, when the ICT revolution started (Faini and Sapir, 2005).
19. Although on average the Italian model is characterized by 'vertical negative' specialization – that is the average unit value of imports is higher than the average unit value of exports (Chiarlone, 2001) – this is not the case for all sectors. In the clothing industry, for example, the average unit value of Italian exports in 2002 was 4.8 times higher than the world average (Onida, 2003).
20. In terms of expenditure in education Italy is largely in line with the other industrialized countries, although still below the EU average. In terms of outcomes, however, in spite of remarkable progress in recent decades, Italy is still behind the European average in university education.
21. The expression is Pietro Modiano's, head of the Istituto S. Paolo, an important Italian private bank (Vianello, 2008). See also Ginzburg (2005) for an early criticism of this thesis.
22. While small size can be an obstacle to taking full advantage of scale economies, new technology, delocalization and foreign market penetration, the fact is overlooked that small firms often do not operate in isolation. The unit of analysis, to which to compare the minimum efficient scale, should thus be applied to the system of small enterprises, be it the group, the district or the vertically integrated value chain, in which the single firm is integrated (Ginzburg, 2005).
23. Poorly educated women account for a low share of the working female population: lack of job opportunities, greater difficulties in reconciliation (due also to the features of unskilled jobs) and low economic incentives for second earners (as a combined result of low earnings and high reconciliation costs) may explain the lower share in Italy when compared to other EU countries.

References

Acemoglu, D. (1998), 'Why Do New Technologies Complement Skills? Directed Technical Change and Wage Inequality', *Quarterly Journal of Economics* 113(4): 1055–89.
AGCM (Autorità Garante della Concorrenza e del Mercato) (2005), *Relazione annuale sull'attività svolta*, Rome.
Barbieri, P. and Scherer, F. (2005), 'Le conseguenze sociali della flessibilizzazione del mercato del lavoro in Italia', *Stato e Mercato* 74 (8): 291–321.
Barca, F. (2005), *Italia frenata*, Rome: Donzelli.
Becattini, G. (ed.) (1987), *Mercato e forze locali: il distretto industriale*, Bologna: Il Mulino.
Berloffa, G. and Villa, P. (2007), 'Inequality Across Cohorts of Households: Evidence from Italy', Dipartimento di Economia, Università degli Studi di Trento, Discussion Paper, 11/2007.
Bettio, F. and Plantenga, J. (2004), 'Comparing Care Regimes in Europe', *Feminist Economics* 10 (1): 85–113.

Bettio, F. and Villa, P. (1999), 'To What Extent Does it Pay to be Better Educated? Education and Market Work for Women in Italy', *South European Society and Politics* 4 (2): 150–70.
Bettio, F., Simonazzi, A. and Villa P. (2006), 'Change in Care Regimes and Female Migration: The "care drain" in the Mediterranean', *Journal of European Social Policy* 16 (3): 271–85.
Brandolini, A., Casadio, P., Cipollone, P., Magnani, M., Rosolia, A. and Torrini, R. (2007), 'Employment Growth in Italy in the 1990s: Institutional Arrangements and Market Forces', pp. 31–68 in N. Acocella and R. Leoni (eds), *Social Pacts, Employment and Growth*, Heidelberg: Physica-Verlag.
Brusco, S. (1989), *Piccole imprese e distretti industriali*, Torino: Rosenberg & Sellier.
Bugamelli, M. (2001), 'Il modello di specializzazione internazionale dell'area dell'euro e dei principali paesi europei: omogeneità e convergenza', *Bank of Italy, Temi di Discussione* 402.
Chiarlone, S. (2001), 'Evidence of Product Differentiation and Relative Quality in Italian Trade', *Rivista italiana degli economisti* 6 (2): 147–68.
Cipolla, C. M. (1995), *Storia facile dell'economia italiana dal medioevo ad oggi*, Milano: Mondadori.
Costi, R. and Messori, M. (eds) (2005), *Per lo sviluppo. Un capitalismo senza rendite e senza capitale*, Bologna: Il Mulino.
Fabiani, S., Schivardi, F. and Trento, S. (2003), 'Quale impresa italiana investe in tecnologie digitali?', pp. 125–50 in S. Rossi (ed.), *La nuova economia. I fatti dietro il mito, The New Economy*, Bologna: Il Mulino.
Facchini, C. and Villa, P. (2005), 'La lenta transizione alla vita adulta in Italia', pp. 61–104 in C. Facchini (ed.), *Diventare adulti. Vincoli economici e strategie familiari*, Milano: Guerini Scientifica.
Faini, R. and Sapir, A. (2005), 'Un modello obsoleto? Crescita e specializzazione dell'economia italiana', pp. 19–77 in T. Boeri, R. Faini, A. Ichino, G. Pisauro and C. Scarpa (eds), *Oltre il declino*, Bologna: Il Mulino.
Ferrera, M. (1996), 'The "Southern Model" of Welfare in Social Europe', *Journal of European Social Policy* 6 (1): 17–37.
Giacomelli, S. and Trento, S. (2005), 'Proprietà, controllo e trasferimenti nelle imprese italiane. Cosa è cambiato nel decennio 1993–2003?', *Bank of Italy, Temi di Discussione* 550.
Ginzburg, A. (2005), 'Le porte del cambiamento. A proposito di alcune recenti interpretazioni del ristagno dell'economia italiana', *Economia & Lavoro* 39 (2): 5–20.
Ginzburg, A. and Simonazzi, A. (2005), 'Patterns of Industrialisation and the Flying-geese Model: The Case of Electronics in East Asia', *Journal of Asian Economics* 15 (6): 1051–78.
Ichino, A., Mealli, F. and Nannicini, T. (2005), 'Temporary Work Agencies in Italy: A Springboard Toward Permanent Employment?', *Giornale degli Economisti e Annali di Economia* 64 (1): 1–27.
Istat (2005), *Rapporto annuale. La situazione del Paese nel 2004*, Rome.
Istat (2006), 'L'innovazione nelle imprese italiane. Anni 2002–2004', *Statistiche in breve*, November.
Istat (2007), *Rapporto annuale. La situazione del Paese nel 2006*, Rome.
Karamessini, M. (2008), 'Continuity and Change in the Southern European Social Model', *International Labour Review* 147 (1): 43–70.
Mediobanca (2000), *Le privatizzazioni in Italia dal 1992*, Milan.

Melitz, M. and Ottaviano, G. (2005), 'Market Size, Trade, and Productivity', *NBER Working Paper Series* 11393.
Molina, O. and Rhodes, M. (2007), 'The Political Economy of Adjustment in Mixed Market Economies: A Study of Spain and Italy', pp. 223–52 in B. Hancké, M. Rhodes and M. Thatcher (eds), *Beyond Varieties of Capitalism*, Oxford: OUP.
Morlicchio, E. and Pugliese, E. (2004), 'Il modello italiano di povertà', *Economia & Lavoro* 38 (2–3): 183–202.
Naticchioni, P. and Lucidi, F. (2006), 'What's Behind the Italian Structural Economic Crisis? Specialisation vs. Liberalization Issues', FGB and Dynamo WP. http://www.dynamoproject.eu
Naticchioni, P., Ricci, A. and Rustichelli, E. (2007), 'Far Away from a Skill-Biased Change: Falling Educational Wage Premia in Italy', *CEIS – University of Rome Tor Vergata Discussion Paper* 260.
Onida, F. (2003), 'Growth, Competitiveness and Firm Size: Factors Shaping the Role of Italy's Productive System in the World Arena', *CESPRI Working Papers* 144.
Picchio, M. (2006), 'Wage Differentials and Temporary Jobs in Italy', *Université Catholique de Louvain, Discussion Paper* 33.
Piore, M. J. and Sabel, C. F. (1984), *The Second Industrial Divide: Possibilities for Prosperity*, New York: Basic Books.
Putnam, R. (1993), *Making Democracy Work: Civic Traditions in Modern Italy*, New Jersey: Princeton University Press.
Rosolia, A. and Torrini, R. (2007), 'The Generation Gap: Relative Earnings of Young and Old Workers in Italy', Bank of Italy, *Temi di discussione*, n. 639, September.
Schneider, F. and Enste, D. (2002), *The Shadow Economy: An International Survey*, Cambridge: Cambridge University Press.
Simonazzi, A. (ed.) (2006), *Questioni di genere, questioni di politica. Trasformazioni economiche e sociali in una prospettiva di genere*, Roma: Carocci.
Simonazzi, A. (2009), 'Care Regimes and National Employment Models', *Cambridge Journal of Economics* (in press, 10.1093/cje/ben043).
Simonazzi, A. and Villa, P. (2009), '"La grande illusion". 'How Italy's "American Dream" Turned Sour', in D. Anxo, G. Bosch and J. Rubery (eds), *Welfare States and Life Transitions*, Cheltenham: Edward Elgar (forthcoming).
Streeck, W. (1997), 'Beneficial Constraints: On the Economic Limits of Rational Voluntarism', pp. 197–219 in J. R. Hollingsworth and R. Boyer (eds), *Contemporary Capitalism*, Cambridge: Cambridge University Press.
Vianello, F. (2008), 'Sistemi di imprese. A proposito della nuova raccolta di saggi di Sebastiano Brusco (e della precedente)', *Economia & Lavoro* 42 (1): 109–21.

9
From a State-Led Familistic to a Liberal, Partly De-familialized Capitalism: The Difficult Transition of the Greek Model

Maria Karamessini

Introduction

This chapter examines the transformation of the Greek socio-economic model since the beginning of the 1990s, analyses the main drivers for change and evaluates its success/shortcomings in achieving high job growth rates, job quality and social cohesion while maintaining competitiveness.

I argue that, since the early 1990s, the Greek socio-economic model has been moving way from a *state-led familistic capitalism* and heading towards a *liberal de-familialized* capitalism. Economic policy over this period has steadily reduced state intervention in the economy and the weight of public ownership in the production system and has created ample investment opportunities and favourable profitability conditions for private capital. However, up until now it has not succeeded in preventing deterioration in competitiveness or in laying the foundations for long-term economic growth and social progress. Social policy over the same period has mainly aimed at reinforcing the financial sustainability of the pensions system and combating poverty among low-income pensioners, but it has not improved unemployment compensation. Moreover, it has only belatedly and inadequately tried to lift the burden on families in terms of financial support and care provided to children and the elderly. In short, transition towards a liberal capitalism has not yet produced a sustainable development model, while the degree of de-familialization of the welfare regime is low and the pace of change rather slow.

In the next section I analyse the key features of the model at the end of the 1980s by tracing their origin in the post-war decades and the key changes after 1974, the year when the military dictatorship ended and the economic crisis began. I then go on to describe the more recent challenges to the model and trace the path of institutional change since the beginning of the 1990s. Finally, I assess the capacity of the transformed model to fulfil basic socio-economic goals in the present and near future.

State-led familistic capitalism (1945–89)

The particularity of Greek post-war capitalism until the mid-1970s is that it was state-led, familistic and authoritarian. *Statism* involved mainly the protection of the domestic market, state control of credit distribution and interest rates, and direct and indirect state intervention in wage-setting and labour market regulation. On the other hand the role of the state as entrepreneur was limited and the welfare state underdeveloped. *Familialism* refers to the crucial role played by the family in spheres of both production and reproduction in an agrarian society that was undergoing a process of rapid industrialization. In particular it refers to the great weight of family businesses in the production system, the familial governance of small and large firms and the strong solidarity, protection and care provided by the family to its offspring as well as to its unemployed, sick and elderly members. Familialism was accompanied by a rigid gender division of labour, discouraging women from involvement in paid employment after marriage. It was also reflected in the derived rights of women to social security and the numerous early-retirement schemes for those with working careers. *Authoritarianism* was a basic feature of the political regime of those times. All parliamentary right-wing governments ruled through state control of the unions and political repression of communists and their sympathizers, while the military dictatorship suspended most democratic rights between 1967 and 1974.

The 1960–73 period of strong economic growth, combined with the raised expectations following the fall of the military regime in 1974, resulted in a number of major challenges for the Greek economy and society. In particular it had to deal with huge social demands for enhanced civil, political and social rights in a period of international economic instability. This situation led to severe industrial conflict, double-digit inflation and falling profit and investment rates. In 1981 Greece's integration into the European Economic Community (EEC) coincided with the economy entering a phase of prolonged stagnation at the same time as the election of the socialist party (PASOK) stimulated a new round of social demands for enhanced civil and social rights and improved social conditions for the working classes.

The traditional model and its continuity/change after 1974
Production regime, employment structure and skills development
Until the early 1960s Greece's economy was mainly agrarian, combined with a limited industrial base created through protection of the internal market from imports. In 1960 57 per cent of all employed were occupied in agriculture and 17 per cent in industry but by 1975, after 15 years of spectacular economic growth and intensive industrialization, the share of agriculture had dropped to 36 per cent and that of industry had risen to 28 per cent. Another major feature of the employment system was the large share

of the self-employed and unpaid family workers in all economic sectors, reflecting the great weight of small family businesses/farms in the production system.

Apart from its large investments in infrastructure and the provision of financial incentives to private capital, the state encouraged industrialization through the protection of the domestic market and the direct control of interest rates and the distribution of credit. Foreign investments in manufacturing were at the forefront of the industrialization process. New industries of intermediary consumption and capital goods appeared (steel and metal, cement, chemicals, shipyards, oil refineries) next to traditional industries such as food, beverage, tobacco and textiles. During the early post-war decades the main clusters of international specialization of the production system were found in *agricultural products, raw materials* and *shipping*. In 1961 Greece signed an association agreement with the EEC and launched a strategy aimed at the promotion of *manufacturing exports*. As a result the share of manufacturing in total exports of goods rose from 5 per cent of the value of exports in 1960 to 52 per cent in 1976, surpassing for the first time the 50 per cent benchmark used by the World Bank for classifying a country as newly industrializing (NIC). Textiles, steel, chemicals, oil products and cement dominated manufacturing exports in the 1970s, while food products and clothing manifested a greater dynamism in the 1980s. In the 1960s and 1970s *tourism* also emerged as an important cluster of international specialization.

From 1974 there was a gradual phasing out of tariffs in view of Greece's accession to the EEC in 1981, but the complete removal of tariff and non-tariff barriers was achieved only in 1989. The competitive pressure on domestic firms from gradual elimination of market protection was offset until 1987 by the devaluation of the national currency.

The economic performance of manufacturing and construction decelerated after the first oil shock and the return to democracy. The conflict between capital and labour over the distribution of value added and the growth in capital intensity caused a drastic fall in profitability and investments. From 1980 both sectors entered a long period of stagnation that lasted until 1993 and services became the only sector of net job creation in the economy.

The industrial crisis of the 1980s mainly hit large and medium firms, leading to closure and downsizing. At the same time the development of extensive subcontracting networks in the clothing and food industries and the growth of tourism according to a *'diffused industrialization pattern'* (Hadjimihalis and Vaiou, 1987) stimulated the proliferation of small family businesses. The share of the self-employed in overall employment in industry and services increased in the 1980s, while that of unpaid family workers also rose slightly in industry but remained stable in services. Home-working and informal work acquired significant dimensions. Informality was the main reaction of small and medium-sized enterprises (SMEs) to the growing labour costs resulting from the improvement of employee and social rights during this period.

Another important structural change during 1974–89 was the expansion of the state's share of capital ownership in the production system. After the fall of the dictatorship, air transport, the bus service of Athens, an oil refinery and a big private group of banks, insurance companies, hotels, shipyards, fertilizer plants etc. were all nationalized, while the armaments industry was created with public funds. Moreover, a number of new food industries were founded by the state-owned Agricultural Bank that kept a majority control of their capital. A second wave of nationalizations in the first half of the 1980s brought under state control heavily indebted and loss-making industrial firms, judged important by their size and leadership in 'strategic' industries. As a result, in 1988 Greece possessed the third highest share of public enterprises in gross domestic product (GDP) in western Europe after Portugal and Italy.[1]

The increase in the weight of public enterprises in the production of value added and the expansion of small private firms along with informal work intensified *labour market segmentation* between 1974 and 1989.

Corporate governance and work organization remained largely unchanged during this period. The former could be regarded as *familial*. Most big Greek companies had a high degree of ownership concentration and a limited separation between ownership and management, while the main role in the ownership structure and management of both big companies and SMEs was played by the owner and the members of his/her family. As far as work organization is concerned, micro/small enterprises applied artisan production forms that not only involved direct participation by the owner and his/her family, but also the multi-skilling of core workers and direct forms of work control alongside paternalistic employment relations (Georgakopoulou, 1983). However, medium and large firms used to implement more sophisticated forms of division of labour, together with Taylorist principles of work organization.

In the 1950s and 1960s the craftsman apprenticeship was regarded as the royal route to skill development among the urban working class. Alongside the informal system that catered for the needs of SMEs, the Labour Force Employment Organization founded, first from 1953, schools for apprenticeship and later, in the 1960s, centres for accelerated vocational training directly linked to the skill needs of certain big industrial firms (Konstantinopoulos, 1993). However, the newly mobilized labour of rural origin, employed primarily by big manufacturing plants to carry out un/semi-skilled tasks, tended to be trained in-house and on the job.

At this time the majority of such blue-collar workers had *at most* completed primary school education, while the majority of white-collar workers had undergone a six-year secondary education. Education was a field that experienced major institutional changes after 1974. In 1976 lower-secondary education became compulsory, new vocational training schools were introduced and a vocational stream was created in upper-secondary education. Moreover, the vocational training schools for technicians, founded in 1970, were transformed in 1982 into higher technological education institutes. Finally, from the mid-1970s to the mid-1980s, higher education was gradually opened up to more students as a way to satisfy social demand for more education.

Employment regime and labour market structure

Strong state intervention in industrial relations and labour market regulation characterized the traditional post-war employment regime. Industrial relations during the post-war period until 1974 can be best described as *étatiste* or *corporatist* (Mavrogordatos, 1988; Karamessini, 1992; Kritsantonis, 1998; Ioannou, 2000). The state intervened to ensure political control and exclusion of the Left. It controlled the official trade unions through judicial intervention that imposed government nominees at the top of the organizations and the creation of rubber-stamp unions and a caste of pro-regime leaders supporting government policies. The freedom to unite and strike being guaranteed by the Constitution, independent unions also operated prior to the dictatorship; the colonels abolished the rights to strike and closed down the unions controlled by the Left.

Even though the state indirectly controlled the claims of the *officially recognized* unions, it still did not allow free collective bargaining to set wages. It kept the prerogative to intervene directly or indirectly in wage determination. From 1945 to 1952 and from 1969 to 1974 the national minimum wage was directly set by the government. In 1955 Law 3239 on collective bargaining established that the Minister of Labour had the right to reject or correct any collective agreement or arbitration decision providing for wage increases surpassing by 3 percentage points the incomes policy norm, and to unilaterally prolong any collective agreement or arbitration decision as well as to unilaterally extend them to non-unionized employees. Indirect state regulation of wages operated through compulsory arbitration.

Economic growth in the period 1960–73 was remarkably strong but literally jobless. The incapacity of the urban sector to absorb the huge pool of labour liberated from agriculture led the state to adopt an *active emigration policy* entailing bilateral agreements with host countries. The mass emigration between 1955 and 1977 of about one-third of the Greek population aged 15 to 44 years allowed for full employment at home in the early 1970s.

The state also actively promoted labour market segmentation as a political instrument for class division. The main divide was between the public and the private sector (Karamessini and Kaminioti, 1999). Employment in public administration, pubic utilities and state-controlled banks was a privilege reserved for the social strata that were loyal to the post-civil war parliamentary regimes and, later on, to the military dictatorship. Employment in the public sector involved greater security and higher pay than in the private sector. Pay differences by size of firm were also important within the private sector. Furthermore, uninsured work and non-payment of full social security contributions were more widespread in SMEs than in large firms. Segmentation was also produced through formal discrimination between types of employees. Female employees were entitled to lower wage rates than men for the same work and blue-collar employees enjoyed much weaker protection from dismissals than their white-collar counterparts.

After the 1974 collapse of the military dictatorship a series of changes and new phenomena transformed the state corporatist model of industrial relations into a more democratic version. The first was the *collapse of state control of the unions* and the introduction of explicit *political factionalism* in which all main leftist parties – newly legalized after 30 years – were represented (Kritsantonis, 1998). A second important change was the development of genuine *collective bargaining* after the abolition in 1975 of all forms of direct state regulation of wages. A third was the rise of *industrial conflict*. Strike activity in Greece in the second half of the 1970s was the highest in western Europe, along with that of Spain and Italy (Ioannou, 1989), and this high level of conflict was maintained during the 1980s. A final new phenomenon was the *de facto* recognition by employers of *union activity in the workplace* and *company collective agreements*, although both were not permitted by existing legislation. Only in 1982, after the PASOK had taken power, was union activity within firms officially recognized and protected and the freedom to strike enlarged.

State intervention in wage determination continued in this high-inflationary period through incomes policy. In 1982 the incomes policy allowed for ex-post indexation of wages to past inflation but this was replaced in 1986 by ex-ante indexation of wages to target inflation. The state also attempted to control wage increases through compulsory arbitration and suspension of the right to collective bargaining in 1983, 1986 and 1987.

The abrupt rise of unemployment in the early 1980s led to a major institutional innovation: employment policy. *Job creation in the public sector* and *defensive nationalizations* were its basic pillars. *Active labour market policy* (ALMP) became the third pillar after resources were provided through the European Social Fund (ESF). Employment protection legislation underwent marginal changes during 1974–89. The definition of collective dismissals, for which prior administrative approval had been required since 1967, became stricter after 1974 and even more so in 1983. In 1979 the use of fixed-term contracts – and later on of service contracts – was permitted in the public sector for seasonal, temporary and extraordinary needs. This legislative change allowed the creation of large numbers of temporary jobs in the public sector, later transformed into permanent ones. These jobs were distributed by the government parties through patronage networks to a clientele of job-seekers in exchange for votes. The fixed-term contracts also expanded through the ALMP schemes subsidizing new jobs in the private sector for special groups of unemployed.

Judging the period as a whole, it can be argued that the political radicalism of the post-dictatorship period and the ensuing industrial conflict succeeded in advancing the living standards of Greek employees even during a period of economic crisis and growing unemployment and in spite of state intervention aimed at controlling labour demands. This is true with respect both to wages and other aspects of the wage relationship. For example, between 1975 and 1983 there was a gradual reduction of the working week from 48 to 40 hours and from six to five days, a substantial increase in paid holidays and the abolition of different wage rates for men and women.

Welfare state and family model

In the early post-war decades the Greek regime displayed all the features of the southern European model of social protection and welfare identified in the relevant literature. These features included general underdevelopment of state provision combined with extreme fragmentation of social insurance and a residual social assistance system. This resulted in great gaps in social protection provision (Leibfried, 1992; Ferrera, 1996; Petmesidou, 1996).

Public expenditure on social protection as a percentage of GDP was very low, while pensions and healthcare benefits were provided by a great number of insurance funds. In 1969 308 independent insurance funds were delivering pensions, 43 of them main pensions with the remainder providing supplementary pensions and mutual-aid and end-of-service allowances. Likewise, 52 insurance funds distributed health benefits. This fragmentation was based on occupational and corporatist status divisions and was associated with large differences in entitlements.

The strong familialism and gender bias of the welfare regime, mentioned by Esping-Andersen (1999) as distinctive features of the conservative welfare regime and its southern European variant, were reflected in Greece in:

(1) The residual character of the unemployment compensation system, which although founded in 1945 and generalized in 1951 still provided low coverage and income replacement;
(2) The residual character of family policy, such that family allowances, provided since 1958, were at a deplorable level, while publicly-funded care services were totally lacking;
(3) The lower legal age of retirement for women and the special pre-retirement schemes for married women and mothers of children under 18.

The designers of the social protection system thus expected that the unemployed, children and the elderly should be financially assisted and cared for by their families, while the 'favourable treatment' of working women by the pensions system proved that they were primarily seen as wives and mothers and only ancillary or temporary breadwinners.

However, the gender division of labour in the family during the post-war decades was more complex. The 'family economic gender model' (Pfau-Effinger, 1998) in which both sexes contribute substantially to the survival of the family business (farm or craft) and women work as unpaid family members was prevalent in agriculture but also frequent in the urban centres. The 'male-breadwinner/female-home-carer model' was prevalent in the urban centres among middle and working class families. However, women in the poorest families worked intermittently or for longer periods, mostly on an informal basis, while a small but increasing share of high-educated women worked continuously in the public sector.

The period 1974–89 is characterized by a process of catching up with the welfare states of more developed European economies. Social protection expenditure increased from 11.4 per cent of GDP in 1974 to 23.1 per cent in 1988. Catching up was mainly observed in the field of *pensions,* where expenditure rose from 6.7 per cent of GDP in 1974 to 15.8 per cent in 1988.

The rise in spending on pensions was due to the arrival of the system to maturity, the relaxation of eligibility requirements and an increase in the generosity of benefits. In 1978 the right to retirement with 35 years of contribution record, which up to then had only applied to public sector employees, was extended to private sector employees, leading to a very high number of workers taking retirement between 1978 and 1980 (Provopoulos, 1985). In the same year the minimum pension was fixed at 60 per cent of the minimum wage and linked to variations in the latter. In the 1980s the socialist governments increased the ratio first to 70 per cent in 1982 and then to 80 per cent in 1985 and also linked the minimum pension to the system of indexing wages to prices. Such increases had an automatic, positive impact on the whole scale of pensions. Moreover, in 1979 insurance for complementary pensions (on top of main pensions) was made mandatory. Consequently, the rate of employees covered by complementary pensions rose from 26 per cent in 1958 to 42 per cent in 1979, and gradually reached 100 per cent in the following years (Hadjidimitriou, 1991), while the formal replacement rate of contributory pensions was raised to 100 per cent of the final wage received by the employee. The above-mentioned changes made the Greek pensions system unique in the world, since it comprised two pillars of strictly identical main and complementary pensions in that they were mandatory, contributory and pay-as-you-go (Manassis, 1991).

Although the level of benefits increased during the period examined here, the basic features of the traditional pensions system were maintained. Its contributory character was reinforced but the fragmentation was not really tackled. The number of insurance funds did decline in the decade after 1978 but only from 380 to 325 (and from 41 to 33 for main pension funds). Insurance funds for sickness also declined from 76 to 42 across the same period, but here the main change was the establishment of the National Health System (NHS) in 1983.

Until the mid-1980s the Greek healthcare system was funded through compulsory social insurance but delivered by a mix of public and private services. In 1974 94 per cent of the population was already covered by healthcare and the remaining gaps were partly filled in the early 1980s through extensions to the agricultural population. But in 1983 the PASOK government established a universal system of healthcare free at the point of use, ensuring full population coverage and aimed at reducing inequalities in access. To accomplish these goals the NHS law expanded the public hospital sector by nationalizing not-for-profit hospitals and improved primary healthcare by founding about 200 rural and semi-urban health centres coordinated by the Ministry of Health. Additionally, the 1983 reform prohibited the establishment of new private hospitals, prevented existing private hospitals from changing their functions and banned private practice for public hospital doctors.

The unemployment protection system was reformed in 1985, for the first time since its creation in 1951. The contributions record required for the first award of benefits was relaxed, the limit on the cumulative duration of benefits over a four-year period abolished and the duration of benefits extended for seasonal workers in the construction, tourism, mining and fishing industries. Moreover, benefits were set at 40 per cent and 50 per cent of the previous daily or monthly wage respectively, while their maximum duration of grant was set at eight months and later on at 12 months. Yet, even though the reform slightly increased coverage and entitlements, the Greek system remained the most residual in the EU.[2]

As for family policy, the main change was the entitlement of employees of both sexes to several care leaves, first introduced in 1984. However, legislation did not have any serious impact on take-up rates since most leaves were unpaid or not enforced. In sum, marginal changes in the unemployment protection system and family policy, along with the continuing gender bias in the pensions system, preserved the strong familialism of the social protection system as an element of continuity of the Greek welfare regime through the period 1974–1989.

From an authoritarian to a democratic state-led familistic capitalism

Notwithstanding intensive institutional change from 1974 to 1989, the Greek model of capitalism changed only at the margin. Authoritarianism disappeared after democratization of the political regime and the union movement, but statism was reinforced even though some of its forms were abandoned. The preparation for and accession to the EEC led to the gradual removal of tariff and non-tariff protection in the goods market but was immediately compensated by exchange rate policy which became the basic policy tool for restoring competitiveness. Direct state intervention in wage-setting in the private sector was abandoned, except for a short while with the suspension of the constitutional right to collective bargaining in 1985–87, but the role of incomes policy was greatly reinforced. On the other hand the role of the state as entrepreneur, employer and welfare provider in the fields of pensions, education and healthcare was extended. As for the familialism of the model, it remained constant for a number of reasons. Firstly, the development of the welfare state was minimal in the fields traditionally undertaken by the family. Moreover, the role of small family businesses in the production system was enhanced because of their better endurance of economic crises compared to large firms. Finally, corporate governance remained familial during this period. In short, between 1974 and 1989 Greek capitalism remained state-led and familistic, but became democratic.

A model in transition (1990 to the present day)

By the beginning of the 1990s the Greek economy had still not recovered from stagnation and was facing serious macroeconomic problems. In 1990 inflation was still 20.4 per cent, the public deficit stood at 16 per cent of GDP and public debt had climbed to 80 per cent of GDP, from 25 per cent in 1980. Mounting indebtedness of the state and the anaemic recovery of private investment and economic growth after 1986 pointed to the limited effectiveness of state management of distributional conflicts during a structural economic crisis.

The election of a liberal government in 1990 marks the reversal of policy priorities and a move towards monetary stability, reduction of budget deficits and public sector ownership and activity, liberalization of financial services and public utility markets, and labour market flexibility. The aim was to sponsor private investment through the promotion of economic liberalism. Furthermore, the new phase of European integration launched with the European Single Act and ratified by the Maastricht Treaty became a powerful driver for change of the Greek model towards economic liberalism.

Apart from macroeconomic imbalances and EU obligations, the beginning of the 1990s also generated a number of both old and new challenges: increased international competition, high youth and female unemployment, growing female activity rates, mass immigration and ageing of the population. From here on I study the changes of the model in response to challenges.

Liberal capitalism and external imbalances

The turn of economic policy towards liberalism was preceded by the move towards monetarism in the mid-1980s when the first stabilization plan was adopted. From 1987 onwards exchange rate policy became one of the basic tools of disinflationary macroeconomic policy and was translated into an overvalued exchange rate that pushed firms to adjust (Ioakimoglou and Milios, 1992). This kind of policy was reinforced by the requirements of nominal convergence towards the targets defined for EMU by the Maastricht Treaty. As a result the drachma was over-valued for 15 years. Furthermore, a highly uncompetitive rate was used for the conversion of the drachma to the euro in 2002 when Greece joined the EMU. Since Greece is a *price-taker* in international trade, the overvaluation of the drachma compelled domestic producers to reduce either profit margins or production costs in order to defend their market shares (Karamessini, 2002). Marginal production units, unable to cope with foreign competition and the recession of 1990–93, closed down. The remaining production units responded to intensified competition in two different ways: some sectors modernized their production and organization methods while others tried to survive through deterioration in the working conditions and living standards of employees (Ioakimoglou, 1996).

Paradoxically, the increased competitive pressures on domestic producers resulted in an increase in the number of micro/small capitalist firms in all the sectors of economic activity. This is the sector that made the most intensive use of migrant (irregular) labour in the 1990s and 2000s due to the increasing unavailability of young women and men for unpaid family work amid a growing distaste for manual work.

However, the most important qualitative change in the production system over the period was the restructuring of capital ownership in the large-firm sector. This occurred through privatizations of public firms, contracting out to private firms of important public projects and market deregulation in banking and finance, as well as in public utility sectors where state monopolies operated. EU Single Market directives and EMU criteria for fiscal discipline have acted as a catalyst for change. But privatizations and deregulation have also been seen by right-wing elites and reform-minded socialists as more than mechanisms of adjustment or as money-raisers but as part of a wider programme of transformation of the economy (Wright and Pagoulatos, 2001). Yet, by international comparison, the Greek privatization process has been rather slow and evolutionary, starting from partial privatization in order to gain the approval or tolerance of public opinion and interested parties for full privatization (Savva-Balfousia, 2005).

In fully or partially privatized companies and organizations, voluntary redundancies and early retirement have been the favoured ways to cut personnel since they bypass union opposition. The power of unions in public enterprises had already been eroded by the downsizing of the sector but a new law on public utilities and services passed in 2005 has attempted to reduce it still further by permitting different terms and conditions of employment for newly hired employees, and by imposing changes by collective agreement or law on Staff Regulations in those companies with negative operating results or receiving subsidies from the state. However, change in Staff Regulations has yet to take place because of strong resistance by unions.

Market liberalization in services started with financial services: in the 1980s domestic financial institutions and their activities were deregulated and in the 1990s the financial markets were liberalized (Gibson et al., 2001). In 1987 state control over interest rates and the portfolio allocations of banks was eliminated, while that on capital flows was gradually removed between 1988 and 1994. In the 1990s successive reforms of financial markets increased the volume of transactions in the stock market and created a market for debt instruments. As a result there has been a clear trend towards a greater reliance by firms and the state on financial markets for credit. Finally, a wave of privatizations of state-owned/controlled banks and mergers since 1998 has led to the formation of a small number of big groups based on partnerships of domestic and foreign capital. Market deregulation in the public utility sectors (energy, water supply, transport and telecommunications) started in the late 1990s, in application of EU directives. However, in spite of these changes, in 2003 Greece still had the most stringent regulation and state control of the product market in the OECD after Italy (OECD, 2005). These changes in firm ownership and in financial markets have been accompanied by changes in corporate management. The separation of ownership and management and the protection of minority shareholders have advanced and familial governance has retreated.

The creation of private oligopolies and cartels in most of the 'liberalized' economic sectors increased prices and profits substantially, thus fuelling inflation and resulting in producers and consumers incurring higher costs than in the period of state control. Market deregulation in sectors previously dominated by state monopolies or strongly controlled/regulated by the state has thus betrayed expectations of lower prices through increased competition. In fact, since 2002 inflation in Greece has been systematically higher than in the rest of the euro-zone countries. The inflation differential, along with the overvaluation of the euro relative to the dollar, is responsible for the substantial rise of the real effective exchange rate in the post-2002 period. This rise follows a longer-term trend that started in 1987 and has led to the erosion of price competitiveness of domestic production and a severe deterioration in the balance of current transactions with the rest of the world. The current transactions deficit, which equalled only 0.9 per cent of GDP in 1995, had climbed to 11.4 per cent in 2006, in spite of EU transfers equal to 2.7 per cent of GDP in the same year.

As for the international specialization of production, the most important change since the 1990s is the sharp decline in clothing exports as a result of competition from low labour cost countries, the share of clothing in manufacturing exports declined from 37 per cent in 1990 to 13 per cent in 2005. As regards export of services, shipping increased its share after a long period of retreat and recently took the lead from tourism. Tourism faced a severe downturn between 2000 and 2003 but has recovered since due in part to the

2004 Olympics; however, the rise of new cheap tourist destinations is undermining the growth potential of the sector.

The collapse of labour-intensive manufacturing exports, exhaustion of the dynamics of the 'sea and sun' model of tourism and huge and growing deficits in the balance of current transactions with the rest of the world cast doubt on the capacity of liberal capitalism to ensure long-term economic growth. Greece is a weakly industrialized and rapidly tertiarizing country that has lost its comparative advantage in low labour costs and is facing a continuous rise in its real effective exchange rate. It has only belatedly started to develop in the advanced technology and knowledge economy. Today Greece is the OECD country with the second lowest research and development (R&D) expenditure as a percentage of GDP and the second lowest share of information and communication technology (ICT) in total investments (OECD, 2007). It also has the fourth lowest share of all employed with ICT user-skills in the EU-27 after Romania, Bulgaria and Portugal (European Commission, 2008).

Last but not least the 1990s and 2000s saw a spectacular increase in private and social investment in education. The proportion of the population aged 20–24 years completing at least upper-secondary education climbed from 71 per cent in 1992 to 84 per cent in 2005, while the number of entrants in tertiary education doubled between 1990 and 2000. However, in 2004 Greece still had the fifth highest share (40.8 per cent) of low-educated in the working age population in the EU-25. Furthermore, the quality of education provided is seriously undermined by the extremely low public expenditure per student and institutional features of the education system that condition its performance.

Less conflict in industrial relations and more labour market flexibility

As previously mentioned, prior to 1990 there was considerable tension in the relations between capital and labour. Given the incapacity of incomes policy to control a two-digit inflation rate and wage drift, and its contribution to industrial conflict and political discontent, a law on 'free collective bargaining' was passed in 1990. This law abolished compulsory arbitration and attributed the main responsibility for collective regulation of wages to social partners. Compulsory arbitration was replaced by a new voluntary system of conciliation, mediation and arbitration by independent specialists of a tripartite organization. In the same year the system of automatic indexation of wages to inflation was abolished by law. Since then the projected inflation rate has been used as a basis for national-level bargaining on national minimum wage increases between the General Confederation of Greek Workers (GSEE), which is the only trade union confederation for private sector employees, and employer organizations. Moreover, in the late 1990s the bargaining rounds between management and the strong unions in public utilities and banking were decoupled from those between GSEE and peak employer organizations on the national minimum wage. The basic mechanisms of wage drift through articulated bargaining[3] have thus been broken (Ioannou, 2000).

By eradicating state intervention in industrial relations and wage-setting the legislative reforms of 1990 gave an impetus to collective bargaining and reduced conflict in industrial relations. Moreover, the economic recession of 1990–93, the ideological impact of the collapse of the communist bloc on the union factions of the Left, and the accession to power of a liberal government that remained in office during 1990–93 contributed to a turn by the majority of trade unionists towards a *social-partnership* approach to industrial relations, away from the *adversarial* approach of the previous period. This was reflected in the decline in the number of strikes, from 207 in 1989 to 38 in 1998, and the fall in the share of arbitration decisions in all collective regulations, from 43.7 per cent in 1975–91 to 13.6 per cent in 1992–2005. Economic recession and the abolition of automatic indexation produced a fall of real wages between 1990 and 1993. Since 1993 real wages have increased; at lower rates than productivity until 2000 and in line with it from 2001 onwards (Table 9.1).

Table 9.1 Main economic indicators, Greece

	1961–73	1974–85	1986–90	1991–95	1996–2000	2000–06
GDP (real)	8.5	1.7	1.2	1.2	3.4	4.4
Employment	−0.5	1.0	0.7	0.5	1.4	1.4
Unemployment rate	4.4	3.8	6.6	8.3	10.7	10.0
Real wages per head	6.4	2.7	−0.7	−1.5	2.3	3.5
Labour productivity	9.0	0.7	0.5	0.7	2.8	3.2
Private consumption deflator	3.6	18.2	17.6	13.8	5.6	2.8
Gross fixed capital formation	9.7	−3.2	0.8	−0.4	9.0	7.2
Profitability index (1961–1973 = 100)	100	76.3	55.8	71.7	77.0	91.4
Exports of goods and services	11.5	5.5	3.6	4.3	12.0	2.2
Imports of goods and services	12.8	3.0	8.4	3.5	12.1	2.6
Real effective exchange rate index (1995 = 100)	120.1	92.9	88.2	92.3	105.4	108.5
General government budget (% of GDP)	0.5	−5.0	−12.0	−11.2	−5.2	−5.4
Public debt end of period (% of GDP)	17.5	53.6	79.6	108.7	111.6	108.8

Source: European Economy Statistical Annex (Spring 2007)
*All figures indicate average annual % changes, except for indexes and public finance rates.

EU integration is an additional determinant of the gradual decline of conflict in industrial relations. Its influence has been exerted through, firstly, the establishment of social dialogue institutions, such as the Economic and Social Committee in 1994 and the National Committees for Employment and Social Protection in 2003, and, secondly, the achievement of social consensus on the country's entry into the EMU, which has persuaded trade unions to moderate their wage claims (Kouzis, 2002). However, while the employers' organizations and the unions seem, by and large, to have overcome their adversarial past, tripartite social dialogue has produced so far only one social pact, in 1997. This is in part due to the temptation of unions to veto reforms because of their close ties with the ruling party. In addition, the absence of gains for employees in exchange for losses and the lack of political consensus over the reforms have made it hard for unions to sell them to their rank and file (Zambarloukou, 2006).

Since 1990 a series of laws have tried to boost formal labour flexibility (atypical forms of work) alongside the informal flexibility (irregular work) that has been a structural feature of the Greek labour market since the postwar era. At the same time these laws have defined the rights of atypical workers. Part-time work was first regulated in 1990, re-regulated in 1998, promoted by incentives for the employee in 2000 and introduced in public services and local government in 2003 and 2004. Home-working, teleworking and contract work were first regulated in 1998 and temporary employment agencies were first authorized in 2001. Recourse by private employers to fixed-term contracts has always been easy in Greece since legislation dating from the 1920s was very permissive. In 2004 the law transposing the EU directive on fixed-term contracts put more restrictions on their use. It specified more concretely the situations in which these contracts can be used, allowed up to two renewals only of the contract and set a maximum of two years for the cumulative duration of successive contracts.

Working-time flexibility is achieved by Greek firms only through overtime work. In 2000 overtime premia were raised in an attempt by the government to discourage recourse to overtime work and to push for job creation. The measure met with employer discontent and in 2005 the previous overtime regime was re-adopted. Flexible working-time arrangements were first allowed by law in 1990 and then re-regulated in 1998 and 2005. However, all laws have required for their implementation the prior consent of trade unions, works councils and company employees. Due to the hostility of the unions and employees all provisions have remained so far ineffective and will most probably remain so in the near future.

In general Greek trade unions have successfully resisted radical reforms of labour market regulation leading to excessive flexibility. Moreover, with the exception of the period 1990–93, they have managed to obtain real wage increases slightly below or in line with productivity gains. On the other hand they have not been able to control the spectacular rise in

Table 9.2 Labour market and social indicators, Greece

Years	1992	2001	2005
Activity rates			
% of population aged 15–64	58.5	63.3	66.8
% of population aged 15–24	38.2	36.5	33.7
% of male population aged 15–64	76.4	77.1	79.2
% of female population aged 15–64	41.8	49.7	54.5
Employment rates			
% of population aged 15–64	53.7	56.3	60.1
% of male population aged 15–64	72.4	71.4	74.2
% of female population aged 15–64	36.2	41.5	46.1
% of population aged 15–24	28.3	26.2	25.0
% of population aged 55–64	39.8	38.2	41.6
Unemployment rates			
Total (% of labour force 15+)	7.9	10.8	9.8
Youth (% of labour force 15–24)	25.2	28.2	26.0
Men (% of labour force 15+)	5.0	7.3	6.1
Women (% of labour force 15+)	12.9	16.2	15.3
Long term (% of labour force)	3.8	5.5	5.1
Temporary employment (fixed term)			
Total (% all employed)	9.6	13.2	11.8
Men (% all employed men)	9.8	11.6	10.1
Women (% all employed women)	9.4	15.7	14.3
Part-time employment			
Total (% all employed)	4.5	4.0	5.0
Men (% all employed men)	2.6	2.2	2.3
Women (% all employed women)	8.1	7.2	9.3
Self-employed			
Total (% all employed)	48.2	41.0	40.8
Men (% all employed men)	49.0	43.3	43.7
Women (% all employed women)	46.7	37.0	36.0
Social protection expenditure			
Total (% of GDP)	21.2	26.7	26.0**
Pensions (% of GDP)	10.8	13.1	12.9**
At-risk-of-poverty rate (%)			
Total population	22.0*	20.0	20.0
People aged 65 years and more	35.0*	33.0	28.0

Source: Eurostat
*1995; ** 2004

unemployment, nor prevent the expansion of project work, service contracts and informal work in the last two decades.

Mass immigration, irregular work and labour market segmentation

By the late 1980s Greece was no longer a labour exporting country; however, immigration was also negligible. Since the beginning of the 1990s it has experienced a mass inflow of economic migrants, coming mainly from the

Balkans, eastern Europe and the Middle East. In 2005 non-EU nationals represented 8.1 per cent of total population and their employment rate was 70.5 per cent against 59.7 per cent for Greeks and other EU nationals. Moreover, their unemployment rate (8.1 per cent) was lower than that of the latter (9.7 per cent).

The first immigration law was hastily passed in 1991 to confront the sudden and massive arrival of immigrants and basically intended to check their flow by making legal work and residence extremely difficult (Glytsos, 1995). In 1997 the policy approach changed in favour of regularizing illegal residence and work by foreigners. However, all laws and amnesties since that year set stringent requirements as well as costly, bureaucratic procedures. The outcome has been the regularization of only a small proportion of the illegally residing population and often to a reversal of the migrant's situation from legality to illegality. Moreover, only the last law of 2005 has provided for long-duration residence permits and measures promoting the social inclusion of immigrants.

For the time being the social inclusion of immigrants takes place mainly through their work and the education of their children in public schools. Their contribution to the containment of production costs and inflation has been widely recognized among scholars, while their role in the reproduction of the underground economy has also been stressed. It is important to note that immigration has renewed the pool of labour available for informal/irregular work traditionally composed by low-educated women, young first jobseekers, students and members of ethnic, cultural and religious minorities. They have thus contributed to the reproduction of a basic feature of the traditional social model that is labour market segmentation.

Still residual protection against unemployment

Unemployment increased sharply in the 1990s, the rate climbing from 6.4 per cent in 1990 to 12 per cent in 1999. To tackle the problem, active labour market policies were extended using resources from EU Structural Funds, with training emerging as their most important component. On the other hand no reforms were made to the unemployment compensation system to improve coverage and income replacement. At the same time inequalities of treatment were introduced into the system. More generous benefits and preferential treatment in active labour programmes were offered to those laid off from strongly unionized industrial firms under control of the state or state banks than were available to their counterparts dismissed from private firms. Moreover, the personnel of public utilities and banks were offered pre-retirement options or attractive financial packages in cases of voluntary redundancy. At the other extreme young first-time jobseekers and women returnees continued to receive either very low compensation or none at all.

Although labour market policy in the 1990s became the principal tool of social management of unemployment, in 2004 total expenditure on such policy was only 0.6 per cent of GDP, the lowest rate among the former EU-15 countries (European Commission, 2006, p. 127). From the 1990s onwards youth unemployment rocketed, its rate today being the third highest in the EU-25 at 26 per cent. Initial vocational training for upper-secondary graduates was established in 1992. Its accreditation system is linked to model occupational profiles and takes place with social partners' participation (Vretakou and Rousseas, 2002). In addition, higher education was further opened up to a growing number of upper-secondary education graduates. The enrolment rate in tertiary education reached 60.2 per cent in 2004, the highest rate in the EU-25 and the OECD. However, the production system did not create sufficient jobs in the type of occupations that young people had studied and prepared for and which matched their career expectations. Today even more highly educated graduates are experiencing difficulties in their transition to work and a high risk of unemployment.

Partially implemented reforms to pensions and healthcare

Reforms of the pensions system since the beginning of the 1990s have aimed at tackling current and future deficits in insurance funds generated by the drop in the ratio of insured to pensioners, the extensive and long-standing evasion of contributions and the continual use by the state of the reserves of the insurance funds deposited at the Central Bank to finance investments and social policy measures.

The reforms of the early 1990s have introduced a number of changes in the system:

(a) Equalization of women's legal age of retirement with men's at 65 years for those insured after 1 January 1993;
(b) Gradual equalization of the legal age of retirement for employees working in the civil service, banks, public utilities and so on with that of private sector employees;
(c) An increase in the minimum insured time for full pension entitlement and reduction of the replacement rate of pensions to prolong the age of exit from the labour force;
(d) Abolition in the public sector of early retirement schemes for married women and for widows, divorced and unmarried mothers with adult unmarried children; and
(e) Tightening of the eligibility criteria for early retirement for women with minor or disabled children in both the public and private sector.

In 1992 it was established for the first time that general taxation would contribute to the insurance funds, accounting for one-third of total contributions due by those insured after 1 January 1993. This was a decisive rupture initiating a trend away from a purely contribution-based social security system towards a mixed-funded one. The second half of the 1990s and the

2000s saw structural but piecemeal changes. These included the transformation of the farmers' insurance fund from a general taxation-based to a contributions-based fund; the merger of all main and supplementary funds of private sector employees into a single fund; the introduction of a means-tested pension supplement to low basic pensions; the contribution of 1 per cent of GDP per year from the state budget to the main insurance fund for private sector employees; permission to invest a proportion of the reserves of the funds in financial products; and the creation of occupational funds based on capitalization.

Most of the changes just described are *incremental* and *path-dependent*. The most radical of them have either advanced slowly (mergers) or not at all (creation of occupational funds based on capitalization principles), while the investment of reserves in financial products has recently resulted in many funds incurring considerable losses.

Similarly, *institutional legacies* have prevailed over attempts at structural reform in public healthcare (Sotiropoulos, 2004). Due to their links to political parties the members of the privileged social insurance funds have constituted an effective blocking minority at attempts to reduce the great disparities in the levels of cover and access to healthcare providers between the different groups of the population (Davaki and Mossialos, 2006). Furthermore, medical professors have successfully resisted a reform obliging them to choose between practising in private clinics or in public university hospitals. As a result, a series of reforms have focused on the improvement of efficiency in the provision and funding of services through the introduction of managerial techniques, but even these have not been fully implemented (Katrougalos, 2003). Undoubtedly, the most important change since 1990 is the declining share of public expenditure and the rising share of private expenditure in total health expenditure. Private expenditure takes the form of direct payments by patients for private consultations and other medical services (for example hospital and diagnostics), hospital out-patient consultations, co-payments for prescriptions and unofficial out-of-pocket payments by patients to doctors of public hospitals (informal market). In 2002 health expenditure rose to 9.5 per cent of GDP, of which 47 per cent was private.

Female emancipation and inadequate de-familialization

The female activity rate has continued to follow the upward trend evident since the 1980s (Table 9.2). The most important contribution to this increase was made by women aged 25–54. Yet the rate among 55–9 year olds also rose significantly, indicating a later exit from the labour force than in previous decades. In 2003, couples where only the man was working represented 44 per cent of all couples aged 20–49 with at least one person working (Aliaga, 2005). This is evidence that the male-breadwinner/family home-carer model is still very strong but no longer dominant.

The increase in female labour market participation has not been followed by an adequate policy for reconciliation of work and family life. It was only in 1997/98 that an important effort by policymakers to improve publicly funded childcare infrastructure and develop programmes of domiciliary care for the elderly got underway. It is thus no surprise that Greece has today the lowest coverage rate of children and elderly by care services in the former EU-15. Because of the low coverage of formal childcare services (7 per cent of children aged 0–3 years, 60 per cent of those aged 3–6 years in 2003), the most usual care strategies adopted by working parents are the mobilization of grandparents and the hiring of nannies (Symeonidou et al., 2001). Owing to the inadequacy of public care services for the dependent elderly, the most usual strategy adopted by their working children is to hire live-in immigrants to look after them. Paid domestic care though does not fully replace informal care by family members.

Growing female emancipation has coincided with an increasing demand for family solidarity due to the increase in the years spent by young people in education, the extremely high youth unemployment rates and the residual character of the unemployment protection system. More years spent in education, difficulties in the transition from education to work and changes in youth culture towards greater individualization have delayed the average age of leaving home. In the mid-1980s the co-residence rate of men aged 25–9 with their parents was 50 per cent, but in 2002 this had risen to 70 per cent (Becker et al., 2005). Delay in leaving the parental home has increased the cost of having children and has both encouraged female activity and discouraged fertility decisions. In 2005 the total fertility rate was 1.28 children, down from 1.43 in 1990 and 2.23 in 1980. Only eastern European countries today have lower fertility rates than Greece in Europe as a whole.

Towards a liberal, partly de-familialized capitalism

Since the beginning of the 1990s the Greek socio-economic model has been heading towards a form of liberal capitalism, while since the end of the 1990s it has been undergoing a process of de-familialization. Two of the main drivers of change towards liberalism have been public indebtedness and European integration. Growing public indebtedness from the mid-1980s onwards pointed at an early stage to the limits of statism in a stagnating capitalist economy with low private investment. European integration imposed economic liberalism through a series of institutional constraints (Single Market directives, EMU, Stability Pact) while at the same time promoting social partnership and dialogue and the coordination of national policies in the fields of employment, social inclusion and social protection. As for de-familialization, this was encouraged by the European Employment Strategy and the availability of ESF funds. It responded to growing social dissatisfaction, especially of working couples, with the increasing cost of having children and caring for the elderly.

With the reduction in industrial conflict, the growth of collective bargaining free from state intervention and the development of social dialogue, it might be possible to imagine that the Greek model since the 1990s has been heading towards a 'coordinated' or 'negotiated capitalism'. However, this is very far from reality. In fact, the adversarial culture and the use of party affiliations and political rivalry between parties to obtain concessions from employers and their organizations are still key features of Greek trade unionism. Moreover, liberalism and labour market flexibility advance only when the unions are defeated. Namely, all privatizations and law provisions introducing labour market flexibility were not negotiated but imposed, although strong resistance has attenuated their impact. In fact, only moderate forms of employment and working-time flexibility have been introduced by law and were accompanied by adequate security rights for workers. As for informal forms of labour flexibility, they thrive in the Greek labour market because they are beyond the reach of the unions.

The sustainability of the new model is questionable on several grounds. First, market liberalization and privatization do not bring competitive advantage by themselves and may even undermine the prospects of high and sustainable economic growth. There is a need for appropriate structural and macroeconomic policies. Second, the rate of job growth has been quite high in the last decade but clearly insufficient to absorb high unemployment among youth and women. At the same time the one million irregular and low-quality jobs occupied today by immigrants who have arrived since the beginning of the 1990s suggest that a very important part of the jobs created in the economy do not match the occupations and skills or the quality expectations of high and medium-educated young people. Third, partial de-familialization of the welfare regime is incapable of putting an end to the unprecedented 'birth strike', while full de-familialization requires adequate resources for the expansion of the welfare state. Fourth, the pensions system is going to face severe deficits by 2010 and its funding is not yet ensured. Fifth, although the incidence of poverty in old age has been reduced due to the means-tested supplements for low-income pensioners, it remains very high and substantially above the already high overall poverty rate. Last but not least, the lack of concern among policymakers for the social inclusion of immigrants and their children will certainly create social tensions in the near future.

Even leaving aside the issue of social resistance, it can be seen that the transition of the Greek socio-economic model from a state-led familistic to a liberal de-familialized capitalism is difficult in large part because of an unresolved tension. Competitiveness of the economy needs to be restored along with the extension of the welfare state, if the new model is to be economically and socially sustainable in the long term. For the time being

Greece seems to be in a trap. Competition with low-cost countries in an open economy context and the continuously rising real exchange rate reinforce de-industrialization and de-ruralization, fuel the underground economy and keep unemployment at a very high level. Both phenomena undermine the tax base that is necessary to extend the welfare state. In addition, the very high profits generated over the last decade by exploiting rents distributed by the state, oligopolistic conditions in the market and speculation in financial markets and real estate have not yet been used to create new sources of competitive advantage, allowing for sustainable long-term development.

Notes

1. OECD Observer, April–May 1991.
2. The Italian system was even more rudimentary than the Greek for those individually dismissed but was extremely generous for the victims of mass redundancies.
3. Since the 1980s, during negotiations with employer organizations, union federations of private sector employees have used national minimum wage increases as the floor and the best rate achieved by pubic utilities and banking federations as the target.

References

(G) = In Greek

Aliaga, C. (2005), 'Gender Gaps in the Reconciliation between Work and Family Life', *Statistics in Focus*, 4/25, Luxembourg: Office for Official Publications of the European Communities.

Becker, S., Bentolila, S., Fernandes, A. and Ichino, A. (2005), 'Youth Emancipation and Perceived Job Insecurity of Parents and Children', *IZA Discussion Paper* 1836, Bonn: Institute for the Study of Labor.

Davaki, K. and Mossialos E. (2006), 'Financing and Delivering Health Care', pp. 286–318 in M. Petmesidou and E. Mossialos (eds), *Social Policy Developments in Greece*, London: Ashgate.

Esping-Andersen, G. (1999), *Social Foundations of Postindustrial Economies*, Oxford: Oxford University Press.

European Commission (2006), *Employment in Europe 2006*, Luxembourg: Office for Official Publications of the European Communities.

European Commission (2008), *Annual Information Society Report 2008*, Luxembourg: Office for Official Publications of the European Communities.

Ferrera, M. (1996), 'The "southern model" of Welfare in Social Europe', *Journal of European Social Policy* 6 (1): 17–37.

Georgakopoulou, V. (1983), *Morphologie industrielle et emploi: le cas de la petite et moyenne industrie grecque dans les années soixante et soixante-dix*, Mémoire de DEA, Université Paris I, Panthéon-Sorbonne.

Gibson, H., Stournaras, Y. and Tsakalotos E. (2001), 'The Changing Role of Finance in Southern European Economies: Will there be and Improvement in Economic Performance?', pp. 274–305 in H. Gibson (ed.), *Economic Transformation, Democratization and Integration into the European Union. Southern Europe in Comparative Perspective*, Basingstoke and New York: Palgrave Macmillan.

Glytsos, N. (1995), 'Problems and Policies Regarding the Socio-economic Integration of Returnees and Foreign Workers in Greece', *International Migration* XXXIII (2): 155–73.

Hadjidimitriou, F. (1991), 'Complementary Insurance: The Great Irrationality of the Greek System of Social Security', *Syndicalistiki Epitheorisi (Unions' Review)* 75/76: 28–40. (G)

Hadjimihalis, K. and Vaiou D. (1987), 'Changing Patterns of Uneven Regional Development and Forms of Social Reproduction in Greece', *Society and Space* 5 (1987): 319–33. (G)

Ioakimoglou, E. (1996), *Restructuring and Specialization of Manufacturing in Greece*, Athens: Institute of Labour, General Confederation of Workers. (G)

Ioakimoglou, E. and Milios, J. (1992), 'Capital Over-Accumulation and Profitability Crisis in Greece', *Review of Radical Political Economy* 25 (1992): 81–107.

Ioannou, C. (1989), *Salaried Employment and Trade Unionism in Greece*, Athens: Foundation for Mediterranean Studies. (G)

Ioannou, C. (2000), 'Social Pacts in Hellenic Industrial Relations: Odysseus or Sisyphus?', pp. 219–36 in G. Fajertag and P. Pochet (eds), *Social Pacts in Europe – New Dynamics*, Brussels: ETUI (2nd edition).

Karamessini, M. (1992), *Flexibilité du travail et restructuration du capital. La crise du modèle de développement et l'enjeu de la flexibilité*, Thèse de doctorat, Université de Paris VII.

Karamessini, M. (2002), *Industrial Policy, EU Integration and Wage Labour*, Athens: Ellinika Grammata. (G).

Karamessini, M. and Kaminioti O. (1999), 'Labour Market Segmentation in Greece: Historical Perspective and Recent Trends'. *Discussion Papers* 69, Athens: Centre of Planning and Economic Research.

Katrougalos, G. (2003), 'National Health Systems. An Originality of the South?', pp. 123–66 in G. Katrougalos and G. Lazaridis (eds), *Southern European Welfare States. Problems, Challenges and Prospects*, Basingstoke, Hampshire: Palgrave Macmillan.

Konstantinopoulos, C. (1993), *Institutions and Agencies for Combating Unemployment in Greece (1920–1992)*. Athens: OAED. (G).

Kouzis, Y. (2002), 'The Changes in Labour Relations in Greece', in P. Getimis et al. (eds), *Yearbook of Labour 2002*, Athens: Institute of Human Resources and Urban Environment, Panteion University. (G)

Kritsantonis, N. (1998), 'Greece: The Maturing of the System', pp. 601–28 in A. Ferner and R. Hyman (eds), *Changing Industrial Relations in Europe*, Oxford: Blackwell (2nd edition).

Leibfried, S. (1992), 'Towards a European Welfare State? On Integrating Poverty Regimes into the European Community', pp. 245–80 in Z. Ferge and J. E. Kolberg (eds), *Social Policy in a Changing Europe*, Boulder: Westview Press.

Manassis, N. (1991), *Project for the Establishment of a National Pensions System*, Athens: DEN.

Mavrogordatos, G. (1988), *Between Pitiokamptis and Prokroustis: Occupational Organizations in Contemporary Greece*, Athens: Odysseus (G).

OECD (2005), *Greece 2005. OECD Economic Surveys*, OECD: Paris.

OECD (2007), *Main Science and Technology Indicators (MSTI): 2007/2 edition*, OECD: Paris.

Petmesidou, M. (1996), 'Social Protection in Southern Europe: Trends and Prospects', *Journal of Area Studies* 9 (1996): 95–125.

Pfau-Effinger, B. (1998), 'The Modernization of Family and Motherhood in Western Europe', pp. 60–79 in R. Crompton (ed.), *Restructuring Gender Relations and Employment. The Decline of the Male Breadwinner*, Oxford: Oxford University Press.

Provopoulos, G. (1985), *The Crisis of Social Security: the problem of IKA*, Athens: IOBE. (G)
Savva-Balfousia, S. (2005), 'The Progress of Structural Changes and the Challenges of the New Economic Environment', *Economic Developments* 9 (2005): 36–48, Athens: KEPE. (G)
Sotiropoulos, D. (2004), 'The EU's Impact on the Greek Welfare State: Europeanization on Paper?', *Journal of European Social Policy* 14 (3): 267–84.
Symeonidou, H., Mitsopoulos, G. and Vezyrgianni K. (2001), 'The Division of Paid and Unpaid Work in Greece, European Network of Policies and the Division of Unpaid and Paid Work', WORC Report 01.02.002, Tilburg University.
Vretakou, V. and Rousseas P. (2002), *Vocational Education and Training in Greece. Brief Description*, Cedefop Panorama Series, 50, Luxembourg: Office for Official Publications of the European Communities.
Wright, V. and Pagoulatos G. (2001), 'The Comparative Politics of Industrial Privatization: Spain, Portugal and Greece in a European Perspective', pp. 231–73 in H. Gibson (ed.), *Economic Transformation, Democratization and Integration into the European Union. Southern Europe in Comparative Perspective*, Basingstoke and New York: Palgrave Macmillan.
Zambarloukou, S. (2006), 'Collective Bargaining and Social Pacts: Greece in Comparative Perspective', *European Journal of Industrial Relations* 12 (2): 211–29.

10
The Transformation of the Employment System in Spain: Towards a Mediterranean Neoliberalism?

Josep Banyuls, Fausto Miguélez, Albert Recio, Ernest Cano and Raúl Lorente

Introduction

Since the first democratic elections after the Francoist dictatorship (20 June 1977), important changes have taken place in Spain. These have affected the economic and social structure, culture, labour relations, gender relations and everyday life. The changes have been influenced by both external factors (globalization, European integration) and internal factors (political democratization, territorial restructuring, social demands and cultural changes). This context of deep and rapid transformation in the socio-economic model must be taken into account in order to understand the puzzle that is the current employment system. The drivers of these changes are diverse, as we will see. Our hypothesis is that there have been significant breaks with the past, but these are not of a radical nature and are instead combined with significant degrees of continuity.

The socio-economic model of the late years of the Franco system has been characterized as both *unfinished peripheral fordism* (Toharia, 1986; Lipietz, 1997) and as a *coordinated market economy*. Although the Spanish economy operated primarily as a closed economy, its adoption of an external trade liberalization policy in 1959 led to a phase of economic expansion associated with the arrival of multinational firms and the start of tourism. This rise in activity boosted consumption and allowed a period of intensive capital accumulation. Nevertheless, the economy retained the characteristics of peripheral fordism: production was mainly oriented to the domestic market and limited by the high proportion of small and very small firms, wages were low and unions banned. In addition, the dependency on foreign technology was very high and skilled labour was in short supply. On the other hand the state exerted a powerful influence on economic activity, both direct, through the state-owned firms and indirect, through strong regulation of many activities that frequently generated oligopolistic structures. It is within these latter structures that the core of Spanish capitalism (banking, utilities and so on) was, and still is, located. In this sense the old Spanish model can be also classified as a *coordinated market economy*.

However, these two classifications of the characteristics of the Spanish 'variety of capitalism' relate only to the nature of the business system, which is not sufficient in itself to characterize an employment model. In terms of social structure and welfare regime Spain was in fact clearly a southern country (Karamessini, 2007): the family played a central role providing services, and public services (including education and health) were underdeveloped. Also, one of the main effects of this social model was a significant gender division of labour, associated with low female participation in the labour market. Overall, the model combined economic growth with poor labour and social conditions and very high inequalities by class and gender.

The forces of change have come from different directions. On the one hand, with the arrival of democracy, strong social movements demanded improvements in social conditions and reductions in inequality. There was a general demand for the expansion of public services (health, education, urban renewal, pensions and so on) that put pressure on the new democratic institutions and generated one of the drivers for modernization. On the other hand there were pressures to liberalize the economy and to change both product and labour regulations, stemming from the increasing internationalization of the economy and its integration into the European Union. While in some respects economic liberalization may promote productive modernization, in others it acts in contradiction to the demands for greater equality. The overall direction of change is the outcome of the interaction of these contradictory forces (and the inertia of old institutions and behaviours), thereby rendering it very difficult to characterize the current Spanish socio-economic model by a single reference. In reality, as we will show, while much progress has been made in both welfare and employment outcomes, many of the same institutions and the same economic and social problems remain. Economic progress has been apparently particularly strong over the past ten years but there are question marks over the sustainability of the model. In the following sections we analyse the puzzle of the current employment model, focusing on the main trends and the drivers that explain them.

Changes in the productive structure

Changes in the Spanish production structure have been taking place over the last three decades, explaining much of the character of the new jobs that have been created. In recent years economic development has been mainly in labour-intensive activities with low productivity. The other key factor in the Spanish employment model is labour management flexibility. The difficulties experienced by many sectors in establishing a new accumulation model have increased the pressure on labour costs and led to employers seeking increased control over the labour force. The transformation of the production structure combines prior trends with transformations that are, to some extent, a break with the past. An analysis of the changes at sector level (see Table 10.1) highlights the significant decline in agricultural activity in absolute and relative terms: from 21 per cent of employment in 1976 to less than 5 per cent in 2006. This tendency is the result of the intensification of the disagrarization process, which began in the 1960s, and the introduction of technological innovations. It can be expected to continue into the future.

Over the same period manufacturing employment declined from 27 per cent to 16 per cent. This trend in decline has involved more intensive employment loss in the recession and more limited employment growth in the upswing than for the Spanish economy as a whole. This tendency can be explained by the restructuring promoted by economic recessions. During recessions many firms in sectors where long-term competitiveness is in serious doubt (for instance clothing, footwear, electronics and some auto-parts firms) have either closed or relocated to other countries. In addition, some activities have been outsourced from manufacturing towards the tertiary sector. Overall, the decline in manufacturing employment reflects Spanish industrial companies' weak competitive position in the new international context, which in turn partly explains their preference for external labour flexibility and low wages. Throughout this period the construction sector has undergone even more intense cyclical changes than manufacturing. However, since 1996 it has increased in relative importance with its share of total employment rising from 9 to 13 per cent (20 per cent of male employment, with a significant share of immigrants), five points above the EU-15 level. In fact, construction has been one of the main drivers behind economic growth in recent years and the sector has reached very high levels of employment that will be impossible to consolidate in the medium term.

Table 10.1 Employment by economic activity (in percentages), Spain 1976–2006, EU-15 2006

	1976	1979	1987	1996	2006 Spain	2006 EU-15
Total	100.0	100.0	100.0	100.0	100.0	100.0
Agriculture, livestock farming and fishing	21.6	19.5	14.3	8.1	4.9	3.7
Manufacturing	27.4	27.2	24.2	20.2	15.9	17.4
Construction	9.9	9.4	8.3	9.6	12.6	8.1
Services	41.1	44.0	53.2	62.1	65.7	69.6

Source: Data for 1976 to 1996, National Statistics Institute, Labour Force Survey. 2006 data, EUROSTAT. Data given for 2006 are not strictly comparable with the previous years because employment is calculated on 15 years and over while the previous years are calculated on 16 years and over.

Services have experienced the most intensive and relatively continuous expansion, increasing from 41 per cent of employment in 1976 to 66 per cent in 2006. This tendency is the result of various factors including the relatively stable behaviour of traditional services such as trade, transport and finances, the expansion of hotels and restaurants (linked to tourism), the intensive creation of employment in business service companies and the expansion of education, health and social services, managed as public services or business (Cuadrado and Iglesias, 2003). The growth of services can be considered a process of modernization, which is unfinished. Indeed the relative importance of services in the Spanish economy is still lower than in the EU-15. However, much of the expansion of tertiary activities is based on low salaries and labour-intensive activities (hotels and restaurants, domestic services and personal services).

In this context of structural changes it is noteworthy that employment growth has been associated with only a modest level of productivity growth. Despite various governments raising the issue of technological development, investment in research and development (R&D) remains low (1.13 per cent of GDP in 2005) and public activity accounts for nearly half of this investment. There are several reasons for this situation. One of them is the polarized structure of business, with a high proportion of small firms coexisting with only a small number of big firms. Small and medium-sized enterprises (SMEs) experience problems in positioning themselves to be proactive in shaping their competitive position as most of them are dependent on larger companies. These firms base their competitiveness mainly on a reduction of labour costs and external flexibility and, in some cases, still use the black economy (Ybarra et al., 2002). On the other side are the large multinational companies that control key sectors of the production structure (motor, chemicals, electronics, food, commercial distribution) and develop the high technological activities in the country.

Another reason is the fact that the largest Spanish groups are concentrated in sectors such as banking, construction, utilities and public services, retailing and hotels (Giraldez, 2002). Despite some of these being big users of technology, they do not create enough spill-over to the economy as a whole. Part of their business is more devoted to developing fluid relations with public administrators (partly explaining the successful position of these firms in Latin America) and to safeguarding their oligopolistic positions. In addition, the new liberal environment has strengthened opportunities to make large profits in sectors that do not need intensive technological innovation, like real estate, building and tourism.

A clear result of Spanish sectoral specialization is a weak position in the international economy (Banco de España, 2003; Pérez et al., 2004). Spain has in the past been able to maintain some international competitiveness through the use of changes in the exchange rate. With European monetary union, this option is no longer available to the Spanish government and the economy has been losing competitiveness continuously. One explanation is the high specialization of Spain in sectors that are only weakly integrated into the international economy. A detailed analysis of external trade (Pérez et al., 2004) shows that, with the exception of the motor industry, there are no significant industrial activities with permanent comparative advantages in international trade. Only the agro-food and tourism industries score in this context. Tourism is the main export activity in the Spanish economy, reinforcing the focus on construction and the creation of low-quality jobs in services.

A segmented labour relations model

The heritage of the Francoist industrial relations model is still evident in the Spanish employment model. Some authors argue that Francoist regulation created a rigid but paternalistic labour market. From our point of view Franco's labour market regulation is more appropriately labelled as authoritarian. Employment protection rules were oriented to the legitimation of the political regime but employers still had opportunities to use discretionary dismissal: disciplinary dismissal did not require compensation and there were specific contract arrangements for activities facing seasonal or cyclical variations (agriculture, tourism, construction). The prohibition of unions and the lack of a real public system of control allowed managers to impose long working times, discretionary payments and internal flexibility and so on. Labour relations were based on low trust between employers and employees. Despite these adverse conditions, clandestine unions emerged in large firms from the 1960s onwards and increased their membership in the last years of the old regime. This was a highly politicized form of trade unionism, due to its central role in the Franco resistance and the anti-capitalism attitude of those times. In 1976, after the dictator's death, there were massive worker mobilizations demanding union freedoms and improvement of wages and labour conditions. In 1977, before the first democratic elections, unions were legalized.

Moncloa's Pact in 1977, an agreement signed by political parties, provided the blueprint for the main changes in the social model brought about by democratization (union recognition, tax reform, welfare expansion and labour market reform). In addition, it included guidelines on moderating wage increases and other workers' demands. Further reforms and several social agreements resulted in a high institutionalization of trade unions and employers' organizations. Unions became strong political actors even though, except in large and some medium companies, union presence was not significant at the job level; in fact, union delegates are voted on by 40 per cent of workers when elections at company level take place, even though union density barely exceeds 15 per cent. They have thus a great deal of power and extensive negotiating responsibilities, but their ability to ensure compliance with agreements is low. From this situation came two forms of dualism. On the one hand, as national actors, union policies oscillate between the defence of working-class aims and a compromise with 'national economic needs'. On the other hand they only have the capacity to represent employees in large firms efficiently; it is difficult for them to organize union activity in small firms, among temporary workers and so on.

The recent history of labour relations in Spain, including agreements and conflicts, needs to be viewed through this framework. In the National Employment Agreement (1981) the trade unions undertook to moderate their wage demands and maintain social peace in return for the commitment by government and employers to social reforms and job creation. However, a few years later the Economic and Social Agreement (1984) was signed only by the government (PSOE) and by one of the trade unions bodies, the UGT.[1] The other trade union body, the CC.OO. withdrew at the last minute in protest at the change in the Workers' Rights Statute which introduced temporary employment. Both trade union bodies formally moved away from the agreement in 1986, despite the willingness of the government and the employers' association to continue.

The trade unions' response grew more acute as the impact of deregulation on the labour markets became clear. The general strike of 14 December 1988 brought the CC.OO. and the UGT together to challenge the labour market deregulation policy, and they successfully opposed the Apprentice Contracts Act, which would have introduced salaries below the legal national minimum wage for young people in temporary employment (Cachón and Palacio, 1991). The result, as well as preventing this project, was that the government consented in 1990 to introduce some social welfare measures in agreement with the trade unions, but without the participation of the employers.

The labour reform of 1994 led to further disagreement between the trade unions and the socialist government, and to another general strike. In 1997, under a conservative government, the social agents changed their strategy and employers and large trade union confederations signed a proposal for labour reform. The main feature was the introduction of incentives to create permanent employment contracts for young people, long-term unemployed and for holders of temporary contracts in return for reduced compensation levels for redundancy. In 2006, under a socialist government, a new reform in the same direction was also agreed.

The results of this whole process of agreements and conflicts are complex. Those involved in it, trade unions and business organizations, have consolidated their position in political terms and public opinion above and beyond their formal representation. However, results for labour conditions are contradictory. Despite collective agreements covering all employees in one industry at provincial, regional or national level, the effect of the combined processes of a proliferation of new agreements in new service activities, together with the externalization of work to firms and sectors without any effective collective bargaining coverage, has been to produce a sharp variation in wages and the emergence of new low-wage sectors. The same applies to other labour conditions (including dismissals) where unions have not developed effective forms of action for everybody.

These effects can be understood if the interactions between labour market segmentation and trade union activity are considered (Alós, 2005). The unemployed, temporary and part-time workers, those that work in small companies and young people with insecure jobs hardly ever become involved in trade unions. Real negotiation for the flexibility of employment does not therefore take place in sectors with flexible employment. The trade unions have achieved some degree of control over external flexibility by exchanging increases in internal flexibility for job security in large companies and, to a certain extent, in sectors in which they are strong, such as banking, chemicals and the civil service. However, in other areas the flexibility that has been imposed is external and totally controlled by the companies. In the 1997 and 2006 agreements the government intervened to reduce temporary employment by subsidizing companies. Nevertheless, this was only effective while there were subsidies and there was no check on abuses of temporary employment in areas with little trade union presence. Both the dichotomy between trade union influence at national and workplace levels and the political cycles of conflict and compromise have shaped the process of labour market restructuring over the last 30 years.

An all-embracing process of labour market segmentation

The current employment model is also partly a heritage of the former Francoist model. As we pointed out earlier, the economic system was characterized by strong market protection against external competition and a predominance of low-productivity activities and regulations that promoted both large monopolistic groups and a proliferation of small firms. These conditions generated a low-skilled labour force and poor labour standards. Labour regulations offered formal individual guarantees to employees in exchange for giving companies complete freedom to organize the work process and the forbidding of collective protection. Employment of core employees was protected both by laws and by the sustained growth of firms until the 1970s crisis. Things changed significantly with the return of democracy in 1977 and the entry of Spain into the European Economic Community (EEC) in 1986. Nevertheless, it is still possible to identify obvious continuities from the past. With regard to economic growth, the main drivers are still low-tech and low-wage activities, such as tourism and construction and all sectors involved in them. Competitiveness problems remain, external trade disequilibrium is permanent and the dualism in the productive structure between multinational corporations and large companies and the SME sector persist. However, there are substantial changes from the past, especially in social aspects and welfare: education is compulsory up until age 16 and healthcare assistance and pensions are universal.

In the labour market we can also find continuities and breaks. Despite some improvements, job quality is still low and poor labour standards are common in many activities, especially in small firms. The core workforce still places high value on the maintenance of basic labour rights, social security and employment protection. The unskilled workforce remains very important and skills are not always recognized. These aspects are a clear continuity from the past. However, the characteristics of labour force supply have changed dramatically owing to the boost to female labour market participation and the rise in immigration (see below). Likewise, the increase in temporary work and the high degree of precariousness in the labour market, especially for women, young people and immigrants, are clear breaks with the past. As a whole the outcome of these forces is that the Spanish economy, while successful in terms of employment creation, achieves this through 'low-quality jobs' and a highly segmented labour market.

The mainstream explanation for employment dualism is that we are in the middle of a path of reform: so far labour market reforms have been successful at reducing the high unemployment levels and now there is the possibility to improve job quality. A central argument from this point of view is that we are in transition from a highly protected, paternalistic employment system to a flexible labour market (or, perhaps, a future flexi-secure labour market). The official argument for this deregulation policy is that it stimulates economic growth and reduces unemployment by facilitating employment without committing employers to stability. The partiality of the successive labour market reforms (reforms 'on the margin') is explained by the resistance of unions (and insider employees) to a general reform, generating new forms of segmentation.

However, there is an alternative interpretation. Faced with a crisis in the productive model in the 1970s and the first half of the 1980s, some companies focused their labour management on exploiting the *de facto* deregulation of the labour market, regardless of the legal regulations, resulting in the growth of the black and deregulated labour relations economy (Bilbao, 1993). From this perspective the reforms of employment legislation in the 1980s had not so much enabled unemployment to be reduced, but instead had 'legalized' employers' external flexibility practices and brought these back into the regulatory framework by replacing employment in the black economy with temporary flexible contracts (Cano and Sánchez, 1998). Such practices were thereby encouraged, not only to ensure flexibility but also as a means of reducing labour costs and increasing a company's control over its workforce.[2] These practices have become structural for companies, whatever their economic situation, and they act as a disincentive to possible alternatives based on developing higher-quality human resource policies and improved working and employment conditions.

What is more, despite the major change in context since Franco, neither unions nor individual workers are able to exert control over labour conditions in small firms. The poor job conditions persist and the experience of massive unemployment in 1980s and 1990s continues to act as a dampener on protests against these conditions. An example of this union weakness is the high percentage of temporary jobs. To a certain extent these conditions reflect the particular specialization of the Spanish economy, but also the poor labour conditions and low trust policies adopted in a high proportion of firms and industries where unions lack the capacity to exert influence. It is in these areas that the core of precarious jobs are concentrated. The new regulation of the labour market can be explained as a policy of adaptation to the global economy by means of controlling labour costs together with specialization in activities such as construction, low-skilled services and industrial activities in which Spain is not able to develop a high level of international competitiveness. Nevertheless, it has also an element of continuity with the tradition of poor quality of labour conditions.

As a whole, since the establishment of democracy, the Spanish labour market has been characterized by turbulence and continuous reforms. This turbulence has resulted primarily from structural changes in the economy and the global recessions. Labour reforms are justified as the basic way to tackle turbulence in a political context of neoliberal ideology. At the same time there is a struggle between forces trying to set the most liberal possible model and forces trying to establish some degree of regulation in the model. Laws, agreements, policies and strategies have moved between these two poles over the last 30 years. Some minimum standards inherited from Franco's times have been retained, albeit in moderated forms, as corrections to the full force of the neoliberal model: opposition to costless dismissal, maintaining minimum income and universal pensions. Nevertheless, a consistent employment policy with a design appropriate to the new situation has not been developed. The prevailing neoliberalism at international level in the 1980s and 1990s allowed Spanish governments, including left-wing ones, to conclude that there was not enough scope to introduce greater regulation into the internal capitalism. Therefore, neoliberal capitalism has prevailed with some modifications, an approach that the current government is continuing, except for some increases in the incentives for secure employment.

Where more detailed labour market reforms are concerned, the starting point is the 1980 Workers' Rights Statute, which to a considerable extent guaranteed the defence of workers' rights. There have been continuous reforms of the employment regulations, with a clear trend towards increasing the flexibility of the labour market in line with the international consensus (OECD, 1999). A common point of labour policies in Spain has been the aim of encouraging business competitiveness by means of reducing labour costs, rather than promoting productivity increases, cooperation between employers and employees, training and so on (Cachón and Palacio, 1999).

Until the mid-1990s employment reform in Spain was characterized by its encouragement of 'flexibility at the margin' (external flexibility), which permitted practically unlimited temporary employment for new workers, although job security for workers with a permanent contract was protected (Toharia, 2005). The 1984 reform of the Workers' Rights Statute made this clear by introducing a fixed-term contract aimed at stimulating non-causal employment, as well as increasing the general flexibility of temporary employment with respect to requirements and duration. During this period of economic recession two employment and social policy initiatives took place, which further embedded the neoliberal deregulation model (Recio, 1998). Firstly, in 1992 welfare coverage for unemployment was reduced due to financing problems. Secondly, because of the increase in unemployment, the government in 1994 introduced a new labour reform which reinforced flexibility: temporary employment agencies were legalized, grounds for justifiable dismissal were increased, government and trade union supervision of dismissals was reduced and aspects of working conditions that had previously been legally regulated at national level were transferred to collective bargaining.

The 1997 labour reform that provided a subsidy for permanent contracts introduced a change in the trend, albeit short lived. There was a slight fall in the rate of temporary employment in the late 1990s but this reversed again after 2002, and when the subsidy ended in 2006, temporary employment had reached 35 per cent. In June 2006 the government negotiated a new reform with unions and employers' associations. The logic of this reform is similar to the 1997 agreement: on one side it reduces job protection for permanent employees, and on the other it increases public aid to encourage permanent jobs and introduces some punishments for the use of fixed-term contracts. In the short term the reform has shown some moderate effects on the reduction of fixed-term contracts, but it is not clear that this agreement will be enough to transform the labour market.

These labour reforms are related to the main trends of the Spanish labour market over last 30 years. When the democratic period began the country was apparently close to full employment, although only little more than half of the population aged over 16 and 28 per cent of women were active. The situation deteriorated rapidly due to internal reasons (institutional change and the end of tariff-based protectionism) and to external factors (the oil crisis and the world economic recession). Workers demanded improvements in conditions, resulting in tensions over labour costs. But many firms closed down because they were not able to adapt to this new situation. Unemployment rose quickly and inflation and labour disputes increased. In 1985, just one year before Spain joined the EEC, the employment rate was only 38 per cent, lower than at the end of the Franco era, while the unemployment rate exceeded 20 per cent. For some this severe recession, lasting from 1976 to 1985, was caused by the rise in labour costs, associated with the democratization reforms and the maintenance of employment rigidities stemming from the Franco period (Malo de Molina, 1988; García and Sanromà, 2001). However, alternative explanations[3] link the recession to the weaknesses of the Francoist 1960s economic development model; this could only survive in an environment of external trade protectionism and repression of free unionism in a way that had become impossible to maintain by the late 1970s as a result of economic and social changes (Fina and Toharia, 1987). After a strong recovery in the second part of 1980s, the early 1990s again saw an intense loss of employment with unemployment rising back to its highest levels (24 per cent in 1994) and the employment rate falling to its 1985 level. Unemployment was much higher for young people and for women, whose share of the active population continued to increase. The employment decline mostly affected jobs involving permanent labour contracts, as the level of temporary employment increased to 34 per cent of wage earners in 1994.

Since the mid-1990s there has been a significant rate of growth in employment: 54 per cent between 1996 and 2006, compared to 14 per cent for the EU-15. However, the unemployment rate only fell below 10 per cent from 2005 onwards, and the employment rate only reached the 1976 level in 2004. Despite this, the unemployment situation for those aged under 25 remains bleak. The impact of this concentration in temporary employment is very high for young people (see Table 10.2). Although temporary contracts are a means of access to the labour market, many young people suffer from job insecurity, moving between unemployment and temporary employment over many years. In this context it can be said that job insecurity is coming to be regarded as 'normal' among young people (CC.OO., 2004). This lengthens the period of 'youth', if this is defined as a socio-professional

Table 10.2 Temporary employment rate (percentage of wage earners with a fixed-term contract), Spain, 1987–2006

	1987	1991	1994	1996	2004	2006
Total	18.5	32.2	34.3	34.1	33.1	34.6
Men	17.4	29.3	32.4	32.8	31.3	32.6
Women	21.2	38.3	37.8	36.4	35.8	37.4
16 to 19 years old	54.4	80.9	87.9	86.8	84.3	85.2
20 to 24 years old	41.0	66.0	73.4	72.4	63.0	63.2
25 to 29 years old	21.7	43.0	49.9	51.1	44.9	47.2
16 to 29 years old	33.5	57.1	62.4	62.1	54.3	56.1

Source: National Statistics Institute, Labour Force Survey (third quarter data)

transition phase to adult life (Casal, 2000). The precarious nature of integration into employment for young people can only be maintained without social tension because of family support provided over long periods of time. State policies providing support for young people (in housing for example) remain very limited.

Despite the progress made in terms of women's employment participation (partly due to female immigration), gender differences remain above the European Union average. Furthermore, the increase in female participation has taken place mainly in temporary employment, accounting for 37 per cent of employed women in 2006, while a significant proportion (22 per cent) are also involved in part-time employment. There is a general problem of precariousness with regard to the situation of women in the labour market. Although a group of qualified women work in the public sector and in big companies, the vast majority work in unskilled services. The increase in dual-earner couples has not been accompanied by an assumption of responsibilities at home by men (CES, 2004) and the reconciliation of family life and employment is only a utopian dream for the majority of women (Carrasco et al., 2003; Torns et al., 2004). Nevertheless, there has been a break with one of the aspects of the traditional Mediterranean family model (Bettio and Villa, 1998) as a relatively high share of young women remains in the labour market after marriage or motherhood (Cebrián et al., 1997). Today immigrant women play an important role in covering some care activities, reinforcing, at the same time, some traits of female labour market segmentation. Also, a basic recent trend in the Spanish labour market has been the significant and swift assimilation of immigrants, and increasingly those from outside the EU (who accounted for 88 per cent of the working-age foreign population in 2006). The pace of this assimilation is particularly noteworthy. In 1996 1 per cent of the working-age population resident in Spain was foreign. In 2000 this figure was 2 per cent but, by 2006, immigrants not only formed 9 per cent of the working-age population but almost 13 per cent of the active population. Employment rates of this group are thus higher than for the native Spanish population. However, their unemployment rate is also higher. Employed immigrants are concentrated more intensively than Spanish workers in secondary activities: agriculture, construction, hotels, personal services and domestic employment (women in this case), in some cases on an irregular basis. There are several reasons for this. The most important is the increase in the demand for high labour-intensive activities (construction, care, hotels), due partly to changes in family structures and the ageing of the population. Many of these jobs are not attractive to Spanish people on account of the low salaries and poor conditions associated with them.

Any assessment of the employment system must also include aspects related to its capacity to create *decent work* according to the benchmarks of the ILO (Ghai, 2003). Between 25 and 30 per cent of Spanish employees can be estimated as not having decent employment. A major contributor to this is temporary employment that generates a high level of job insecurity; however, the problem goes beyond this phenomenon (Rodgers, 1992; Cano, 2004). Low salaries, deterioration in working conditions and inadequate social protection are also aspects of job insecurity. The minimum wage in Spain, EUR560 per month in 2006, is the lowest in the EU-15. Jobs at low wage levels have increased (Recio, 2001) but generate low income, in part because they are temporary and of short duration, often interspersed with periods of unemployment, and in many cases are not covered by unemployment benefit or involve a short working day (part-time jobs). Part-time employment has increased in importance, accounting for 12 per cent of total employees in 2006. However, it is also associated with problems of low salaries and a high level of insecurity, as, in half of the cases, part-time workers are on only a fixed-term contract. If we consider working conditions (particularly the length of the working day and health and safety in the workplace) the trend in the past towards improvement of these conditions has been halted (Miguélez, 2002; Prieto, 2002). Spain has a very high level of workplace accidents – the highest in the EU-15 since 1995 – in all business sectors, and particularly in construction and in the manufacturing industry. This is the case despite the approval of the Prevention of Workplace Risks Law in 1995, which increased company obligations and introduced participation mechanisms for workers. Also, working time is less regulated than in the past and increasingly is arranged to suit the employers' interests (Prieto, 2002). The most notable feature is the variability of the working day – excessively long and variable hours (in sectors such as trade and hotel/restaurants) and overtime – which puts obstacles in the way of conciliation of personal, family and social life.

These various aspects come together to characterize the form of labour market segmentation. The high level of temporary employment has led to a view that the distinction between permanent and temporary wage earners is the only relevant dimension of segmentation. As such, segmentation is often presented as an inefficient result of institutional intervention in the labour market, an example of the insider-outsider model (Ferreiro et al., 2004). However, the source of the various faces of segmentation of the Spanish labour market may be linked to the employers' practices of labour management. In particular, externalization policies between firms is an important mechanism of segmentation (Recio, 1999).

In this respect temporary employment varies significantly between production sectors.[4] In practice employers use it differently within the same regulatory framework, depending on market conditions, the structure and size of the companies and their strategies for competitiveness and adjustment to a more or less globalized and unstable environment. These employers' policies generate large differences in labour conditions (wage, job tenure, skill recognition, union representation and so on) between employees, suggesting that there are several lines of segmentation, related to the influence of public regulations, firm strategies, the collective agreement system and so on.

Welfare system and social policies

Spain in the 1970s could be characterized as a Mediterranean model. The underdevelopment of public services and transfers, the extended role of the family and a low level of taxes (and general acceptance of tax avoidance) explained in part the large inequalities in income distribution and welfare. In the democratic transition, important social movements demanded changes and an enlargement of the welfare state. Moreover, this became a core element of tacit and implicit social agreements of these years (for instance in the Moncloa Agreements): on the one side, social moderation (including wages) and on the other, improvements in the welfare system.

Comparing the present context with the situation 30 years ago, we can see a real growth in the role of the state in providing services and transfers and breaks with the traditional Mediterranean model. Nevertheless, this development has been limited both by the force of neoliberal policies oriented to reducing the shape of the public sector and the continuity of structures and cultures of the Mediterranean regime. Tax avoidance, for instance, is a point of confluence of both neoliberal aims and Mediterranean traditions. In general we are confronted with two alternative demands: service expansion versus reductions in budgets. The result is a situation in which the family continues to have a central role in the organization of everyday life, where old gender divisions continue despite changing family structures as women seek to participate actively in the labour market.

In recent years the EU policy of social cohesion has forced the introduction of new items onto the political arena: active labour policies, gender inequalities and life-long learning. These new objectives, especially those related to gender inequality, are welcomed at a social level, especially for women, who carry at the same time the burdens of domestic work and the inequalities of the labour market. In this context, with the new government after the 2004 elections, Spain has entered into a new phase of welfare reforms. It is not clear, however, if they will have the capacity to transform completely the traditional Mediterranean model, especially in view of the lack of financial funds to support the endeavour.

The particular structure of Spanish policies is visible in many areas. For example, in the case of labour market policies, the burden of active, passive and intermediary policies in terms of GDP (in 2003) is clearly below the EU-15 average. Active policies account for only 0.6 per cent of GDP, although Spain is coming closer to the European average thanks to a widespread decline in this expenditure in the EU as a whole. However, there are significant differences in the internal structure of spending compared to other

European countries (Alujas, 2004). The highest percentage of expenditure is on employment subsidies, followed by direct creation of employment and training. In comparison with other European countries, both training and the policies aimed at groups with specific needs have been less significant in Spain. It should also be stressed that there has been less spending in intermediation in the labour market.

The greatest shortcomings are in the area of family policies and, especially, in those that focus on children and dependent people (CES, 2003). Spain is at the bottom of the European Union table in terms of the conditions provided by legislation for balancing family and working life (CES, 2004). In 1999 the government transposed the European Council Directive of parental leave into law, mainly motivated to promote fertility rather than an adequate balance between the labour market and personal life for men and women. This half-hearted and contradictory approach is reflected in a clause that made it difficult to implement the directive: 'Workers may exercise their right to reconciliation, providing that this does not affect the company's operations or the interests of other workers'. This limitation has not been removed in collective bargaining processes, and the idea that reconciliation is mainly for women, in order for them to reconcile having two jobs (domestic and in the market), has not been overcome.

A particular problem is the fact that although the salaries of women are low they are essential for the family budget. The low family income level makes it difficult to work in the market fewer hours in order to spend more time looking after the family. The wage gap between men and women can be explained by job discrimination both in terms of concentration in secondary segment and lack of opportunities for training and promotion. Similarly, long and irregular working hours and shift working make it difficult to reconcile labour market participation and private life (Papers, 2007). Some progress is being made with the Concilia Plan for civil servants[5] (approved in 2005), extending the leave for mothers with children aged less than 12 months and increasing the right to a reduction in the working day to care for children until 12 years of age or a seriously ill close family member. These last measures are open to men and women in order to eliminate gender bias. The private sector, however, is not applying the same measures, and this is opening up a new gap between public and private sector workers and between women of different social status (women working in public services are mainly graduates).

According to a recent survey (Instituto de la Mujer, 2005) reconciliation in lower-income families is based on the family's internal resources (an increase in the dual worker-housewife role, the assistance of grandmothers). In higher income groups reconciliation takes place with the use of the support services available on the market, which are mainly provided by immigrants. The gender regime in Spain is moving from a model based on a male breadwinner to a model in which some degree of new gender agreements are beginning to appear. However, these are weak because they are not sufficiently based on education, employment and social policies. The flexible working time imposed in many service and manufacturing activities competes with domestic needs (Carrasco et al., 2003). Despite the higher female participation in the labour market, women do not have opportunities to change ways of organizing work, or to change the basis of the public policies promoted by government, because they are mostly in positions with little public influence and with little decision-making power over regulations, behaviour, attitudes and ideas.

A third important issue in the welfare system is retirement pensions. Due to the characteristics of the Spanish labour market, many people are on low incomes. In order to guarantee the financial equilibrium of the system, the successive reforms (1985, 1995, 2001) reduced the payout from contributions, especially for those unable to remain in employment until retirement age (including those in large firms who took early retirement). Increases in flexible working over recent years create new problems for the future of many people. The low level of pensions is one of the main reasons why, according to official figures, nearly 20 per cent of the Spanish population are in poverty.

Training, education and employment systems

The education system represents another example of continuity and adaptation. Until 1980 Spain did not have a real system of compulsory education. In the past there was a clear separation between the private schooling system (controlled mainly by the Catholic Church) used by high and urban middle classes, and a public system in rural and working class areas. In those times a university degree guaranteed access to a privileged job. Despite the successive education reforms, including the extension of compulsory and free education up to age 16 and the expansion of universities, many problems remain. One is the maintenance of dual private-public networks (the private financed by public resources) that generates social differentiation. Another problem is that major investments have been devoted to university degrees and not to vocational studies. Education systems reflect in part the culture and aims of politicians and employers and, for many years, their assumption has been that the Spanish labour market does not need skilled workers, only the highly educated and the unskilled. This has not only driven political decisions but is also reflected in the attitudes and expectations of society, as many do not consider vocational training a gateway to good jobs. Combined with the low educational background of previous cohorts, this explains the paradox of the Spanish education structure, which combines high numbers of university students with very low rates of those following vocational studies and almost 30 per cent of young people still not completing secondary education.

There is also a confirmed low quality and inefficiency within the Spanish education system compared to those of other countries, related in the main to the continuous low level of public investment that has been allocated to education. In 2002, the most recent year for which comparative data are available, Spain spent little more than 4 per cent of its GDP on educational expenditure, compared to 6 per cent or 8 per cent in other European countries, while university education expenditure accounted for 0.9 per cent, compared to a EU average of 1.6 per cent. There are, of course, other factors such as the large number of changes and reforms since 1985 and the low social standing of teachers. Low investment in public sector education is creating a dangerous educational segmentation at young ages, with the arrival *en masse* of immigrant children who enter public schools, while the Spaniards who are able to pay send their children to private schools.

This educational polarization is behind two phenomena. On the one hand many young people leave the educational system poorly prepared for employment while, on the other, many others are over-educated when they attempt to join the labour market (Oliver, 2005). This is of course over-education in terms of the demands of the labour market, rather than in terms of life aspirations. Consequently, large sectors of the production system pay low wages to many over-educated workers as if they were a labour force with low qualifications.

Conclusion

The employment system in Spain presents contradictory views according to different considerations. If we focus on GDP growth, employment growth, internationalization of firms, urban modernization and so on, the last ten years appear as a successful story. Income has risen to 98 percent of the EU-25 average countries in 2006, and Spanish employment and unemployment rates in 2006 were almost at the EU-15 average level. Indeed, if we consider some questions, such as women's participation in the labour market, the change can be considered rather revolutionary. Nevertheless, there is still a dark side to the Spanish miracle. Unemployment at 8 per cent and an employment rate of 65 per cent for the working-age population hardly meets conventional definitions of full employment and falls well below the objectives of the European employment strategy. Moreover, although there has been an obvious improvement in female employment levels, it remains below the male employment level and far below the EU female employment rate average. Labour conditions are poor, employment insecurity prevails in many jobs, the proportion of low wages is high, real wages have stagnated through the boom years of the 2000s, injuries at work are very high, and family debt is dramatic due to the price of housing. Despite construction being the driver of Spain's recent economic expansion, housing is the most important problem for people below 30 years of age. What is more, the proportion of the population in poverty remains very high, as does the gap between wages for men and women.

The same contradictions can be found if we analyse other economic indicators. Trade balance disequilibrium is one of the most important problems due to the incapacity of the Spanish economy to generate product exports with higher competitiveness. The underlying problem is an unbalanced economic structure that combines large firms in financial, construction and some services, foreign multinational companies that control basic manufacturing activities and a large group of small and medium-sized firms without the capacity to compete in the international arena. The strengthening of specialization in construction and tourism in recent years has deepened this unbalanced structure. The other side of the model is the unsustainable aspect of the form of development. Spain is the European leader of growth in the generation of CO_2, and this is only one of many environmental problems (desertification, soil erosion, pollution, water consumption and so on). Both in social and productive terms, Spain's modernization has important throwbacks to its former model.

In terms of welfare, the crisis of the Mediterranean model presents the same contradictory forces. On the one hand it generates claims towards a more social-democratic model, based on state provision of reproductive services, reducing social gaps (particularly the gender gap), the articulation of the labour market and everyday life and so on. But on the other hand the pressures for liberal competitiveness and the inertia of all Mediterranean institutions (family provision, Catholic culture, tax avoidance tradition) have blocked this alternative and created contradictory situations in which the organization of people's everyday lives is sometimes very difficult. In contrast to the claims to be moving towards a social-democratic model, a more accurate analysis reveals the limited coverage of welfare, the maintenance of large inequalities and the persistence of the family as provider of services. Spain lies at the bottom of European rankings in health, education and welfare expenditures. Consequently, the quality of welfare is low and can be described as a *low-quality universal welfare system*.

In terms of typologies of the economic system, globalization has effectively destroyed the old peripheral Fordism model based on developing the internal market. Moreover, according to some indicators, Spain has moved from a highly coordinated market economy towards a more liberal one (measured for example by product and labour market regulations). Nevertheless, other features show an opposite tendency: there is evidence of persistence of close relations between the state and some firms in the core of Spanish capitalism (mainly in construction, utilities and business services), and in the high level of union and industrial relations institutionalization (in contrast to the low density of unionization). Together, these factors could justify its characterization as a *mixed market economy* (Crouch, 2005). The problem of classification, in some sense, lies in the use of typologies themselves. While functional as a means of highlighting differences in a cross-sectional comparison, they are less useful for explaining long-term changes, especially if, as in the Spanish case, changes are the result of contradictory forces. From our point of view the Spanish employment model, both in the past under Franco and today, combines characteristics of different productive and welfare regimes that are difficult to include in one particular category.

The changes that we have tracked have not occurred in a single direction or under a single set of influences. In the Spanish case they have been the result of a dynamic of social and political actions that take place within a specific economic and institutional context, including globalization, economic cycles and integration into the European Community (Royo, 2007). Both the economic institutions and the agents or actors have undoubtedly played an important role in shaping the changes. For example, the persistence of high levels of unemployment has reinforced the social influence of business, whose demands have been backed in turn by the rhetoric of both international economic institutions (IMF, OECD) and national institutions (the Spanish Central Bank and the Ministry of Economy) and the opinion of many experts and research centres. These same opinion formers have promoted neoliberal approaches to economic and social policy and, in particular, measures for deregulating the labour market, social security system reforms, restrictions on public sector growth, liberalization of the housing sector and the absence of industrial policies. Parts of these policies have been easy to apply because they have fitted well with the old Mediterranean tradition of family provision, gender division of labour and low taxes, thereby allowing the provision of public services to continue to be limited.

Nevertheless, these tendencies in the Spanish context have been strongly contested in several ways. The most important agents in the resistance to these pressures have been the trade unions, which, despite being weak at the company and workplace level, are still strong at an institutional level and continue to enjoy high legitimacy in the public sphere. They have combined a policy of engaging in negotiating long-term reforms with a strong capacity to use social mobilization in response to changes that they consider harmful, particularly in the labour market, as demonstrated by the series of general strikes in 1985, 1988, 1994 and 2002 that prevented the adoption of more profound neoliberal reforms. At times the trade unions have been supported by other social movements and as a consequence of the Socialist Party having been in government for many years (1982–96, 2004 to the present day) there has been some scope for social demands to influence policy outcomes. However, the political agenda is influenced by the economic situation: in the recession periods, neoliberal proposals have been reinforced, but when employment grows, egalitarian demands have reappeared.

The improvements in the Spanish economic and social position in fact have not taken place gradually, but instead have occurred over the last ten years and especially since 2000 when economic growth has been fuelled by the expansion of tourism, construction, transport and personal services, and also by a stable but low interest rate, which has pushed up internal consumption. Part of the employment expansion is also a result of public sector growth, both direct and by means of funding many private activities. However, many of the 'emergent' productive sectors are rather short-term speculative activities that the authorities dare not control because of the fear of damage to the growth engine. The other side of this model is, as we have identified, the persistence of a trade balance deficit, increasing personal debt, poor labour conditions and a high level of environmental damage. The instability of the new structure is already becoming apparent. At the end of 2007 the most recent economic boom appeared to be over: construction growth ended and unemployment increased. The need to change the employment and economic model has become common place in political and economic debate, but nobody seems to have a real alternative programme. The country has experienced a dramatic modernization in the last 30 years, which has been accompanied by inequalities and various side-effects. The most important challenge today is how to develop for the future a more sustainable (in economic, social and environmental terms) and a more equitable employment model.

Notes

We had valuable help from Isabel Hernandez, Isabel Olivares and Maria Amigo.

1. There are two main unions in the whole country, CC.OO. and UGT, and two minor ones, USO and CGT. The weight of collective bargaining at national level is carried out by the first two. In two of the three 'historical regions' of Spain there are also very important specific unions: ELA and LAB in the Basque country and CIG in Galicia, all with the capacity to bargain in their territories. There is no significant nationalist union in Catalunya. Besides them, there are also autonomous unions in some sectors like education, health, and public administration (the most important being CSIF) and other professional unions (pilots, train drivers and so on).
2. In fact, labour management practices combine the use of temporary employment with company discretion on a worker's continued employment. This has encouraged the efforts of temporary workers, who accept deterioration in working conditions to 'win' continued employment; in turn this has put pressure on the pace of work of the workforce as a whole (Bilbao, 1988; Prieto, 1989). The differences in working conditions that have arisen between temporary and permanent employees, as a result of the employers' policy, has become another tool for controlling the workforce, as it undermines solidarity between workers and their collective organization.
3. Interpretations which put in question the effect of wage increases on unemployment and the inflexibility of the Spanish labour market, emphasizing the macroeconomic aspects (concerning the cycle and economic policy) and the problems in the Spanish productive structure and its integration in the international division of labour (Torres, 1999).

4. The highest rates of temporary employment in 2006 were in agriculture (with 61 per cent of temporary wage earners), construction (57 per cent) and hostelry (46 per cent), followed by personal services (35 per cent), health and social services (33 per cent), business services (31 per cent), education (29 per cent), retail (28 per cent), transport and communications (26 per cent), manufacturing industry (25 per cent), the civil service (24 per cent, although this has increased significantly) and financial brokerage (17 per cent).
5. Also, with the Equality Act, passed in February 2007, women's opportunities have increased in the social sphere. For instance, gender representation amongst candidates standing for political elections must be at least 40 per cent; parents have access to increased length of parental leave; companies with over 250 employees are obliged to negotiate an equality program.

References

Alós, R. (2005), *Relacions laborals i condicions d'ocupació en els centres de treball*, Barcelona: CONC.
Alujas, J. A. (2004), 'La política de fomento del empleo: Eje fundamental de las políticas activas de mercado de trabajo en España', *Revista del Ministerio de Trabajo y Asuntos Sociales* 51 (2004): 15–28.
Banco de España (2003), 'Los factores determinantes de la competitividad y sus indicadores para la economía española', *Boletín Económico* September 2003.
Bettio, F. and Villa, P. (1998), 'A Mediterranean perspective on the breakdown of the relationship between participation and fertility', *Cambridge Journal of Economics* 22 (1998): 137–171.
Bilbao, A. (1988), 'El trabajador socializado', *Sociología del Trabajo* 4 (1988): 107–127.
Bilbao, A. (1993), *Obreros y ciudadanos. La desestructuración de la clase obrera*, Madrid: Trotta.
Cachón, L. and Palacio, J. I. (1999), 'Política de empleo en España desde el ingreso en la UE', pp. 273–304 in F. Miguélez and C. Prieto (eds), *Las relaciones de empleo en España*, Madrid: Siglo XXI.
Cano, E. (2004), 'Formas, percepciones y consecuencias de la precariedad', *Mientras Tanto* 93(2004): 67–81.
Cano, E. and Sánchez, A. (1998), 'La economía sumergida en el proceso de extensión del trabajo precario', pp. 221–50 in J. A. Ybarra (ed.), *Economía sumergida: el estado de la cuestión en España*, Murcia: Iniciativas de futuro.
Carrasco, C., Alabart, A., Coco, A., Domínguez, M., Martínez, A., Mayordomo, M., Recio, A. and Serrano, M. (2003), *Tiempos, trabajos y flexibilidad: una cuestión de género*, Madrid: Instituto de la Mujer.
Casal, J. (2000), 'Modalidades de transición profesional y precarización del empleo', in L. Cachón (ed.), *La inserción profesional*, Alzira: Germania.
CC.OO. (2004), *Jóvenes: la nueva precariedad laboral*, Madrid: Cuadernos de Información Sindical.
Cebrián, I., Moreno, G. and Toharia, L. (1997), 'Transiciones laborales de las mujeres casadas en España', *Información Comercial Española* 760 (1997): 129–43.
CES (2003), *Segundo informe sobre la situación de las mujeres en la realidad sociolaboral española*, Madrid: CES
CES (2004), *Panorama sociolaboral de la mujer en España*, Madrid: CES.
Crouch C. (2005), 'Models of Capitalism', *New Political Economy* 10(4): 439–56.

Cuadrado, J. R., and Iglesias, C. (2003), *Cambio sectorial y desempleo en España: un análisis de la relación entre terciarización, cambio cualificativo y movilidad laboral en España*, Bilbao: Fundación BBVA.
Ferreiro, J., Bea, E., Gómez, M. C. and Intxausti, M. A. (2004), 'Teoría insider-outsider y temporalidad en el mercado de trabajo español', *Revista del Ministerio de Trabajo y Asuntos Sociales* 51 (2004): 31–54.
Fina, L. and Toharia, L. (1987), *El paro en España: un punto de vista estructural*, Madrid: Fundación IESA.
García, G. and Sanromà, E. (2001), 'Mercado de trabajo', pp. 291–336 in J. L. García Delgado, R. Myro and J. A. Martínez Serrano (eds), *Lecciones de economía española*, Madrid: Civitas.
Ghai, D. (2003), 'Trabajo decente. Concepto e indicadores', Revista Internacional del Trabajo 122 (2): 125–60.
Giraldez, E. (2002), *La internacionalización de las empresas españolas en América Latina*, Madrid: CES.
Instituto de la Mujer (2005), *Estudio sobre la conciliación de la vida familiar y la vida laboral: situación actual, necesidades y demandas*, Madrid: Instituto de la Mujer.
Karamessini, M. (2007), *Changes in the Southern European social model*, Geneve: IILS discussion papers.
Lipietz, A. (1997), 'The Post-Fordist World: Labour Relations, International Hierarchy and Global Ecology', *Review of International Political Economy* 4 (1): 1–41.
Malo de Molina, J. L. (1988), 'Política de empleo y reforma del mercado de trabajo', pp. 11–32 in J. L. Malo de Molina (ed.), *El debate sobre la flexibilidad del mercado de trabajo*, Madrid: Obra Social CECA.
Miguélez, F. (2002), '¿Por qué empeora el empleo?', *Sistema* 168 (2002): 37–52.
OECD (1999). *Employment Outlook*.
Oliver, J. (2005), 'Capital humano y cambio ocupacional en España', in E. Genescà (coord.), *La industria en España: claves para competir en un mundo global*, Barcelona: Ariel.
Papers (2007), *Special Issue on Work-life Balance in Collective Bargaining*, 83.
Pérez, F. (dir.), Chorén, P., Goerlich, F. J., Mas, M., Milgram, J., Robledo, J. C., Soler, A., Serrano, L., Ünal-Kesenci, D. and Uriel, E. (2004), *La competitividad de la economía Española*, Barcelona: La Caixa.
Prieto, C. (1989), 'Políticas de mano de obra en las empresas españolas', *Sociología del Trabajo* 6(1989): 33–50.
Prieto, C. (2002), 'La degradación del empleo o la norma social del empleo flexibilizado', *Sistema* 168 (2002): 89–106.
Recio, A. (1998), 'La política laboral: acuerdo y conflicto en un contexto de reforma continua', pp. 113–32 in R. Gomà and J. Subirats (eds), *Políticas públicas en España. Contenidos, redes de actores y niveles de gobierno*, Barcelona: Ariel.
Recio, A. (1999), 'La segmentación del mercado de trabajo en España', pp. 125–50 in F. Miguelez and C. Prieto (eds), *Las relaciones de empleo en España*, Madrid: Siglo XXI.
Recio, A. (2001), 'Low Pay in Spain', *Transfer* 2 (2001): 331–7.
Rodgers, G. (1992), 'El debate sobre el trabajo precario en Europa Occidental', pp. 15–41 in G. Rodgers and J. Rodgers (eds), *El trabajo precario en la regulación del mercado laboral*, Madrid: Ministerio de Trabajo y Seguridad Social.
Royo, S. (2007), 'Varieties of Capitalism in Spain: Business and the Politics of Coordination', *European Journal of Industrial Relations* 13 (1): 47–65.
Toharia, L. (1986), 'Un fordismo inacabado, entre la transición política y la crisis económica', pp. 161–84 in R. Boyer (ed.), *La flexibilidad del trabajo en Europa*, Madrid: Ministerio de Trabajo y Seguridad Social.

Toharia, L. (ed.) (2005), *El problema de la temporalidad en España: un diagnóstico*, Madrid: Ministerio de Trabajo y Asuntos Sociales.

Torns, T., Borràs, V. and Carrasquer, P. (2004), 'La conciliación de la vida laboral y familiar: ¿Un horizonte posible?', *Sociología del Trabajo* 50 (2004): 111–38.

Torres, J. (1999), 'Sobre las causas del paro y la degradación del trabajo', *Sistema* 151 (1999): 37–69.

Ybarra, J. A., Hurtado, J. and San Miguel, B. (2002), 'La economía sumergida en España: un viaje sin retorno', *Sistema* 169 (2002): 247–82.

Index

active labour market policy (ALMP)
  and Austria, 144–5
  and France, 42–3, 190–1
  and Greece, 228, 239
  and Hungary, 166, 167, 170–1
  and Sweden, 83, 85, 87–9, 102;
    cutback in, 99–100; integration of immigrants, 93; integration of unemployed, 88; social legitimacy, 88
actors and national employment models, 18–19
  and interest groups, 40–2
  and new actor configurations, 15
ageing population, 7, 14, 35
  and Hungary, 172
  and Italy, 207–8, 216
  and pension reform, 39–40
architecture of national employment models, 18
  and challenges across production-employment nexus, 32–5
  and challenges across welfare-employment nexus, 35–40
  and impact of differences in, 31–2
  and meaning of term, 53 n11
  and political will, 32
Australia, 66
Austria
  and active labour market policy, 144–5
  and austerity policy, 145
  and Central and Eastern Europe (CEE), 140–2
  and changes in model, 25–6, 138, 149
  and childcare, 148
  and collective bargaining, 25–6;
    attitudes towards, 41; erosion of, 147; sector/company agreements, 133; sector-specific differences, 139–40; stability of, 146–7
  and competitiveness, 141, 142, 143, 149
  and consensual capitalism, 133
  as coordinated market economy, 24, 132, 133, 151
  and corporate governance, 138, 142
  and corporatism, 25, 133–4, 147
  and crisis in system, 138
  and economic growth, 137
  and education and training, 135, 140, 142–3
  and European Union membership, 138, 140, 145, 149
  and features of post-war model, 133–8
  and foreign direct investment, 135, 140, 141
  and heterogeneity of economy, 148
  and historical context, 132
  and incremental change, 132, 149–50
  and inequality, 136, 148
  and institutional continuity, 146–9, 150
  and internationalization of economy, 140–2
  and labour market, 143–5;
    flexibilization, 144; segmentation of, 136
  and labour protection, 134
  as liberal market economy, 132, 149
  and minimum wage, 136, 147
  and negotiated capitalism, 134, 147
  and outsourcing, 143
  and part-time work, 143–4
  and pension reform, 145–6
  and political will, 43
  and privatization, 25, 43, 132, 139–40
  and production system, changes in organization, 142–3
  and public social expenditure, 36
  and relationship with Germany, 131;
    investment by, 135
  and research and development, 135
  and Rhenish capitalism, 133
  and role of the state sector, 134–5
  and shareholder value, 139
  and small and medium-sized enterprises, 135–6
  and social partnership, 133–4, 146, 150

and strike activity, 146
and tax policy, 146, 149
and trade unions, 133, 136; weakening of, 140
and unemployment, 138
and welfare state, 136–7; as conservative regime, 26, 137, 148–9; family model, 148–9; male breadwinner model, 137; reform of, 145–6
and women's labour market participation, 38, 137, 144, 148
Austrian Trade Union Federation, 133

Balladur, Edouard, 185
Bank of England, 62
birth rate, and decline in, 35
Blair, Tony, 57, 66
Brown, Gordon, 65, 66

Cap Gemini, 192
capitalism, *see* varieties of capitalism
Central and Eastern Europe (CEE), and Austria, 140–2
Central European Bank, 188
childcare, 14
 and Austria, 148
 and Germany, 112, 124, 127 n2
 and Greece, 242
 and Hungary, 168
 and Sweden, 92, 94, 95
 and United Kingdom, 73
cluster analyses, and national employment models, 9
codetermination, and Germany, 108, 109
collective bargaining
 and Austria, 25–6; attitudes towards, 41; erosion of, 147; sector/company agreements, 133; sector-specific differences, 139–40; stability of, 146–7
 and employers' attitudes towards, 40–1
 and France, post-war period, 180
 and Germany, 25, 34, 108; attitudes towards, 40–1; erosion of, 121; introduction into East Germany, 112–13
 and Greece: establishment of free, 235; post-dictatorship changes, 228; role of the state, 227

and Hungary, 163, 164–5; weakening of, 165
and Sweden, 24, 34, 82; Agreement on Industry, 89; changes in, 87, 89–90; solidaristic wage policy, 82–3; two-tier system, 90, 91, 100–1
and United Kingdom, 34; erosion of, 58–9, 71
see also trade unions
comparative advantage, and quality of work, 3
comparative institutional advantage
 and coordinated market economies, 5–6
 and institutional complementarities, 6
 and liberal market economies, 6
 and national employment models, 12
competitiveness
 and Austria, 141, 142, 143, 149
 and compatibility with social protection, 14
 and education and training, 24
 and France, 181, 188, 192
 and Germany, 108, 114, 120
 and globalization, 12
 and Greece, 223, 225, 231, 234, 243
 and Hungary, 173, 174
 and Italy, 203, 205, 209, 210, 211, 212, 213, 217
 and national employment models, 4–5
 and Spain, 249, 250–1, 253, 255, 256, 264
 and Sweden, 84, 91, 99
conflicts of interest, and national employment models, 15–16, 40–2
consensual capitalism, and Austria, 133
conservative welfare regimes, 7
 and Austria, 26, 137, 148–9
 and France, 27, 181
 and Germany, 24, 25
 and Italy, 28
continental European model of capitalism, 9
continental welfare regimes, *see* conservative welfare regimes
conversion, and institutional change, 17; Austria, 150

coordinated market economies (CMEs), 5–6
  and Austria, 25, 132, 133, 151
  and Germany, 24
  and Hungary, 173, 174, 175
  and institutional complementarities, 6
  and reduced scope of actors, 40
  and Spain, 247–8, 264
  and Sweden, 23
corporate governance
  and Austria, 138, 142
  and France, 180, 191–2
  and Germany, 107; changes in, 115–18
  and Greece, 226, 232, 234
  and Hungary, 160
  and Italy, 210
corporatism, and Austria, 25, 133–4
Council for Mutual Economic Assistance (COMECON), 141, 157
country size, and national employment models, 13, 45
crises
  and Austria, 138
  and change in national employment models, 11
  and Germany, 111–14
  and Sweden: early 1990s, 85–6; late 1970s, 84–5
cycles
  and national employment models, 11, 45
  and United Kingdom, 57

decent work, 3, 51 n2
  and Germany, 126
  and Spain, 258–9
  and United Kingdom, 75
decentralization, and France, 27, 185
deregulation
  and France, 33
  and Germany, 33
  and Greece, 233, 234
  and impact of, 32–4
  and Italy, 201, 206–7
  and labour standards, 32–4, 48
  and Nordic countries, 33
  and Spain, 254–5, 256
  and Sweden, 98

  and United Kingdom, 33; disadvantages of, 67; financial sector, 23; low regulation economy, 66–7
displacement, and incremental change, 17
drift, and institutional change, 17; Austria, 150

economic growth
  and Austria, 137
  and France, 187–8, 189
  and Germany, 105, 106, 111, 114, 126
  and Greece, 223, 224, 227, 232, 235
  and Hungary, 155, 157, 159
  and Italy, 202, 203
  and Spain, 247, 253, 266
  and Sweden, 84, 86, 97
  and United Kingdom, 67
education and training, 14
  and Austria, 135, 140, 142–3
  and competitiveness, 24
  and France, 195; post-war period, 179–80
  and Germany, 107–8; deficiencies in school system, 120; firms' reluctance to offer training, 120; innovation, 120; underinvestment in, 126
  and Greece, 226–7, 235, 240
  and Hungary, 169–71
  and Italy, 212–13; women, 215
  and Spain, 262–3
  and Sweden, 24, 88
  and United Kingdom, 59; focus on higher education, 71–2; skill problems, 72–3
elites
  and France, 182, 183–4, 185
  and increasing exit options, 14–15
employers' organizations
  and France, 183–4
  and Germany, 108
  and Hungary, 164
  and Spain, 251
  and Sweden, 83
European Central Bank, 11, 113, 126
European Commission, 15
European Court of Justice, and Laval case, 34, 91

Index 273

European Employment Strategy, 48
  and Greece, 28, 242
European Social Fund (ESF), and Greece, 28, 228, 242
European social model
  and basis of, 2
  and challenges to, 2–3
  and core principles of, 44
  and Hungary, 174
  and ruptures within, 49
European Structural Funds
  and Greece, 239
  and Hungary, 172–3
European Union (EU)
  and deregulation of product markets, 32–3
  and directives of, 14
  and influence at national level, 44
  and integration of new members, 49
  and macroeconomic constraints of, 50–1
  and neglect of production-employment interactions, 51
  and Posted Worker Directive, 91
  and reduced scope for national action, 49–50
  and reform, 2
  and role of state actors, 47
  and strengthening of national executives, 15
exhaustion, and institutional change, 17

familialist welfare regime, 7
  and access to, 31
  and Austria, 148
  and Greece, 229–30, 242
  and Italy, 28, 218 n5
  and social protection, 7
financial sector, and United Kingdom, 23, 57, 59, 66
Finland, 52 n5
flexibility, 3
flexicurity, 3, 50
foreign direct investment
  and Austria, 135, 140, 141
  and France, 188
  and Hungary, 156, 161–2
  and United Kingdom, 67
France
  and activation policy, 42–3

and active labour market policy (ALMP), 190–1
and balance of trade, 188–9
and changes in model, 27, 197
and collective bargaining, post-war period, 180
and competitiveness, 181, 188, 192
and continuity in model, 197
and corporate governance, 191–2; post-war period, 180
and deregulation, 33
and difficulty in classifying, 178
as dirigist state, 182
and economic growth, 187–8, 189
and education and training, 195; post-war period, 179–80
and employers' organizations, 183–4
and employment growth, 190; public sector, 191; subsidized jobs, 191
and European Union, influence of, 183
and foreign direct investment, 188
and governance structure: decentralization, 27, 185; political/administrative elites, 182, 183–4, 185; territorialization, 185–6
and immigration policy, 198
and increased importance of stock exchange, 32
and incremental change, 179, 197; social policy, 183
and industrial concentration and restructuring, 192
and industrial relations: fragmentation, 186–7; post-war period, 180–1
and inequality, 193
and labour market: age structure, 194; labour cost reductions, 193; post-war period, 180; subsidized jobs, 191; unskilled jobs, 195; working time, 195
and labour standards, worsening of, 194–5
and macroeconomic policy, 182; deflationary strategy, 182
and manufacturing, 192
and minimum wage, 27, 180, 182, 193, 197

274 Index

France (contd.)
  and nationalized industries, 181, 182
  and neoliberalism, 183
  and paradoxical policies, 178–9
  and part-time work, 195
  and political will, 42–3
  and privatization, 27, 32, 184, 191–2
  and public expenditure: growth of social expenditure, 190–1; reduction in, 184, 189
  and public sector employment, 181, 186, 191
  and research and development, 184
  and role of the state, 178–9, 192; changes in, 184–6; economy, 181–2; industrial relations, 181; as prime mover, 185, 186
  and service economy, 194–5
  and small and medium-sized enterprises, 192
  and social policy, 183, 185
  and social protection, 196–7
  and social stratification, 179
  and state-enhanced capitalism, 27, 32, 178, 179, 197
  and state-led capitalism, 27; employment regime, 179–81; pressures on model, 179
  and trade unions, 181; weakening of, 184
  and unemployment, 187, 190, 192–4; impact of, 192–3, 196
  and welfare regime: as conservative regime, 27, 181; conservative welfare regime, 181; incremental change, 183; post-war period, 181–2; reform of, 196; segmentation of, 196–7
  and women's labour market participation, 193–4, 197–8
  and work organization, 194–5
  and young people, 198

Germany
  and changes in model, 24–5, 116–17; status of, 12
  and childcare, 112, 124, 127 n2
  and codetermination, 108, 109
  and collective bargaining, 25, 34, 108; change in employers' attitudes, 40–1; erosion of, 121; introduction into East Germany, 112–13
  and competitiveness, 108, 114, 120
  and coordination, 24–5
  and corporate governance, 107; changes in, 115–18
  and crisis in system, 111–14
  and criticism of model, 105–6
  and deregulation, 33
  and dual labour system, 125
  and economic growth, 105, 106, 111, 114, 126
  and education and training, 107–8; deficiencies in school system, 120; firms' reluctance to offer training, 120; innovation, 120; underinvestment in, 126
  and employers' organizations, 108; declining membership, 121, 122
  and essence of model, 105, 124
  and export-oriented production, 105, 106; dependence on success of, 125; pressure on labour costs, 125–6; revitalization of, 125
  and financial market capitalism, 126; increased importance of stock exchange, 32, 118; trend towards, 115–18
  and gendered nature of model, 111
  and geographic divide, 25, 112
  and healthcare, 118
  and industrial relations, 108, 120–1; upheavals in, 121–2; wage dispersion, 121–2
  and institutional/social fragmentation, 124–5
  and labour law, 108
  and labour market policy, 108; part-time work, 122–3; reforms, 123, 125
  and low-wage sector, 34, 122, 123, 125
  and macroeconomic policy, 113–14; Maastricht criteria, 114, 126
  and manufacturing, 105, 109; competition, 111; declining importance of, 114–15; innovation, 119; reorganization of, 119
  and minimum wage, 25, 26, 122, 127
  and the Mittelstand, 107

and neoliberalism, 111, 113
and parental leave, 124
and part-time work, 122–3
and 'patient' capital, 32, 107, 126
and policy challenges, 126–7
and political will, 43; reunification, 113
and privatization, 113, 115, 118, 122
and production system, modernization of, 118–19
and public social expenditure, 36
and reunification of, 105; impact of, 106, 111–13, 126
and Rhenish capitalism, 105
and segments of economy, 109; changes in employment in, 115; changes in employment model, 116–17; regulation of, 110
and service economy, 106; lack of model for, 126
and trade unions, 30, 40–1, 108, 109; decline in influence, 114, 121
and unemployment, 105, 111, 126
and welfare state: as conservative regime, 24, 25; criticism of, 106; features of, 108; gender bias, 111, 124; reforms, 123–4; unemployment benefits, 123
and women's labour market participation, 38, 124
globalization
and impact of, 32, 45–6
and labour standards, 49
and nation states, 15
and pressures for change, 13–14
and United Kingdom, 66
governance structures
and changes in, 32
and France: decentralization, 27, 185; political/administrative elites, 182, 183–4, 185; territorialization, 185–6
and multi-level governance, problems with, 50–1
see also corporate governance
Greece
and active emigration policy, 227
and active labour market policy (ALMP), 228, 239
and changes in model, 28–9, 223

and childcare, 242
and collective bargaining: establishment of free, 235; post-dictatorship changes, 228; role of the state, 227
and competitiveness, 223, 225, 231, 234, 243
and corporate governance, 226, 232, 234
and deregulation, 233, 234
and economic growth, 223, 224, 227, 232, 235
and economic policy, 223
and education and training, 226–7, 235, 240
and employment policy, 228–9
and employment structure, 224–5
and European Union membership, 224; impact of, 232, 237, 242
and financial market liberalization, 234
and immigration, 238–9
and incomes policy, 228
and incremental change, 241
and industrial crisis, 225
and industrial relations, 227; eradication of state intervention, 235–6; post-dictatorship changes, 228; reduction in conflict, 236–7; social partnership approach, 236
and industrialization, 225
and inflation, 234
and labour market: flexibility, 237; irregular work, 237, 239; segmentation of, 226, 227–8
and liberal capitalism, 242
and macroeconomic policy, 232–3; Maastricht criteria, 232–3
and manufacturing, 225
and minimum wage, 227, 235
and part-time work, 237
and pension reform, 240–1
and political will, 43
and privatization, 29, 233, 234
and production system, 224; international competition, 233; international specialization, 225, 234–5; nationalization, 226; stagnation, 225

Greece (*contd.*)
  and public debt, 242
  and public sector employment, 227–8
  and research and development, 235
  and small and medium-sized enterprises, 225–6
  and social partnership, 236–7
  and social policy, 223
  and state-led familistic capitalism, 224; post-dictatorship changes, 231–2
  and strike activity, 228, 236
  and sustainability of new model, 243–4
  and trade unions, 41, 43, 227, 228, 233, 243
  and unemployment, 237–8, 239–40
  and welfare state: de-familialization, 242–3; familialism, 229–30, 242; family policy, 231; features of, 229; fragmentation of, 229; gender bias, 229–30; healthcare, 229, 231, 241; increased spending on, 230; pension policy, 230; unemployment protection, 231
  and women's labour market participation, 241–2
  and work organization, 226

healthcare
  and Germany, 118
  and Greece, 229, 231, 241
  and Hungary, 167, 169
  and Italy, 203, 217 n1
  and Spain, 248, 250, 254
  and Sweden, 84, 85, 92, 97, 98, 99
  and United Kingdom, 59, 62, 64
housing boom, 11
  and Spain, 11
  and United Kingdom, 67
Hungary
  and active labour market policy (ALMP), 166, 167, 170–1
  and changes in model, 26–7
  and childcare, 168
  and collective bargaining, 163, 164–5; weakening of, 165
  and competitiveness, 173, 174
  as coordinated market economy, 173, 174, 175
  and corporate governance, 160
  and development path, 155–6
  and economic growth, 155, 157, 159
  and education and training, 169–71
  and employers' organizations, 164
  and European Union membership, 155, 158, 169; funding from, 173; Lisbon strategy, 172–3; Maastricht criteria, 159, 173
  and foreign direct investment, 156, 161–2
  and foreign trade structure, 157
  and healthcare, 167, 169
  and industrial relations, 163–5
  and inequality, 167
  and labour market: ageing population, 172; changes in, 165–7; early retirement, 169; low employment rate, 169; regional differences, 166; wage elasticity, 167
  as liberal market economy, 173, 174–5
  and Lisbon strategy, 172–3
  and macroeconomic policy, 157–9
  and management practices, 163
  and minimum wage, 158, 160, 164, 165, 172, 175
  and model-building, distinct periods of, 175–6
  and national tripartite forum (National Interest Reconciliation Council), 164
  and obstacles to reform, 176–7
  and political conflict, 159
  and post-communist transition, 155, 156–9; economic policy, 157–9; initial conditions for, 156–7; transition recession, 156, 157, 166
  and privatization, 26, 156, 160
  and public social expenditure, 36
  and research and development, 162–3
  and Roma, 166, 170
  and small and medium-sized enterprises, 160–1
  and trade unions, 163–4
  and unemployment, 156, 165, 166, 167
  and welfare state: early retirement, 169; family policy, 167–8; maternalist, 167; premature welfare state, 168; reform of, 156, 167–9;

in socialist period, 167; trends in, 168–9
and women's labour market participation, 168
ideology, and pressures for change, 14
immigrants/immigration
and France, 198
and Greece, 238–9
and Spain, 258
and Sweden, 93
income distribution, *see* inequality
incremental change, 132
and Austria, 149–50
and France, 179, 197; social policy, 183
and Greece, 241
and national employment models, 17
and United Kingdom, 68–70
industrial districts, and Italy, 28, 202–3, 212
industrial relations
and France: fragmentation, 186–7; post-war period, 180–1
and Germany, 108, 120–1; upheavals in, 121–2; wage dispersion, 121–2
and Greece, 227; eradication of state intervention, 235–6; post-dictatorship changes, 228; reduction in conflict, 236–7; social partnership approach, 236
and Hungary, 163–5
and Spain: under Franco, 251; post-Franco, 251–3
and Sweden, 89–91, 100–1
see also collective bargaining; employers' organizations; trade unions
inequality
and Austria, 136, 148
and employment relationship, 1
and France, 193
and Hungary, 167
and labour standards, 48
and social protection, 48
and Sweden, 84
and United Kingdom, 59, 68, 76
institutional change
and societal effects, 2
and types of, 17

institutions
and institutional complementarities, 6, 131–2
and need for multi-level institution building, 48–51
and role of, 1
interest groups, and national employment models, 40–2
international agreements, and pressures for change, 14, 46
international governance, and pressures for change, 14
International Labour Organization (ILO), and decent work, 3, 51 n2
Italy
and ageing population, 207–8, 216
and changes in model, 28
and competitiveness, 203, 205, 209, 210, 211, 212, 213, 217
and corporate governance, 210
and dual production systems, 28, 201
and economic growth, 202, 203
and education and training, 212–13; women, 215
and employment growth, 204–5
and exchange rate policy, 203
and financial market capitalism, 210
and gender roles, 215–16
and healthcare, 203, 216, 217 n1
and industrial districts, 28, 202–3, 212
and informal economy, 202, 214–15, 217, 218 n4
and job quality, 215
and labour market: deregulation, 201, 206–7; income policies, 205–6; protected sectors, 204; regulatory framework, 203–4; segmentation of, 202, 206
and macroeconomic policy, 205
and main features of social model, 202–4
and manufacturing, 211–12
and North-South divide, 201, 202, 214–15, 217; explanations of, 203
and obstacles to reform, 201–2, 216–17
and part-time work, 37, 219 n9
and pension reform, 40, 208–9
and political will, 43
and privatization, 28, 201, 202, 209–10

Italy (*contd.*)
  and production system, 202–3; export performance, 211–12; frozen specialization, 211–12; innovation, 213; structural weakness, 212; structure of, 211; upgrading, 213–14
  and research and development, 212
  and social protection, 203–4
  and unemployment, 214; women, 216
  and welfare state: as conservative regime, 28; familialism, 28, 218 n5; lack of reform, 216; southern model of welfare, 203–4
  and women's labour market participation, 39, 214, 216
  and young people, 207, 208

Japan, and changing status as model, 12
job quality, 3
  and comparative advantage, 3
  and Italy, 215
  and labour standards, 48
  and social protection, 48
  and Spain, 254, 255, 258–9
  and United Kingdom, 75

Keynesianism, 10
Kornai, János, 168

labour markets
  and Austria, 143–5; flexibilization, 144
  and European Union regulation, 34
  and France: age structure, 194; labour cost reductions, 193; post-war period, 180; subsidized jobs, 191; unskilled jobs, 195; working time, 195
  and Germany, 108; reforms, 123, 125
  and Greece: flexibility, 237; irregular work, 237, 239; segmentation of, 226, 227–8
  and Hungary: changes in, 165–7; early retirement, 169; low employment rate, 169; regional differences, 166; wage elasticity, 167
  and impact of product deregulation, 33–4
  and Italy: deregulation, 201, 206–7; income policies, 205–6; protected sectors, 204; regulatory framework, 203–4; segmentation of, 202, 206
  and non-standard work forms, 48
  and polarization of, 48
  and Spain: deregulation, 254–5, 256; flexibility, 256; gender pay gap, 261; job insecurity, 257, 259; low-quality jobs, 254, 255; opposition to reforms, 252; reducing labour costs, 255–6; reform of, 252, 254, 255–6; segmentation of, 259–60; temporary jobs, 255, 256, 259, 266 n2, 267 n4; transitional phase, 254; turbulence in, 255; young people, 257–8
  and Sweden: integration of immigrants, 93; integration of unemployed, 88; large companies, 98; low employment growth, 99; regulation of, 33–4, 91; total employment, 99
  and United Kingdom: job quality, 75; segmentation of, 74
  and women's participation, 7, 8, 14, 35–6, 37–9; Austria, 38, 137, 144, 148; France, 193–4, 197–8; Germany, 38, 124; Greece, 241–2; Hungary, 168; Italy, 39, 214, 216; Spain, 39, 258; Sweden, 92–3; United Kingdom, 39, 73
  see also active labour market policy (ALMP); part-time work
labour standards
  and deregulation, 32–4, 48
  and globalization, 49
  and income distribution, 48
  and insider-outsider labour competition, 48
  and non-standard work forms, 48
  and offshoring, 49
  and quality of work, 48
  and wages and employment security, 48–9
  and weakening of, 49
layering, and institutional change, 17; Austria, 150
liberal market economies (LMEs), 5–6
  and Austria, 132
  and Hungary, 173, 174–5
  and institutional complementarities, 6
  and Spain, 264
  and United Kingdom, 23, 58
liberal welfare regimes, 7

liberalization, and incremental change, 17
Lisbon strategy, 12, 48, 70
  and education and training, 213
  and France, 194, 197
  and Hungary, 172–3

Maastricht criteria, 11
  and Germany, 114, 126
  and Greece, 232–3
  and Hungary, 159, 173
macroeconomic policy
  and France, 182; deflationary strategy, 182
  and Germany, 113–14; Maastricht criteria, 114, 126
  and Greece, 232–3; Maastricht criteria, 232–3
  and Hungary, 157–9
  and Italy, 205
  and national employment models, 10–11, 45
  and Sweden, 82, 83; reorientation of, 87, 100
  and United Kingdom, 62, 74
manufacturing
  and France, 192
  and Germany, 105, 109; competition, 111; declining importance of, 114–15; innovation, 119; reorganization of, 119
  and Greece, 225
  and Italy, 211–12
  and Spain, 249
  and Sweden, 97
  and United Kingdom, 58, 59, 70–1
market-based model of capitalism, 9
market state, 23
  and United Kingdom, 23, 65, 76
maternity leave, and United Kingdom, 73
  see also parental leave
Mediterranean model of capitalism, 9
Meidner, Rudolf, 83
minimum wage, 30, 34
  and Austria, 136, 147
  and France, 27, 180, 182, 193, 197
  and Germany, 25, 26, 122, 127
  and Greece, 227, 235
  and Hungary, 158, 160, 164, 165, 172, 175

  and Spain, 252, 259
  and United Kingdom, 23, 39, 59, 65, 69
Mitterand, François, 182
mixed market economies (MMEs), 52 n6
  and Spain, 264
Mouvement des Entreprises de France, 184
multi-level governance, and problems with, 50–1
multinational companies, and pressures for change, 14

nation state
  and continuing importance of, 19, 47–8
  and political will, 42–3
  and reduced scope for action, 49–50
national employment models
  and actors in, 18–19
  and architecture of, 18; challenges across production-employment nexus, 32–5; challenges across welfare-employment nexus, 35–40; impact of differences in, 31–2; political will, 32
  and challenges to, 2; responses to, 2–3
  and changes in, 4; balance of power, 30; degree of liberalism, 31; lack of purposeful design, 31; variations in, 20–2, 30–1
  and commonalities among, 2
  and competitiveness, 4–5
  and country size, 13, 45
  and cycles, 11, 45
  and developing analyses of changes in, 44–5; expanding factors accounting for employment performance, 45; expanding range of challenges, 45–6; hybrid typologies, 46–7; importance of actors, 47–8; political will, 47–8
  and development of, 15–16
  and diversity in, 2
  and employment relationship, 1
  and forms of change, 15–20; conflicts of interest, 15–16; environmental change, 16–17; historical perspective, 18; incremental, 17; power relations, 15–16; rupture, 17–18

national employment models (*contd.*)
    and globalization, 13–14, 32, 45–6
    and macroeconomic policy, 10–11, 45
    and multi-level institution building, 48–51
    and political will, 19, 42–3
    and pressures for change, 13–15; external, 13–14, 45–6; internal, 14, 46; new actor configurations, 15
    and societal effects, 2
    and specialization, 12, 45
    and status of, 11–12
    and typologies of, 4–10; cluster analyses, 9; institutional complementarities, 6; value of, 5; varieties of capitalism approach, 5–6, 8–9; welfare regime approach, 7–9
    and varieties of capitalism, 1–2, 5–6, 8–9; criticism of approach, 15
    and welfare regimes, 5
    see also individual countries
negotiated capitalism, and Austria, 134, 147
neoliberalism
    and France, 183
    and Germany, 111, 113
    and Spain, 255
    and United Kingdom, 58
Nordic countries
    and deregulation, 33
    and labour market regulation, 33–4

offshoring, 49
    and United Kingdom, 71
Organization for Economic Co-Operation and Development (OECD), 2
outsourcing, 48
    and Austria, 143
    and United Kingdom, 64
ownership, and changes in, 32

parental leave
    and Germany, 124
    and Spain, 261
    and Sweden, 92, 94–5
    see also maternity leave
part-time work
    and Austria, 143–4
    and France, 195
    and Germany, 122–3

    and Greece, 237
    and Italy, 37, 219 n9
    and Spain, 37, 259
    and Sweden, 39, 92
    and United Kingdom, 39
    and women's labour market participation, 37–9
pension policy/reform, 39–40
    and Austria, 145–6
    and Greece, 230, 240–1
    and Italy, 40, 208–9
    and Spain, 262
    and Sweden, 24, 39–40, 96; actors' attitudes, 41
    and United Kingdom, 40, 67–8, 75–6
political will
    and architecture of national employment models, 32
    and national employment models, 19, 42–3, 47–8
Portugal, 52 n5
poverty reduction, and United Kingdom, 59, 65, 75
poverty traps, and United Kingdom, 67
power relations, and national employment models, 15–16
privatization, 7
    and Austria, 25, 43, 132, 139–40
    and France, 27, 32, 184, 191–2
    and Germany, 113, 115, 118, 122
    and Greece, 29, 233, 234
    and Hungary, 26, 156, 160
    and Italy, 28, 201, 202, 209–10
    and Sweden, 98
    and United Kingdom, 34, 58, 67
production system
    and changes in, 2
    and elements of, 18
    and employment relationship, 1
    see also individual countries
public discourse, 14
public social expenditure
    and Austria, 36
    and Germany, 36
    and Hungary, 36
    and Sweden, 36, 81
    and United Kingdom, 23, 36–7, 62
    and variations in, 36–7

quality of work, *see* job quality

radical change, and national
  employment models, 17–18
Rehn, Gösta, 83
research and development
  and Austria, 135
  and France, 184
  and Greece, 235
  and Hungary, 162–3
  and Italy, 212
  and Spain, 250
  and Sweden, 98, 99
  and United Kingdom, 70
Rhenish capitalism
  and Austria, 133
  and Germany, 105
  see also coordinated market economies (CMEs)
ruptures
  and European social models, 49
  and national employment models, 17–18

service economy, 5
  and development of, 35–6
  and France, 194–5
  and Germany, 106; lack of model for, 126
  and growth patterns in, 8
  and Spain, 250
  and Sweden, 98
  and United Kingdom, 70, 71, 74
  and welfare regimes, 8
Siemens, 141
small and medium-sized enterprises
  and Austria, 135–6
  and France, 192
  and Greece, 225–6
  and Hungary, 160–1
  and Spain, 250
social cohesion, 3
social-democratic model of capitalism, 9
social-democratic welfare regimes, 7
  and Sweden, 23
social policy
  and France, 183, 185
  and Greece, 223
  as productive factor, 48
  and Sweden, 92
social protection
  and the family, 7
  and flexibility, 3
  and income distribution, 48
  and maintenance of, 3, 37
  and quality of work, 48
  and weakening of, 49
social services
  and provision of, 37
  and women's employment in, 37
societal effects
  and institutional change, 2
  and national employment models, 2
  and technological change, 14
southern model of welfare
  and Italy, 203–4
  and Spain, 248, 260
Spain, 260
  and changes in model, 29; contested by trade unions, 265; factors influencing, 247, 248, 265; pace of, 265–6
  and competitiveness, 249, 250–1, 253, 255, 256, 264
  and construction sector, 249
  and contradictory views of employment system, 263–4
  as coordinated market economy, 247–8, 264
  and decent work, 258–9
  and difficulty in classifying economic system, 264–5
  and economic growth, 253, 266; under Franco, 247
  and education and training, 262–3
  and employers' organizations, 251
  and employment rates, 256–7
  and environmental problems, 264
  and European Union membership, impact of, 260
  and healthcare, 248, 250, 254
  and housing boom, 11
  and immigrants, 258
  and industrial relations: under Franco, 251; post-Franco, 251–3
  and international trade, 251
  and job quality, 254
  and labour market: deregulation, 254–5, 256; flexibility, 256; gender pay gap, 261; job insecurity, 257, 259; low-quality jobs, 254, 255, 258–9; opposition to reforms, 252;

Spain (*contd.*)
  reducing labour costs, 255–6; reform of, 252, 254, 255–6; segmentation of, 259–60; temporary jobs, 255, 256, 259, 266 n2, 267 n4; transitional phase, 254; turbulence in, 255; Workers' Rights Statute (1980), 255, 256; young people, 257–8
  and liberal capitalism, 264
  and manufacturing, 249
  and minimum wage, 252, 259
  as mixed market economy, 264
  and neoliberalism, 255
  and part-time work, 37, 259
  and peripheral Fordism, 247, 264
  and production system, 248–51; dual business structure, 250, 253–4; employment structure, 249–50; productivity, 250; sectoral specialization, 250
  and research and development, 250
  and service economy, 250
  and small and medium-sized enterprises, 250
  and trade unions, 29, 30, 41–2, 251–3, 265, 266 n1; weakness of, 255
  and unemployment, 256–7
  and welfare regime: family policy, 261; growth in role of state, 260; impact of EU policies, 260; life-work balance, 261–2; low quality of, 264; parental leave, 261; pension reform, 262; southern model, 248, 260
  and women's labour market participation, 39, 258
specialization, and national employment models, 12, 45
state-enhanced capitalism, *see* France
state-led capitalism
  and France, 27, 179–81
  and Greece, 224, 231–2
stock markets, and increasing importance of, 32
  Austria, 133, 139, 145
  France, 32
  Germany, 32, 118
  Greece, 234
  Italy, 210
strategic alliances, and coordinated market economies, 6

Sweden
  and active labour market policy (ALMP), 83, 85, 87–9, 102; cutback in, 99–100; integration of immigrants, 93; integration of unemployed, 88; social legitimacy, 88 and actors' role, 41
  and central bank, 87
  and changes in model, 23–4; status of, 12
  and childcare, 92, 94, 95
  and collective bargaining, 24, 34, 82, 87; Agreement on Industry, 89; changes in, 87, 89–90; solidaristic wage policy, 82–3; two-tier system, 90, 91, 100–1
  and competitiveness, 84, 91, 99
  and deregulation, 98
  and devaluation, 84, 85, 86
  and economic growth, 84, 86, 97
  and economic performance, 97; crisis of late 1970s, 84–5; employment crisis of early 1990s, 85–6; post-1994 recovery, 86
  and education and training, 24, 88
  and employers' organizations, 83
  and future direction of, 100
  and healthcare, 84, 85, 92, 97, 98, 99
  and household-related services, 98–9
  and industrial relations, 89–91, 100–1
  and inequality, 84
  and labour market: integration of immigrants, 93; integration of unemployed, 88; large companies, 98; low employment growth, 99; regulation of, 33–4, 91; total employment, 99; women's participation, 92–3
  and macroeconomic policy, 82, 83; reorientation of, 87, 100
  and maintenance of model, 48
  and manufacturing, 97
  and parental leave, 92, 94–5
  and part-time work, 39, 92
  and pension reform, 24, 39–40, 96; actors' attitudes, 41
  and privatization, 98
  and production system, 97–9
  and public sector employment, 85
  and public social expenditure, 36, 81

Index 283

and Rehn-Meidner model, 83
and research and development, 98, 99
and service economy, 98
and sickness benefits, 97
and social protection system, 94–7, 101
and tax policy, 95–6, 99
and trade unions, 24, 83, 89, 90, 91
and traditional model, 82–4;
  egalitarianism, 92; revival of, 82,
  100; strengthening of, 87
and unemployment, 81, 83, 85, 86,
  100; crisis of early 1990s, 85–6
and welfare state, 82; characteristics
  of, 92; egalitarianism, 92;
  individualization of social policy, 92
Swedish Confederation of Trade Unions
  (LO), 83, 90
Swedish Employers' Confederation
  (SAF), 83
system effects, and pressures for change,
  14

tax policy
  and Austria, 146, 149
  and Sweden, 95–6, 99
technology, and pressures for change, 14
territorialization, and France, 185–6
Thatcher, Margaret, 58, 64, 67
tipping points, and United Kingdom,
  70–3
trade unions
  and Austria, 133, 136
  and coordinated market economies,
    5–6
  and decline in power of, 42
  and France, 181; weakening of, 184
  and Germany, 30, 40–1, 108, 109;
    decline in influence, 114, 121
  and Greece, 41, 43, 227, 228, 233, 243
  and Hungary, 163–4
  and Spain, 29, 30, 41–2, 251–3, 265,
    266 n1; weakness of, 255
  and Sweden, 24, 83, 89, 90, 91
  and United Kingdom, 58, 65; decline
    of, 71

unemployment
  and Austria, 138
  and France, 187, 190, 192–4; impact
    of, 192–3, 196

and Germany, 105, 111, 126
and Greece, 237–8, 239–40
and Hungary, 156, 165, 166, 167
and Italy, 214, 216
and Spain, 256–7
and Sweden, 81, 83, 85, 86, 100; crisis
  of early 1990s, 85–6
United Kingdom
  and assessment of model, 76
  and balance of payments, 74
  and Bank of England, 62
  and changes in model, 23, 60–1;
    incremental change, 68–70; nature
    of, 60; tipping points, 70–3; turning
    points, 62–4
  and characteristics of, 58;
    re-evaluation of, 68; reinforcement
    of, 66–8
  and childcare, 73
  and collective bargaining, 34; erosion
    of, 58–9, 71
  and continuity in model, 66–8
  and credit expansion, 67
  and cyclical volatility, 57
  and debt, 59; consumer, 67
  and deregulation, 33; disadvantages
    of, 67; financial sector, 23; low
    regulation economy, 66–7
  and dual-earner households, 73
  and economic growth, 67
  and education and training, 59;
    absorption of graduates, 68; focus
    on higher education, 71–2; skill
    problems, 72–3
  and employment growth, 10–11, 59,
    64, 71
  and employment relations, 69–70
  and employment rights, 69
  and English language, 68
  and financial sector, 66; collapse of,
    57; deregulation, 23; reliance on,
    59
  and fiscal policy, 11
  and foreign direct investment,
    67
  and fragility of, 57, 75
  and globalization, 66
  and healthcare, 59, 62, 64
  and housing boom, 67
  and inequality, 59, 68, 76

United Kingdom (*contd.*)
  and internationalization of economy, 65–6
  and labour market: job quality, 75; segmentation of, 74
  as liberal market economy, 58; characteristics of, 58–9
  as low-wage/low-skill economy, 58
  and macroeconomic policy, 62, 74
  and manufacturing, 58, 59, 70–1
  and the market state, 23, 65, 76
  and maternity leave, 73
  and minimum wage, 23, 39, 59, 65, 69
  and non-union private sector, 71
  and offshoring, 71
  and outsourcing of public services, 64
  and part-time work, 39
  and political choice, 42, 65; Bank of England independence, 62; remaining outside Euro zone, 62
  and poverty reduction, 59, 65, 75
  and Private Finance Initiative (PFI), 66, 76 n1
  and privatization, 34, 58, 67
  and public sector employment, 64
  and public social expenditure, 23, 36–7; employment impact, 64; future of, 75; growth of, 62, 63, 64
  and research and development, 70
  and retail sector, 70
  as role model for Europe: assessment of, 76; Blair's claims for, 57; debate on, 74–6
  and service economy, 70, 71, 74
  and shareholder finance system, 68–9
  and specialization, 12
  and status of model, 12
  and trade unions, 58, 65; decline of, 71
  and transformation into neoliberal model, 58
  and turning points, 62–6; poverty reduction, 65; rise in public expenditure, 62–4
  and United States: differences from, 52 n4; similarities to, 59
  and wage bargaining in public sector, 69–70
  and welfare state: pension policy, 40, 67–8, 75–6; poverty traps, 67;
  raising of safety nets, 70; recommitment to, 59; residual, 57, 58; as targeted system, 67
  and women's labour market participation, 39, 73
  and work first policy, 65
  and work-life policies, 59
United States
  and changing status as model, 12
  and social protection, 48

varieties of capitalism
  and coordinated market economies, 5–6
  and core hypothesis of, 5
  and criticism of approach, 15
  and institutional complementarities, 6, 131–2
  and large-country focus of approach, 131
  and liberal market economies, 5–6
  and mixed market economies, 52 n6
  and national employment models, 1–2; typologies of, 5–6, 8–9, 178
  and weakness of approach, 6–7; coherence, 131–2; interdependence, 131; pace and extent of change, 132

welfare regimes
  and elements of, 18
  and national employment models, 5; typologies of, 7–9
  and service economy, 8
  and typology of, 7–8
  see also individual countries
women, and labour market participation, 7, 8, 14, 35–6, 37–9
  Austria, 38, 137, 144, 148
  France, 193–4, 197–8
  Germany, 38, 124
  Greece, 241–2
  Hungary, 168
  Italy, 39, 214, 216
  Spain, 39, 258
  Sweden, 92–3
  United Kingdom, 39, 73
World Trade Organization (WTO)
  and pressures for change, 14
  and reform, 2